The Social Foundations of German Unification 1858-1871

Ideas and Institutions

The Social
Foundations of
German Unification
1858-1871

Ideas and Institutions

Theodore S. Hamerow

PRINCETON UNIVERSITY PRESS
Princeton, New Jersey
1969

Preface

THIS BOOK represents an attempt to answer a number of questions which occurred to me originally several years ago while I was working on a study of the interrelationship of economics and politics in the German Confederation. I realized then for the first time how little we actually know about the process of national unification in Central Europe during the middle years of the nineteenth century. To be sure, the political and diplomatic developments of the 1850's and 1860's have been studied so extensively that little remains to be added, except perhaps a nuance here or a footnote there. But the preoccupation of most scholars with the problems of statecraft has caused them to neglect the social matrix of civic activity. Trying to prove that the liberals were right rather than the conservatives, or the Prussians rather than the Austrians, or the Germans rather than the French, they have largely ignored the material forces and class interests behind the establishment of the German Empire. They have continued to fight the fights of their fathers and grandfathers, trying to justify or condemn with the written word what had been achieved on the battlefield or in the legislative chamber.

Only today, a hundred years later, can we finally turn to new issues, because the old ones have ceased to seem vital to us. They have lost their timeliness. It no longer matters a great deal whether crown or parliament had justice on its side during the constitutional conflict in Prussia, whether the Habsburgs or the Hohenzollerns were better qualified to lead Central Europe toward unity, or whether it was worth destroying an empire in France in order to create one in Germany. We are ready to deal with other problems. For example, what was the connection between industrialization and nationalism in the German Confederation? What groups in society

favored political reform? What was the effect of economic change on civic ideology? What was the relationship between affluence and authority in the state? Such
are the questions I have tried to answer in this book.

As I proceeded with the writing, I began to feel that
I could not do justice to the theme within the scope of
a single volume. I therefore decided to examine first
the economic, social, and ideological framework within
which the national consolidation of Germany took place.
This section of the work is topical and analytical rather
than chronological and narrative. The second volume,
which I expect to complete in a year or two, will study
the political developments of the period of unification
in the light of the categories and patterns described in
the first volume. While the over-all dimensions of the
book will not become fully apparent until the comple-
tion of the second half, I hope that the part now published will make a contribution in its own right to a
better understanding of an important era in German
history.

One of the reasons for the sense of satisfaction I feel
at the appearance of this volume is that it gives me an
opportunity to acknowledge the obligations I have incurred in its writing. There are first of all the many
libraries, both in this country and abroad, which gave
me access to their collections directly or through micro-
film. To enumerate them all would require a long and
tedious list. But some I cannot leave unmentioned.
The Memorial Library of the University of Wisconsin
assisted me not only by making available to me its
substantial holdings, but also by borrowing important
materials from other American libraries. As for European libraries, I am especially indebted to the Univer-
sitätsbibliothek of the University of Erlangen-Nürnberg
and the Stadtbibliothek in Nürnberg. During my trip
abroad in 1962-63 they allowed me to use their resources and obtained for me works from various collec-

tions in Germany. The Bayerische Staatsbibliothek in Munich permitted me to borrow its books, provided me with information regarding the location of materials I needed, and even admitted me to its stacks, a rare privilege. Finally, the Deutsche Staatsbibliothek in Berlin helped me by letting me examine its holdings, by sending me microfilms, and, most important, by informing me about the collections of other libraries in the German Democratic Republic.

The writing of this book was also made possible by the financial assistance I received from three sources. The Graduate School of the University of Wisconsin was both generous and patient in providing funds for research assistants and research materials year after year, while the Social Science Research Council and the Committee on International Exchange of Persons (the Fulbright Program) awarded me concurrent fellowships which enabled me to spend a year in Europe examining historical data unavailable in this country. Without this stay abroad I would not have been able to complete my work. In conclusion, some of my friends who are experts in the field of nineteenth-century German history kindly agreed to read the manuscript: Francis L. Loewenheim, Otto Pflanze, and George G. Windell. Their comments and suggestions were very helpful, and I want to express my thanks to them.

THEODORE S. HAMEROW
Madison, Wisconsin
June 1969

Contents

PREFACE   V

PART ONE: THE PATTERN OF SOCIETY
   1. The Economic Environment   3
   2. The Social Structure   44
   3. Class and Reform   84

PART TWO: THE CLASH OF IDEOLOGIES
   4. The Liberal Creed   135
   5. Conservatism and the Old Order   181
   6. The Emergence of Socialism   222

PART THREE: THE SYSTEM OF POLITICS
   7. Status and Power   269
   8. Civic Organizations   308
   9. Public Opinion   359

        ALPHABETICAL LIST OF CITED WORKS   401
        INDEX   427

THE PATTERN OF SOCIETY

ONE

++

The Economic Environment

IT WAS March 1858. Germany lay in the grip of an economic depression. A boom built on paper profits and wild hopes had just collapsed, bringing in its wake panic, bankruptcy, unemployment, and hunger. In the pervasive mood of bitter disillusionment there was little inclination to commemorate those other March days of ten years before, when the nation had risen in revolution to seek security through freedom and unity. But in Frankfurt am Main an anonymous publicist contrasted the spirit of the spring of 1848 with that which he felt about him now: "Our nation of 'forty million dreamers and idealists' has learned a good deal in the hard school of reality, and it has also fortunately forgotten some things. Above all, it has become more practical. Romanticism and sentimentality, transcendental philosophy and supranaturalism have now withdrawn from the public life of our people into private life. For realism and steam, machines and industrial exhibitions, the natural sciences and practical interests now fill the great market place of life and work at the humming loom of our time."[1]

The Germany which was about to enter upon a new period of political turmoil was indeed less romantic and sentimental, less interested in the transcendental and supranatural. The late 1840's with their famine, depression, revolution, and civil war had been followed by years in which the efforts of the nation had turned from politics to economics. It was as if the popular energies frustrated in the task of national unification had now

[1] *Nach zehn Jahren: Auch eine Rundschau (März 1848–März 1858)* (Frankfurt am Main, 1858) , p. 30.

3

concentrated on the creation of material well-being. The 1850's became the period of a great capitalistic boom, displaying all the characteristic traits of an expanding industrial economy. A bold program of railroad construction created the foundations of a modern transportation system. Mines, foundries, and factories proliferated in an atmosphere of high profits and higher expectations. Lending institutions organized on the joint-stock principle began to compete with older private banks, providing a significant volume of risk capital for industrial undertakings. On the stock exchange new issues were oversubscribed five, ten, and twenty times by jobbers who knew that a show of spurious confidence would enable them to sell their shares to a gullible public at inflated prices. The annual report of the Cologne chamber of commerce for 1855 boasted that "probably in no country on the Continent has industry made more rapid progress these last years than in the Zollverein. A few more years of peace and unrestricted exercise of all our forces in this field, and the Zollverein will be in a position of complete equality with France and Belgium." Even three years later, after the bubble had burst, the liberal economist Max Wirth looked back with pride at what German industriousness had achieved:

The stagnation, the utter paralysis of business in the years 1848, 1849, and 1850 had ended after the fall of the French republic. The totally depleted warehouses had to be filled again, and when at the same time the effects of the introduction of California gold and of the low discount rate made themselves felt by way of England, there gradually developed a spirit of enterprise more powerful than any experienced in Germany up to that time. And although now the magnificent wave of expansion has to be paid for with a business depression, its appearance was so beautiful that we can never forget it. The steamboat traffic on the rivers, the shipment of goods on the railroads, the construction of ships and machinery grew at an extraordinary rate. Railroads and machine shops, coal mines and iron foundries, spinneries and rolling mills seemed to spring out of the ground, and especially in the industrial regions of Saxony, the Rhineland, and Westphalia smokestacks sprouted from the earth like mushrooms.[2]

There were those, to be sure, who had recognized the risks inherent in the mania of promotion and speculation. About eighteen months before the crash, the eminent financier David Hansemann warned the directors of the Disconto-Gesellschaft that "we are at present on the road leading to a not insignificant crisis. The gambling fever in shares is more and more affecting almost all classes of the population. Almost everybody is buying, not to retain, but to sell again at a profit after the first installment payment or even earlier, if possible. However impressive the rise in prosperity may be, not enough new capital is being created to absorb this mass of new values in any sound fashion, since nearly every day creates not a few but very many millions of these values suitable for speculation, and the people who have thus acquired or are still acquiring a large fortune are insatiable." The danger signs soon began to multiply. The price of coal reached its highest point in 1856 and then began to decline, while iron passed its peak even earlier. It was disturbing that the shares of an important enterprise like the Darmstädter Bank, which stood at 417 on July 1, 1856, fell by the end of the year to 346. Those of the Disconto-Gesellschaft went from 146 to 122, and those of the Cologne-Minden Railroad from 162 to 156. On September 22 the conservative state-controlled Preussische Bank, sensitive to every shift in the wind, raised its discount rate from 5 to 6 per cent, keeping it at that level for almost half a year before reducing it again. An important Hamburg firm reported in April 1857 that a vague uneasiness

[2] Max Wirth, *Geschichte der Handelskrisen* (Frankfurt am Main, 1858), p. 348. Cf. *Preussisches Handelsarchiv* (1856), I, 488.

5

seemed to prevail on the stock exchange, that despite the sizable importation of silver the discount rate remained at a high 7 per cent, and that merchants were encountering difficulty in selling their commodities because of the shortness of credit.[3]

What finally toppled the house of cards was the economic crisis which started in the New World and then overwhelmed the Old. The Swabian publicist A.E.F. Schäffle compared its course with that of an elemental force of nature:

> The avalanche from the banks of the Ohio, where it was set in motion by the insidious activities of a few speculating rascals, advanced with devastating violence irresistibly eastward. It crushed the Atlantic states of the great republic, and after a mighty leap across the ocean fell upon England and the mainland of the European continent, reaching as far as the plains around the Baltic Sea (North Germany, Poland, Scandinavia). Everywhere it has brought all branches of business more or less to a standstill. Like a thief in the night it has surprised the world of speculation and production which had climbed to dizzying heights. In a time of the most profound political peace, after a generally rich harvest, that same edifice collapses which in years of scarcity and of a great war had towered on high like a fairy castle springing out of the wilderness. Its rise as well as its fall border on the incredible.

Admittedly, not all parts of Germany were equally affected by the financial collapse. Agricultural regions like Bavaria or East Prussia were less vulnerable than

[3] Alexander Bergengrün, *David Hansemann* (Berlin, 1901), p. 678; Alfred Jacobs and Hans Richter, *Die Grosshandelspreise in Deutschland von 1792 bis 1934* (Hamburg, 1935), pp. 40-41; Jürgen Kuczynski, *Studien zur Geschichte der zyklischen Überproduktionskrisen in Deutschland, 1825 bis 1866* (Berlin, 1961), pp. 124-125; H. von Poschinger, *Bankwesen und Bankpolitik in Preussen* (3 vols., Berlin, 1878-79), II, 382; Julius Kahn, *Geschichte des Zinsfusses in Deutschland seit 1815 und die Ursachen seiner Veränderung* (Stuttgart, 1884), pp. 155-156.

the industrialized Rhineland or Saxony, while most factory towns were not as hard hit as mercantile Hamburg, Leipzig, and Frankfurt am Main. Yet when wholesale prices were falling drastically, some by nearly a third; when shares on the stock exchange were selling for as little as half of par; when the foreign trade of the Zollverein was declining by 300,000,000 marks; when the nominal value of the national wealth was estimated to have shrunk by 25 per cent or more, everyone was bound to feel the hard times directly or indirectly.[4]

The economic depression was all things to all men. Baron Heinrich von Testa, the Austrian minister to the Hanseatic cities, wrote to his government during the days of panic in November 1857 that the ultimate cause of the catastrophe was the "abandonment of patriarchal morality, that weakness for senseless luxury, that resentment of wealth engendered by pride, that overstimulation of the spirit of speculation." The daughter of the eminent Hamburg merchant Justus Ruperti, on the other hand, was convinced that the disaster was an expression of divine displeasure: "It is surely the punishment for the excessive luxury and presumption of our city in recent times. For it certainly cannot be denied that they have been very widespread. Just think of the luxury of the parties and costumes of last winter. The contrast with this winter is truly frightening."[5]

Across the North Sea in England, Marx and Engels were inclined to read a dialectical rather than providential meaning into the economic collapse. Although his father's firm in Barmen was close to bankruptcy,

---

[4] [A.E.F. Schäffle], "Die Handelskrisis, mit besonderer Rücksicht auf das Bankwesen," *Deutsche Vierteljahrs-Schrift*, XXI (1858), no. 1, p. 256; A. Sartorius von Waltershausen, *Deutsche Wirtschaftsgeschichte, 1815-1914*, 2nd edn. (Jena, 1923), pp. 188, 193-194; Hans Rosenberg, *Die Weltwirtschaftskrisis von 1857-1859* (Stuttgart and Berlin, 1934), pp. 140-143, 156; J. Kuczynski, *Studien zur Geschichte der Überproduktionskrisen*, pp. 129-130.

[5] Percy Ernst Schramm, *Hamburg, Deutschland und die Welt: Leistung und Grenzen hanseatischen Bürgertums in der Zeit zwischen Napoleon I. und Bismarck* (Munich, 1943), p. 562.

7

Engels exulted at the prospect of exchanging his life as a businessman *malgré lui* for that of a revolutionary leader. He found it "absolutely impossible to think of anything except the general crash. I could neither read nor write." The time for action was finally approaching. "Everything is now at stake. Therefore my military studies will at once become more practical. I shall immediately devote myself to the study of the existing organization and basic tactics of the Prussian, Austrian, Bavarian, and French armies, and beyond that only to riding, that is, fox hunting, which is the only real school." At the same time Marx, more comfortable at his desk than on horseback, was preparing for the impending crisis of capitalism by dropping his hack work for the *New American Cyclopaedia* and returning to theoretical analysis: "I am working like a madman day and night on the synopsis of my economic studies, so that I will at least have the outline clear before the deluge." The deluge never came, but the synopsis on which he worked with such intensity appeared two years later as *Zur Kritik der politischen Ökonomie*.[6]

For most Germans the depression meant above all business failures, lost savings, falling incomes, and disappointed hopes. What made it even worse was that there appeared to be no rational explanation for the disaster which had overtaken them. "All relationships seemed to be topsy-turvy," puzzled the *Preussische Jahrbücher*. "Amid supplies of merchandise greater than ever before, amid rich harvests there was universal privation; in the presence of excellent means of transportation there was no exchange of goods anywhere; notwithstanding large imports of precious metals there was everywhere a shortage of money; despite the most extensive credit institutions there was a rate of interest higher than any the century had known."[7]

6 Karl Marx and Friedrich Engels, *Briefwechsel* (4 vols., Berlin, 1949-50), II, 302, 314, 334.

7 [O. Gildemeister], "Die Verkehrskrisis des Jahres 1857," *Preussische Jahrbücher*, I (1858), 98.

The financial crisis ended even more abruptly than it began. The stock market, which had been declining slowly but steadily since the summer of 1856, began to fall precipitously in September 1857. Two months later it reached bottom. But by the end of the year it had managed to stage a mild recovery, and the worst was over. The movement of the discount rate of the Preussische Bank during those critical weeks told the story. It had risen to 7.5 per cent on November 7 at the height of the panic, was then reduced to 6.5 on December 21, on January 5 it fell again to 5.5, then on January 16 to 5, and finally on February 2 it was set at 4 per cent, the lowest point in about a year and a half. Yet the economy at large was slow to respond to this display of revived confidence by the banking community. There had been too many bitter losses and thwarted hopes. The index of wholesale prices for articles of commerce (1913 = 100) went from 99.5 in 1857 to 84.2 in 1858, then up to 86.0 in 1859, and 94.2 in 1860. The foreign trade of the Zollverein, which had totaled 2,988,000,000 marks in 1857, declined to 2,688,000,000 in 1858 and 2,661,000,000 in 1859, before rising again to 3,018,000,-000 in 1860. The turnover of the Preussische Bank, amounting to 2,667,000,000 marks in 1857, stood at 2,463,000,000 in 1858, 2,448,000,000 in 1859, and 2,298,-000,000 in 1860. During the years 1855-57, 67 joint-stock companies had been formed in the Zollverein in mining, 43 in metallurgy, and 29 in textiles. During 1858-60 the corresponding figures were 9, 2, and 1.[8]

For that matter, the entire decade following the crash was a period of economic insecurity. Just as the political stagnation of the 1850's had coincided with a financial boom, so the achievement of national unification during

[8] J. Kuczynski, *Studien zur Geschichte der Überproduktionskrisen*, pp. 125, 129-130; H. v. Poschinger, *Bankwesen und Bankpolitik*, II, 382-383; J. Kahn, *Geschichte des Zinsfusses*, pp. 156-158; H. Rosenberg, *Weltwirtschaftskrisis*, pp. 140-143, 156, 170; A. Jacobs and H. Richter, *Die Grosshandelspreise in Deutschland*, p. 41; Pierre Benaerts, *Les origines de la grande industrie allemande* (Paris, 1933), p. 266.

the 1860's took place in an atmosphere of recurrent business recessions. No sooner had the effects of the crisis of 1857 begun to wear off, than the outbreak of the war in Italy, which threatened to involve the states of the German Confederation, produced a minor depression. Prussian treasury bills which in January 1859 sold for 83.75 sank in the course of the next few months to 72, while the 4.5 per cent government bonds went from 101 to 86.5. By the end of the year the money market had recovered, but in view of the tense international situation a feeling of uneasiness persisted. Then, after a period of moderate expansion, came another setback in the wake of the Danish War of 1864. Paradoxically, economic conditions remained fairly stable as long as the conflict was in progress. But once victory had been achieved, the outflow of silver became so pronounced that on September 8 the Preussische Bank was forced to raise its discount rate from 5 to 6 per cent and, on October 6, to 7 per cent. Other lending institutions raised their charges to still higher levels, and it was not until December that the cost of credit began to decline.[9]

The most severe financial crisis of the 1860's coincided with the coming of the Seven Weeks' War, although the disintegration of the German Confederation intensified rather than initiated the economic difficulties. The end of the American Civil War and the renewal of the Zollverein in 1865 stimulated the demand for credit at the very time when the Paris Bourse was buzzing with the news of the Mexican fiasco and several important London firms were declaring bankruptcy. The threat of an Austro-Prussian conflict completed the disruption of the money market until the reorganization of Germany had been achieved. Between the middle of March and the end of May 1866 the discount rate on the Berlin stock exchange rose from 6 to 9 per cent, in Hamburg from

[9] Wolfgang Köllmann, *Sozialgeschichte der Stadt Barmen im 19. Jahrhundert* (Tübingen, 1960), pp. 282-283; H. v. Poschinger, *Bankwesen und Bankpolitik*, II, 383, III, 23, 29, 48-49.

4 to 8, and in Frankfurt am Main from 4.5 to 7 per cent. Shares of the Preussische Bank fell from 155.5 to 115, of the Rhenish Railroad from 118 to 94, of the Schaaffhausenscher Bankverein from 126 to 110, and of the Kölner Bergwerksverein from 64 to 57. The Gleiwitz chamber of commerce in its report for 1866 described how "in the second quarter conditions became more and more troubled in every respect, leading naturally to continually falling prices. But when in the month of June the outbreak of war became unavoidable and imminent, business came to an almost complete standstill. The short duration and fortunate outcome of the war could not effect the immediate revival of trade." Long after hostilities had come to an end, economic progress remained fitful. Diplomatic tension between France and the North German Confederation, labor unrest in the Rhineland, famine in East Prussia, all had an unsettling effect on the world of finance. Only with the victorious outcome of the Franco-Prussian War could the government in Berlin justly claim that "the entire economic life in Prussia rests on a healthy and sound foundation." In 1871 as in 1849 the end of political upheaval introduced a period of business expansion.[10]

While the money market was particularly sensitive to the diplomatic crises and military struggles of the years

[10] Alexander Bergengrün, *Staatsminister August Freiherr von der Heydt* (Leipzig, 1908), p. 327; Hans-Joachim von Collani, *Die Finanzgebarung des preussischen Staates zur Zeit des Verfassungskonfliktes, 1862-1866* (Düsseldorf, 1939), p. 48; Fritz Löwenthal, *Der preussische Verfassungsstreit, 1862-1866* (Munich and Leipzig, 1914), p. 283; Rudolph von Delbrück, *Lebenserinnerungen, 1817-1867* (2 vols., Leipzig, 1905), II, 371-372; J. Kuczynski, *Studien zur Geschichte der Überproduktionskrisen*, pp. 154, 160-161; J. Kahn, *Geschichte des Zinsfusses*, pp. 164, 179-180, 212, 217, 219, 221; "Aus dem kommerziellen Leben des Jahres 1866," *Vierteljahrschrift für Volkswirtschaft und Kulturgeschichte*, IV (1866), no. 4, p. 180; *Preussisches Handelsarchiv* (1867), III (Jahresberichte der Handelskammern und kaufmännischen Korporationen des preussischen Staats für 1866), 443; W. Köllmann, *Sozialgeschichte der Stadt Barmen*, p. 45; *Fürst Bismarck als Volkswirth*, ed. Heinrich v. Poschinger (3 vols., Berlin, 1889-91), I, 33; *Europäischer Geschichtskalender*, ed. H. Schulthess (1868), p. 35.

11

following 1857, the rate of return on industrial investment was also bound to be affected. It is true that the economy as a whole continued to grow, but the dramatic gains of the boom years could not be matched. Of the 79 new enterprises in mining and metallurgy formed in Prussia between 1851 and 1870 with a capitalization of 275,400,000 marks, no fewer than 59, representing an authorized capital of 212,100,000 marks, were established in the period 1852-57. The production of pig iron in the Zollverein increased in value by 173 per cent between 1848 and 1857, climbing from 24,606,000 to 67,228,000 marks, whereas between 1860 and 1870 it advanced 103 per cent, from 52,287,000 to 106,365,000 marks. Figures for the output of foundries including nonferrous metals were even less favorable. During the period 1848-57 the value of Zollverein production rose 168 per cent, from 44,329,000 to 118,937,000 marks. Between 1860 and 1870, on the other hand, the growth was only 74 per cent, from 101,412,000 to 176,457,000 marks.[11]

To be sure, it would be a mistake to minimize the achievements of the German economy during the 1860's. The volume of pig iron production more than doubled, equaling the rate of growth of the previous decade, while the manufacture of steel increased fivefold. The exports of wrought iron and raw steel, moreover, were on the whole greater than imports. Indeed, the Zollverein was third among the industrial powers of Europe as a producer of iron and steel, surpassed only by England and France. The growth in the output of coal was equally impressive. In 1860 Germany was mining approximately 17,000,000 metric tons including lignite, as

[11] H. Rosenberg, *Weltwirtschaftskrisis*, p. 65; *Jahrbuch für die amtliche Statistik des preussischen Staats*, I (1863), 428; Georg von Viebahn, *Statistik des zollvereinten und nördlichen Deutschlands* (3 vols., Berlin, 1858-68), II, 421, 488; *Statistisches Jahrbuch für das Deutsche Reich* (1880), I, 34, 36; Gertrud Hermes, "Statistische Studien zur wirtschaftlichen und gesellschaftlichen Struktur des zollvereinten Deutschlands," *Archiv für Sozialwissenschaft und Sozialpolitik*, LXIII (1930), 150.

compared with 81,000,000 for Great Britain, 9,600,000 for Belgium, and 8,300,000 for France. By the time of the establishment of the empire eleven years later German production had risen to more than 37,500,000 tons, while the figure for Great Britain was 118,000,000 and for France and Belgium only 13,000,000 to 14,000,000 each. Yet granted that the economy was expanding at a substantial rate, it was incapable of repeating the miracle of the 1850's. During the period 1851-60 the index of production for capital goods (1860 = 100) more than doubled over what it had been during 1841-50, rising from 37 to 81. For the decade 1861-70, on the other hand, it grew by barely a half, from 81 to 123. There was an obvious and logical correlation between political and economic insecurity which the chamber of commerce of Elberfeld and Barmen recognized in its report for 1867:

> In view of the intimate reciprocal relationship prevailing between the diplomatic and economic intercourse of nations, it is natural that in moments when great and fateful decisions have either just been reached or are about to be reached, commerce and industry should regard these disturbances with great concern and avoid all enterprise. This great uncertainty of the European situation has produced a profound listlessness in all the larger centers of commerce. It has uselessly piled up money and capital in all the banks. In addition there were the higher and unavoidable providential dispensations of our time. The widespread epidemic of cholera and rinderpest intensified the general concern as well as the feeling of social malaise, completely paralyzing the will toward any progress or greater business enterprise.[12]

[12] *Preussisches Handelsarchiv* (1868), III (Jahresberichte der Handelskammern und kaufmännischen Korporationen des preussischen Staats für 1867), 133. Cf. *Statistisches Jahrbuch für das Deutsche Reich* (1880), I, 30, 34; Walther Lotz, *Die Ideen der deutschen Handelspolitik von 1860 bis 1891* (Leipzig, 1892), p. 95; Ivo Nikolai Lambi, *Free Trade and Protection in Germany, 1868-1879* (Wiesbaden, 1963), pp. 12, 16;

Not only did political tension have an unfavorable effect on business conditions; economic insecurity in turn threatened to weaken government policy. Prussia embarked on the course of blood and iron in a strong financial position. The income which the treasury derived from state-controlled railroads, from public lands, and from the royal mines and foundries grew steadily throughout the 1860's, rising from 41,500,000 to 100,-600,000 marks annually. There was, furthermore, a tax surplus of about 15,000,000 marks in 1862 and again in 1863, so that the cost of the war against Denmark could be covered by funds on hand. A foreign diplomat marvelled that while "all states incur debts, Prussia wages war and still has money left over." As for Bismarck, jubilant over the successes of his statecraft, he boasted of the resources available to him in a letter of March 24, 1865, to Karl Friedrich von Savigny, Berlin's representative at the diet of the German Confederation: "Our financial balance for last year (64) shows that we need only 2 (two) million from the state treasury for the Danish War. Everything else is covered by the surpluses for 63-64. This information, although very gratifying, is to be kept secret because of the legislature. The financiers are pressing loans on us without requiring legislative approval, but we could wage the Danish War twice over without needing one." Four months later Minister of War Albrecht von Roon echoed his chief's optimism, assuring his cousin Moritz von Blanckenburg that "there is money at our disposal, enough to give us a free hand in foreign policy, and if necessary, to mobilize the entire army and pay it for the duration of a campaign. That gives our stand against Austria the necessary aplomb."[13]

P. Benaerts, *Les origines*, p. 632; Jürgen Kuczynski, *A Short History of Labour Conditions under Industrial Capitalism: Germany, 1800 to the Present Day* (London, 1945), p. 66.

[13] *Denkwürdigkeiten aus dem Leben des Generalfeldmarschalls Kriegsministers Grafen von Roon*, 5th edn. (3 vols., Berlin, 1905), II, 354. Cf. W. G. Hoffmann and J. H. Müller, *Das deutsche Volksein-*

The financial prospects, however, were not always rosy. In 1862, as the constitutional conflict between crown and parliament was entering a critical stage, the government experienced considerable difficulty in placing a 4 per cent railroad loan. Worse still, the plan to convert the bond issues of 1850 and 1852 from 4.5 to 4 per cent met with the approval of only about half of the holders. The situation improved after the first victories of Bismarck's diplomacy had revived public confidence in the regime. Yet prior to the Seven Weeks' War, after the government had painfully increased its reserves to 180,000,000 marks by selling the option to acquire the Cologne-Minden Railroad, by utilizing credits approved by the legislature for railway construction, and by drawing on the balance in hand, it turned out that the available funds would support military operations not for a year, as the minister of war had assumed, but only six months. Could the cabinet have raised more money if the campaign of 1866 had dragged on? Only with the greatest difficulty. Between March and June of that year Prussian state bonds had declined about 10 per cent, and in the event of prolonged hostilities the drop would surely have become calamitous. What saved the government from the consequences of its miscalculation was the rapid defeat of the Austrian army.

But late in the decade the cabinet's financial luck began to run out. Bismarck's confidant Robert von Keudell recalled in his memoirs that "economic conditions in Prussia as well as in the North German Confederation were uncertain. After 1866 a heavy burden weighed on business, industry, and commerce, because in view of all the reports regarding the consistently hostile attitude of the Parisian political world, people felt that they must reckon with the possibility of a sudden outbreak of war. In Prussia, consequently, govern-

---

kommen, 1851-1957 (Tübingen, 1959), pp. 30, 81-82; *Bismarck als Volkswirth*, ed. H. v. Poschinger, I, 23; Otto von Bismarck, *Die gesammelten Werke* (15 vols., Berlin, 1924-35), XIV/II, 693.

ment receipts lagged behind the estimates. Some of the measures to facilitate trade which the legislature had approved produced a temporary decline in income, while certain emergencies led to increased expenditures. At the conclusion of the fiscal year 1868 there was an unexpectedly high deficit" of approximately 16,000,000 marks. The forces inhibiting private enterprise were now also making themselves felt in the financial affairs of the state.[14]

Despite these ups and downs, the economy of Germany was undergoing a rapid industrialization. Although its most impressive achievements were not to come until after the Franco-Prussian War, the foundation of those achievements must be sought in the 1850's and 1860's. The transition to the factory system, however, was not a clear-cut process. For a long time there were branches of manufacture virtually untouched by mechanization, while others were experiencing a revolutionary transformation. More than that, within the same field of enterprise old and new methods of production often coexisted, neither strong enough to overcome the other, though time was clearly on the side of innovation. The textile industry was the most important in the Zollverein, employing in 1861 more than 600,000 persons in weaving and almost 150,000 in spinning, compared with about 394,000 in the building trades, 363,000 in metallurgy, and 151,000 in the construction of machinery. Of the 2,069 factories in Prussia with at least 50 workers, 131 were spinneries and 773 weaving plants. The preponderance of textile manufacturing was even more marked in the category of enterprises with

14 J. Kahn, *Geschichte des Zinsfusses*, pp. 142-143, 212; Heinrich von Srbik, *Deutsche Einheit: Idee und Wirklichkeit vom Heiligen Reich bis Königgrätz* (4 vols., Munich, 1935-42) , IV, 270; Robert von Keudell, *Fürst und Fürstin Bismarck: Erinnerungen aus den Jahren 1846 bis 1872*, 3rd edn. (Berlin and Stuttgart, 1902) , p. 412; Karl Zuchardt, *Die Finanzpolitik Bismarcks und der Parteien im Norddeutschen Bunde* (Leipzig, 1910) , p. 64; Erich Marcks, *Der Aufstieg des Reiches: Deutsche Geschichte von 1807-1871/78* (2 vols., Stuttgart and Berlin, 1936) , II, 310.

500 or more workers. Of 100 such enterprises, 53 were engaged in the production of cloth and yarn, 36 turned out iron and iron wares, and 11 were scattered in miscellaneous fields. Yet side by side with these highly rationalized industrial establishments were numerous small shops operating in accordance with traditional handicraft methods, and an even larger number of homes in which a family income usually derived from farming or a trade was supplemented by part-time labor at the spinning wheel or loom. Within the Zollverein as a whole, weaving factories employed 144,000 persons, while 469,000 artisan masters and journeymen lived under working conditions no different in any essential respect from what they had been a hundred years before. In the manufacture of linen, the most backward segment of the textile industry, there were 350 mechanical looms, 120,000 hand looms worked on a full-time basis, and 371,000 hand looms in part-time use.[15]

The metal industry was by its nature more responsive to technological progress. Involved in the manufacture of producers' goods, it derived a powerful stimulus from the railroad and construction boom of the 1850's, which withstood the hardships of the depression late in the decade. With some 57,000 factory workers as of 1861, it was far behind the textile mills and shops in the size of its labor force. Even considering only the larger enterprises with 50 or more employees, weaving and spinning plants in Prussia were nearly twice as numerous as foundries and metalworks. Yet there were giants among the ironmasters no less than among the cloth manufacturers. Alfred Krupp was already employing more than 8,000 persons and recording annual sales of some 24,000,000 marks. There were also the firm of Haniel and Huyssen and the Hörder works, each with more than 3,000 mill hands, the Phönix Company with 2,100, and the Stumm Brothers with 1,100. The pattern

[15] G. v. Viebahn, *Statistik Deutschlands*, III, 1121; G. Hermes, "Statistische Studien," pp. 141-144, 153-154.

of private investment, moreover, reflected a widespread confidence in the future growth of heavy industry. Of 107 industrial joint-stock companies formed in Prussia during the period 1850-59, about two-thirds were in mining and smelting, as compared with barely a tenth in textiles.

The mechanization of production was also more pronounced in the capital goods industries. By the early 1860's the mines and foundries of the Zollverein, employing 2,100 steam engines with 72,000 horsepower, were far ahead of weaving and spinning, where the comparable figures were 1,400 and 31,000. While in the Prussian textile factories there were still 28,000 hand looms against only about 15,000 mechanical ones, the proportion of blast furnaces using coke rather than charcoal grew from 37 per cent in 1852 to over 76 per cent in 1862. The result was that production not only could keep pace with a swiftly mounting demand for metals but succeeded in supplying an increasing share of the domestic market. Between 1851 and 1857 the German output of pig iron more than doubled, rising from 219,000 to 536,000 metric tons annually. Yet the need for imports from abroad remained unchanged, since domestic manufacture could only satisfy between 66 and 76 per cent of demand. During the following decade, however, the Zollverein began to approach self-sufficiency in iron. Yearly production expanded from 558,-000 metric tons in 1858 to 905,000 in 1864, when it amounted to 93 per cent of total consumption.

Still, the process of industrialization in metallurgy, extensive though it was, remained incomplete. The expanding size of the manufacturing units, the growing mechanization of production, the increasing acceptance of the joint-stock principle, all suggested an advanced stage of economic development. And yet even in heavy industry tradition could not be easily uprooted. Throughout the Zollverein small enterprises continued to compete with the great mills, most of them clinging to preindustrial methods of operation. In 1861 there were still 120,000 artisan shops engaged in the manufacture of heavy metal goods and another 20,500 in specialized metallurgical trades, employing a total of about 277,000 persons. In other words, the average handicraft establishment provided work for barely two people, one of them probably a master tradesman who was also in all likelihood the proprietor, the other a journeyman or apprentice. But the aggregate of those earning a livelihood under this domestic system of output was about five times as great as that in the factories. The vestiges of an older economic order thus remained clearly discernible in the metal industry despite rapid changes in the method and organization of production.[16]

Mining was so closely related to metallurgy that, despite the importance which it had in its own right, much of the contemporary statistical data made no distinction between them. Such a distinction would in any case have been difficult, since numerous enterprises in heavy industry combined the extraction of coal and ore with the founding and refining of metal. In Prussia during the 1850's, 75 firms with an authorized capitalization of 244,360,200 marks were formed in mining and metallurgy, most of them apparently engaged in both operations. In the preceding decade of slower growth, when only seven companies officially capitalized at 43,070,001 marks came into existence, collieries and blast furnaces were also very frequently under common ownership. Yet while the volume of investment

16 G. v. Viebahn, *Statistik Deutschlands*, III, 1034, 1121; G. Hermes, "Statistische Studien," pp. 151-152, 154; Horst Blumberg, "Die Finanzierung der Neugründungen und Erweiterungen von Industriebetrieben in Form der Aktiengesellschaften während der fünfziger Jahre des neunzehnten Jahrhunderts, am Beispiel der preussischen Verhältnisse erläutert," in Hans Mottek, Horst Blumberg, Heinz Wutzmer, and Walter Becker, *Studien zur Geschichte der industriellen Revolution in Deutschland* (Berlin, 1960), p. 176; H. A. Mascher, *Das deutsche Gewerbewesen von der frühesten Zeit bis auf die Gegenwart* (Potsdam, 1866), p. 524; J. Kuczynski, *Short History*, p. 70; P. Benaerts, *Les origines*, pp. 457, 461-462.

in mines apart from foundries cannot be determined with any precision, there is adequate information regarding their technical progress. Judged by the extent of mechanization, mining was the most advanced sector of industry. As of 1861 it employed close to 20 per cent of all steam engines in the Zollverein with 38 per cent of the total horsepower, far ahead of textiles and metals, which were in second and third place. The results were reflected in the index of productivity for Prussian coal miners (1850 = 100). After climbing steadily to reach 108 in 1858, it suddenly jumped two years later to 119, and by 1865 had reached 150. Thereafter its average rate of growth declined, so that at the beginning of the following decade it was still only 155.

For the mining industry no less than for the economy as a whole the 1850's were boom years. Its output tripled in value between 1848 and 1857, rising from 44,653,000 marks to 137,280,000, while the labor force did not quite double, rising from 88,000 to 169,000. Here was another indication of technological improvement. After the economic crisis of 1857 the industry resumed its growth, but at a less rapid pace. Between 1860 and 1869 its over-all production grew from 18,854,000 to 39,665,000 metric tons, and from 125,902,000 to 240,429,000 marks. The most important branch of mining was coal, accounting in 1857 for about 60 per cent of total value, and to this amount should be added another 8 per cent for lignite. Far behind were zinc and iron, each with approximately 9 per cent, then came lead with 6 per cent, silver with 3 per cent and copper and manganese with less than 2 per cent each. The collieries were also the most developed mining enterprises in the Zollverein, characterized by a high concentration of capital and intensiveness of production. While their number was rising by only 8 per cent from 591 in 1848 to 636 in 1857, their combined output came close to tripling, from 4,384,000 to 11,279,000 metric tons, and their labor force more than doubled from 36,000 to 78,000. The average coal mine, employing some 122 workers and producing 17,700 tons annually toward the end of the 1850's, was a large-scale undertaking even by the standards of a later age. The industry, moreover, continued to grow steadily throughout the following decade. By 1864 it was providing a livelihood for 99,000 miners and digging 19,409,000 tons, by 1867 the yield was 23,808,-000, and by 1871, 29,373,000 tons.

In most other branches of mining, however, small enterprises and traditional methods were still the rule. Lignite was an important supplement of coal, in 1857 employing 11 per cent of all workers in the pits and accounting for 8 per cent of the combined worth of mine production. Yet there were 683 companies in the field, 47 more than in coal, so that average employment in each was only 26 workers and average value of annual output 16,500 marks. Iron mining was another case in point. It was second only to the collieries in the size of its labor force, while in value it was in third place, after coal and zinc. The industry was particularly important in Westphalia, the Ruhr, the Harz mountains, Thuringia, Upper Silesia, the Spessart range, and the upper valley of the Lahn. In 1857 there were 3,000 iron pits in the Zollverein with 28,000 workers and an output of 11,654,000 marks. For each mine there were thus fewer than 10 miners and an annual production of less than 4,000 marks. Modest as these figures were, they represented a significant improvement over the conditions of 1848, when there were 2,000 works, each on an average with 8 workers and a yield of 1,900 marks. Even as late as 1864, when the labor force had risen to 24,000 men and production to 12,964,000 marks, iron mining had advanced only a short distance beyond the level of a handicraft.[17]

[17] *Jahrbuch für die amtliche Statistik des preussischen Staats*, I (1863), 425-428; P. Benaerts, *Les origines*, pp. 377-378; H. A. Mascher, *Das deutsche Gewerbewesen*, p. 524; J. Kuczynski, *Short History*, p. 84; G. v. Viebahn, *Statistik Deutschlands*, II, 365, 371, 377, 407; *Statistisches*

For that matter, so modern a form of industrial enterprise as machine construction was in the social origin of its leaders, the dissemination of its technology, and the form of its organization not far removed from the world of trade guilds. Its beginnings went back to the late eighteenth century, when mercantilist civil servants of the Prussian state began to build engines and engine factories on the British model, hoping to improve production in the royal mines and foundries. In the 1820's the aging Goethe was disturbed by the incipient mechanization of economic life noticeable even in provincial Weimar. "Machinery, which is gaining the upper hand, worries and alarms me," he confessed in *Wilhelm Meisters Wanderjahre*. "It rolls on like a thunderstorm, slowly, slowly. But it has taken aim, it will come and strike." By that time the manufacture of machinery had ceased to be primarily a state enterprise. It was now more and more dominated by a group of inventive and energetic self-made men, many of them of lower-class background, who had left some skilled craft or modest countinghouse to become the pioneers of a new industry. August Borsig had learned the carpenter's trade before receiving technical training in the Gewerbeinstitut in Berlin and founding his own machine shop. The bellmaker Carl Anton Henschel transformed his foundry in Kassel into a plant for the construction of steam engines. Josef Anton Maffei, who established in Munich the first locomotive works of southern Germany, was originally a dealer in groceries. Richard Hartmann had come to Chemnitz as a wandering journeyman blacksmith, then in 1832 he hired three workmen and opened a small repair shop, in 1841 he built his first engine, and by 1845 he was employing 350 men. These were typical success stories of the early period of machine-building in Central Europe.

Jahrbuch für das Deutsche Reich, I (1880), 30-32; G. Hermes, "Statistische Studien," pp. 148, 150-151; A. Sartorius von Waltershausen, *Wirtschaftsgeschichte*, pp. 166-167.

Ways of acquiring skill and experience were equally uncomplicated. There were no trade journals or professional publications, and schools of technology were few in number. Many founders of new enterprises, therefore, began as employees of older firms, gradually acquiring the knowledge needed to start out on their own. This was essentially the time-honored training method of the guild system adapted to the needs of a youthful industrialism. In their business practices, moreover, the machine-builders resembled master artisans from whom they were often descended more than capitalistic entrepreneurs. Sober and hardheaded, running their factories the way their fathers had run their shops, they looked with suspicion on newfangled financial devices which divorced ownership from management. Only 4 joint-stock companies with a capitalization of 18,150,000 marks were formed in the Prussian machine industry in the 1850's, although there were over 300 companies in the state engaged in the construction of engines. For Germany as a whole, of some 320 joint-stock companies which had come into existence during the decade with a capital close to 2,400,000,000 marks, no more than 8 with 25,500,000 marks were in machinery-building. Was this business conservatism also responsible for the relative decline of mechanization in the machine industry? Whatever the reason, it was incongruous that the same manufacturers who were providing engines for mines and foundries could not themselves keep pace with the technological advance of other sectors of the economy. Their workers almost tripled between 1846 and 1861, rising from 13,000 to 37,000, while their machines increased from 139 to 618 and their horsepower from 1,700 to 6,600. Yet their percentage of the Zollverein total for the number of machines fell from 9 to 6, and for the volume of horsepower from 6.4 to 3.5. The great period of German engine-building was to come later, well after the middle of the century, when the era of rugged individualism had come to an end, and the financier and technician had begun to counsel or even displace the self-made craftsman and inventor.[18]

It was symptomatic of an early stage of industrialism that before 1871 the most important area of investment was not in production but transportation. The railroad was king on every stock exchange in Germany. More than half of the approximately 3,000,000,000 marks at which joint-stock companies were capitalized on the eve of the Franco-Prussian War had gone into the construction of railway lines. Enterprises of such vast dimensions completely overshadowed mines and foundries with 360,000,000 marks and machine factories with a mere 33,000,000 marks. In Berlin stockbrokers were trading in 175 railroad issues, almost half of all offerings. Only government bonds could hold their own on the money market against rail shares. What attracted the investor was the prospect of a quick and ample profit. In the late 1860's the Leipzig-Dresden Railroad was paying dividends of 25 per cent, the Saxon Coal Railroad 23 to 24 per cent, the old Nürnberg-Fürth Railroad 19 per cent, and the Magdeburg-Leipzig Railroad 18 per cent. These were notable achievements which tended to obscure the fact that many companies could show only a modest return. Some of the better lines, however, continued to pay 15 to 20 per cent for years, and the average for all Prussian railroads in 1865 was a respectable 6.25 per cent. The steady flow of investment capital promoted

[18] Johann Wolfgang Goethe, *Wilhelm Meisters Wanderjahre: Wilhelm Meisters theatralische Sendung* (Zurich, 1949), p. 460; Fritz Redlich, "The Leaders of the German Steam-Engine Industry during the First Hundred Years," *Journal of Economic History*, IV (1944), 143-145, 147-148; Franz Schnabel, *Deutsche Geschichte im neunzehnten Jahrhundert* (4 vols., Freiburg im Breisgau, 1929-37), III, 403-405; Heinrich Bechtel, *Wirtschaftsgeschichte Deutschlands* (3 vols., Munich, 1951-56), III, 158-159; H. Blumberg, "Die Finanzierung der Neugründungen," pp. 176-177; P. Benaerts, *Les origines*, pp. 266-267, 377-378, 389; H. A. Mascher, *Das deutsche Gewerbewesen*, p. 524; Ludwig Pohle and Max Muss, *Das deutsche Wirtschaftsleben seit Beginn des neunzehnten Jahrhunderts*, 6th edn., (Leipzig and Berlin, 1930), pp. 14-15.

the growth of the German rail network from 5,800 kilometers in 1850 to 11,000 in 1860, and 18,600 in 1870. Only the United States and Great Britain could surpass these figures.[19]

The form of railroad ownership in the German Confederation varied from state to state. Some of them like Hanover and Baden adopted the principle of state proprietorship which the Belgians had introduced. In the Bavarian Palatinate and for a time in Mecklenburg-Schwerin private enterprise was the rule. Hesse-Kassel and Nassau favored a mixed system under which public and private lines existed side by side. All in all, as of 1860, state railroads totaled 5,200 kilometers, private railroads under government management 1,400, and private railroads with administrative autonomy 4,600. In Prussia the conservative bureaucracy of the late 1830's, distrustful of innovation almost as a matter of principle, followed a policy of watchful waiting with regard to railway companies. Then in 1842 a new period opened, when the state began to encourage construction by subscribing to the capital of important new lines or guaranteeing the interest on their obligations. But direct government ownership did not begin on any significant scale until after 1848, when August von der Heydt became minister of commerce. A political trimmer with a remarkable talent for administration, he devoted himself during his fourteen years in office to the creation of a network of public railroads. Sometimes the state would engage directly in the building of a new line, as

---

[19] H. Bechtel, *Wirtschaftsgeschichte Deutschlands*, III, 164, 453; Werner Sombart, *Die deutsche Volkswirtschaft im neunzehnten Jahrhundert und im Anfang des 20. Jahrhunderts*, 5th edn. (Berlin, 1921), pp. 242-243, 489, 493; Werner Sombart, *Der moderne Kapitalismus: Historisch-systematische Darstellung des gesamteuropäischen Wirtschaftslebens von seinen Anfängen bis zur Gegenwart*, 6th edn. (3 vols., Munich and Leipzig, 1924-28), III, 163; Friedrich Lütge, *Deutsche Sozial- und Wirtschaftsgeschichte* (Berlin, Göttingen, and Heidelberg, 1952), p. 367; L. Pohle and M. Muss, *Das deutsche Wirtschaftsleben*, pp. 16-17; *Zeitschrift des königlich preussischen Statistischen Bureaus*, XV (1875), 430; *Statistisches Handbuch für den preussischen Staat*, II (1893), 299.

with the Eastern Railroad, or it would purchase an established company like the Niederschlesisch-Märkische
Railroad, or it might take over the management of a
private enterprise such as the Bergisch-Märkische Railroad. By 1860 some 2,800 of the 5,700 kilometers of
Prussian railroads were under government ownership
or administration.

After von der Heydt resigned his post two years later,
the pendulum swung back in favor of free enterprise.
The cabinet, determined to carry out the royal program
of military reform even without a legal budget, was reluctant to assume an additional financial obligation by
embarking on new railway ventures. The rising tide of
economic liberalism, moreover, began to carry the bureaucracy with it. Count Heinrich von Itzenplitz, the
new minister of commerce, maintained that it did not
matter who built the railroads, as long as someone did.
It was particularly difficult for the business community
to reconcile the ideal of laissez faire which it increasingly
professed with the leading role of the state in the transportation system. The prominent industrialist and politician Friedrich Hammacher insisted at a meeting of
representatives of the German chambers of commerce
that "the turn of fate placing the railroads in the hands
of the state governments . . . means nothing other than
practicing communism. It means nothing other than
confiscating private property in the interest of the state
and the public welfare, and paralyzing the railroads in
the fulfillment of their industrial mission for the common
good. No one of us will doubt that he would certainly not
be inclined to invest capital in railroad enterprises if the
state had the power under any conditions whatever to
destroy the property of the railroads." To many statesmen and businessmen alike this logic seemed irrefutable. During the 1860's the mileage of private railroads
in Prussia increased twice as much as that of state-owned
lines. Elsewhere the reaction against public ownership
was not so pronounced. But throughout Germany dar

ing entrepreneurs like the "railroad king" Bethel Henry Strousberg formed companies, issued stock, promoted, borrowed, and kited, until the pyramid collapsed in the depression of the following decade.[20]

An increase in commerce accompanied and reflected the expansion of industry and transportation. To be sure, the foreign trade of Germany was only about half that of the United Kingdom, and the difference in the rate of growth increased in favor of the latter after the middle of the century. In the competition for second place in the commerce of Europe, moreover, the French were usually successful, although only by a narrow margin. Yet the rise in the total value of the imports and exports of the Zollverein was impressive. It went from 1,067,000,000 marks in 1850 to 2,173,000,000 in 1860 and 4,834,000,000 in 1869. The population was also growing at a steady rate, but even on a per capita basis, foreign commerce more than tripled, the figures being 36, 63, and 125 marks. During most of the period 1850-69 the balance of trade was unfavorable; only in 1853, 1854, 1858, and 1864 did exports exceed imports. The resultant burden of indebtedness, however, was not heavy. In two decades the total for the states of the Zollverein was no more than 1,113,000,000 marks, almost 90 per cent of it incurred during the years 1866-69. Such a minor imbalance posed no problem for an advancing economy.

The pattern of exportation, however, suggested that the progress of German industrialism was uneven and intermittent. While the greatest proportional increase among goods shipped abroad was in the products of

---

[20] A. Sartorius von Waltershausen, *Wirtschaftsgeschichte*, pp. 104-105, 277-278; Walther Lotz, *Verkehrsentwickelung in Deutschland seit 1800*, 4th edn. (Leipzig and Berlin, 1920), p. 35; F. Lütge, *Sozial- und Wirtschaftsgeschichte*, p. 366; *Deutsches Verkehrsbuch*, ed. Hans Baumann (Berlin, 1931), pp. 7, 11, 14, 25; P. Benaerts, *Les origines*, p. 320; *Verhandlungen des Dritten Deutschen Handelstages zu Frankfurt am Main, vom 25. bis 28. September 1865* (Berlin, 1865), p. 34; *Statistisches Handbuch für den preussischen Staat*, II (1893), 299.

mining and smelting, followed by manufactured wares, agricultural produce, and semifinished articles, these changes were not considerable enough to alter the basic distribution of the components of foreign trade. The largest single category of exports from the Zollverein remained manufactures, amounting to 47 per cent of the total in 1850, 52 per cent in 1864, and 44 per cent in 1869. Within this category textiles consistently accounted for more than half. Raw materials and semifinished products were in second place, with between 27 and 33 per cent. Foodstuffs, ranging from 17 to 20 per cent, were the last of the important elements of exportation. Not until the great expansion of heavy industry after 1871 did these ratios begin to change substantially. As for retail trade, it was still the domain of the small storekeeper, who like the master tailor and shoemaker practiced a time-honored craft in a tradition-bound way. Toward the end of the 1850's there were in Prussia 39,300 proprietors of commercial establishments with 22,900 helpers. Even in a sizable city like Breslau the 500 provision merchants had only 800 employees, so that the typical grocer's shop could hardly have changed much since the time more than a hundred years before when Silesia first became Prussian.[21]

The passing of the old order was more apparent in banking. The demand for new sources of risk capital engendered by the progress of industry was bound to affect the world of finance more than foreign or retail trade. It led in fact to the formation of a number of important new lending institutions distinguished from older banks by both the form of their organization and the character of their investment. In the first place, they were built on the joint-stock principle, thereby seeking to tap a source of funds greater than that available to private financiers. Secondly, they were prepared to ad-

[21] W. Sombart, *Die deutsche Volkswirtschaft*, pp. 224, 521; Gerhard Bondi, *Deutschlands Aussenhandel, 1815-1870* (Berlin, 1958), pp. 145-146; G. Hermes, "Statistische Studien," pp. 158-159.

vance loans for industrial ventures, more hazardous but also potentially more profitable than the government bonds favored by the established firms. The increasingly self-confident tone of their statements of purpose is a gauge of their success as well as of the advance of the economy as a whole. At the time of its establishment in 1851 the directors of the Disconto-Gesellschaft announced modestly that they expected "to provide credit for handicraftsmen and small businessmen by discounting notes or by cash advances." The Darmstädter Bank in 1853 hoped "to transfer temporarily to German industry the funds needed for its operations in the form of current accounts paying interest, but without at the same time encouraging agiotage or directing capital toward unproductive speculation on the stock exchange." By 1856 the Berliner Handelsgesellschaft promised that it would engage in "the operation of bank, commercial, and industrial enterprises of all kinds, as well as the organization, amalgamation, and consolidation of joint-stock companies." And in 1870, with Germany on the threshold of a new era of worldwide economic activity, the Deutsche Bank proudly boasted that it would pursue banking activities of every sort, "particularly the advancement and facilitation of commercial relations between Germany, the other European states, and overseas markets."

There were good financial reasons for this self-confidence. Between the Revolution of 1848 and the depression of 1857 about fourteen major joint-stock banks were established in Germany, starting with the A. Schaaffhausenscher Bankverein of Cologne and ending on the eve of the crash with the Handelsgesellschaft in Berlin, the Allgemeine Deutsche Credit-Anstalt in Leipzig, the Mitteldeutsche Creditbank in Meiningen, and the Norddeutsche Bank in Hamburg, among others. "Each city, each state, however small, wants to have its bank and its lending establishment," observed the French consul in Leipzig in a dispatch to his government of March 14, 1856. "There are many people who are somewhat frightened by this enthusiasm which they find not entirely in keeping with the real needs and financial means of Germany. . . . It seems as if there is as much determination to cover Germany with a network of credit institutions as there was to cover her with a network of railroads." The comparison was apt. Of the nearly 2,400,000,000 marks invested in new joint-stock companies during the 1850's, about 1,000,000,000 were in transportation, 800,000,000 in banking, and 600,000,000 in industry. The ten largest investment banks of northern Germany represented as much capital as all the joint-stock companies of the Zollverein engaged in mining and smelting. Is it any wonder that many investors preferred to put their money into ventures like the Disconto-Gesellschaft or the Handelsgesellschaft rather than collieries and foundries? Out of a total of 359 issues traded on the Berlin stock exchange at the end of 1870, 175 were in railroads, 99 in government loans, both domestic and foreign, 76 in various banking institutions, and only 9 in industrial enterprises.

The victory of the new banks, however, was neither immediate nor complete. In finance as in industry tradition was a powerful force. Even the great Darmstädter Bank, organized with the aid of French capital on the model of Crédit Mobilier, proved a disappointment at first. Its report of May 22, 1854, spoke of the difficulties it had encountered because of "political circumstances and the hostility of a great many people," complaining that its critics were spreading the view that it was "an essentially dangerous institution established to excite speculation to an excess, to aid agiotage, and to feed the manipulations of the bourse." The opposition to joint-stock financing could at times prove insurmountable. For example, in Frankfurt am Main, a historic stronghold of the private bank, the great firms like Grünelius, Metzler, and of course Rothschild succeeded in frustrating most plans for new credit institutions. There were many instances, on the other hand, in which farseeing financiers of the old school participated in the formation of investment companies designed to meet the needs of industry. The Handelsgesellschaft, established with the support of such banking houses as Sal. Oppenheim Jr. & Co. of Cologne and Mendelssohn & Co. of Berlin, was a case in point. Abraham Oppenheim collaborated with the brilliant entrepreneur Gustav Mevissen in organizing the Darmstädter Bank. There was the Waaren-Kredit-Gesellschaft founded at Königsberg in which Gerson Bleichröder and Jacob Cassel, both of them engaged in private underwriting, played an important role. In view of these interconnections between the old banks and the new, it would be misleading to make a sharp distinction between their interests.

Whatever their structural differences, moreover, they often undertook the same sort of financial operations. In its early lean days the Darmstädter Bank acted as the fiscal agent for the Hessian state, underwrote a portion of the French Crimean War bonds, and participated in a loan to the government of Baden. By the same token even the Rothschilds, after achieving greatness as moneylenders for the rulers of Europe, began to promote such ventures as the Upper Silesian Railroad and the Machine Construction Company of Karlsruhe. The ubiquitous Oppenheim brothers joined forces with the Disconto-Gesellschaft to help form the Aachen-Höngen Mining Company; S. Bleichröder as well as the A. Schaaffhausenscher Bankverein were members of the consortium which reorganized the Kissing & Schmöle metalworks in Westphalia; Cohn, Bürgers & Co. and the Darmstädter Bank took the lead in financing the Berlin-Potsdam-Magdeburg Railroad; and M. A. v. Rothschild & Sons and S. Bleichröder collaborated with the Disconto-Gesellschaft and the Darmstädter Bank on the Thuringian Railroad.

How meaningful then is the usual textbook differentiation between the old banks and the new, when applied to the middle years of the nineteenth century? The latter institutions undoubtedly helped by their example to demonstrate the possibilities of industrial investing and promoting. Yet the undeveloped state of the German credit system precluded a high degree of specialization in finance. All types of banking houses shared in the prosperity of the years 1850-70. In Cologne the number of private lending firms rose from 11 to 24, and even those establishments engaged only in money changing increased from 7 to 13. The resources of the joint-stock banks were not yet sufficient to give them a decisive advantage. As of 1857 the largest among them had an average capitalization of barely 30,000,000 marks. The value of the acceptance bills of nine big banking companies in Berlin was a mere 8,200,000 marks, while in Prussia as a whole there were only 602 establishments with 1,172 employees dealing in money and credit. At the beginning of the twentieth century a spokesman for the Dresdner Bank, contemplating the growth of financial operations during his lifetime, concluded with substantial accuracy: "It is from 1871 that our real development dates, and it is since that year our great banks have been organised."[22]

Yet even during the years before the achievement of national unification the economy had begun to display tendencies symptomatic of industrial capitalism. The most obvious of these was the growing mechanization of

[22] J. H. Clapham, *The Economic Development of France and Germany, 1815-1914*, 4th edn. (Cambridge, 1951), p. 390. Cf. A. Sartorius von Waltershausen, *Wirtschaftsgeschichte*, pp. 555-556; Jürgen Kuczynski, *Die Bewegung der deutschen Wirtschaft von 1800 bis 1946*, 2nd edn. (Berlin and Leipzig, 1947), p. 71; P. Benaerts, *Les origines*, pp. 266-267, 273-278; G. Hermes, "Statistische Studien," pp. 155-156; W. Sombart, *Die deutsche Volkswirtschaft*, pp. 178, 489; Rondo E. Cameron, "Founding the Bank of Darmstadt," *Explorations in Entrepreneurial History*, VIII (1956), 118-119, 123-125; Alfred Krüger, *Das Kölner Bankiergewerbe vom Ende des 18. Jahrhunderts bis 1875* (Essen, 1925), pp. 143, 151, 167-169, 195; W. Sombart, *Der moderne Kapitalismus*, III, 210.

production. In 1850 the horsepower employed in German industry was 260,000, as compared with 370,000 for France and 1,290,000 for the United Kingdom. Ten years later Germany was still in third place with 850,000, while the French figure was 1,120,000, and the British 2,450,000. But the German rate of increase had been the largest, and by 1870 a significant change had taken place in the relative positions of the three leading industrial powers of Europe. Germany with 2,480,000 horsepower was now well ahead of France, which had 1,850,000. More than that, the United Kingdom's total of 4,040,000 was not even twice that of Germany, whereas twenty years before it had been five times as large. This technological advance of Central Europe was clearly reflected in the growing productivity of labor. The number of coal miners in the Zollverein increased 119 per cent between 1848 and 1857, while the amount of coal mined increased 157 per cent. In the extraction of iron ore the working force expanded 82 per cent and the volume of output 183 per cent. Laborers employed in blast furnaces grew 41 per cent as compared with a rise in the production of pig iron of 155 per cent. During the 1860's the increase in productivity was equally impressive. The average annual output of a worker in coal mining grew about 33 per cent, in copper mining 24 per cent, and in iron smelting 71 per cent. While more rational methods of organizing production accounted in part for this progress, most of it was the effect of an improvement in industrial technology.[23]

As significant as the mechanization of production was its incipient tendency toward concentration. The large-scale enterprise was already beginning to jeopardize the economic existence of the countless small workshops and countinghouses whose roots were still in the preindustrial age. The result in many cases was a decline in the total number of establishments engaged in a given field

[23] J. Kuczynski, *Short History*, pp. 85, 87, 89, 116, 151, 153; G. v. Viebahn, *Statistik Deutschlands*, II, 365, 377, 421.

of manufacture accompanied by a marked increase in the size and strength of those which had emerged victorious in the struggle for existence. This trend was most pronounced where industrialization was farthest advanced. Metallurgy and metalworking were an apt illustration. Those factories in the Zollverein engaged in the production of basic materials like pig iron and requiring the largest amount of capital and equipment decreased slightly between 1849 and 1861, from 720 to 656, while the average number of workers in each factory more than doubled, from 25 to 56. Similarly, enterprises involved in transforming and refining operations, that is, forges, rolling mills, and steel works, diminished by about a half, from 2,567 to 1,311, but the labor force per unit rose from not quite 5 to 16. By contrast, plants turning out specialized metal products such as wire, tools, and machines increased from 498 to 1,103, at a more rapid rate than the number of employees, so that the workers in an average shop actually declined from 27 to 25.

The process of concentration was also discernible in railroading, where a policy of consolidation could be profitably combined with speculation on the stock exchange. The Bergisch-Märkische Railroad, for example, enjoyed great success in expanding its network in the Rhine valley despite the fact that its administration was controlled by the Prussian government. It absorbed the Düsseldorf-Elberfeld line in 1857, the Prince Wilhelm in 1863, and the Aachen-Düsseldorf, the Ruhrort–Krefeld–Kreis Gladbach, and the Elector Friedrich Wilhelm's Northern Railroads in 1866. Even among private bankers there was a growing disparity between the large firms and the small, as the experience of Cologne suggested. The number of banking houses in the city, exclusive of those engaged only in money changing, rose from 9 in 1835 to 33 in 1875. Yet in fact wealth was increasingly concentrated in the six leading companies, whose combined resources were probably more than ten times as large as those of all the other middle and small banks put together.[24]

Finally, the spread of joint-stock financing bespoke the opening of a new economic age. It represented the accommodation of the money market to the demands created by the mechanization of transportation and production, so that its effect was greatest in precisely those sectors of the economy most adaptable to the techniques of industrial capitalism. The railroad, a product of the nineteenth century and thus free from ties to an established handicraft tradition, received far and away the largest share of the funds provided by the general public for new business ventures. In manufacture it was heavy industry, particularly mines and foundries, which adjusted most successfully to changing forms of entrepreneurial organization. And in finance itself investment banks and insurance companies, serving the needs of the industrializing process, utilized the resources of the small investor to challenge the established private lending firms. As yet the possibilities inherent in the joint-stock principle were not fully realized, primarily because they had not been thoroughly explored. There were still those who felt that the struggle between the old and the new mode of financing would end in stalemate and coexistence. But as early as 1856 Gustav Mevissen presented a remarkably penetrating analysis of the fundamental changes in business structure which were beginning to take place:

> The alliance within the field of industry of capital and intellectual forces in the form of the joint-stock company has increasingly become a striking feature of the present time. . . . On the basis of what has already occurred, it seems clear today after the passage of a few decades that the joint-stock company has developed in modern society with the energy and speed of a force of nature. As a result

[24] P. Benaerts, *Les origines*, p. 497; *Deutsches Verkehrsbuch*, ed. H. Baumann, p. 17; A. Krüger, *Kölner Bankiergewerbe*, p. 40.

of conditions in Europe and America, it has arisen simul-
taneously in all states which have assumed the great task
of material progress; it has in a sense re-established the
corporate association on the ruins of a bygone era. The
energies united within its form have in the course of a
few decades created works of material civilization before
which even the great works of antiquity and the Middle
Ages must bow. Like all natural manifestations of the
spirit of a given period, it has found no pre-existent forms.
Its legal position and the legislation which governs it are
divergent. The extent of the authority granted to this new
corporate association varies enormously, depending on
the differences among the states, from fearful mistrust and
the most minute supervision of its every move to the most
complete and unconditional acceptance of its creative
power. Besides, the resistance which develops against all
new creations bearing the seeds of a great future has not
been and is not absent. But so far the young giant has
overcome all his opponents, and every day enlarges his
power. . . . The newest achievements of modern times,
the railway and steamship companies, allied with the
banks and insurance companies belonging to an earlier
period, were the first to be molded in the form of the
joint-stock company. Based on these fields, the form has
gradually gained control of a number of branches of industry in which capital plays the leading role, and individual activity and talent a secondary one. It seeks to
penetrate deeper and deeper into the domain of industry.[25]

Agriculture was also profoundly influenced by the
spirit and method of industrial capitalism. For in the
cultivation of the soil as in the manufacture of goods

[25] Joseph Hansen, *Gustav von Mevissen: Ein rheinisches Lebensbild,
1815-1899* (2 vols., Berlin, 1906), II, 532-533. Cf. W. Sombart, *Die
deutsche Volkswirtschaft*, pp. 84-85; A. Sartorius von Waltershausen,
Wirtschaftsgeschichte, p. 189; H. Bechtel, *Wirtschaftsgeschichte Deutschlands*, III, 453; J. Kuczynski, *Short History*, pp. 67-68; P. Benaerts, *Les
origines*, pp. 266-267; L. Pohle and M. Muss, *Das deutsche Wirtschaftsleben*, pp. 16-17; H. Blumberg, "Die Finanzierung der Neugründungen,"
pp. 176-178, 185.

the advantages of rationalized technique and large-scale output were becoming obvious. Mevissen was even convinced that "we are standing on the threshold of an age when the form of the joint-stock company will also draw the tillage of the land within its sphere and bring agriculture into the closest relationship with industry." He may have been mistaken regarding the specific form of landownership which would result from the modernization of farming, but he recognized the basic similarity in the development of industrial and agricultural production. Both were attempting to adjust their organization and procedure to the conditions of a new economic era. In the fifty years following the War of Liberation the large estate owners of Prussia extended their possessions by close to 1,000,000 hectares at the expense of smaller peasant proprietors. In addition, the area under cultivation in the kingdom grew more than 1,500,000 hectares between 1849 and 1864, while the proportion of wasteland decreased from 19 to 7 per cent of the total. East of the Elbe many of the aristocratic landholders were learning to combine the growing of rye and wheat with the refining of sugar, baking of brick, and distilling of alcohol. Throughout Germany, moreover, the consolidation of scattered holdings and the division of common lands were making possible more efficient methods of tillage.

Yet the improvement of agriculture was an expensive process. In Prussia even the big landowners, whose peasants had paid them about 260,000,000 marks as compensation for abolished manorial dues, were forced to borrow heavily in order to modernize their estates. The burden of their indebtedness had remained fairly constant during the period of depression and revolution in the 1840's, but then it rose 13 per cent during 1850-55 and another 12 per cent during 1855-60. At the time of the establishment of the North German Confederation it amounted to more than 500,000,000 marks. The result was bound to be a growing mobility in the ownership of land. As of 1885 scarcely 25 per cent of the latifundia beyond the Elbe had been in the possession of the same family more than fifty years. During the years 1835-65, 11,800 large Prussian estates in the eastern provinces and Westphalia changed hands some 23,600 times, 7,900 of them by inheritance, 14,400 by voluntary sale, and 1,300 by foreclosure. The traditional distinction between aristocratic and bourgeois forms of property was clearly breaking down under the growing influence of capital in agriculture. The number of middle-class landowners continued to expand throughout the early and middle decades of the century, until by the 1880's noble proprietors were in a minority even in the east. But the infusion of bourgeois energy and wealth provided a powerful stimulus to rural enterprise, and the resultant improvement in farming methods helped the aristocracy retain economic importance in a period of rising industrialization.

What made landownership an attractive form of investment despite increasing indebtedness was its prosperous state. For agriculture no less than industry flourished during the mid-century. Indeed, while bankers and millowners still had to cope with obstacles like antiquated usury laws and restrictions on the formation of joint-stock companies, enterprising landholders were free to proceed with the modernization of their estates as they saw fit. The legal transition from manorialism to a system of free proprietorship had been completed in the wake of the Revolution of 1848, and during the decades which followed farming boomed as never before. Thanks to advances in organization and technology the yield of rye on 100 hectares of medium quality soil rose from 94 metric tons in 1840-50 to 103 in 1850-60 and 135 in 1860-70. Agricultural prices remained high, and some even tended to rise, so that net proceeds from husbandry approximately doubled between 1850 and 1880. A hundredweight of rye which cost, on an average, 6.13 marks in 1841-50 sold for 8.02 in 1851-60 and 7.37

in 1861-70. At the same time the price of a pound of beef was increasing from 28 pfennigs to 35 and 43, and of a pound of butter from 60 to 73 and 89 pfennigs. The growing value of farm land reflected rural prosperity. In Posen large estates which could be purchased for 274 marks per hectare in 1841-50 were realizing 340 in 1851-60 and 459 in 1861-70. By 1867 the price of eastern latifundia was about four times what it had been eighty years before. Foreign consumption of grain from Central Europe was beginning to decline, especially after 1864 when Danish attacks on Prussian and Hanseatic shipping gave the wheatgrowers of America an advantage in the English market which they never relinquished. But the increase in domestic demand arising out of the expanding industrialization of Germany made up for losses suffered abroad. Agriculture continued to thrive until well into the 1870's.

While the great landowners were the principal beneficiaries of this prosperity, the peasantry also managed to improve its lot. During the Hungry Forties unrest engendered by overpopulation and crop failure had culminated in a rural uprising in the spring of 1848. Fifteen years later the masses of the countryside were only impassive observers of the renewed struggle between progressive and traditionalist political principles. Good harvests and rising incomes had reconciled them to the status quo. For those who could not make a go of it on the farm, there was the alternative of emigration, either abroad to the fertile fields of the New World, or within Central Europe to the factories of the city. The hope of enlightened statesmen early in the century that a vigorous class of independent peasant proprietors would emerge out of agrarian reform had been frustrated, partly by the rapid growth of population on the land, partly by the conservative social policies of government authorities. But after 1850 even the small peasant proprietor along the Neckar or the Main was able to profit from the expansion of the domestic market for foodstuffs, while beyond the Elbe the real income of farm hands on the great estates rose close to 50 per cent during the twenty years preceding the establishment of the German Empire. By 1873 landowners were complaining that it was becoming increasingly difficult to find agricultural labor at wages they could afford to pay. Yet good times also allayed discontent in the villages, and the aristocracy could derive comfort from the assurances of the well-known sociologist Wilhelm Heinrich Riehl that "the conservatism of the peasant is a way of life with him." Whether it was a matter of habit or prosperity, the countryside remained loyal to the established order throughout the period of national unification.[26]

In agriculture no less than in industry, the introduction of advanced techniques of production was essential for material progress. More than that, attitudes as well as methods had to change. Yet the abandonment of what had for centuries been a familiar way of life was a difficult process, both technologically and psychologically. It meant a fundamental alteration in the beliefs, customs, hopes, and expectations of important social groups suddenly forced to adjust to new economic realities. The

[26] J. Hansen, *Mevissen*, II, 533; Max Sering, *Deutsche Agrarpolitik auf geschichtlicher und landeskundlicher Grundlage* (Leipzig, 1934), p. 29; Alexander Gerschenkron, *Bread and Democracy in Germany* (Berkeley and Los Angeles, 1943), p. 23; Gunther Ipsen, "Die preussische Bauernbefreiung als Landesausbau," *Zeitschrift für Agrargeschichte und Agrarsoziologie*, II (1954), 48; Siegfried von Ciriacy-Wantrup, *Agrarkrisen und Stockungsspannen: Zur Frage der langen "Welle" in der wirtschaftlichen Entwicklung* (Berlin, 1936), pp. 37, 41-42, 46, 118, 378; W. Sombart, *Der moderne Kapitalismus*, III, 245, 334-335; J. Conrad, "Agrarstatistische Untersuchungen: Die Latifundien im preussischen Osten," *Jahrbücher für Nationalökonomie und Statistik*, L (1888), 138, 140, 152; Theodor von der Goltz, *Geschichte der deutschen Landwirtschaft* (2 vols., Stuttgart and Berlin, 1902-03), II, 350; Theodor von der Goltz, *Vorlesungen über Agrarwesen und Agrarpolitik* (Jena, 1899), pp. 44-45; I. N. Lambi, *Free Trade and Protection*, pp. 19-21; W. Sombart, *Die deutsche Volkswirtschaft*, pp. 358, 360; H. Bechtel, *Wirtschaftsgeschichte Deutschlands*, III, 182; L. Pohle and M. Muss, *Das deutsche Wirtschaftsleben*, p. 107; W. H. Riehl, *Die bürgerliche Gesellschaft*, 2nd edn. (Stuttgart and Tübingen, 1854), p. 41.

mechanization and concentration of manufacture, for example, undermined many of the handicraft trades which provided a livelihood for the mass of skilled artisans. The first to feel the adverse effects of industrialization were the ancillary employments practiced in the villages to supplement an income derived primarily from agricultural pursuits. The decline in the weaving of linen cloth, largely a rural part-time occupation, illustrates this development. Between 1837 and 1861 the number of linen looms decreased from 11,600 to 7,900 in Silesia, from 13,500 to 9,000 in the Province of Saxony, and from 26,900 to 18,400 in Westphalia. As of the early 1860's there were still 250,000 of them in Prussia as a whole, but twenty years later only about 30,000 remained. The brewing and distilling of alcohol, another important industrial supplement of agriculture, was beginning to diminish in the country districts. In Saxony the number of rural distilleries fell 39 per cent during the period 1840-65, while in the Prussian provinces rural breweries declined 47 per cent. Gristmills driven by water or wind were now being replaced by steam mills, some of them employing as many as 70 workers; in Prussia alone the number of steam mills grew from 115 to 664 between 1846 and 1861.

Even more serious was the plight of those whose full-time occupations were threatened by the advance of industrialism. Since the peasant's main source of income was farming, he could manage without a still or a hand loom, especially when the price of grain was rising. But for the independent handicraft spinners of linen thread, the mechanization and consolidation of manufacture were an economic tragedy. Of the 84,000 in Prussia in 1849 no more than 14,500 were left in 1861, when even the most diligent workers could barely earn more than six pfennigs a day. In the textile industry the position of the skilled artisan was likewise deteriorating. Factories were beginning to dominate the weaving of wool, and the Chemnitz chamber of commerce reported in 1863

that "in the surrounding districts . . . , where the weaving of cotton by hand is still very widespread, the high
price of the raw material and the competition of the
power looms have reduced production to a third or a
fourth of its former importance." After 1840 the small
tailor shop had to face urban manufacturers of ready-
made clothes who were even preparing to expand into
the countryside. By 1852 an establishment like Hermann Gerson in Berlin was already employing more
than 200 skilled craftsmen, seamstresses, clerks, and
supervisors in its workshops and salesrooms. The process
of economic concentration was also apparent in such
other diverse fields as the luxury trades and mining.
Surveying the situation of the coal industry in 1860, the
Statistical Bureau of Saxony concluded that "the prevailing course of development leads to the abandonment of the little enterprises without prospects for the
future."

In some regions and occupations, to be sure, handicraftsmen succeeded in holding their own. The demand
for goldsmiths, silversmiths, copper workers, needlemak-
ers, and beltmakers actually increased around Nürnberg
and Fürth after 1847. Elsewhere in Bavaria wood carving and basket weaving managed to extend their markets and earnings. But even most of the well-to-do
artisans sensed that they were facing a bleak future.
The young economist Gustav Schmoller, on the threshold of a brilliant career, noted in the late 1860's that
"they seek to practice their trade as their fathers and
grandfathers had done. They do not understand the
new age. They only see that despite all their work they
are getting poorer and poorer." The victory of industrial capitalism in Germany was not yet complete. The
craftsman's shop continued to compete with the factory;
handiwork resisted the machine; corporative guild regulations restricted the freedom of action of millowners
and promoters; divergencies in coinage systems, weights
and measures, commercial laws, and economic policies

hampered the flow of trade; and a rural, conservative distrust of urban forms of wealth stood in the way of the development of banking. But in economics as in politics the period of national unification marked a decisive breakthrough, creating conditions under which a new order could once and for all destroy the old. More than that, there was a powerful interaction between the processes of civic and material consolidation. The veteran democrat Franz Ziegler was one of many contemporary observers who recognized what was taking place. On April 5, 1866, as Prussia and Austria girded for their decisive test of strength, he wrote in a mood of bitter discouragement: "Legitimacy, Caesarism, republic, etc., all of that is intertwined with cotton, brandy, coal, and iron. A terrible time is coming for thinking men, but the bourgeoisie will wallow in rapture and bliss. . . . People want to trade, earn, enjoy, and get along; they want not a state but a trading company."[27]

[27] Ludwig Dehio, "Die preussische Demokratie und der Krieg von 1866: Aus dem Briefwechsel von Karl Rodbertus mit Franz Ziegler," *Forschungen zur brandenburgischen und preussischen Geschichte*, xxxix (1927), 241. Cf. W. Sombart, *Der moderne Kapitalismus*, iii, 341-343; J. H. Clapham, *Economic Development*, p, 291; Gustav Schmoller, *Zur Geschichte der deutschen Kleingewerbe im 19. Jahrhundert* (Halle, 1870), pp. 125-126, 399, 667; L. Pohle and M. Muss, *Das deutsche Wirtschaftsleben*, p. 84; W. Sombart, *Die deutsche Volkswirtschaft*, pp. 283, 291; P. Benaerts, *Les origines*, pp. 395, 431.

TWO

✦✦

The Social Structure

THE transformation of the German economy was partly a cause, partly an effect of basic changes in the pattern of society. The most obvious was a rapid rise in population, which increased from about 25,000,000 to 40,000,000 between the Congress of Vienna and the Franco-Prussian War. This rate of growth, amounting to some 60 per cent for a period of 55 years, was still behind that of Great Britain, where the corresponding figure was 70 per cent, but it was also far ahead of Austria with 50, Italy with 43.3, and France with 33.6 per cent. Yet the course of demographic development in Central Europe was neither uniform nor constant. Sensitive to political, economic, and social influences, it reflected a historical process as much as a biological one.

During the tranquil years of the Restoration between 1815 and 1845 the number of inhabitants of Germany grew 37.7 per cent, from 25,000,000 to approximately 34,500,000. Three decades of uninterrupted peace, the improvement of agriculture, the development of commerce, the advance of communication, the beginning of industrialism, the liberalization of economic practice, all provided an environment favorable to the expansion of population. By the same token, during the years of struggle for national unification between 1845 and 1870 the growth was only some 6,000,000, or 17.6 per cent, the rate of increase being scarcely half of what it had been in the previous period. The most important factor in this decline was the famine and depression of the late 1840's. Aggravated by revolution and the danger of war, its effects continued to be felt well into the following decade despite the revival of the economy. The average annual rise in population, after reaching 1.42 per cent in 1816-37, fell to 0.85 for the years 1837-58. In Prussia the triennial increase, which was 641,854 for 1843-46, dropped to 218,249 for 1846-49, climbed back to 604,233 for 1849-52, but then sank again to 267,411 for 1852-55. In Saxony there was a growth of 78,633 in 1843-46, 57,534 in 1846-49, 95,052 in 1849-52, and 51,133 in 1852-55. Some of the states of the German Confederation actually diminished. Württemberg, for example, had 1,752,538 inhabitants in 1846 and 1,669,720 nine years later. The figures for Baden during approximately the same period were 1,349,884 and 1,314,837. Bavaria declined by 12,213 between 1852 and 1855, while in Mecklenburg-Schwerin the loss was 4,106, from 543,337 in 1851 to 539,231 in 1857. The prosperity of the following decade partly counterbalanced the forces inhibiting the growth of population, but the sense of political insecurity aroused by the policy of blood and iron slowed demographic as well as economic expansion. The rate of increase, which had amounted to 12 per cent in the 1820's and 11 in the 1830's, fell to 8 in the 1840's, 7 in the 1850's, and 8 again in the 1860's. Only after the establishment of the empire had dispelled widespread doubts about the future of Germany did the tempo quicken once more, reaching 11 per cent in the 1870's, 9 in the 1880's, and 14 in the 1890's.

The increase in population varied from region to region, depending on the ability of the economy to absorb an expanding labor force. The flourishing agricultural districts of the east, underpopulated at the beginning of the century, almost doubled during the fifty years following the War of Liberation. In the crowded towns and villages of the south and west, on the other hand, the rise was only about 23 per cent. Of the larger states, Saxony had the highest rate of growth thanks to her rapid industrialization, the average annual increment between 1837 and 1858 being 1.36 per cent. Prussia was not far behind with a figure of 1.21 per cent. But here the critical factor was the progress of agriculture rather than industry. Such eastern provinces as Pomerania, East and West Prussia, and Posen, where artistocratic latifundia predominated, rose 1.29 per cent each year, while to the west in the industrially more advanced Rhine Province and Westphalia the increase was only about 1.07 per cent. Even the purely agrarian states of the north like Holstein with 0.89, Mecklenburg-Strelitz with 0.74, Mecklenburg-Schwerin with 0.59, and Oldenburg with 0.60 per cent were growing faster than Hesse-Darmstadt with 0.41, Bavaria with 0.33, Baden with 0.27, and Hesse-Kassel with 0.01 per cent. The political consequence of these demographic developments was to strengthen the government in Berlin in relation to the particularistic and Austrophile regimes south of the Main. Between 1815 and 1864 the inhabitants of Prussia increased 87 per cent, from 10,319,993 to 19,254,649. In Bavaria during approximately the same period the rise was no more than 30 per cent, from 3,707,966 to 4,807,440, and in Württemberg it was 24 per cent, from 1,410,327 to 1,747,187. This divergence in long-range population growth had a significant effect on the outcome of the struggle for national unification.

The demographic expansion of the first half of the nineteenth century was due in large measure to a rural lower-class increase in population. This increase, however, was subject to considerable local variation. During the years 1835-71 the average annual number of births per 10,000 inhabitants was 447 in the Province of Posen, 446 in East and West Prussia, 405 in Silesia, and 398 in Pomerania, while in the Rhine Province the figure was 373 and in Westphalia 362. The obvious conclusion would seem to be that farming districts were growing more rapidly than centers of manufacture. Yet in agricultural Bavaria the average annual increase in the number of inhabitants during the period 1837-58 was only 0.33 per cent, whereas in industrialized Saxony it was 1.36. The point is that economic opportunity had a profound influence on the geographic distribution of population growth. The overcrowded, subdivided lands of the south and west were simply incapable of yielding a significantly higher volume of produce within the framework of what Friedrich List in the 1840's had described as a "dwarf economy." But east of the Elbe the rationalization of agriculture on the large estates and the more intensive exploitation of an underpopulated soil generated a demand for farm labor which encouraged fertility and minimized emigration. As of 1858 the Hohenzollern kingdom was still twenty-sixth among the states of the German Confederation in density of population. In its rate of growth, however, it was in sixth place, exceeded only by the municipal republics Hamburg, Bremen, and Frankfurt am Main, by tiny Reuss-Greiz, and by booming Saxony. Moreover, while in 1816 the Rhine Province and Westphalia had about 82,000 inhabitants more than Pomerania, East and West Prussia, and Posen, forty years later the latter were the more populous by close to 750,000. In other words, at the time of the Prussian constitutional conflict in the 1860's the rural strongholds of the conservative aristocracy were gaining both demographically and economically.[1]

The growth of population was not due to any increase in longevity until well after 1871. Indeed, on the eve of the Franco-Prussian War Gustav Schmoller was arguing that life expectancy actually diminished as a result of industrial progress: "Mortality has grown. The assertion that there has been an extension of the mean

[1] P. Benaerts, *Les origines*, pp. 131-134, 136, 138; G. v. Viebahn, *Statistik Deutschlands*, I, 341, 349, 361, II, 43, 171, 251, 258, 261; Bruno Moll, *Die Landarbeiterfrage im Königreich Sachsen* (Leipzig, 1908), p. 52; F. Lütge, *Sozial- und Wirtschaftsgeschichte*, p. 306; "Beiträge zur Statistik des Deutschen Reiches," *Zeitschrift des königlich preussischen Statistischen Bureaus*, XVII (1877), 277.

span of life has long ago been consigned by science to the realm of fairy tales. The only scientific estimate for Prussia dealing with the average age of those dying every year shows that it has successively decreased from the beginning of the century to the present. Life has on the average become a shorter phenomenon. Work and pleasure are destroying it. The struggles and fortunes befalling the lives of most people are more variable and make this result seem natural." But his social conscience had gotten the better of his judgment. The fact was that mortality had not increased, although it had not decreased either. The Prussian annual death rate per 10,000 inhabitants was 297 in 1816-30, 299 in 1931-40, 295 in 1841-49, 298 in 1850-59, and 286 in 1860-69. For Germany as a whole it was 268 in the 1840's, 266 in the 1850's, and 270 in the 1860's. The average of 268 for the entire period 1841-70 was much more favorable than the Austrian figure of 316, but it was also substantially greater than the 229 for Great Britain, 235 for France, 235 for Belgium, and 257 for the Netherlands. In regard to life expectancy, a more sensitive measure of mortality than the death rate because less dependent on the age distribution of the population, Germany was also behind her neighbors to the west and north. The average span of life of a German male in 1875 was 35.6 years, compared with 41.4 for an Englishman, 45.3 for a Swede, 48.3 for a Norwegian, 39.1 for a Frenchman as of 1865, and 36.4 for a Dutchman as of 1855.

What accounted for the growth of population in the German Confederation was the fact that the birth rate was consistently higher than the death rate. Their relationship could be expressed in graph form by two roughly parallel curves moving horizontally. If proportionately more people were dying in Germany than in Western Europe, more were also being born. The average birth rate per 10,000 inhabitants for the decades 1841-70 was 362, less than in Austria, where it was 385, but also considerably higher than the 340 in Great

Britain, 266 in France, 308 in Belgium, and 339 in the Netherlands. In Germany, moreover, the average excess of births over deaths, 95, was greater than in any of the neighboring states to the west and south except Great Britain with 116. During the twenty-five years prior to the Seven Weeks' War it would at times depart drastically from the mean, dropping to 42 in 1848 and 41 in 1855, or rising to 120 in 1845 and 131 in 1860. Yet by and large it tended to fall within a range between 85 and 115.

There were, however, important differences among the states of the German Confederation, depending on the extent to which economic conditions encouraged fertility and reduced disease. From the 1830's through the 1860's the favorable balance of demographic change amounted to an average annual figure of 100 per 10,000 inhabitants for Prussia, 84 for Württemberg, and 60 for Bavaria. Infant mortality was also consistently high, so that during the period 1820-70 the deaths of those less than a year old reached 20 per cent of all live births in Prussia and 30 per cent in Bavaria, even exceeding 40 per cent in some districts like Swabia. But the fact that population growth was due to a large birth rate rather than an increase in life span meant that the country was young and vigorous. This was especially true of Prussia, where in the 1850's and 1860's about 46 per cent of the inhabitants were under 20 years, 41 per cent were between 21 and 50, and only 13 per cent were over 50. In most of the other states the age distribution was less advantageous, but not substantially different. Here then was a people in the prime of life, capable of working and procreating, capable of fighting and dying for a statecraft of blood and iron.[2]

[2] G. Schmoller, *Geschichte der Kleingewerbe*, p. 692; P. Benaerts, *Les origines*, pp. 137-138, 141-142; S. v. Ciriacy-Wantrup, *Agrarkrisen und Stockungsspannen*, pp. 164-165; Paul Mombert, *Studien zur Bevölkerungsbewegung in Deutschland in den letzten Jahrzehnten mit besonderer Berücksichtigung der ehelichen Fruchtbarkeit* (Karlsruhe, 1907), p. 105; C.F.W. Dieterici, *Handbuch der Statistik des preussischen Staats* (Berlin, 1861), p. 191.

Demographic development, however, did not depend entirely on the relationship of the birth and death rates. It also reflected the movement of population within the German Confederation as well as beyond its frontiers to foreign countries. But until the coming of the Hungry Forties emigration abroad was not a common solution to the problems arising out of economic hardship. Between 1821 and 1840 only some 176,000 persons crossed the Atlantic from Germany, the vast majority of them seeking land and opportunity in fabled America. Much more important was the flow from the impoverished and overpopulated regions of southern Germany, Austria, and even Russian Poland to the expanding economy of the northeast. Prussia, for example, attracted about 177,000 migrants in the difficult years 1816-19 which followed the end of the Napoleonic wars. During the 1820's the volume of immigration declined considerably, but then it rose again, reaching 154,000 in 1831-34, 142,000 in 1834-37, and 343,000 in 1837-40, when it amounted to more than two-thirds of the increase due to the surplus of births.

The depression of the following decade changed the pattern of population movement drastically. What had been a trickle of wanderers overseas became a human flood desperate to escape from the hunger of Central Europe. In 1841-43 around 64,000 persons left Germany; in 1844-46 the number was 101,000; during the crisis period 1847-49 it swelled to 306,000; there was a slight decline to 294,000 in 1850-52; then another increase to 474,000 in 1853-55; and finally a leveling off at 133,000 in 1856-58 and 137,000 in 1859-61. All in all, approximately 1,500,000 people left the German Confederation between 1841 and 1860, the bulk of them in search of material improvement more than political emancipation. Gustav von Struve, who had himself been forced into exile in the United States because of his republican predilections, acknowledged that most emigrants "would prefer to find in the German fatherland what they now seek with a great expenditure of time, effort, and money on the other side of the ocean, namely, the freedom to settle down, to marry, and to acquire civic rights, as well as land at cheaper prices."

The economic motivation of the great wave of emigration which reached its peak during 1848-54 is apparent from the geographic distribution of its sources. To be sure, in virtually all the states of the German Confederation, even the most prosperous, there was an outflow during those terrible years. Prussia, where prior to the great depression immigration had consistently exceeded emigration, suffered a net loss due to population movement of 81,000 in 1846-49, 32,000 in 1849-52, and 86,000 in 1852-55. Whereas during the years 1824-48 the state had enjoyed a favorable balance of over 769,000 inhabitants, in 1849-66 hard times and political unrest produced a deficit of 225,000. Similarly, in Saxony the number of emigrants, which had amounted to barely 1,800 in 1841-43, grew to 11,000 in 1844-46, dropped to 2,000 in 1847-49, rose again to almost 21,000 in 1850-52, and then remained between 11,000 and 13,000 per three-year period until 1861.

More than 90 per cent of the exodus, however, originated in lands west of the Elbe, although the populations separated by the river were almost equal. While the center of emigration was the southwest, the crucial factor here was not demographic growth or density, but an uneconomical mode of cultivation resulting from the fragmentation of peasant holdings. Bavaria illustrates this point. In the Palatinate, where the size of the average farm did not exceed 3 hectares, the rate of emigration per 10,000 inhabitants for 1848-54 was 727; in Swabia the corresponding figures were 6 and 108; and in Upper Bavaria 8 and 38. The situation in Württemberg was strikingly similar. The Neckar Province, where the per capita amount of land devoted to agriculture was only about 0.42 hectares, had an emigration rate of 494; for the Black Forest Province the corresponding figures were 0.53 and 435; for the Jagst Province 0.78 and 282; and for the Danube Province 1.00 and 243. The statistical information for Baden is less complete, but here the intensity of potato cultivation may be taken as an index of rural impoverishment. In the Middle Rhine Province approximately 14 potatoes were being raised per square kilometer, while the rate of emigration was 540; in the Lower Rhine Province the two figures were 13.6 and 500; in the Upper Rhine Province they were 8 and 380; and in the Lake Province 4 and 320. These data illuminate the underlying material causes of population movement at the mid-century.

During the late 1850's the first great wave of emigration from Central Europe began to subside, but its effects could be felt throughout the period of national unification. Even after the opening of the new decade the exodus of population continued at a much faster pace than before the great depression, totaling more than 800,000 persons for the period 1861-70. This was an outflow almost twice that of the 1840's and five times that of the 1830's. It took a long time to make good the losses suffered during the years of economic crisis. In the course of 1854 alone emigrants equaled 1.25 per cent of the population in Württemberg, 1.6 per cent in Baden, 1.8 per cent in Hesse-Darmstadt, 1.8 per cent in Mecklenburg-Schwerin, and 1.9 per cent in Hesse-Kassel. Not until 1864 did the number of inhabitants of Württemberg surpass the figure for 1849. During the same decade and a half some 90,000 people left Mecklenburg-Schwerin, more than 15 per cent of the total, while the remaining population of the grand duchy increased by not even 30,000. In some regions the deficits of the 1850's were still not completely wiped out twenty years later. For example, the countryside of northern Hesse-Darmstadt, where the high cost of food and shrinking economic opportunity drove villagers across the ocean by the tens of thousands, continued to decline long after the Seven Weeks' War.

Nor did the victory of Bismarckian statecraft in the struggle against Austria reduce the flow of population. Indeed, the end of the American Civil War encouraged the migration of hard pressed peasants from the Old World to the cheap lands of the New, while the introduction of a conscription period of three years in the provinces conquered by the Hohenzollern armies made the free republican institutions of the United States seem all the more appealing. The decay of artisan trades unable to withstand the rise of industrialism, and the increasing competition of overseas grain growers in the British market further intensified the transatlantic movement. Figures published by the American government showed that there were 32,000 German immigrants in 1861, 28,000 in 1862, 33,000 in 1863, 57,000 in 1864, and 83,000 in 1865. Then, after the triumph of the North had assured the survival of the Union, the number swelled to 116,000 in 1866, 133,000 in 1867, 123,000 in 1868, and 125,000 in 1869. By the time of the outbreak of the Franco-Prussian War the second great wave of emigration from Central Europe was in full swing.[3]

Yet in the long run the most important population movement in Germany during the nineteenth century was not from south to north or from the Eastern Hemi-

[3] Gustav Stolper, *German Economy, 1870-1940* (New York, 1940), p. 39; P. Benaerts, *Les origines*, pp. 136, 139; G. v. Viebahn, *Statistik Deutschlands*, II, 251, 258-259, III, 1175; P. Mombert, *Studien zur Bevölkerungsbewegung*, pp. 48, 105; Gustav Struve, *Diesseits und jenseits des Oceans* (4 vols., Coburg, 1863-64), I, 75; Alexis Markow, *Das Wachstum der Bevölkerung und die Entwickelung der Aus- und Einwanderungen, Ab- und Zuzüge in Preussen und Preussens einzelnen Provinzen, Bezirken und Kreisgruppen von 1824 bis 1885* (Tübingen, 1889), p. 162; Marcus L. Hansen, "The Revolutions of 1848 and German Emigration," *Journal of Economic and Business History*, II (1930), 632-635, 657-658; H. Bechtel, *Wirtschaftsgeschichte Deutschlands*, p. 442; H. Rosenberg, *Weltwirtschaftskrisis*, p. 43, n. 4; *Europäischer Geschichtskalender*, ed. H. Schulthess (1864), p. 158; Eugen Katz, *Landarbeiter und Landwirtschaft in Oberhessen* (Stuttgart and Berlin, 1904), pp. 29-39; A. Sartorius von Waltershausen, *Wirtschaftsgeschichte*, pp. 221-222; *Statistisches Jahrbuch für das Deutsche Reich*, I (1880), 19.

sphere to the Western, but from the country to the city. The urban environment was a great social solvent, undermining loyalties which the village had bred in the course of centuries, and arousing ambitions unrealizable within the framework of the old order of society. Between 1816 and 1871 the population of Germany increased by 63 per cent; but while the growth of the countryside was only 43 per cent, municipalities gained 262 per cent. The rise of the city, moreover, reflected the industrial boom after the mid-century. For example, in Prussia the expansion of urban and rural districts between 1816 and 1849 was about the same, 59 and 58 per cent respectively. Then came a marked divergence in their rates of increase coinciding with the prosperity of the 1850's, so that by the end of the decade the percentages had changed to 82 and 67.

The most rapid increase occurred in the big cities, where the demand for labor was most intense. The proportion of the Prussian population living in municipalities of less than 10,000 inhabitants declined between 1834 and 1864 from 18.6 to 15.2 per cent, whereas in the category between 10,000 and 50,000 inhabitants it rose from 3.7 to 7.2 per cent, and in the category above 50,000 it went from 3.4 to 7.4 per cent. The same tendency was apparent in Bavaria. Out of a total urban population gain in the provinces east of the Rhine amounting to 90,000 for 1847-61, almost 80,000 was recorded by the four largest cities of the kingdom, Munich, Nürnberg, Augsburg, and Würzburg. The small provincial town, dependent economically on the surrounding countryside, was being left farther behind by the great industrial and commercial centers growing pell-mell during the middle decades of the century at an annual rate of 3.73 per cent for Dresden, 3.42 for Breslau, 3.15 for Leipzig, 2.83 for Nürnberg, 2.62 for Magdeburg, and an extraordinary 4.09 for Berlin.

The rise of the city, to be sure, was not swift enough to change the essentially rural character of Central

Europe. At the time of the Congress of Vienna more than 90 per cent of the German population lived in the countryside; forty years later, at the conclusion of the Crimean War, the ratio had declined to 72 per cent; and fifteen years after that, when William I was proclaimed emperor in the Hall of Mirrors at Versailles, it stood at 64 per cent. As of the late 1850's none of the states of the German Confederation except the four municipal republics had more than about a third of its population residing in urban communities. The percentages were as follows: Prussia 30, Saxony 35, Bavaria 22, Württemberg 20, Baden 25, Hanover 26, Hesse-Kassel 27, Hesse-Darmstadt 26, Nassau 17, and Oldenburg 9. The figure of 28 per cent for Germany as a whole compared favorably with 27 per cent for France and 26 per cent for Belgium, but it was far behind Great Britain's 50 per cent. More than half of the German town dwellers, moreover, lived in communities with less than 10,000 inhabitants.

Yet the city had an importance out of proportion to its size. It dared reject the values of agrarian tradition, encouraging the spread of new political ideologies like liberalism, democracy, and socialism. It favored bourgeois forms of wealth based on manufacture and commerce. It became the center of the process of industrialization which was transforming the economy of Central Europe. And it attracted the surplus population of the countryside, especially the youthful, the vigorous, and the enterprising. In Prussia as of 1858, persons under 16 constituted 40.3 per cent of the total in rural districts and 35.8 per cent in the municipalities; for the age span from 17 to 39, however, the percentages were 35.6 and 40.2; and for those over 39 they were about equal, 24.1 and 24.0. What accounted for the growth of cities, in other words, was not primarily a favorable balance of births over deaths, but the influx of hundreds of thousands of rustics, many of them in their best years, seeking to attain in the new urban environment a security which the ancestral village could no longer provide.[4]

Is it any wonder that for most aristocrats the mid-century was a period of trial? The conservative politician Baron Philipp von Künssberg-Mandel, frightened by the spreading disintegration of social authority, found the early 1860's a time out of joint: "No class is any longer satisfied with the lot assigned to it; each man wants to climb higher. Everybody seeks only one goal, namely, wealth and pleasure. Everything is sacrificed to this idol, and today appearances count for more than realities." It was the perennial lament of the orthodox believer doomed to live in a time of changing loyalties. Friedrich Engels, on the other hand, was favorably impressed by the social transformation which Germany was experiencing. During a trip to his native Barmen occasioned by the death of his father he marveled at the development of Rhenish industry and the growth of bourgeois constitutionalism. "An enormous change has taken place since 1848," he wrote to Marx on April 8, 1860, "although there is still enough of the old leavening left."[5]

As for Bismarck, he was too much the Prussian Junker to overcome a deep-seated suspicion of the city, the breeding ground of democracy and radicalism. In the fall of 1870, while waiting in headquarters at Versailles for starving Paris to surrender, he held forth at the dinner table about the fundamental difference between the rustic and the townsman. Big cities were less practical than the countryside, which came into closer con-

[4] G. Ipsen, "Die preussische Bauernbefreiung," p. 49; *Jahrbuch für die amtliche Statistik des preussischen Staats*, I (1863), 110; G. Schmoller, *Geschichte der Kleingewerbe*, pp. 132, 189-191, 193; Ernst Bruch, "Wohnungsnoth und Hülfe," *Berlin und seine Entwickelung: Städtisches Jahrbuch für Volkswirthschaft und Statistik*, VI (1872), 18; G. v. Viebahn, *Statistik Deutschlands*, II, 147, 161, 188; W. Sombart, *Der moderne Kapitalismus*, III, 389.

[5] K. Marx and F. Engels, *Briefwechsel*, II, 584. Cf. Philipp von Künssberg-Mandel, *Auf zur That! Ein Zuruf an meine Standesgenossen und alle loyalen Deutschen* (Dresden, 1861), p. 6; Gustav Mayer, *Friedrich Engels: Eine Biographie* (2 vols., The Hague, 1934), II, 108.

tact with life and nature, and hence formed sounder judgment. "Where so many people are close together," he expatiated, "individual qualities can easily cease to exist, they intermix. All sorts of opinions arise out of the air, out of hearsay and repetition, opinions which have little or no foundation in fact. But they are spread through newspapers, public meetings, conversations over a glass of beer, and then they become fixed, indestructible. . . . That is the case in all big cities." So he went on, inveighing against "mass belief," "mass superstition," "stupidities," and "absurdities," eternalizing the prejudices of a country squire into immutable laws of human nature.[6]

And yet his animus was not altogether unjustified. Behind it lay a realization that the attitudes formed by the big city were basically inconsistent with the kind of society he was seeking to preserve. Perhaps he even sensed that one day the forces generated by urbanization would destroy his lifework. For the time being, however, the danger was not insurmountable. Most Germans continued to live in rural communities, and husbandry remained their most important source of livelihood. Around 1830 some 80 per cent of the population was economically dependent on farming pursuits, as of 1860 the percentage had fallen to 60, and in 1870 it was no more than about 50. During those forty years, moreover, the relative value of agrarian production declined steadily, while that of manufacture was close to doubling. But only in Saxony had industrialism clearly gained the upper hand. There as early as 1849 only 32 per cent of the labor force was engaged in agriculture and forestry, compared with 48 per cent in industry, mining, and metallurgy, and 5 per cent in commerce. By 1861 the ratios had shifted still farther in favor of urban occupations, amounting to 25, 52, and 6 per cent respectively. Around 1871 they were 16, 52, and 10 per cent.

In Prussia, the second most highly industrialized state

6 O. v. Bismarck, *Werke*, VII, 389-390.

of Germany, agricultural occupations including farming, gardening, fishery, and forestry continued to predominate, supporting 78 per cent of all inhabitants in 1816, 64 per cent in 1849, and 48 per cent in 1867. As of 1858 farming alone provided a source of livelihood for more than 8,000,000 people or 45 per cent of the entire population. Of this number proprietors, lessees, and tenants totaled 1,217,000, and members of their families 4,928,000; about 1,074,000 were stableboys, herdboys, barnmen, milkmaids, and kitchen help; and 838,000 worked as day laborers and farm hands. While persons practicing husbandry on a full-time basis and their dependents diminished from 6,592,000 in 1849, to 6,310,-000 in 1852, 6,263,000 in 1855, and 5,878,000 in 1858, those supported by part-time agrarian employment increased from 1,776,000 to 2,252,000 and 2,317,000, before falling off slightly to 2,177,322. Not until the end of the 1850's did the sum total of both categories constitute less than half of all inhabitants. At the beginning of the following decade every one of the Prussian provinces, west as well as east, still had at least 40 per cent of its labor force in husbandry except Brandenburg, where the population of Berlin reduced the percentage to 35. And these figures do not include large numbers of people technically in manufacture or commerce, but subsisting upon a local rural market. The decline of farming was a gradual process which did not substantially alter the agrarian base of German society until well toward the close of the century.[7]

The power of the nobility rested on that base. The ownership of land, historically a mark of high birth, re-

[7] P. Benaerts, *Les origines*, p. 133; *Die landwirthschaftliche Statistik des Königreichs Sachsen*, ed. K. von Langsdorff (Dresden, 1886), pp. 38-39; A. Sartorius von Waltershausen, *Wirtschaftsgeschichte*, p. 7; L. Pohle and M. Muss, *Das deutsche Wirtschaftsleben*, p. 20; *Tabellen und amtliche Nachrichten über den preussischen Staat für das Jahr 1858* (Berlin, 1860), pp. 326-327; G. v. Viebahn, *Statistik Deutschlands*, II, 251, 603-604, 607; *Jahrbuch für die amtliche Statistik des preussischen Staats*, I (1863), 286.

mained an accurate gauge of the degree of aristocratic influence in state and society. In the south and west the prevalence of small peasant holdings restricted the economic importance of the seigneurial houses and facilitated the process of political reform. Representative institutions could easily take root in a region of family farms and bustling towns with a long tradition of municipal autonomy. Similarly, the nobleman of central Germany lacked the material resources to withstand for any length of time the demand for a parliamentary form of government. By the beginning of the 1860's only about 18 per cent of the arable land of industrial Saxony was in the possession of the aristocracy, while for rural Hanover the figure was even smaller, barely 6 per cent. Both states had to make concessions to constitutionalism, although the Guelph kings never reconciled themselves to the passing of the old order.

East of the Elbe, on the other hand, the nobles could effectively oppose any threat to the status quo. What chance did a middle-class liberal have in Mecklenburg-Schwerin, where large estates and crown lands accounted for about 90 per cent of the entire territory? As for Prussia, holdings of more than 150 hectares amounted to 63 per cent of all farm properties in Pomerania, 57 per cent in Posen, 51 per cent in Silesia, 50 per cent in Brandenburg, and 43 per cent in East and West Prussia. To be sure, many of the great landowners were commoners. By the early 1880's about half of the latifundia were in bourgeois hands. But aristocrats made up 68 per cent of the biggest proprietors, those with more than 1,000 hectares. The efficient organization of production made possible by large-scale operation, and an increasing tendency toward entailment protected them against the vicissitudes of the grain market. Agriculture thus provided a strong economic foundation for the political activity of the nobility of the east.[8]

8 Wilhelm Kellner, *Taschenbuch der politischen Statistik Deutschlands oder Aufstellung der staatlichen Einrichtungen Gesammt-Deutsch-*

Yet landownership alone cannot account for the continuing importance of the Junker in Prussian society. Property was only a means toward the maintenance of his dominant role in the processes of government. The real source of the influence which the aristocracy exerted was its strategic position within the apparatus of administration. There was first of all the legal power which it wielded over the countryside. Before 1849 it exercised court jurisdiction over about a fourth of the population, while its right to enforce police regulations and appoint village mayors was not abolished until 1872. More important was its preponderance in the higher ranks in the army and bureaucracy. When William I became king of Prussia in 1861, some 65 per cent of the officers were noble, and among generals and colonels the percentage was 86. Of the chief administrative officials, the minister of the interior and 5 of the 8 provincial governors were of high birth. More than 70 per cent of the holders of leading diplomatic positions, including all the important ambassadors and ministers, were aristocrats. The Saxon officer corps, on the other hand, was composed of 352 noblemen and 329 commoners, while in Bavaria the corresponding figures were 1,213 and 2,844. Detailed statistical information regarding the armed forces of Württemberg is not available, but there too the proportion of middle-class officers grew considerably after 1815, except in the case of a few old, exclusive cavalry regiments like the 26th Dragoons or the 19th Uhlans.

The bureaucracy of the secondary states below the Main was also less restrictive, even at the highest level. Of the 13 Bavarian foreign ministers during the period 1818-71, 11 bore titles of nobility, as did 19 of the 21 ministers of the interior. In Prussia the ratio was almost

lands sowohl als der einzelnen deutschen Staaten (Frankfurt am Main, 1864), pp. 19, 102; G. v. Viebahn, Statistik Deutschlands, II, 564; J. Conrad, "Latifundien," pp. 140-141; Lujo Brentano, "Familienfideikommisse und ihre Wirkungen," Volkswirtschaftliche Zeitfragen, XXXIII (1911), no. 2, pp. 18-21.

the same in the first category, 15 out of 18, while in the second it was only 7 out of 15. Yet whereas in Munich 4 of the 13 foreign ministers and 14 of the 21 ministers of the interior belonged to families only recently ennobled or still bourgeois, in Berlin the proportions were 3 out of 18 and 6 out of 15. In other words, no more than 47 per cent of the Bavarian cabinet members under consideration were descended from the old aristocracy, whereas in Prussia the percentage was 73. There was generally much greater social mobility in southern and western Germany. For a commoner of ability, service to the state could be the means of advancement to the ranks of the ruling class. But east of the Elbe the noble caste was more firmly entrenched by virtue of its greater economic strength and administrative function. Here the conflict between aristocrat and bourgeois was bound to assume a more uncompromising form.[9]

There were also significant differences which came to prevail in the status of the peasantry in various parts of Central Europe. The problem of transforming a manorial mode of landholding into a system of unencumbered ownership appropriate to an age of capitalistic property relationships was everywhere the same. And everywhere the final result was the creation of a large class of free farmers whose customary servile dues and obligations had been commuted into money payments or land cessions. Yet the economic and social consequences of this agrarian reorganization differed greatly from region to region. In the southwest the high nobility, content with the genteel role of absentee landlord and rentier, withdrew more and more from both husbandry and politics. The peasant became a small independent proprietor, al-

[9] [Heinrich Berghaus], *Statistik des preussischen Staats: Versuch einer Darstellung seiner Grundmacht und Kultur, seiner Verfassung, Regierung und Verwaltung im Lichte der Gegenwart* (Berlin, 1845), pp. 500-501; Karl Demeter, *Das deutsche Offizierkorps in Gesellschaft und Staat, 1650-1945*, 2nd edn. (Frankfurt am Main, 1962), pp. 26, 30, 37, 44-46; Nikolaus von Preradovich, *Die Führungsschichten in Österreich und Preussen (1804-1918)* (Wiesbaden, 1955), pp. 84-87, 92-93, 101, 108-111, 118, 167-168.

though overpopulation often led to the fragmentation of landholding and the exhaustion of the soil. The situation in the northeast was precisely the opposite. The reform of agriculture made possible the rationalization of production and an increase in output, but the framework of rural society remained unchanged. Around the middle of the nineteenth century there were only some 17,700 big estates of more than 150 hectares in all of Prussia, as compared with more than 269,000 large farms and 407,000 small ones in the eastern provinces alone. And yet the legal emancipation of the peasantry made little difference in the class structure of the countryside. The position of the Junker remained unassailable afterward as before.

To be sure, once the rustic had paid for freedom by surrendering a part of his land to the nobleman, latifundium and farm remained in a state of equilibrium. Between 1816 and 1859 the total area of peasant holdings in Prussia exclusive of the Rhine Province diminished by approximately 440,000 hectares, or 5 per cent, not a drastic rate of decline. But it was precisely the maintenance of this equilibrium which perpetuated Junker domination of the region beyond the Elbe. Nothing less than a revolution in agrarian property relations could have broken the power of the aristocracy over the countryside, and such a revolution was inconceivable under the alliance of crown and nobility on which the Hohenzollern state had been built. Indeed, as the century wore on, the structure of rural society became increasingly stratified and inflexible. There was progressively less opportunity to rise in the world, to acquire property, to attain security, and to become an independent farmer.

East Prussia illustrates this trend. During the period 1805-67 the average annual growth of the rural population of the province was 10.1 persons for each 1,000 inhabitants. In the category of big landholders including both owners and lessees the rise was 14 per mill, well above the mean. The increase of the well-to-do peasant proprietors, on the other hand, was only 3 per mill, the lowest of all. The class of household servants and hired hands, occupying a semi-servile status on the large estates or middle-sized farms, also grew slowly. Its yearly increase was 5 per mill. The highest rate of expansion occurred among the small landowners, with holdings of less than 4 hectares as a rule, whose increase was 21 per mill. Among the artisans and craftsmen of the countryside, who were often engaged in part-time agricultural pursuits, the rate was 19 per mill. And among the day laborers and farm workers, usually propertyless except perhaps for a garden plot or vegetable patch, it was 16 per mill. There was thus a clear tendency toward the concentration of landownership. In the course of some sixty years of agrarian reform the proportion of those, whether noble or peasant, whose properties were sufficiently large to provide economic security and independence declined from 39 to 26 per cent of the rural population. Not only were the entirely or nearly landless classes expanding rapidly, but their composition was undergoing a significant alteration. Household servants and hired hands, an inefficient form of agricultural labor more suited to manorialism than to a capitalistic mode of cultivation, were increasing at only about a third the rate of day laborers and farm workers. In husbandry as in manufacture the rationalization of production meant the rise of a propertyless proletariat, legally free but socially subordinate, deriving a marginal livelihood from an impersonalized economy.[10]

A drastic change in the pattern of society, however, was taking place in the city. The urban bourgeoisie, free from the domination of a hereditary noble caste,

[10] C.F.W. Dieterici, *Handbuch der Statistik*, p. 303; Georg Friedrich Knapp, *Die Bauern-Befreiung und der Ursprung der Landarbeiter in den älteren Theilen Preussens* (2 vols., Leipzig, 1887), I, 257; T. Bödiker, "Die Auswanderung und die Einwanderung des preussischen Staates," *Zeitschrift des königlich preussischen Statistischen Bureaus*, XIII (1873), 25; G. Ipsen, "Die preussische Bauernbefreiung," pp. 51-54.

was creating a new economic system which threatened to undermine the traditional class relationships of Central Europe. The danger to the established order was recognized by its defenders, and yet the force of circumstance obliged them to tolerate it. What else could they do? No government dared risk the military defense of its interests without the support of railroads, foundries, factories, and banks, in short, the entire apparatus of modern industrialism. Reactionary publicists lamented that "money today plays the role of lever and tool of a definite political policy which proposes to eliminate the last remnants of the old state institutions in order then to bring about the unchallenged domination of the bourgeoisie." But the bureaucracy had to accept the creative economic forces on which it relied for the execution of public policy. All it could hope for was to maintain a little longer the discrepancy between material affluence and political power. In the meantime the process of industrialization was hastening the day when crown and aristocracy would be compelled to reach an accommodation with the manufacturer and banker.

While the growth of the urban middle class was unmistakable, its size and constitution are hard to determine. An anonymous contributor to the conservative *Berliner Revue* insisted that "the bourgeoisie . . . is not a class but, to put it briefly, a 'swamp' in which are gathered all the unclean discharges of the private economy, elements which have forgotten their duty to labor. . . . The bourgeoisie actually consists of few people among whom remnants and traces of all class differentiations are recognizable. It is a frightful concoction, a gray on gray." He was right, at least to the extent that the middle class was indeed small in number and varied in composition. What held its members together was an economic dependence on manufacture, commerce, or the learned professions, a generally similar intermediate position within the social order, a common minimum level

64

of income and education, and a pervasive hostility to the hierarchical structure of authority.

The government statistics of the mid-century, while detailed regarding the make-up of rural society and the size of the urban labor force, say little about the bourgeoisie. Figures for Prussia during the early 1860's show that there were some 44,000 persons holding managerial and supervisory positions in factories and other establishments engaged primarily in large-scale production, 14,000 wholesale traders and commission merchants, and 600 bankers and money dealers. But how useful are such fragmentary data? They say nothing about the industrialists, mineowners, entrepreneurs, promoters, investors, journalists, lawyers, academics, and civil servants who considered themselves and were considered to be part of the bourgeoisie. An attempt to determine the dimensions of this class by means of occupational groups is doomed to fail for lack of sufficient information.[11]

Income and taxation data provide a more promising approach. At the beginning of the 1850's the Prussian Statistical Bureau in Berlin published an estimate that only about 82,000 persons, or 0.5 per cent of the population of the kingdom, were members of families with an annual income above 3,000 marks. It admitted that "these are very general calculations," but tax figures issued late in the following decade tended to support its appraisal. They revealed that out of a total of 5,062,000 income tax payers in Prussia around the mid-century, 43,500, or 0.9 per cent, were classified as having more than 3,000 marks a year. The well-to-do middle class clearly belonged in this category, but so did the great landowners, the wealthy rentiers, the court aristocrats, the military leaders, and the higher civil officials. The

---

[11] "Die Debatte über das Wuchergesetz," *Berliner Revue*, XX (1860), 513; v. X., "Preussische Briefe: Neue Folge," *ibid.*, XXI (1860), 458; "Die Ergebnisse der Volkszählung und Volksbeschreibung nach den Aufnahmen vom 3. December 1861, resp. Anfang 1862," *Preussische Statistik*, V (1864), 40, 43.

upper bourgeoisie thus included at the most 1 to 2 per cent of all inhabitants, although it also drew reinforcement from the 531,000 persons, or 3.25 per cent of the population, who, according to the Statistical Bureau, were members of families with an income between 1,200 and 3,000 marks. Among the latter would be found much of the salaried supervisory and clerical personnel, the less successful practitioners of the professions, master tradesmen, retail merchants, and neighborhood shopkeepers. Clinging to its small measure of property and learning, the symbols of superior social status, this petty bourgeoisie often led a marginal existence between the upper middle class to whose ranks it hopelessly aspired and the proletarian masses threatening to submerge it. Despite its pretensions to genteel respectability, it was condemned to play a subordinate role in society. When the Prussian prime minister Otto von Manteuffel privately confessed to "a thorough contempt for the present generation, especially the so-called educated class" characterized by "a combination of arrogance and cowardice, both sprung from godlessness," he was thinking above all of the wealthy bankers, industrialists, and businessmen, and of their allies in the law offices and professorial chairs who were advancing a program of reform designed to destroy the privileged position of the landed aristocracy.[12]

The middle class varied greatly in the social origins and economic activities of its members. It included the traders, shippers, promoters, and legislators who made up the urban patriciate of the Hanseatic states, men like the big merchants Johann Cesar Godeffroy of Hamburg and Hermann Heinrich Meier of Bremen; Johann

[12] *Mittheilungen des Statistischen Bureau's in Berlin,* IV (1851), 226-227; Ernst Engel, "Die Ergebnisse der Classensteuer, der classificirten Einkommensteuer und der Mahl- und Schlachtsteuer im preussischen Staate," *Zeitschrift des königlich preussischen Statistischen Bureaus,* VIII (1868), 83; *Preussens auswärtige Politik, 1850 bis 1858: Unveröffentlichte Dokumente aus dem Nachlasse des Ministerpräsidenten Otto Frhrn. v. Manteuffel,* ed. Heinrich v. Poschinger (3 vols., Berlin, 1902), I, 141.

Smidt, the pastor's son who founded Bremerhaven to safeguard the commercial interests of the lower Weser, and Arnold Duckwitz, who helped establish the first direct steamship connection between the United States and the mainland of Europe; and burgher statesmen such as Karl Sieveking and Johann Gustav Heckscher, who won a national reputation during the Restoration and the Revolution of 1848. Among the financiers were established banking families like the Bethmanns of Frankfurt am Main or the Oppenheims of Cologne, but also those whose affluence was more recent. David Hansemann's father had been a preacher, Ludolf Camphausen's a merchant, Hermann von Beckerath's a bailiff, Ernst Wilhelm Arnoldi's a grocery dealer, and Gustav Mevissen's a thread manufacturer.

Most of the leading industrialists were of petty bourgeois or even lower-class background. There were exceptions, to be sure. Alfred Krupp belonged to a family which had been well-to-do in the days when Essen was still a free city, although he himself had been forced to leave school at fourteen to help support his widowed mother. Emil Kessler, the son of an army officer, had studied at a polytechnical institute before founding engine factories in Karlsruhe and Esslingen. The Mecklenburg machine industry owed its beginnings to the oculist Ernst Alban, son of a clergyman. Johann Friedrich Klett, the wealthy merchant from Nürnberg, became an important manufacturer of steam boilers and railroad equipment. Many of the others, however, came from more modest homes. The construction of engines, for example, was dominated until about the middle of the century by self-made entrepreneurs who had started out in life as skilled craftsmen, as locksmiths, blacksmiths, carpenters, or cabinetmakers. As for the jurists, publicists, doctors, engineers, and academics who provided the bourgeoisie with much of its leadership, they were usually men of unpretentious middle-class origin who had managed to rise above the parsonage or count-

67

inghouse of their childhood, and who were determined to rise still higher.

The cohesion of the bourgeoisie derived from a community of interest rather than tradition. Its members may have been descended from various strata of society, but they were all engaged in urban pursuits and directly or indirectly dependent on capitalistic undertakings. An examination of the occupational backgrounds of the founders of industrial joint-stock companies in Prussia during the 1850's reveals the economic interdependence of the diverse elements constituting the middle class. Of 480 promoters responsible for the formation of 61 enterprises, about 32 per cent derived their income from commercial activity, 15 per cent owned factories, mines, and foundries, 13 per cent were state officials, 11 per cent were bankers, 7 per cent were great landholders, and 5 per cent were lawyers, physicians, engineers, and members of other skilled professions. Even rentiers and officers were ready at times to help establish collieries and blast furnaces, although there were cases no doubt when they did little more than provide a façade of aristocratic names behind which plebeian entrepreneurs could operate with greater effectiveness. More striking is the extent to which all the segments of the middle class, including merchants, manufacturers, bankers, and professional men, collaborated in the rationalization of production. This commitment to the progress of industrialism and the need to establish a political system consistent with it determined the class interest of the bourgeoisie.[13]

The growth of a capitalistic economy was also transforming the social structure of urban labor. Until the beginning of the nineteenth century the working class of Central Europe developed within the framework of the handicraft system. Dominated by the ideal of a corporative organization of production appropriate to

---

[13] F. Schnabel, *Deutsche Geschichte*, III, 404, 408-409; H. Bechtel, *Wirtschaftsgeschichte Deutschlands*, III, 159, 163; F. Redlich, "Leaders of the German Steam-Engine Industry," pp. 139, 145, 147; H. Blumberg, "Die Finanzierung der Neugründungen," p. 196.

a preindustrial age, it accepted the hierarchical distribution of occupational rights and responsibilities of which the guilds were an institutional expression. During the spring of 1848, long after the advance of mechanization had undermined the traditional way of life of the skilled craftsman, the artisans of Leipzig still looked back with nostalgia to an idealized era of Arcadian simplicity which the industrial revolution had destroyed:

> In former times every single master, even if he was only a citizen of low birth, could still feel that he was a member of a highly respected guild. Just as the apprentice and the journeyman saw in his superior a master and member of the same class, and therefore displayed toward him not merely an outward but also an inward, a voluntary obedience and respect, so the master had the same attitude toward the authorities in the city. Just as the master's chair had not been inaccessible to him, so could he reach a position of civic authority. Thus the guild system maintained harmony, cooperation, and mutual help among the citizens, and this harmony prevailed despite all differences. The struggle of the cities against the robber barons and against the enemies of the cities in general demonstrated what manly strength, what a manly spirit was dominant in the guilds of those days.[14]

While the progress of industrialism sapped the handicraft system, it also led to the growth of a factory proletariat. This new working class recruited its members from two main sources. There were first of all the degraded artisans forced into a new occupation by shrinking economic opportunities in the skilled crafts. But the majority of what Marx called the "industrial reserve army" came from the surplus rural population which had deserted the land to seek subsistence in the big cities. What separated the craftsman from the mill

[14] *Offener Brief an alle Innungen Deutschlands so wie zugleich an alle Bürger und Hausväter: Von zweiundzwanzig Innungen zu Leipzig* (Leipzig, 1848), pp. 13-14.

hand was his unique relationship to the process of work and his distinct status within the structure of society. The trade guilds had been designed to provide a method of training by which in the course of time the apprentice might achieve the expertness and prestige of a master. There was something patriarchal in the attitude of employer toward employee, both working on the same bench, eating at the same table, sleeping under the same roof. The reward for long years of arduous training was in theory if not always in fact the command of a technical proficiency providing a secure livelihood.

The condition of the factory worker was of a different order, because he existed within a different economic context. His connection to the millowner was of necessity nothing more than the impersonal cash nexus, while the skills required of him were frequently elementary and unchallenging. He lived in the insecure social environment created by an industrial capitalism which hailed unrestrained competition as the instrument of progress. Perhaps worst of all, he was consigned for all time to the lowest element of the community, the uprooted and propertyless urban mob. It was this loss of status and hope which made proletarianization such a frightening prospect. "See the dreadful abyss of the proletariat," warned the artisans of Bremen in 1848. "One step farther along this road, and the handicraftsman is irretrievably lost as the heart of the middle estate."[15]

Statistical data on the size of the industrial working class are ample but undiscriminating. According to contemporary estimates there were about 1,421,000 persons employed in the factories of the Zollverein as of 1861, a figure equivalent to 4.1 per cent of the population. In Prussia, which accounted for almost half of the total, the ratio was 3.7 per cent. But there was a wide diver-

[15] Bundesarchiv Abteilung Frankfurt am Main, *Akten der Nationalversammlung: Volksw. Ausschuss*, 21 II (Memorial of the Bremen Civic Association) .

gence among the provinces, ranging from percentages of
0.9 for East and West Prussia, 1.3 for Posen, and 1.5
for Pomerania to 6.2 for the Rhine Province and 4.7 for
Westphalia and the Province of Saxony. The other members of the German Confederation also differed considerably, depending on the degree of their industrialization. The Kingdom of Saxony was of course in first place
with 9.6 percent, then came the Thuringian principalities with 6.2, Württemberg with 4.9, and Baden with
4.6 per cent. At the bottom of the scale were the agrarian states of the northwest: Hesse-Kassel with 3.1, Oldenburg with 2.8, Waldeck with 2.5, and Hanover with 2.4
per cent. Even urban communities varied greatly in the
proportion of their inhabitants working in industrial
establishments. That Barmen, Elberfeld, and Krefeld,
where the figures were 27.8, 26.1, and 16.9 per cent,
should be far ahead of Posen, Bromberg, and Stettin
with 1.6, 1.7, and 2.3 per cent is not surprising. But
some towns in the east, Brandenburg, for example, with
12.5, Görlitz with 9.9, Potsdam with 6.6, and Elbing
with 5.5, not to mention Berlin with 8.0 per cent, surpassed such western cities as Münster with 2.8, Koblenz
with 3.4, Düsseldorf with 4.6, or even Cologne with 5.8
per cent.

The weakness of these data, however, lies in their inadequate delimitation of the category of factory labor.
They lump together light and heavy industries and
mechanized and manual occupations, intermixing the
337,000 persons in the alimental trades with the 746,000
textile operatives and 57,000 metallurgical workers.
While they comprise wood carvers, toymen, and paper-
makers, they omit coal and ore miners. In short, they do
not make a sufficiently fine distinction between industrialized and merely non-artisan areas of economic enterprise. But an approximate compensation for these statistical deficiencies can be made. In Prussia during the
early 1860's, large manufacturing establishments with
50 or more workers employed a total of 330,000 persons,

about half of the entire number categorized as factory labor. Here is a rough gauge of the manpower in the service of large-scale rationalized production. A more discriminating analysis based primarily on the number of employees of sizable enterprises in the fields of heavy and semifinished metallurgy, machine construction, spinning, weaving, mining, and chemicals suggests a figure of only 450,000 persons for the entire Zollverein, not even a third of those classified as industrial workers in the calculations of economists like Georg von Viebahn or Gustav Schmoller. Assuming that for every member of the labor force there were on an average two dependents, the population deriving a livelihood directly or indirectly from some form of factory employment would amount to 12 per cent of all inhabitants of the Zollverein. Yet only about 4 to 6 per cent could properly be considered the working class of big industry. The others were in an intermediate stage between skilled artisans and mill operatives, no longer part of the handicraft system, but not yet completely assimilated by mechanized manufacture.[16]

The position of the industrial worker was precarious at best, and in times of economic depression it could become calamitous. Toward the end of the prosperous 1850's a report of the Cologne chamber of commerce acknowledged the obvious: "In spite of all the well-intentioned plans and suggestions of the state government, in spite of all the sickness and savings funds, the great increase in wages has only in rare cases led to a transformation from a propertyless to a propertied working class. A special investigation might well reveal in several factory districts that . . . the workers were on an average just as propertyless and even here and there weighed down with a greater burden of indebtedness than ten years ago." The government factory inspector

---

[16] G. v. Viebahn, *Statistik Deutschlands*, III, 561, 1034, 1121, 1131; G. Schmoller, *Geschichte der Kleingewerbe*, pp. 281, 292, 307-308; G. Hermes, "Statistische Studien," p. 154; P. Benaerts, *Les origines*, pp. 573-575.

for the Aachen district painted a much bleaker picture during the business collapse of 1857. Mill hands were subsisting almost entirely on a diet of bread and so-called coffee water supplemented occasionally with a few potatoes prepared with oil. As for the employers, told that a man earning less than a mark for a twelve-hour day could barely survive, their reply would usually be that "if they get more, they drink more," or "they become insolent" and "no longer want to work."

By the end of the decade the situation had improved, but in 1863 an official report from Gladbach in the Rhine Province still found that "the welfare of the industrial population remains largely subject to fluctuations which produce temporary distress and even lasting impoverishment," while the county commissioner of Neurode in Silesia related how "the hired weavers and ordinary factory workers earn so little that they must be content with the worst nourishment, potatoes without butter, bad bread, dumplings or soups made with so-called black flour, etc. In addition, the hired weavers often work through the whole night, and workers in the spinning and finishing mills labor up to eighteen hours a day." When five years later the Erfurt chamber of commerce described the plight of the lower classes, its language was milder, but the meaning was not essentially different: "Since earnings have been low and all foodstuffs have increased in price by nearly half compared with previous years, the situation not only of our workers but also of our handicraftsmen and businessmen can hardly be considered favorable. Demands must everywhere be severely restricted, if expenditures are not to exceed income."[17]

17 *Preussisches Handelsarchiv* (1868), III (Jahresberichte der Handelskammern und kaufmännischen Korporationen des preussischen Staats für 1867), 466. Cf. *ibid.* (1858), II, 260; Alphons Thun, *Die Industrie am Niederrhein und ihre Arbeiter* (2 vols., Leipzig, 1879), I, 34-35; "Die arbeitenden Classen und die Arbeits- und Lohnverhältnisse," *Jahrbuch für die amtliche Statistik des preussischen Staats*, II (1867), 306, 324.

Yet despite prevalent hardship and insecurity, the position of the industrial worker improved between the Revolution of 1848 and the establishment of the German Empire. The growth of the factory system meant that the employment opportunities open to him were multiplying, while the mechanization and rationalization of manufacture were promoting his efficiency. The annual earnings of a miner in the Saar district rose from 386 marks in 1850 to 634 in 1860 and 729 in 1869. During the same years the Krupp plant in Essen raised the daily wage of metal workers from 1.25 marks to 2.06 and then 2.86. In the Württemberg textile plants cotton weavers who had been paid 1.37 marks a day during the 1850's were getting 2.34 by 1872. The weekly income of a Leipzig mason increased from 8.88 marks in 1850 to 12.00 in 1860 and 14.52 in 1869. The demand was greatest for trained labor, but the pay even of unskilled workers improved. In the building trades of Hamburg, for instance, it grew from 1.43 marks daily in 1848 to 1.80 in 1856 and 2.25 in 1868. For Germany as a whole the index of average gross money wages in industry based on small and scattered samplings (1900 = 100) climbed from 45 in 1850 to 53 in 1860 and 66 in 1870. Although these calculations can be considered no more than an approximation, they are in general supported by contemporary observations. The Cologne chamber of commerce, to give an example, estimated in 1858 that since the beginning of the decade the pay of day laborers had risen 20 to 30 per cent, and that of factory operatives 30 to 50 per cent. "While only ten years ago the wages of the German labor force were far below the wages in England and Belgium, they are today in many branches of industry almost equal to those in the former country and decidedly higher than in Belgium."[18]

The improvement in the standard of living of industrial labor was not due entirely to the law of supply and

18 *Preussisches Handelsarchiv* (1858), II, 260. Cf. J. Kuczynski, *Short History*, pp. 74-76, 101-106; P. Benaerts, *Les origines*, pp. 598-601.

demand. The expansion of factory production and its impersonalization of economic relationships tended to encourage among many workers the concept of collective resistance against employers. The result was a wave of strikes which continued throughout the period of national unification. Between 1850 and 1859 there were all told 107 organized work stoppages in Germany, more than a third of them in the crisis year 1857. During the following decade the number rose to about 230, clear evidence that working-class discontent was becoming more pronounced.

The technique of the strike, which was first adopted by skilled craftsmen, soon won support in the ranks of industrial labor. Its first major successful test took place in the Wupper valley in 1857, about twenty years later than in England and America, when more than 800 journeyman dyers left their jobs in order to obtain a wage increase. Not until the book printers of Leipzig won a partial victory in 1865 was there a work stoppage of comparable dimensions. But soon thereafter the construction workers of Berlin walked out, then came labor unrest in Hamburg and Augsburg, and on the eve of the Franco-Prussian War the first great coal strike took place in the Waldenburg collieries in Silesia. To be sure, most battles ended unfavorably for the strikers. Hunger would usually force them to compromise or surrender before their objectives had been secured. But even their defeat often persuaded the millowner to treat the claims of labor thereafter with greater circumspection. Some businessmen no doubt approved the proposal of the Hanover chamber of commerce that employers form an association to resist demands for higher wages. Others perhaps agreed with a speaker before the General Civic Society of Barmen that "from now on we see as the main task for times of peace the reconciliation of the bourgeois with the worker, so that through the solution of the 'social question' we can prevent a certain catastrophe." In any case, for the working class fear or even hostility on the part of industrialists was in the long run preferable to complete indifference.[19]

There were occasions, moreover, when the factory worker received a measure of support from the state. The higher bureaucracy, suspicious of middle-class ambitions, was prepared to assist labor to a limited extent for the sake of the general welfare. In Prussia, for example, the authorities frequently failed to enforce the prohibition against strikes introduced in 1845. During the twenty years following its promulgation it was invoked in no more than twenty-six cases, although organized work stoppages were taking place with growing frequency. Even when the law was applied, the courts often imposed the minimum penalty, one to three days in jail. Similarly, the legal restriction of child labor in factories derived from the readiness of some governments to subordinate the freedom of contract to the physical and moral well-being of the lower classes. The limitations on the employment of minors established by the laws of 1839 and 1853 in Prussia, 1840 and 1854 in Bavaria, 1840 in Baden, and 1861 in Saxony represented a considerable gain for the industrial workers of Germany. To be sure, enforcement was altogether inadequate. To expect three inspectors to maintain supervision over all Prussian industrial establishments was manifestly unrealistic. And yet the fact remains that whereas in 1846 about 9.7 per cent of the factory workers in the kingdom were under the age of 14, by 1858

---

[19] Elisabeth Todt, *Die gewerkschaftliche Betätigung in Deutschland von 1850 bis 1859* (Berlin, 1950), pp. 98-100, 104-117; Walter Steglich, "Eine Streiktabelle für Deutschland, 1864 bis 1880," *Jahrbuch für Wirtschaftsgeschichte* (1960), no. 2, pp. 247-254; W. Köllmann, *Sozialgeschichte der Stadt Barmen*, pp. 159, 184; Franz Mehring, *Geschichte der deutschen Sozialdemokratie* (2 vols., Stuttgart, 1897-98), II, 154, 285-286; A. Sartorius von Waltershausen, *Wirtschaftsgeschichte*, pp. 229-230; *Europäischer Geschichtskalender*, ed. H. Schulthess (1865), pp. 59, 83 (1869), p. 139 (1870), pp. 35-36, 39; Alexander Wirminghaus, *Die Industrie- und Handelskammer zu Köln: Ihre Geschichte und ihre Wirksamkeit (1797-1914/33)* (Manuscript, *Rheinisch-Westfälisches Wirtschaftsarchiv*, Cologne), C. Die Wirksamkeit der Handelskammer (1797-1871), Abschnitt x-xiv, p. 189.

the percentage had fallen to 3.3. Not enough is known about the effectiveness of such other measures as the instruction seeking to restrict Sunday work which the ministry of commerce in Berlin issued in 1851, the enactment of the Saxon government in 1855 directed against the truck system of wage payment, or the Bavarian ordinance of 1863 designed to protect mill operatives against chemical injury. Yet in all probability their net result, though modest, was not insignificant.[20]

While factory workers were thus slowly improving their position, for independent artisans the years of the mid-century were the final phase of a tragic social decline. Industrial labor had already begun to adjust to the new realities created by the factory system. In the struggle for economic survival it managed to hold its own, and even a little more than its own, thanks to the increasing rationalization of production. It was perfecting the technique of the strike as a weapon for the advancement of its interests. Before long it would find in the trade union a source of strength to challenge the employer, and in the socialist movement a faith to sustain it amid a poverty-stricken existence. But the material and spiritual foundations of the handicraftsman's way of life were disintegrating. An entire world of traditions, loyalties, beliefs, and aspirations was about to succumb. The unskilled mill hand could survive ideologically as well as physically because he was an indispensable element in the most vital sector of the national economy. The master guildsman, on the other hand, was impris-

[20] Karl Erich Born, "Sozialpolitische Probleme und Bestrebungen in Deutschland von 1848 bis zur Bismarckschen Sozialgesetzgebung," *Vierteljahrschrift für Sozial- und Wirtschaftsgeschichte,* XLVI (1959), 32-34; Theodore S. Hamerow, *Restoration, Revolution, Reaction: Economics and Politics in Germany, 1815-1871* (Princeton, 1958), pp. 18-19, 234-236; Josef Kaizl, *Der Kampf um Gewerbereform und Gewerbefreiheit in Bayern von 1799-1868* (Leipzig, 1879), pp. 114-115; J. Kuczynski, *Short History,* pp. 98-99; Alphons Thun, "Beiträge zur Geschichte der Gesetzgebung und Verwaltung zu Gunsten der Fabrikarbeiter," *Zeitschrift des königlich preussischen Statistischen Bureaus,* XVII (1877), 67, 79, 91; "Die arbeitenden Classen," p. 242.

oned in a constricting environment of reduced opportunity, intensified competition, bewilderment, hopelessness, and resentment. The result was the demoralization of an important class of society. Analyzing the economic condition of Germany during the 1850's, Frédéric Le Play concluded in his classic *Les ouvriers européens* that "the promoters of the new industrial order have not known how to maintain a certain harmony between that order and the old ruined institutions. They have made a revolution out of what was supposed to be only a social transformation. . . . They have dealt a serious blow to the moral sense of the laboring classes."[21]

Yet the crisis confronting the artisan class had no immediate effect on its size. Not only did it remain substantially larger than the industrial labor force, but it continued to grow relatively as well as absolutely. Between 1846 and 1861 the ratio of handicraftsmen to all inhabitants rose from 4.8 to 5.6 per cent in Prussia, 6.1 to 6.9 per cent in Bavaria, 7.4 to 8.0 per cent in Saxony, 5.7 to 7.2 per cent in Hesse-Darmstadt, 5.5 to 6.0 per cent in Hesse-Kassel, and 3.1 to 8.6 per cent in the Thuringian principalities. Only in the case of Baden was there a slight decline, from 6.4 to 6.2 per cent. In the Zollverein as a whole there were at the beginning of the 1860's some 2,201,000 persons engaged in artisan occupations out of a population of 34,658,000, a percentage of 6.3, whereas those classified as factory workers numbered 1,421,000, or 4.1 per cent. Of the entire manufacturing labor force, 50 per cent were employed in handicraft shops, 38 per cent in industrial establishments, and 4 per cent in the decorative and technical trades. In every state with the exception of Saxony there were more skilled tradesmen than mill operatives.

Under favorable economic conditions, moreover, the two groups could coexist in a state of equilibrium, neither affected directly by the growth of the other. Among the leading states of the Zollverein, the two with

[21] F. Le Play, *Les ouvriers européens* (Paris, 1855), p. 139.

the highest proportion of artisans, Württemberg and Saxony, also had the highest proportion of industrial workers. In some cities, to be sure, a sizable class of handicraftsmen coincided with a small factory labor force. For Königsberg the relevant percentages of the population were 10.3 and 2.8, for Danzig 7.3 and 0.9, for Breslau 12.8 and 4.5, and for Frankfurt an der Oder 11.5 and 3.8. But in other cases the situation was different. For Halberstadt the percentages were 11.8 and 7.2, for Aachen 9.1 and 15.0, for Dortmund 10.1 and 9.3, and for Essen 7.7 and 13.4. Where a prosperous economy generated a substantial demand for manufactured goods, the skilled tradesman could survive in the face of large-scale industry.

While artisan establishments still dominated such fields of manufacture as the metal and construction trades, their strength was concentrated more and more in occupations like tailoring, leathermaking, wood carving, toymaking, and decorating. In other words, they were progressively being forced out of the production of industrial goods into ancillary and servicing employments. But even more important were the changes in the structure of the handicraft system. The growth of the artisan class during the decades of the mid-century was due largely to an increase in the number of journeymen and apprentices, the employee groups whose hopes of achieving an independent economic status could no longer be satisfied by the diminished opportunities within the skilled trades. In Württemberg during the period 1852-62 master tradesmen in the 26 most important handicrafts grew 4.5 per cent, while the size of their labor force was expanding 76 per cent. Figures for 36 artisan occupations in Saxony show that between 1849 and 1861 the average number of employees per employer rose from 1.6 to 2.0 in rural districts, from 0.9 to 1.1 in small towns, and from 1.7 to 2.4 in cities. In 1849 there were in Prussia 76 journeymen and apprentices for every 100 masters, a proportion which increased slowly at first to 81 in 1852 and 83 in 1855, and then with mounting rapidity to 93 in 1858 and 104 in 1861.

Confined to a narrowing segment of the economy, the handicraft system was becoming stratified. The pressure exerted by industrialization upon the skilled trades gradually began to create the same social gulf between master and journeyman which already existed between millowner and mill hand. The change in the ratio of employers to employees, moreover, meant that the percentage of the total population dependent on the handicrafts for its livelihood was declining. Since journeymen and apprentices were as a rule unmarried, while the family of a master craftsman numbered on an average about 5 persons, the percentage of the inhabitants of Prussia belonging to the artisan class rose initially from 12.8 in 1843 to 14.0 in 1846 and 16.5 in 1849, but then it fell to 16.0 in 1852, 15.7 in 1855, 15.5 in 1858, and 14.9 in 1861.[22]

The accounts of contemporary observers support the statistical evidence of a crisis in the handicraft occupations. There were countless bitter complaints from the artisans themselves, all in agreement that the economic position of the skilled tradesman was worsening. "Big industry allied with capital and science has destroyed the entire legal foundation of his rights," was the lament of master weaver Rewitzer of Chemnitz. "For other people who are not members of a guild also practice his trade. . . . Many of our handicraftsmen have therefore already succumbed to their fate, and many others will follow them." The official reports of local authorities in Prussia reached the same conclusion. From Weissenfels in the Province of Saxony, for example, came a graphic description of the decay of the urban artisan class: "The worse the situation of the small handicraftsman in the cities becomes because of

[22] G. Schmoller, *Geschichte der Kleingewerbe*, pp. 70-71, 94-95, 112, 281, 292, 298-299, 307, 308-309, 335-336, 358-359, 366-367, 665; G. v. Viebahn, *Statistik Deutschlands*, III, 561, 742, 745, 1034, 1121, 1131.

expensive housing, high municipal taxes, the competition of capital, etc., the more the handicrafts move to the countryside. But they do not gain thereby, because seldom do the handicraftsmen, at least shoemakers and tailors, manage to acquire property of their own free of debt." Gustav Schmoller was dismayed to discover that the younger masters were often ready to exchange their independence for a secure livelihood: "They want to give up their shop, if only they have the prospect of a job as a houseman, as a doorkeeper with free lodging or a few marks, if they can become laborers for a railroad at 300 marks a year." Even the Aachen chamber of commerce, representing the interests of industrialists and merchants, admitted that the condition of the handicraft worker had deteriorated: "Instead of living in the house of his master on the same footing as the family, knowing that he was protected against want until the end of his days by the appropriate corporate guild, he now went to work in the factories. Once he became unemployable, he was left unprotected to his fate. In exchange for his lost independence he has at best the poorhouse."[23]

For many artisans the disintegration of their class was the work of a dark conspiracy directed against the foundations of a just economic system. Cupidity, doctrinairism, and Semitic cunning had joined to destroy the handicraftsman's Arcadia. Master mason C. Pesche of Breslau described to an assembly of tradesmen the authors of their misfortune:

The first opponents . . . are the factory owners, because we compete with them. The second opponents are the idealists who talk and discourse and actually believe that

[23] *Preussisches Handelsarchiv* (1867), III (Jahresberichte der Handelskammern und kaufmännischen Korporationen des preussischen Staats für 1866), 486. Cf. *Zweite Versammlung des Congresses deutscher Volkswirthe zu Frankfurt a. M. vom 12. bis 15. September 1859: Stenographischer Bericht* (Frankfurt am Main, 1859), p. 22; "Die arbeitenden Classen," p. 274; G. Schmoller, *Geschichte der Kleingewerbe*, p. 669.

once the word "freedom" has merely been uttered, it alone constitutes all bliss. The third opponents are the intriguers. They are the men who first want to create a situation in which the handicraftsman will be reduced to hunger, so that through hunger he will be led astray to crime. And these people call that "economics." (Stormy applause.) The fourth opponents are the Jews. They want to become masters without having learned a handicraft.

A petition to the upper chamber of the Prussian legislature requested "the protection of the authorities against the parasitic growths of the modern 'industrial state,' against the swindle of speculation and ruthless competition, against the exploitation of honest labor and the despotic power of big finance capital." As for the economic advantages of free enterprise, they were meaningless to independent handicraftsmen facing ruin. "What good is it to a poor shoemaker or tailor," asked master baker H. Böhlen of Aachen, "that he has the right to become a banker or cloth manufacturer or to establish a factory, when he can make no use of that right? What good is it to me that I am allowed to climb to the moon, when I cannot do it?"[24]

The decline of the artisan class was part of a fundamental process of economic and social change which coincided with the political and diplomatic transformation of Central Europe. In the countryside, to be sure, the rationalization of agriculture failed to produce a significant alteration in the pattern of society. Throughout the first half of the nineteenth century the small peasant proprietor west of the Elbe continued to struggle against the effects of fragmentation and overpopulation of the land, while to the east the prevalence of the

---

[24] *Der zweite deutsche Handwerkertag zu Frankfurt a. M. vom 25. bis 28. September 1863* (Frankfurt am Main, 1863), p. 52. Cf. *Die stenographischen Verhandlungen des deutschen Handwerkertags zu Weimar vom 5. bis 8. September 1862* (Berlin, 1862), pp. 46-47; *Die Gewerbefrage in Preussen: Zwei Petitionen an die hohen Häuser des allgemeinen Landtages* (Berlin, 1861), p. 4.

latifundia perpetuated the hegemony of a hereditary aristocratic caste. The passivity of the village in politics reflected the stability of its class structure. In the cities, however, the growth of industrialism led to a social metamorphosis. One of its manifestations was the decline of the handicraft trades and the decay of guild organizations. Another was the emergence of a factory proletariat, composed largely of uprooted peasants and declassed tradesmen, shaping a purpose of its own out of the harsh experience of the mill and the colliery. Yet the most important social consequence of the industrial revolution was the rise of a new bourgeoisie, small in numbers, but energetic, ambitious, dissatisfied, and above all affluent. Its effect on the fabric of society was bound to be disruptive, for a shift in the distribution of wealth engendered demand for a shift in the distribution of power. Here was the heart of the political conflict of the mid-century which found its resolution in the achievement of national unification.

THREE

++

Class and Reform

THE creation of the German Empire took place in an environment of increasing material well-being. There were those, to be sure, whose way of life was adversely affected by the advance of industrialism. Among the skilled artisans in particular the introduction of new techniques of manufacture had disastrous social consequences. But most inhabitants of Central Europe were enjoying an unprecedented prosperity in which their standard of living reached a new height. The dissatisfaction with the established order revealed in the growth first of liberalism and then of socialism was not the result of economic stagnation. On the contrary, it reflected rising hopes and aspirations inspired by the unprecedented business boom of the mid-century. In the age of Frederick the Great the status quo had been tolerable because it appeared inevitable. But a hundred years later the contemporaries of Bismarck were in rebellion because the great gains which they had achieved were accompanied by still greater expectations. Intermingled with the movement for national unification were the forces of class interest and private ambition, employing the rhetoric of civic reform to establish a new society. In the summer of 1859, when after a decade of reaction public attention began to turn once more to political issues, the chamber of commerce in Worms emphasized this dependence of ideology on economics: "While it is a recognized fact that in the first place and for the most part German scholarship, through its representatives in the great gatherings of men of learning, awakened the loftier enthusiasm for the great fatherland, we still ought not to shut our eyes to the fact that for the great masses of the people it is not the spiritual but the corporeal needs which through their satisfaction lead to understanding, so that among the people trade and commerce have achieved more than the ideals and calculations of the scholars."[1]

Thanks to the growth of the economy, those corporeal needs were being met more successfully than ever before. Imports into the Zollverein rose from 545,000,000 marks in 1850 to 2,559,000,000 marks in 1869, a rate of growth far ahead of demographic expansion, so that the per capita value of goods purchased abroad climbed from 18.30 to 65.90 marks. Figures for the over-all rise of industrial production cannot be ascertained with any degree of precision. But the available data on mining, metallurgy, and manufacture generally support the estimate that the index of production for consumers' goods (1860 = 100) increased from 35 in the 1840's to 75 in the 1850's and 109 in the 1860's. Between 1850 and 1869 the number of savings accounts in Prussia grew from 278,000 to 1,046,000, while their combined value expanded even more rapidly, from 54,360,000 to 343,-820,000 marks. The nominal annual per capita income of the German population was climbing steadily from 266 marks in 1851-55 to 292 in 1856-60, 307 in 1861-65, and 325 in 1866-70. Part of this gain was wiped out by the simultaneous increase in the cost of living, but the accumulation of wealth outstripped the advance of the price level. The index of wholesale values (1913 = 100) rose in the case of agricultural products from 48.1 in 1850 to 75.5 in 1860 and 79 in 1870, and more slowly for basic industrial commodities including coal, iron, and textiles, from 86.7 to 102 and then down again to 98. The real annual per capita income calculated from this index amounted to 295 marks in 1851-55, 303 in 1856-60, 326 in 1861-65, and 333 in 1866-70. Not even the political tensions of the period of national unifica-

[1] *Preussisches Handelsarchiv* (1859), II, 399.

85

tion could repress the vitality of the German economy.[2]

Yet the production and income figures which bespeak a general increase in affluence tell nothing about its distribution. Did all classes of society share in the prosperity of those boom years? There can be no doubt that manufacturers, entrepreneurs, financiers, and merchants derived substantial benefits from the industrial growth of the mid-century. Landowners, both large and small, were similarly in a favorable economic position bolstered by the rationalization of agricultural output and the growing demand for foodstuffs generated by urbanization. But what of the vast propertyless proletariat immersed in the unending daily struggle for survival? Max Wirth, a protagonist of economic liberalism, insisted that "wages rose 25 to 50 per cent, depending on the occupation, not infrequently as much as 100 per cent, and even at such unheard-of wages many employers were at a loss to find men." Ferdinand Lassalle, on the other hand, crusading for lower-class support of the socialist cause, estimated that "96¼ per cent of the population is in an oppressed, impoverished condition." According to the data published by the Prussian government, there were as of 1855 some 288,000 persons in the kingdom dependent entirely on alms, while the Statistical Bureau lamented, "Nothing shows more clearly the growing economic decay of the working class of Berlin than the expenditures for poor relief, which have been increasing during the last decades at a frightening rate." At the same time, however, the Cologne chamber of commerce was complaining that "if we properly take into account the greater average productivity of the English worker, then for many branches of industry the current wages of labor along the Rhine and in Westphalia appear even higher than in England." An

---

[2] G. Bondi, *Deutschlands Aussenhandel*, p. 145; J. Kuczynski, *Short History*, pp. 14-16, 66; *Statistisches Handbuch für den preussischen Staat*, II (1893), 384; W. G. Hoffman and J. H. Müller, *Das deutsche Volkseinkommen*, pp. 13-15; A. Jacobs and H. Richter, *Die Grosshandelspreise in Deutschland*, pp. 82-83.

anonymous conservative publicist argued, moreover, that the position of the agricultural laborer was actually superior to that of the industrial worker, because "in the country many remainders of that feudal outlook still survive, making possible the persistence of a certain relationship of reciprocity, a sort of feeling of attachment between employer and employee." There is thus no simple answer to questions regarding the condition of the proletariat during the years of national struggle.[3]

The most comprehensive portrayal of lower-class living conditions is the collection of summarized reports for the period 1858-66 by the county commissioners which the government of Prussia published shortly after the Seven Weeks' War. The men who composed these accounts were for the most part conservative bureaucrats, inclined to extol the past at the expense of the present. Their descriptions, moreover, deal by and large with the situation in towns and villages rather than big cities. Yet in the aggregate they form a social document of major importance depicting the way of life of the laboring population in every province of the kingdom. They make clear first of all that the inadequate nourishment of many lower-class families made mere physical survival a widespread problem. "At noon and in the evening potatoes with salt and usually with fat, in addition black bread and coffee mixed with chicory, these are the chief means of subsistence of the population" in Adenau near Koblenz. Around Schleiden on the Belgian frontier "potatoes, coffee, and bread and butter are almost the only diet of the peasants." Farther north in Jülich "the potato along with coffee and bread consti-

3 M. Wirth, *Geschichte der Handelskrisen*, p. 350; Ferdinand Lassalle, *Gesammelte Reden und Schriften*, ed. Eduard Bernstein (12 vols., Berlin, 1919-20), III, 80; *Tabellen und amtliche Nachrichten über den preussischen Staat für das Jahr 1855* (Berlin, 1858), p. 197; "Ueber die Verschlechterung der physischen Beschaffenheit der Berliner Bevölkerung in neuerer Zeit," *Mittheilungen des Statistischen Bureau's in Berlin*, XIII (1860), 149; *Preussisches Handelsarchiv* (1858), II, 260; "Zur Arbeiterfrage" (Part 1), *Berliner Revue*, XXXII (1863), 399.

tutes the chief article of food consumption; meat is generally eaten only at church fairs and on the most important holidays." And from the Posen district at the other end of the kingdom came the same account: "The chief article of food consumption of the worker is the potato, the harvest of which therefore has a vital influence on his condition."

The position of the artisan class was especially precarious. All the reports are in agreement on this point. One county commissioner in Westphalia explained that "small handicraftsmen often lack energy, skill, or working capital. . . . Many people unfortunately establish a household of their own without means or savings, and then as soon as they get sick, they fall back on the charity of others." Another described the harsh existence of the skilled tradesman: "The handicrafts have little significance. Most handicraftsmen practice husbandry on the side. Many tailors, joiners, cartwrights, and even many shoemakers work in the homes of their customers for board and a daily wage. Journeymen often earn barely as much as farm hands." Conditions in Brandenburg were no better: "The small handicraftsmen are dependent on the inadequate wage rates granted to them by the industrial masters and proprietors of big plants, since independent small masters diminished more and more following the introduction of machines in the plants." In the Neustettin district of Pomerania the artisan trades were overcrowded and impoverished: "Because they are relatively too numerous, most handicraftsmen have a small volume of business, and therefore they practice husbandry at the same time or even accept work as day laborers." The county commissioner of Rosenberg in West Prussia also portrayed the hard lot of the independent artisan: "The handicraftsmen earn a miserable livelihood, traveling to trade fairs in search of customers, but then they run the risk of selling their wares below cost to cover the expenses of the trip." According to the report from Öls in Silesia, the ultimate reason for the decline of the handicrafts was the progress of free enterprise: "A large part of the skilled trades groans under the burden which the complete dissolution of the guilds necessarily brought with it wherever output and demand reached a state of imbalance, and wherever voluntary associations could not oppose the newly emerging force of capital."

Yet for workers outside the artisan occupations the standard of living was apparently rising. While the industrial and agricultural proletariat could not match the impressive gains of the business community, many of the county commissioners acknowledged that its position had generally improved. Conditions in the Province of Saxony were particularly favorable: "Higher wages have provided a better livelihood for the workers" of Sangerhausen. In County Rossla "the situation of the workers has recently become better because of an almost universal increase in wages and a simultaneous decline in the price of grain." Around Magdeburg "conditions have decidedly improved, because there is no labor surplus, wage scales are higher, and the winters were mild. The factories provide livelihood even in winter time for those who are temporarily unemployed in their own trades." The handicrafts of Oschersleben were generally declining, but in other occupations there was unaccustomed prosperity. "All in all, the needs of the workers are everywhere covered by their earnings, despite their growing preoccupation with amusements, especially since the scarcity of labor has raised those earnings." The situation in Wernigerode was still more favorable, for working-class families "often achieve ownership of a small plot of land or even a small house." Nor were mill hands the only ones to profit from the growth of the economy. According to the county commissioner of Torgau, "the position of the workers has unmistakably gotten better, because the more intensive practice of agriculture demands greater forces, and the

89

work required to maintain the dikes on the Elbe provides remunerative employment."

Reports from the other provinces, although more ambiguous, also suggest that the living conditions of the masses in the early 1860's were improving. For workers in the Silesian textile industry, for example, the economic situation was on the whole satisfactory. The county commissioner of Neurode estimated that "at the moment the position of the laboring classes is in general unusually favorable because of the good harvests; even the weavers find tolerable employment despite the American disturbances." In the nearby Reichenbach district, where the cotton mills employed more than 800 persons, "the position of the workers has improved excepting the weavers who work for wages." While two-thirds of the small artisans of Meseritz in the Province of Posen were forced to seek employment on the side as hired hands, "the construction of highways has improved the position of the day laborers through steady employment and an increase in remuneration for piecework." From the town of Königsburg in Brandenburg came a similar account of the depressed condition of the artisan class, but "the urban handworkmen are somewhat more secure." Descriptions of the situation in the west also dwelt on the hardships of proletarian life mitigated by a gradual improvement. "The position of the laboring classes is not unfavorable," reported Gladbach in the Rhine Province, although "the welfare of the industrial population remains largely subject to fluctuations." To the south in the Eifel region the diet of the rural masses was inadequate, "yet the consumption of meat has grown." In the Westphalian city of Lippstadt even handicraftsmen could get ahead with a little luck and know-how. "The industrious ones, especially if they work with journeymen, live better than minor officials." Despite substantial variation from district to district and from occupation to occupation, the reports of the county commissioners leave the over-all impression that the standard of living of the lower classes was slowly rising.[4]

This impression is reinforced by taxation statistics which suggest that the income of most classes of the Prussian population was increasing during the period of national unification. For the largest major category of taxpayers comprising those with earnings below 600 marks annually, that is, the mass of agricultural workers including both day laborers and farm hands, industrial employees, artisan journeymen, hired help, and even many small peasant proprietors and master craftsmen, the average yearly income rose from 467 marks in 1851 to 491 in 1856, 511 in 1861, 537 in 1866, and 582 in 1871, a total increase of 25 per cent for the two decades. The index of the cost of living based on wholesale prices (1913 = 100) moved at a considerably lower rate from 90.2 for 1851-55 to 96.3 for 1856-60, 94.3 for 1861-65, 97.6 for 1866-70, and then a spurt to 103.4 for the postwar years 1871-75. The living conditions of the masses measured by the real earnings of more than 85 per cent of all income tax payers were thus clearly improving, although progress was at times sluggish and spotty.

Those whose earnings were between 600 and 3,000 marks annually, a group including highly skilled workers, the lower and middle ranks of the civil service, white-collar employees, members of the learned professions, well-to-do farmers, retail merchants, and small businessmen, totaled about 11 per cent of the income tax payers. Their average yearly receipts grew from 1,073 marks in 1851 to 1,131 in 1856, 1,149 in 1861, 1,154 in 1866, and 1,166 in 1871, a rise of only some 9 per cent for the entire period 1851-71, barely ahead of the increase in the cost of living. As for the approximately 1 per cent of all taxpayers with an income above 3,000 marks, their average annual earnings went from 6,391 in 1851 to 6,781 in 1856, 6,724 in 1861, 6,927 in 1866, and 7,156 in 1871. The total rise for this group,

---

[4] "Die arbeitenden Classen," pp. 268, 272, 286, 289, 306, 310-313, 318, 320, 330-332, 341.

91

composed of men of means in industry and agriculture, amounted to 12 per cent.

Yet the generalization that low-income groups were progressing more rapidly than those in the middle and upper range is valid only when applied to broad categories of taxpayers composed of several distinct economic strata. Its statistical validity must not obscure the fact that there were actually substantial class differences in the rate of income growth which constituted an important factor in the aggravation of social tension. To be sure, the material well-being of society as a whole was increasing, but at the same time the gap between rich and poor was widening. Between 1852 and 1867 those with annual earnings below 300 marks, the propertyless and impoverished proletariat, increased slightly, from 71.6 to 72.5 per cent of all income tax paying residents of Prussia. Their share of the entire personal income in the state, however, declined from 26.9 to 21.5 per cent. The petty bourgeoisie, loosely delimited by an income range between 300 and 3,000 marks a year, diminished somewhat from 27.5 to 26.4 per cent of the population, while its portion of the total wealth remained about the same, 56.9 and 56.6 per cent. The middle class proper, on the other hand, composed of those with yearly incomes between 3,000 and 9,600 marks, improved its position both numerically and financially. Its percentage of the income tax payers rose from 0.8 to 1, and its share of the combined taxable revenues from 10.4 to 12.9 per cent. The most impressive gains, however, were made by the very wealthy, those with receipts above 9,600 marks a year. Their number almost doubled, from 5,300 to 9,900, still a minute fraction of the more than 6,000,-000 persons subject to the income tax, but the most rapidly growing economic stratum of the population. Even more important, their proportion of the earnings of all classes of society was expanding at the fastest rate, from 5.8 to 9 per cent.

The advance of industrialism thus produced significant shifts in the distribution of wealth which were of vital importance in the social and political conflicts of the mid-century. First of all, the income of the mass of wage earners and small proprietors diminished from 84 to 78 per cent of the total in the course of some fifteen years, while the revenues of men of property subsisting largely on investments grew correspondingly from 16 to 22 per cent. This tendency was especially pronounced at the two ends of the economic scale. Those on the borders of destitution derived the least benefit from the great expansion of factory production. Indeed, their average earnings may have even diminished because of the drastic decline in the income of the artisan class. For those in a position to organize and finance the growth of manufacture, on the other hand, the era of national unification marked a decisive breakthrough in the struggle for domination of the economy of Central Europe. Throughout the period of the boom large fortunes increased at a much more rapid pace than those of medium size. During the twelve years preceding the outbreak of the Danish War the number of individuals earning more than 36,000 marks annually grew from 94 to 219 in Brandenburg, from 92 to 147 in the Rhine Province, and from 78 to 120 in Silesia. The number of taxpayers in the state with an income above 60,000 marks a year, a group increasingly comprised of the giants of industry, banking, and commerce, rose from 106 in 1852 to 183 in 1857 and 246 in 1867. Centers of manufacture and finance, moreover, registered the largest increment, centers like Berlin, Düsseldorf, Aachen, Cologne, Arnsberg, Breslau, and Oppeln. In the industrial provinces of the kingdom yearly personal receipts of more than 120,000 marks multiplied from 26 in 1853 to 43 in 1863 and 137 in 1873, while in the agricultural provinces the comparable figures were 4, 9, and 20. Here was graphic evi-

93

dence that economic power was passing from the landed aristocracy into the hands of the bourgeoisie.[5]

Alarmed by this sudden alteration in the pattern of society, the defenders of the established order began to resist innovation as a matter of principle. A few of their more sophisticated spokesmen sought to elaborate a program of conservative economic reform behind which all classes threatened by industrial wealth could rally. But for the typical Junker the subtleties of traditionalist social theory were confusing. He ingenuously saw himself in the forefront of a conflict between right and wrong, between the eternal verities of his fathers and the false doctrines of an impious new age. The newspapers he read reinforced his conviction that the nobility must lead the good fight against "the extremes of moneyed rule, of unauthorized industrialism, of the usurious exploitation of agriculture and the handicrafts under the pretext of free exchange, the extremes of government by Jews, of the dissolution of discipline and morality through dechristianization of marriage and the school, of the destruction of the church through the transformation of the old parishes organized in a stable order into a constitutional electorate." The political organizations he supported demanded "protection and respect for honest labor, for every form of property, right, and class; no favoritism and exclusive rule of moneyed capital; no abandonment of the handicrafts and landed property to the false teachings and usurious tricks of our times." Frightened at the prospect of losing its privileged position, the landowning nobility preferred rhetoric to reflection. There were those conservatives who recognized the futility of a policy of pure negation. In a letter of September 18, 1861, Bismarck agreed with his old friend Alexander von Below-Hohendorf that "a political party cannot survive with only a feeble defensive position, much less conquer terrain and followers." But such

[5] W. G. Hoffmann and J. H. Müller, *Das deutsche Volkseinkommen*, pp. 14-15, 59-61, 63-66; P. Benaerts, *Les origines*, pp. 576-580.

94

strictures were rare. The aristocracy as a class proved unable to formulate an economic program going beyond a die-hard defense of the status quo.[6]

The material interests of the middle class, on the other hand, obliged it to seek reform. The rationalization of production in the face of a political and legal system designed for a hierarchical agrarian community produced a growing disparity between the economic basis of society and its institutional framework. The great boom of the 1850's in particular encouraged bourgeois agitation for a program of reform favorable to the growth of industrial capitalism. One of the leaders of that agitation, the liberal economist Victor Böhmert, recalled in his memoirs the feel of those years when heaven was smiling on the aspirations of manufacturers and bankers:

> The entire current of the time, the splendid victory of the English free-trade movement, the development of modern commerce into a world economy which was revealed to the peoples of the earth at the first international exhibition in London in the year 1851 and again at the second international exhibition in Paris in 1855, and also the needs of German big industry which grew powerful soon after the establishment of the Zollverein, all drove the German economy to progress in the direction of industrial and commercial freedom, to the abolition of German river tolls and transit duties, and to reforms in the postal, telegraph, and railroad systems as well as in money and coinage, in weights and measures, in the legislation governing trade and bills of exchange, and in numerous other areas.

The movement for economic innovation became inextricably intertwined with the movement for political unification, both drawing strength from the transforma-

---

6 *Volksblatt für Stadt und Land,* March 22, 1862; *Europäischer Geschichtskalender,* ed. H. Schulthess (1861), p. 45; O. v. Bismarck, *Werke,* XIV/1, 578.

tion of society which industrial capitalism was effecting.[7]

The reports of the Prussian chambers of commerce submitted annually to the authorities in Berlin provide the clearest formulation of the middle-class program of economic reform. They express the wishes of the business community, respectful in tone, but explicit in asserting what the bourgeoisie wanted from the state. First of all, there was the insistent demand for the introduction of industrial freedom. Restrictions on the organization and operation of manufacturing establishments, so the argument ran, while possibly justified in the pre-industrial age of handicraft production, became an intolerable anachronism in an expanding economy of factories and collieries. "Free movement in all areas of labor and productive activity," maintained the businessmen of Essen, "is and remains the necessary watchword of the present time, and our fatherland will reach the level of commercial and industrial development which is its due only when the constantly repeated demand for full industrial freedom has been met." The failure to give scope to the economic talents of the German entrepreneur played into the hands of his foreign competitors, warned a report from Frankfurt an der Oder: "The compulsory examination of occupational skill, the stipulation of a fixed number of years of training as an apprentice and journeyman, the division and delimitation of trades, the prohibition against the simultaneous practice of several crafts by the same person, the restriction on factories as well as master artisans in the employment of artisan journeymen, etc., they prove more and more to be obstacles to the faster development of business pursuits and the free unfolding of popular energies, which therefore often find employment in foreign countries and serve to advance their industries to our disadvantage."

[7] Victor Böhmert, *Rückblicke und Ausblicke eines Siebzigers* (Dresden, 1900), p. 14.

For that matter, explained the chamber of commerce in Aachen, the artisans themselves favored industrial freedom or at least should have favored it:

> Every Prussian must be able freely to apply his intelligence and labor, as long as he does not do so in a way harmful to the community. Otherwise the handicrafts will perish, or rather the energetic handicraftsmen will emigrate on a much larger scale than hitherto. Although there were for a long time some handicraftsmen who sought salvation in the guild system instead of in diligence and effective, unrestrained striving for improvement, today there can only be very few left who do not recognize their mistake and do not realize that on their own two feet they are bound to go farther than on the leading strings and crutches of the guild. If there had been compulsory guild membership for physics, chemistry, mechanics, and the natural sciences, we would be without railroads and telegraphs and the countless inventions which enhance life. Let the handicrafts therefore also move without restraint.

The ultimate justification of free enterprise, however, was not contingent on popular support. The perennial struggle for economic existence was a prod to human industriousness; conflict was the price of progress. "A handicraft which cannot survive in free competition with factories," expounded the merchants and manufacturers of Cologne, "is outdated. To give it an artificial existence by legislative coercion would be contrary to the principles of economics and an injustice to those classes of the population which earn their livelihood in and from factories." In economics as in nature only the fit could expect to survive.[8]

---

[8] *Preussisches Handelsarchiv* (1866), III, (Jahresberichte der Handelskammern und kaufmännischen Korporationen des preussischen Staats für 1865), 712, 747; *ibid.* (1861), III (Jahresberichte der Handelskammern und kaufmännischen Korporationen des preussischen Staats für 1860), 265; Cologne Chamber of Commerce, *Jahres-Bericht für das Jahr 1849* (Cologne, 1850), p. 5.

The chambers of commerce also demanded the freedom of movement without which industrialization would be seriously hampered. The growth of the factory system depended on the flow of manpower from country to city. What was the sense in agitating for the right to establish mills, if there were no mill hands to hire? Yet the movement of labor was restricted partly by the thirty-odd frontiers dividing the German Confederation, but even more by the laws of many states empowering communities to limit the admission of outsiders by means of domicile requirements. In the context of the stable agrarian economy of the early nineteenth century such legislation tended to maintain the equilibrium of the working force and control the vagabondage of the poor. With the rise of industrialism, however, it became an obstacle to the rationalization of production.

This was the point which business circles made over and over again in their reports to the government. "Industrial freedom is obviously only a dead letter as long as complete freedom of movement is not added to it," argued the chamber of commerce in Darmstadt. "From the point of view of economic interests, which cannot be influenced by considerations of foreign policy, the extension of this freedom of movement to outsiders should not be denied under any circumstances, not even when there is no reciprocity. For the inflow of foreign capital, labor, and intelligence can only have a good influence on the development of the country, never a harmful effect." The Breslau chamber of commerce similarly sought to justify the mobility of population on the ground of economic rationality: "Only under the rule of unrestrained freedom of movement can the division of labor develop. . . . It is not enough that freedom of movement be introduced in one state. It is necessary that in general every citizen of a German state be free to apply his energy wherever in his opinion he can do so most advantageously, that industry take its workers wherever it can find them, and that the various regions transfer their labor force or temporary population surplus without hindrance and in accordance with their needs." A report from Düsseldorf emphasized that freedom of movement would safeguard the interests of the proletariat, "so that precisely the worker who does not find a livelihood in one community can seek it in another, without the financial sacrifices which are as a rule beyond his means." Yet from Essen came the contradictory contention that freedom of movement was needed to resist the demands of the proletariat enforced by labor strikes: "If the workers are given the right to shut off the supply of labor within local boundaries by means of mass work stoppages, then by the same token the employers must have the opportunity of seeking to satisfy their demand outside those boundaries. Complete industrial freedom and freedom of movement must form the regulating mechanism, so that when the balance between supply and demand is disturbed by labor unions in one community, it can be re-established within broader boundaries." What made the mobility of manpower important to the middle class was the need of the factory system for a growing labor force.[9]

The bankers and entrepreneurs engaged in financing industrial expansion were also anxious to effect the repeal of usury laws, which in general established a maximum interest rate of 6 per cent. Reflecting the anticapitalistic bias of a rural society, these laws were an inconvenience to the business community, but not an insuperable obstacle. They could be circumvented either by an increase in commission charges or the manipulation of discount rates. As the demand for credit became more intensive, moreover, governments began to modify their restrictive policy by the temporary non-

[9] T. S. Hamerow, *Restoration, Revolution, Reaction*, pp. 231-232; *Preussisches Handelsarchiv* (1864), II, 321; *ibid.* (1866), III (Jahresberichte der Handelskammern und kaufmännischen Korporationen des preussischen Staats für 1865), 352; *ibid.* (1865), III (Jahresberichte der Handelskammern und kaufmännischen Korporationen des preussischen Staats für 1864), 354, 695-696.

enforcement or outright repeal of interest regulations. In Prussia, for example, usury legislation was suspended during the critical years 1809-10 and more briefly during the financial panic of 1857. Most of the states, however, preferred to abolish the restrictions once and for all. As of the early 1850's, only Baden and Württemberg no longer determined the cost of borrowing. But before the decade was out, they were joined by Oldenburg, Bremen, and Saxe-Weimar, then came Saxe-Coburg in 1860, Lübeck in 1862, and Frankfurt am Main and Saxony in 1864. Even in rural Bavaria, where strenuous efforts had once been made to suppress usurious interest rates, the authorities were ready to concede that the establishment of a financial free market was only a matter of time. For the middle class, however, the repeal of legal control over credit transactions did not represent a life-and-death issue, but rather the moral victory of liberal economic principles over irrational agrarian prejudices.[10]

The chambers of commerce were of course overwhelmingly opposed to government regulation of the cost of borrowing. After the brief suspension of the Prussian usury laws in 1857, they hastened to impress on the ministry that a policy which had proved so successful should be made permanent. There were, to be sure, a few dissenting opinions. The report from Minden, for instance, expressed the noncommittal view that "neither the fears of the pessimists nor the hopes of the optimists regarding the adopted measure have been realized," while in the rural Altena district there was even support for the restriction of interest rates: "We have considered a permanent repeal of the so-called usury laws . . . not

[10] Richard Tilly, *Financial Institutions and Industrialization in the Rhineland, 1815-1870* (Madison, Milwaukee, and London, 1966), pp. 88-89; *Konsequenzen des preussisch-französischen Handelsvertrages für unser inneres Staatsleben* (Berlin, 1862), p. 24; "Gutachten des Professor Dr. Goldschmidt zu Heidelberg über die Aufhebung der Wuchergesetze," *Verhandlungen des sechsten deutschen Juristentages* (3 vols., Berlin, 1865-68), I, 239, 253-257, 261-265.

desirable for our local conditions, and we are still convinced today that the rate of interest on sound mortgage loans, which is generally 4 per cent in our county, would gradually rise if the existing limitations were permanently repealed." But these were rare exceptions. The Breslau chamber of commerce spoke for the vast majority in declaring that "we heard of no complaint which the measure evoked, and we could only regret that it was merely temporary." Freedom of credit would not benefit any one class or region, but the economy of the nation as a whole. "The merchants support the abolition of interest restrictions because it is to their advantage," granted an account from Kottbus. "Yet this is not because they alone or even only primarily derive advantage from it, but because the general well-being is also of benefit to them. This liberation, like any other, will undeniably bring dangers and disadvantages to the careless and thoughtless. But we obviously cannot take this into account in any way, because otherwise we would have to prohibit the use of fire and the extraction of iron, things infinitely more dangerous, not to mention steamships and railroads."

The agitation against the usury laws reached its height in 1858, when there was good hope that the government might be persuaded to extend the suspension of interest regulations which it had introduced during the depression. As late as 1865, however, the chamber of commerce in Frankfurt an der Oder was still pleading with the ministry for a more liberal credit policy: "The legal limitations of contractual interest rates, the so-called usury laws, have long been considered antiquated and harmful by modern economic theory as well as by practice. And we must point out over and over again the need to abolish them finally. The opponents of the repeal of those laws are by now to be found almost entirely among the rural landowners, whose opposition, arising out of a supposed self-interest, seems unjustified in view of the general welfare which the usury laws endanger."[11]

The economic reform program of the middle class embraced a number of additional demands whose fulfillment was important for the progress of industrial capitalism. Members of the Cologne chamber of commerce, obliged to transact business in more than forty different kinds of paper money, announced that "we consider a comprehensive regulation of the system of banks of issue in Germany to be one of the most pressing needs of German industry." They also enthusiastically supported government efforts toward "the grand creation of a common German law of commerce." The business community of Düsseldorf urged that "the way . . . be prepared as soon as possible for a uniform system of patent legislation for all of Germany to meet a general need." The merchants of Magdeburg, complaining about the river tolls which Hanover, Mecklenburg-Schwerin, and Lauenburg exacted from commerce on the Elbe, condemned those states "which constantly take pleasure in putting petty obstacles in the way of the free national and economic development of Prussia and of Germany." Finally, the existence of eight distinct monetary systems and thirty-odd standards of measurement was a source of vexation to trade and industry. "The efforts of some German governments to introduce generally uniform weights and measures are most gratifying," declared a report from Halle, while from Frankfurt an der Oder came the concurring opinion that "the creation of a common system of coinage, weights, and measures is a warranted demand" of modern times.[12]

[11] *Preussisches Handelsarchiv* (1865), III (Jahresberichte der Handelskammern und kaufmännischen Korporationen des preussischen Staats für 1864), 649. Cf. *ibid.* (1858), I, 610, II, 357, 488, 520.
[12] Julius Gensel, *Der Deutsche Handelstag in seiner Entwickelung und Thätigkeit, 1861-1901* (Berlin, 1902), p. 2; *Preussisches Handelsarchiv* (1857), II, 318; *ibid.* (1862), III (Jahresberichte der Handelskammern und kaufmännischen Korporationen des preussischen Staats für 1861), 257, 348; *ibid.* (1861), III (Jahresberichte der Handelskammern und kaufmännischen Korporationen des preussischen Staats für 1860),

There was thus a growing tension between the political institutions of the German Confederation established early in the nineteenth century and its material needs emerging fifty years later. The close interconnection between economic and political reform, moreover, was apparent to contemporary observers. Every manufacturer and banker realized on the basis of first-hand experience that national unification would provide a powerful stimulus to industrial expansion. The chambers of commerce, dependent on government authorization, were as a rule reluctant to express themselves on controversial questions of politics. They preferred to speak in hints and nuances. But at times they could be unmistakably forthright. In the summer of 1859, while Germany pondered the Austrian defeats in Italy, the business community of Worms demanded a far-reaching reorganization of the Zollverein for the protection of commercial interests: "Not only the merchant but also the statesman, if he loves his fatherland, must . . . entertain the wish that the movement of trade in Germany be made progressively easier. We must all wish that the Zollverein undergo the improvements which the passage of time has shown to be necessary, especially that it become better adapted to learn and satisfy the needs of states and individuals by means of a 'Zollverein assembly' (composed of the representatives of the German merchant class chosen perhaps by the legislatures of the individual states) , a permanent chief executive authority, and representation abroad (Zollverein consulates) ." And in 1862, after reform of the German Confederation had become a crucial public issue, the Cologne chamber of commerce spoke out even more boldly:

> The division of opinion . . . regarding a timely reform
> of the German federal constitution in a unitary direction

290; *ibid.* (1865) , III (Jahresberichte der Handelskammern und kaufmännischen Korporationen des preussischen Staats für 1864) , 649; Eugene N. Anderson, *The Social and Political Conflict in Prussia, 1858-1864* (Lincoln, 1954) , p. 159.

which has developed between the royal Prussian government and most of the other German governments forces us against our will into the position . . . of expressing from our point of view the wish that the representation of Germany abroad as well as the command and leadership of her armed forces be placed in the hands of a supreme federal authority, and that this authority receive the power to issue, with the approval of a representative assembly of the German people, generally binding laws pertaining to the railroad, postal, and telegraph systems, industrial and patent legislation, weights, measures, and money, river and canal shipping, as well as commercial affairs in the broadest sense, especially import duties. . . . Unity, that is to say, is the fundamental condition for successful creative activity by Germany in the economic sphere, because only unity can remove the unnatural barriers which still hinder the exchange of goods in the domestic market.[13]

The publicists who in the late 1850's began to agitate for the reorganization of the German Confederation were also conscious of the close relationship between political and economic reform. The polemical literature of those years persistently dwelt on the material advantages bound to ensue from national unification. While the chambers of commerce hesitated to express opinions which might alienate the authorities, reformist pamphleteers could afford to be audacious. They may have differed regarding the means of achieving a new civic order, but they were generally eager to enlist middle-class support. Many of them therefore portrayed the exciting opportunities for industry and commerce which a united fatherland would offer. Like the liberal politician and financier Karl Mathy, they recognized that "the desire for a satisfactory discussion between Prussia and Austria concerning better organic institutions for

---

[13] *Preussisches Handelsarchiv* (1862), III (Jahresberichte der Handelskammern und kaufmännischen Korporationen des preussischen Staats für 1861), 372-373. Cf. *ibid.* (1859), II, 399.

the common purposes and vital needs of the German states does not in fact concern castles in the air built out of ideology or doctrine, but palpable material interests. The people who draft and scrutinize balance sheets and bills of exchange are indeed trained primarily to recognize only the immediate causes of their complaints and apprehensions. But to the extent that their tranquillity is disturbed by developments, their faculties begin to observe more sharply."[14]

Constitutional rights and burgeoning factories, liberty and banks, elections and trade, patriotism and profits, all were interrelated in the writings of the publicists whose paper battles preceded the military struggle for supremacy in Central Europe. Some of them hoped to accomplish the reconstruction of the German Confederation under the leadership of a liberalized Prussia. In the pages of the London journal which Gottfried Kinkel edited, for example, democratic refugees from Germany demanded the calling of a national parliament and the immediate formulation by Berlin of a minimum program of federal reform. "This minimum program might well include centralization of foreign policy, of the armed forces, of commercial relations and customs, [and] of the railroad, highway, and postal systems." The liberal jurist Siegfried Weiss argued that a progressive Germany under the Hohenzollern aegis could defy Russia as well as Austria. But the political idealism of the nation would have to be fortified by economic improvements. "We want the removal of industrial constraint throughout Germany, so that labor and industry can develop freely everywhere, because guild privileges shackle all talent for work. . . . Then we want to grant to every German through the state constitutions the full right of domicile, so that every man is free to establish his abode and residence wherever his occupational duties, etc., etc. lead him. . . . Furthermore, we want uniformity in the

14 [Karl Mathy], "Deutsche Interessen und deutsche Politik," *Preussische Jahrbücher*, II (1858), 6.

105

monetary system, so that hereafter only one kind of money will circulate in Germany." The Viennese newspaper editor O. Bernhard Friedmann advocated a peaceful separation of Austria from Germany which would enable both to pursue their separate constitutional destinies, while maintaining the closest diplomatic and economic ties. "A common trade policy, a gradual rapprochement and conformity in commercial, industrial, and tariff legislation, and the greatest possible freedom of communication" would be secured by a treaty between the two governments. "Built on the foundation of international free trade and the closest association and unification of material interests, . . . a treaty of alliance recognized by the law of nations between the Austrian imperial state and the German federal state would provide a firm guarantee of the external security of both lands and of the free development of their internal constitutional structure undisturbed by any extraneous influence."[15]

Many of the protagonists of national unification under Prussian auspices looked to the Zollverein as their point of departure. At the federal diet in Frankfurt am Main, Habsburg diplomacy could always count on the support of the secondary governments. But the customs union was an association of states in which the Hohenzollern primacy remained undisputed. All that had to be done was to extend its competence from commerce to politics, and to transform its administrative apparatus into an instrument of governmental authority. The cautiously liberal *Grenzboten* in Leipzig proposed "a permanent central administration for the Zollverein, and such an administration would follow of its own

---

15 O. Bernhard Friedmann, *Zur Einigung Oesterreichs: Eine Denkschrift* (Stuttgart, 1862), pp. 5, 76. Cf. Hans Rosenberg, *Die nationalpolitische Publizistik Deutschlands: Vom Eintritt der neuen Ära in Preussen bis zum Ausbruch des deutschen Krieges* (2 vols., Munich and Berlin, 1935), I, 101, II, 987, 998; "Was kann Preussen thun?," *Hermann: Deutsches Wochenblatt aus London*, June 11, 1859, p. 178; Siegfried Weiss, *An die deutsche Nation: Oesterreich, Deutschland und das Einheitsproject* (Berlin, 1860), pp. 26-27, 32.

accord as soon as the customs union expressly and consciously makes the establishment of a German federal state its goal." Among the reforms which the Zollverein should consider, moreover, were "the unrestricted right of residence for subjects of the customs union under the same conditions everywhere," and "uniform legislation regarding the conduct of trade and industry (commercial and industrial law, freedom of movement)." The Prussophile Nationalverein, while primarily concerned with political and constitutional questions, was also aware of the advantages which economic integration would provide for the national cause: "To begin with, the Zollverein should rise above the basis of a contractual relationship among sovereign states, and develop into an economic organism. . . . The various branches of a national economy stand in the most intimate relationship to one another. Only after they have obtained a common focus will they be able to do justice to national life."

An anonymous advocate of a vigorous maritime policy saw in the formation of a Zollverein parliament the essential prerequisite for the expansion of German trade overseas: "We must finally cease to consider the Zollverein as simply the most convenient instrument for collecting indirect taxes. . . . Germany on the broadened basis of the Zollverein and under Prussia's precedence must seek to achieve naval power for the protection of the German coast and merchant marine. The Zollverein must breathe more sea air. . . . We need a commercial policy which will win influence for Germany in transatlantic regions." For the political journalist Hermann Robolsky, on the other hand, a reformed customs union was primarily the instrument of economic integration within Germany: "If the Zollverein is to form a centralized totality, if it is to constitute a juristic personality and so develop external power, then it must assume a federal character and receive centralized directive organs of lawmaking and administration. After that, other economic interests of the German people should also be placed within its competence, for instance, the system of money, weights and measures, mercantile representation vis-à-vis foreign countries, and the postal and railroad system." The moderate landowner and politician Baron Anton von Gablenz, while ready to maintain the political connection with Austria, urged that Prussia, acting through the Zollverein, become the champion of the material interests of Germany. "In these times when commerce and industry are the bearers of civilization, when in a sense there is competition among nations to develop free spiritual growth and spread Christian humanism through the improvement of material well-being, when inventions and advances follow one another with lightning speed," the customs union must be transformed into "a German commercial and political association with popular representation." By rallying the economic energies of the nation to their side, the Hohenzollerns could achieve hegemony in Central Europe.[16]

Since the *grossdeutsch* champions of Austria were equally determined to win middle-class support, they too advanced plans of economic improvement. But for them the promotion of material interests could take place only within the framework of the German Confederation. Any diminution of the historic role of the Habsburgs would be a disaster for the nation. They agreed that reform in economics as well as politics was long overdue, but reform must be the result of collaboration at the federal diet between Vienna and Berlin. The brothers August and Peter Reichensperger, voicing the sentiment of the Catholic Rhineland, contended that "a common regulation of credit institutions and of the system of money, weights, and measures should no longer

16 K. M., "Die Zukunft des Zollvereins," *Die Grenzboten,* XIX (1860), no. 4, pp. 9, 45, 47; "Die Bedürfnisse und Bedingungen der deutschen Handelspolitik," *Wochenschrift des Nationalvereins,* May 8, 1860, p. 12; *Die Erstrebung einer maritimen Stellung Deutschlands auf der Basis des Zoll-Vereins* (Berlin, 1859), pp. 41, 52; H. Robolsky, *Der deutsche Zollverein: Seine Entstehung, Entwicklung und Zukunft* (Berlin, 1862), pp. v-vi; Anton von Gablenz, *Die deutsche Einheit nach des Königs Worten aufgefasst* (Breslau, 1861), pp. 5, 16.

be postponed. We must always keep in mind, however, that the main objective is the amalgamation of the two great powers and the rest of Germany in commercial no less than in military affairs." Such views were also frequently expressed in the Protestant north. The Bremen publicist Wilhelm Kiesselbach concluded that if Germany retained the federal principle, the diet in Frankfurt am Main would have to determine common economic policies. "Germany's salvation depends on the harmony of her two Great Powers, in which the other members of the confederation will likewise join." This was also the conviction of the anonymous pamphleteer in Oldenburg who urged the creation of a federal parliament representing the entire nation, "so that the north Germans and the south Germans can discover that their wishes, needs, and sympathies are not different but fundamentally the same, calling for union. Then we need the introduction of uniform laws, uniform communal, provincial, and state constitutions based on self-government, freedom of movement and industrial freedom, [and] uniform commercial institutions, weights, measures, and money."[17]

To the engineer and economist Karl Arnd, moreover, Austria was essential for the fulfillment of the grand destiny of German culture:

It was to a large extent on German scholarship and German inventive genius that the European civilization of today was built. It was to a large extent the voyages of discovery undertaken by Germans which acquainted the Christian world with strange lands. It was to a large extent German factory production and German commerce which made that success possible. Finally, it was to a large

[17] *Deutschlands Lage und Zukunft: Ein freies Wort an Deutschlands Fürsten und Volksstämme* (Oldenburg, 1860) , p. 12. Cf. August and Peter Reichensperger, *Deutschlands nächste Aufgaben* (Paderborn, 1860) , p. 76; W. K., "Handelspolitische Betrachtungen aus der Gegenwart" (Part 1) , *Deutsche Vierteljahrs-Schrift*, xxi (1858) , no. 4, pp. 65, 70; H. Rosenberg, *Die nationalpolitische Publizistik*, ii, 560-561, 990.

extent German emigrants who cultivated and settled many uninhabited regions in unknown parts of the world. But all this was of no advantage to the German nationality and the German influence on the conduct of world politics. We appeared everywhere only as subordinates of the so-called sea powers, without rights of our own. Our historic mission in the world is to act independently as apostles of civilization and morality wherever barbarism, slavery, and coarse ignorance estrange men from their ethical calling. It is our mission to take possession in our own name of the still uncivilized regions of America and Australia, to settle them with industrious inhabitants, and thereby to transform them into the happy homes of many generations of men endowed with reason. But only by means of a common bond holding us together, only by means of a common national flag, a strong navy, and a common representation through embassies and consuls can we achieve this end.[18]

Several other Austrophile publicists stressed the vital role which the Habsburg monarchy could play in the spread of German economic and cultural influence. For most of them, however, the natural sphere of expansion lay not in the New World, but in Central Europe, the Balkans, and the lands of the Mediterranean. From Württemberg A.E.F. Schäffle urged the inclusion of all the Austrian as well as Prussian possessions within a reformed federal union. "Once the inhabitant of the German Confederation can engage in industry, settle down, and travel under the same free law from Munich to Basel and from Bremen to Vienna or Brassó, once he supports a common fleet, once he possesses a common armed force, a supreme court, a general and uniform execution of judicial decisions, once he can find justice under the same law of property, obtain and use a patent easily and profitably throughout the

[18] Karl Arnd, *Gedanken über die Fortbildung des deutschen Bundes* (Frankfurt am Main, 1860), pp. 40-41. Cf. H. Rosenberg, *Die national-politische Publizistik*, ii, 983.

entire country, and have a common consular representation abroad, then this will provide the basis for an
exalting civic consciousness." In Bavaria Friedrich von
Kerstorf, a leading spokesman for the protectionist
industrial circles of the south, portrayed the exciting
possibilities of "a Central European customs and commercial realm of more than 1,000,000 square kilometers
and more than 70 million people, washed by three seas
and possessing the greatest riverain regions, ruled by
the German national element, and institutionally organized in a manner befitting the historically confirmed
system of federation among the numerous German
tribes as well as the maintenance of the independence of
the princes and of the states themselves." The unknown
author of a pamphlet appearing in Stuttgart prophesied
the day when "the road to Austria will be opened for
German commerce and German industry, especially for
the industry of southern Germany. This is its future,
and in this fashion are our conquests to be made, in the
great commercial market of the Orient, through the
Danube and the Black Sea. . . . The immediate and most
pressing task of German policy is the maintenance and
extension of the trade routes to the Orient."

And in the lengthy memoir published shortly after
his tragic suicide, the Austrian statesman Baron Karl
von Bruck maintained that a bold policy of expansion
would safeguard the Habsburg position in Central
Europe:

> Austria should not stand solely on the defensive. She
> must go forward by acting decisively. She must ad-
> vance along with German cultural life, energetic and
> fructifying, up to the very Pontus, accompanied and sup-
> ported by the brisk rise of Austro-German commerce.
> Only in the closest association with Germany will it be
> possible for her to fulfill her external mission on the
> Adriatic Sea as well. The German spirit must also pene-
> trate and animate Austria's maritime development in the
> Mediterranean, so that we can be better prepared than

hitherto for the developments of the future, which have already cast their shadow. We need only to think of the Suez Canal to recognize the great significance of the position of Austria on the Adriatic. But however important for Austria German support in the east and south may be, she has an equal need for the natural economic complement toward the north and west. The north German slope represents for Austria as much as for the rest of Germany the important transatlantic side of her world commerce. With her entire Nordic and transatlantic trade she is directed toward the German river flowing northward, toward the north German seaports, means of transportation, markets, and sources of supply. . . . It would be fatal to think that the German people will be satisfied with no more than occasional measures promulgated by the Confederation regarding commerce, money, weights, measures, and the enforcement of the judicial decisions of German courts in all the German states. It is rather a question of realizing the idea of unity at least in law, in economics, and in foreign relations by means of federal institutions created for that purpose.[19]

While the economic demands of the bourgeoisie were intimately involved in the movement for national unification, to the lower classes the struggle to reorganize the German Confederation was of small consequence. The endless task of earning a daily livelihood left them little time for the great issues of civic reconstruction. The reform programs which they did formulate rarely went beyond bread-and-butter demands for alleviation of the pervasive, grinding poverty. They remained by and large indifferent to the party conflicts whose outcome would determine the future of Central Europe. The peas-

[19] Karl von Bruck, *Die Aufgaben Oesterreichs* (Leipzig, 1860), pp. 54-55, 97. Cf. [A.E.F. Schäffle], "Realpolitische Gedanken aus der deutschen Gegenwart," *Deutsche Vierteljahrs-Schrift*, xxii (1859), no. 3, p. 312; H. Rosenberg, *Die nationalpolitische Publizistik*, i, 70-71; Friedrich von Kerstorf, *Erfahrungen u. Beobachtungen auf handelspolitischem Gebiete, 1848 bis 1862* (Augsburg, 1862), p. 26; *Durch Krieg zum Frieden* (Stuttgart and Wildbad, 1859), pp. 28-29.

antry, for example, the most numerous class of society, was only a passive observer of the political scene. During the Revolution of 1848 it had sought to achieve the abolition of manorialism and the redistribution of landed property, first by a widespread rural uprising, then by petitions to parliamentary assemblies. Fifteen years later it looked on apathetically at the renewed clash between the forces of tradition and reform.

Agricultural prosperity had much to do with this indifference of the countryside toward public affairs, but even more important were the diminished aspirations of the village masses. As long as the process of transforming manorial forms of landowning into individualized proprietorship was incomplete, they could still hope for the expropriation of large estates and the annulment of servile obligations. That was why they joined forces with the revolution during the spring of 1848. In the course of the following decade, however, the reorganization of agriculture begun more than fifty years before came to a conclusion without altering the basic structure of rural society. It was now obvious that neither the liberals nor the conservatives, neither the protagonists of Prussia nor the defenders of Austria would create a prosperous and vigorous class of small independent farmers in Germany. The result was a deepening political apathy of the peasantry which in effect strengthened the established order, an apathy born of disappointment and the feeling of resignation. That ubiquitous gossip Theodor von Bernhardi tried to assure Albrecht von Roon that "the peasants have become very conservative since they have achieved what they especially wanted, namely, the complete division of common lands." But the minister of war remained unconvinced. Writing from Pomerania in the fall of 1863, he professed profound discouragement regarding the countryside: "I live here in the midst of so-called Junkerdom, but my hopes for the future are not thereby strengthened. Supineness, laziness, pusillanimity, these are the chief

113

characteristics of the so-called conservative monarchist majority of the people, which endures everything but also expects everything from the government. Only the rule of the saber can save us!"[20]

Factory workers for the most part displayed no greater interest in public affairs than peasants. Recently uprooted from their ancestral village environment, they lacked the experience and cohesion to formulate a systematic program of economic reform. The most spontaneous expression of their wishes was the growing labor unrest of the 1850's and 1860's, culminating in the great miners' strike in the Waldenburg collieries of Silesia. Sporadic and localized, these work stoppages manifested the preoccupation of industrial labor with practical problems of daily livelihood and its indifference to broad issues of economics or politics. There were those, to be sure, who claimed to speak in its name on fundamental questions of civic policy. But they represented only a fraction of the more than 1,400,000 persons in the Zollverein classified as mill hands. For example, the labor associations organized under liberal auspices, with an active membership in 1865 of not quite 24,000 reflected primarily the attitude of the progressive bourgeoisie in their emphasis on personal liberty, voluntary self-help, and popular education. At their congresses they supported industrial freedom and freedom of movement, urged the establishment of savings and credit cooperatives, and advocated limitation of the working day and security for the sick and aged. But they also deplored the worker's "lack of greater perseverance and thrift as well as his lack of appreciation for the higher values of life, for moral simplicity and moral purity, for conduct and character." Still, these failings could be rectified by training in the basic subjects of the elementary school curriculum supplemented with drawing, bookkeeping, singing, gymnastics, economics, law, his-

[20] Heinrich Otto Meisner, *Der preussische Kronprinz im Verfassungskampf 1863* (Berlin, 1931), p. 165. Cf. *Aus dem Leben Theodor von Bernhardis* (9 vols., Leipzig, 1898-1906), IV, 212.

tory, the natural sciences, and possibly French and English.[21]

As for the socialist movement which Ferdinand Lassalle had founded, his conception of a powerful national state allied with the laboring masses in a program of social welfare was the creation of a brilliant political agitator. Yet it came no closer to winning the support of the factory proletariat than the palliatives of the moderate bourgeois reformers whom he so thoroughly despised. When the would-be tribune of the people with all his boundless energy first threw himself into the task of organizing the working class, he overflowed with high spirits and confidence. Nothing in the world would resist the passion of his eloquence. "An association such as I have described . . . including 1,000,000 workers in Germany with 150,000 talers annually for purposes of agitation and led with energy, that would be a power!" he exulted in March 1863. By May his expectations had diminished somewhat, but he still had hopes of becoming kingmaker. Before a sympathetic audience in Frankfurt am Main, he sounded as sure of himself as ever: "Give me 500,000 German workers entering my association, and our reaction will be no more!" But at the same time, in a letter to the radical military expert Wilhelm Rüstow, he seemed doubtful, even discouraged: "I only want a minority, that is natural. Everything that has happened in the world has been done with minorities. But it must be a respectable minority. I cannot create a political party . . . with a hundred workers. A sect for a later age could be founded with that number, not a

21 G. v. Viebahn, *Statistik Deutschlands,* III, 1034; *Bericht über die Verhandlungen des ersten Vereinstages der deutschen Arbeitervereine abgehalten zu Frankfurt a. M. am 7. und 8. Juni 1863* (Frankfurt am Main, 1863), pp. 5-17, 11-13, 17-25; *Bericht über die Verhandlungen des zweiten Vereinstags deutscher Arbeitervereine. Abgehalten zu Leipzig am 23. und 24. Oktober 1864* (Frankfurt am Main, 1864), pp. 5-10, 18-22; *Jahresbericht über die Thätigkeit des ständigen Ausschusses für den dritten Vereinstag der deutschen Arbeitervereine* (Frankfurt am Main, 1865), p. 6.

party. In that case I was wrong, in that case I came too soon. If my labor association does not have ten thousand workers within the space of a year, then of course I will consider whether I should not give up politics altogether, since all sacrifice would then be useless."

Five months later he could still display a spurious self-assurance toward those whose support he needed. "I can hardly tell you how favorable the situation on the Rhine is," he boasted to the economist Johann Karl Rodbertus-Jagetzow. "Seven times better than I had hoped in my boldest dreams! Furthermore, in all of Saxony, in Hamburg and Frankfurt there is rapid progress. Now I only want to concentrate my energies above all on Berlin! . . . Berlin must be mine before six months are over!" This was also the tone of his appeal to the workers of the Prussian capital: "The most important centers of Germany have been won. Leipzig and the factory districts of Saxony are for us. Hamburg and Frankfurt am Main march under our banner. The Prussian Rhineland is already advancing in double time! With Berlin the movement will become irresistible!" But late that summer he had poured out his heart to his lieutenant Julius Vahlteich in a bitter lament of the prophet without honor: "So there are about 1,000 members in our entire association! Those are for the present the fruits of our labor! Those are the successes I have won by writing my fingers off and talking my lungs out! Don't you agree, dear Vahlteich, this apathy of the masses can drive a man to despair! Such apathy toward a movement which exists only for them, only in their interest; such apathy despite the intellectually enormous means of agitation which have already been employed and which would already have produced tremendous results among a people like the French! When will this unfeeling people finally shake off its lethargy!" At the time of Lassalle's death a year later, the membership of his association had risen to only about 4,600, and toward the end of 1865 it was still under 10,000. The socialist movement remained, as he had feared it might, "a sect for a later age."[22]

The most authentic expression of lower-class aspirations came from the ranks of the skilled artisans. Though petty bourgeois rather than proletarian in their attitude toward social issues, they constituted the largest group of urban workers in Central Europe. In the corporative trade associations, moreover, they possessed established organizations which could voice their demands. And a common sense of danger spurred them to collective action. The advance of the factory system had produced a crisis for the handicraft occupations at a time when the rest of the economy was enjoying a period of prosperity. A threat of social disintegration thus reinforced the class discipline derived from guild tradition, arousing a vigorous protest movement among the independent tradesmen. Its objective was the restraint of industrialism by the maintenance of occupational regulations limiting the size and activity of manufacturing establishments. Throughout the first half of the nineteenth century it continued to oppose the liberalization of economic legislation, until in 1848 the artisan masses turned against established authority in the hope of achieving under a new order what they had been denied by the old. They were disappointed. The men who gained authority during the revolution were liberals to whom free enterprise was as important as parliamentary government or the rights of man. "Now that class privileges have been abolished," expounded the economic committee of the Frankfurt Parliament, "we cannot grant to any class, whether it be the class of all producers or

22 Ferdinand Lassalle, *Nachgelassene Briefe und Schriften*, ed. Gustav Mayer (6 vols., Stuttgart and Berlin, 1921-25) , V, 111, 171, VI, 370; F. Lassalle, *Reden und Schriften*, III, 286, IV, 55; Bernhard Becker, *Geschichte der Arbeiter-Agitation Ferdinand Lassalle's* (Brunswick, 1875) , p. 82; Hermann Oncken, *Lassalle* (Stuttgart, 1904) , pp. 393-394; Franz Mehring, *Die deutsche Sozialdemokratie: Ihre Geschichte und ihre Lehre* (Bremen, 1877) , pp. 32, 54-55; F. Mehring, *Geschichte der deutschen Sozialdemokratie*, II, 102-103, 166-167.

the class of handicraftsmen, the authority to issue rules
. . . restraining other classes." But the ideological consistency of the bourgeois constitutionalists was also their
undoing. They upheld their principles at the cost of
alienating the urban working class, which remained impassive while the authority of the princes was re-established in the spring of 1849 by armed force.

The conservative statesmen who now returned to
power had no similar theoretical commitment to laissez-
faire economics. They quickly recognized, moreover, the
tactical advantages to be derived from an alliance with
the skilled tradesmen. The result was the promulgation
of several industrial measures designed to meet the demands advanced by the artisan movement during the
revolution. In 1849 Nassau introduced residence and
competence requirements for the practice of a craft; in
1850 Frankfurt am Main founded a vocational council
representing the interests of independent guildsmen; in
1851 Saxe-Gotha confirmed the establishment of occupational courts and assemblies authorized provisionally
two years before; and in 1853 Bavaria regulated the employment of apprentices, the sale of handicraft wares,
and the ownership of artisan shops. But the most important attempt to protect the tradesman against unrestrained competition came in Prussia with the law of
February 9, 1849. Anxious to win popular support for
its incipient policy of reaction, the cabinet in Berlin
decreed that in some seventy crafts admission would become contingent on membership in a guild or on demonstration of vocational skill. The truck system of wage
payment was prohibited, and restrictions were imposed
on the simultaneous practice of several occupations.
The most striking feature of the measure was its authorization of local industrial councils, composed of
representatives of the handicraft, factory, and mercantile interests, to investigate economic conditions and advise the government of needed reforms. Here were in-

118

stitutions which in theory at least could express the views of the small shop owner.[23]

Yet in fact the position of the artisan class continued to deteriorate in the 1850's as it had in the 1830's and 1840's. The great economic boom of the mid-century intensified industrialization despite the halfhearted legislative restraints which were imposed on it during the reaction. The hope that factory and handicraft shop could peacefully coexist within the framework of a corporative regulation of the national economy was only a pipe dream. Even the conservative bureaucrats, whose task it was to enforce legislation designed to save the independent tradesman from destruction, were dubious about its wisdom. Minister of Commerce August von der Heydt, architect of the Prussian law of February 9, 1849, reported to the king a few years after its promulgation that the industrial councils were only a device adopted in a time of unrest which had now served its purpose. The failure of the experiment should therefore not be regarded as a misfortune. And toward the end of the 1860's one of the veterans of the artisan movement, master turner Todt of Minden, explained that "by no means did the industrial councils enjoy the protection of the government, and, I say this quite openly, almost the entire Prussian civil service saw the industrial council as an institution which encroached on its rights."

This equivocal attitude of the bureaucracy fostered a feeling of apathy among those whom the industrial councils were supposed to represent. Even in a big city like Cologne it proved impossible to establish a council be-

[23] *Verhandlungen der deutschen verfassunggebenden Reichs-Versammlung zu Frankfurt am Main,* ed. K. D. Hassler (6 vols., Frankfurt am Main, 1848-49), II, 898-899; Theodore S. Hamerow, "The German Artisan Movement, 1848-49," *Journal of Central European Affairs,* XXI (1961), 148-152; T. S. Hamerow, *Restoration, Revolution, Reaction,* pp. 189-190, 192, 231; Heinrich Waentig, "Die gewerbepolitischen Anschauungen in Wissenschaft und Gesetzgebung des 19. Jahrhunderts," *Die Entwicklung der deutschen Volkswirtschaftslehre im neunzehnten Jahrhundert: Gustav Schmoller zur siebenzigsten Wiederkehr seines Geburtstages* (2 vols., Leipzig, 1908), II, no. 25, pp. 22-23.

cause of lack of participation in the choice of members. Of 344 factory owners eligible to vote, not one cast a ballot; almost none of the several thousand factory workers troubled to go to the polls; and among the 1,869 merchants and shopkeepers there were only about 30 voters. The same indifference prevailed in artisan circles. A mere 194 masters out of 4,500 and 53 apprentices out of 4,300 took part in the election. An industrial council was founded in Berlin, but it aroused little interest among the handicraftsmen. In March 1856 the balloting for representatives attracted 32 voters out of 400 eligibles in one district, 18 out of 300 in another, and not even 1 out of 400 in a third. The decline of the councils was bound to be swift. The government had approved the formation of 93, yet no more than 67 could actually be established. By the end of 1854 only 17 were left, and the last 3 went under in 1864. What had been hailed as a bold experiment in occupational self-government turned out to be a paper barrier to the progress of the factory system.[24]

While the statesmen of the reaction felt obliged for ideological reasons to acknowledge the principle of corporative regulation, the revival of liberalism in the late 1850's made the authorities receptive to the argument that legislative enactments should be adapted to economic realities. The first victory of laissez faire came in Austria, where the government had for years been contemplating the introduction of industrial freedom. During the spring of 1859 the ministry of commerce reported to the emperor that "for Austrian industry, which since the fall of the prohibitive system has to struggle in all directions against foreign competition, the grant

[24] A. Bergengrün, *Heydt*, p. 208; *Der dritte Norddeutsche Handwerkertag zu Hannover am 14., 15. und 16. September 1868* (Hanover, 1868), p. 72; A. Wirminghaus, *Die Industrie- und Handelskammer zu Köln*, C. Die Wirksamkeit der Handelskammer (1797-1871), Abschnitt I-II, pp. 125-126; Cologne Chamber of Commerce, *Jahres-Bericht für 1850* (Cologne, 1851), p. 4; Hans Jürgen Teuteberg, *Geschichte der industriellen Mitbestimmung in Deutschland* (Tübingen, 1961), pp. 332-333.

of complete freedom of movement is no longer a question of mere improvement and greater well-being, but a necessary condition of its ability to compete." The last doubts of the Hofburg were dispelled a few months later by the defeats in northern Italy. Free enterprise and constitutional government were now to atone for military failure. On December 20 an imperial patent established freedom of enterprise throughout the Habsburg possessions, and the entire system of corporative industrial regulation in Central Europe began to crumble. Nassau followed the Austrian example in 1860; Saxony, Oldenburg, and Bremen in 1861; Württemberg, Baden, and Saxe-Weimar in 1862; Saxe-Coburg, Saxe-Gotha, and Saxe-Altenburg in 1863; and Brunswick, Hamburg, and Frankfurt am Main in 1864. By the middle of the decade 16 states and 34,000,000 persons in the German Confederation had come under the system of industrial freedom; 7 states inhabited by 7,000,000 people were in the process of transition to the new order; and only 12 states with a population of 3,500,000, among them Hanover, the Mecklenburgs, Holstein, and Lübeck, still adhered to corporative economic restrictions. "The question of extending industrial freedom in Germany . . . may in the main be considered solved," rejoiced that tireless champion of free enterprise, Victor Böhmert.[25]

To the artisan masses, however, the victory of industrial freedom was a tragedy. Unable to comprehend the fundamental economic changes taking place about them, they remained convinced that a just and wise government could save them from destruction by restraining economic competition. Even during the period of reaction, hard pressed tradesmen continued to petition the

[25] *Bericht über die Verhandlungen des siebenten Kongresses deutscher Volkswirthe zu Hannover am 22. 23. 24. 25. August 1864* (Berlin, 1864), p. 11. Cf. Richard Charmatz, *Minister Freiherr von Bruck: Der Vorkämpfer Mitteleuropas* (Leipzig, 1916), pp. 132-135; H. A. Mascher, *Das deutsche Gewerbewesen*, pp. 596, 607-608, 613, 617, 622, 625, 629, 631-634, 636, 641, 662-663, 746, 791-792; W. Kellner, *Taschenbuch der politischen Statistik*, pp. 140-141.

Prussian legislature for guild regulation of production, restriction of department stores selling handicraft wares, demarcation of related occupations, and limitation of the number of new master craftsmen. A report of the committee of the lower house on commerce and industry concluded early in 1856 that "the establishment of such a system of compulsion would in any case also require the restoration of abolished rights of sale, monopoly, and coercion, while the importation into cities of domestic and foreign handicraft articles would have to be prohibited."

With the resurgence of economic liberalism toward the end of the decade, some handicraftsmen began to accept the new order. In 1858 a congress of Hanoverian artisans in Celle came out in support of industrial freedom, while in Nassau representatives of various trade associations gathered at Montabaur voted against corporative regulation. But these were the views of a supple minority which was successfully effecting the transition from guildsman to shopkeeper, from independent craftsman to small businessman. For most skilled artisans the abandonment of their ancestral way of life was a psychological as well as economic impossibility. In an age of mechanization and high finance, they remained defenders of the guild system. Bank director Feustel of Coburg portrayed their outlook before a meeting of liberal economists:

> The class of handicraftsmen is by and large decidedly and resolutely opposed to all industrial freedom. This fact is so positive that it cannot be easily contradicted. . . . Among the artisans it is at most those with greater means and generally a wider sphere of business who are most likely to become reconciled to industrial freedom. They rely on the might of capital, and cast aside the barriers which help the little man. The small handicraftsman, however, when he is opposed by abstract concepts, becomes completely enraged. Perhaps he does not then find the correct expression, perhaps he is confused about first

122

principles. But . . . with the expression "antiquated" or "outmoded" we cannot all at once destroy the concept associated with the honorable title of "master."[26]

The mounting discontent of the artisan masses culminated in the formation of a central organization representing handicraft guilds in all parts of Germany. It was founded on the initiative of Prussian handicraftsmen alarmed by the motion which a group of liberal members of the legislature introduced on March 28, 1860, for the establishment of industrial freedom. Three months later the association of Berlin guildsmen invited all artisan corporations of the kingdom to the Prussian State Convention of Handicraftsmen meeting in the capital from August 28 to 31. Among the subjects on the agenda were an exchange of views regarding the law of February 9, 1849, consideration of the recent legislative move for its repeal, the measures to be taken in combating this effort, and the convocation of a general German assembly of guildsmen. The convention in Berlin late that summer was completely dominated by the advocates of corporative regulation. They condemned free enterprise as "a child of the red republic," opposed the liberalization of economic legislation, demanded the retention of industrial councils, and urged the government to grant financial support for the wholesale purchase of raw materials by guild associations.

Their strongest language, however, was reserved for the denunciation of industrial freedom:

Unconditional industrial freedom is really an extremity. Nothing is unconditionally free; everything is restricted. No part of our body as such is free in itself; it is con-

---

[26] *Zweite Versammlung des Congresses deutscher Volkswirthe 1859*, p. 24. Cf. T. S. Hamerow, *Restoration, Revolution, Reaction*, pp. 243-244; H. Waentig, "Die gewerbepolitischen Anschauungen," p. 24; Prussia, *Sammlung sämmtlicher Drucksachen des Hauses der Abgeordneten aus der ersten Session der IV. Legislatur-Periode, 1855 bis 1856* (6 vols., Berlin, 1856), III, no. 155, p. 8; H. A. Mascher, *Das deutsche Gewerbewesen*, pp. 586-587.

nected with the sinews and ligaments and the entire organism. . . . The stars above in the firmament move in accordance with an eternal order. . . . No clock could function if every single wheel would presume to move forward or be inactive without regard for the movement of the other wheels. . . . Industrial freedom is . . . founded on the pagan principle of egoism, of selfishness. . . . It divides, it pulverizes . . . all of society, because it is founded on the principle of egoism. But therefore it is also the cause of the monopolies of modern times which it ostensibly opposes. . . . In the guilds there was at least self-reliance and independence. But in the world of industrial freedom the predominance of capital is concentrated, all business flows into the hands of a joint-stock company, and the handicraftsman has to be glad to find a very meager wage as a dependent worker of this company.

The anticapitalistic tone of the artisan assembly delighted the conservatives, who had for years been warning the nation against the dangers of industrialism. "We wish and hope that the efforts of the convention of handicraftsmen will have the greatest success," declared the *Neue Preussische Zeitung* in Berlin, the leading newspaper of the reaction. "We rejoice that we can march on the same road. . . . There was a time when the urban guilds often fought the landed aristocracy, not with the weapons of competition and capital, but with sword and mace. That is over now, and the handicrafts are fighting another sort of aristocracy, if it is permissible to apply this noble word to the men of capital."

Before adjourning, the Prussian State Convention of Handicraftsmen appointed a standing committee to formulate its demands and present them to the government and the legislature. Early in 1861, therefore, the minister of commerce and the two houses of parliament received memorials submitted in the name of the artisan population of the kingdom. The equivocal Heydt, "in whom the grateful class of handicraftsmen honors the true author of the now much abused and attacked industrial law of February 9, 1849," was merely urged in a few short paragraphs "to protect the class of handicraftsmen in its political and social position, and for this purpose most graciously to maintain the proven principles of the present industrial law." But the petitions to the legislators expressed an Arcadian philosophy of state and economy appropriate to a venerable class of society facing dissolution. They maintained, to begin with, that "the class of handicraftsmen is the creative and nourishing part of the nation, and is consequently still the true heart of the citizenry." Industrial freedom, "preached as a new gospel," served only the interests of businessmen and Jews. "A few industrialists and a small number of merchants grew rich, but the class of handicraftsmen became impoverished. The middle estate, which in hard times had faithfully borne all the burdens of the state, began to live from hand to mouth, and to degenerate into a propertyless class."

The evils engendered by the factory system were aggravated by the mobility of population. "Freedom of movement or free vagabondage guarantees . . . the influx of labor which then, driven by the competition born of hunger, offers its services at the lowest prices." The same forces of capitalism which sought to reduce the artisan to "a pliable factory worker and serf of money . . . have also been at work a long time to subordinate and dominate governments." If corporative regulation of manufacture were abandoned, "the political life of the cities will also decline more and more, until nothing will be left finally except an aimless, desperate struggle of the working class for a piece of bread, a struggle against an oligarchy of moneyed capital controlling all political and social conditions." The appeal of the artisans concluded with an entreaty "to maintain for the class of handicraftsmen the blessings of current industrial legislation."[27]

But the most significant achievement of the Prussian State Convention of Handicraftsmen was the convocation of a national artisan assembly. The standing committee was authorized to enter into negotiation with guild organizations in other parts of Central Europe. Two years were to elapse, however, before the German Association of Handicraftsmen finally came into existence. Its first meeting, attended by 284 members representing 81 cities, took place in Weimar from September 5 to 8, 1862. The great majority of the participants lived in northern and central Germany, although even here there were important abstentions. Forty-six of the delegates came from Hamburg and 82 from Weimar itself, but none from Austria, Baden, Hesse-Darmstadt, Hesse-Kassel, Saxony, Brunswick, or Holstein.

At the second meeting in Frankfurt am Main, from September 25 to 28, 1863, there were 225 participants, more than a third of them local residents, and only 46 cities were represented. Yet the presiding officer, master painter C.P.C. Schweedt of Hamburg, reported encouragingly that in all the cities of Prussia there were now affiliated organizations, their total number exceeding 70. King William I, moreover, had graciously received a delegation of handicraftsmen seeking his support. Guild corporations in Hanover, Brunswick, Olden-

27 *Die Gewerbefrage in Preussen*, pp. 1, 4, 13-14, 18, 24-25. Cf. Prussia, *Stenographische Berichte über die Verhandlungen der durch die Allerhöchste Verordnung vom 22. Dezember 1859 einberufenen beiden Häuser des Landtages: Haus der Abgeordneten* (5 vols., Berlin, 1860), II, 675; Prussia, *Sammlung sämmtlicher Drucksacher des Hauses der Abgeordneten aus der zweiten Session der V. Legislatur-Periode 1860* (6 vols., Berlin 1860), IV, no. 159, pp. 1-56; Deutsches Zentralarchiv Abteilung Merseburg, *Ministerium für Handel, Gewerbe und öffentliche Arbeiten*, Rep. 120 B I 1 Nr. 62 Bd. 5, "Einladung zum Preussischen Landes-Handwerkertage in Berlin"; *Verhandlungen des im Jahre 1860 vom 27. bis 31. August zu Berlin abgehaltenen Preusz. Landes-Handwerkertages nebst den dabei aufgenommenen Protokollen* (Berlin, 1860), pp. 17, 20, 28, 47-48, 51, 54, 74, 77-79; *Neue Preussische Zeitung*, September 6, 1860.

burg, Württemberg, and Hesse-Darmstadt were about to join the national association. Baden, Nassau, and Holstein were bound to come in sooner or later. There was less optimism, however, about Austria and Bavaria. The chairman was also forced to admit that the *Deutsche Bürger-Zeitung*, the newspaper of the handicraft movement, "had not reached the expected circulation precisely because of the small growth of the association."

The third and final meeting took place in Cologne from September 26 to 28, 1864. By now the association was disintegrating, partly because the continuing legislative victories of industrial freedom rendered its activities pointless, partly because growing differences between the Catholic, Austrophile, moderate artisan organizations of the west and the stanchly conservative trade guilds of eastern Prussia made further collaboration between them impossible. Two hundred and seven names still appeared on the membership list, but ninety-two of them were from Cologne, while the others also came largely from the Rhineland. There were only three participants from the south and one from the east. The same political, ideological, and religious differences driving the nation to civil war had undermined the attempt to organize the artisan class of Germany into an effective force against the advance of industrialism.

The prevailing outlook of the German Association of Handicraftsmen was similar to that of the Prussian State Convention of Handicraftsmen: anticapitalistic, antiliberal, anti-intellectual, and anti-Semitic. There was the same conviction that the artisan class had become the victim of a sinister conspiracy against honest toil. Behind this conspiracy stood the combined might of the financiers, politicians, publicists, and Jews. "As soon as the banks have no more money, there will be an end to swindling," insisted master carpenter Piest of Stettin. In a letter of appreciation to the sympathetic Bishop Wilhelm Emmanuel von Ketteler of Mainz, the executive committee of the association maintained that "the statesmen and lawmakers of our time, possessed and

127

misled by the doctrinaire errors which we are combating, stand almost everywhere in direct opposition against us." Master shoemaker F.M.C. Brandstrup of Hamburg identified "three classes of opponents of industrial regulation: doctors of jurisprudence, men of letters, and democrats." Master saddler J. Hanekamp of Recklinghausen "almost despaired whether a single newspaper . . . is still friendly toward us." The machinations of the Jews were yet another threat to the hard-working tradesman, warned master mason C. Pesche of Breslau. "They want to become masters without having learned a handicraft." As for industrial freedom, the first meeting of the German Association of Handicraftsmen in Weimar voted unanimously "to present most respectfully to all the governments of the German confederate states the declaration that the German class of handicraftsmen considers itself bound by duty both in their and in its own interest to oppose with the greatest resolve this plague of free industrial conditions."

The agitation of the artisan movement culminated in the memorial which it submitted to the governments of the German Confederation in December 1864. This document was the most eloquent expression of the outlook of independent tradesmen threatened by the imminent breakthrough of a new industrial order. Condemning the entire system of liberal economic thought as an alien importation imposed on Central Europe during the French Revolution, it contrasted "that freedom from across the Rhine, which fancied that it had found the salvation of nations in the destruction of all existing institutions," with traditional Teutonic liberty, "which strives for the freest possible movement of every individual within his legitimate sphere." The struggle over the corporative regulation of production involved issues of social morality as much as material advantage. On one side were "the enemies of legal order and civic tranquillity," seeking "to dissolve all bonds and tear down the pillars which support the temple of order." On the other stood the embattled artisan movement. "It does not look for foreign models or precedents; it does not follow the newest and latest benefactors of the people, who arouse the masses with their tales of a never-never land and a never-never time. It wants tranquillity and peace, law and order." As means of protecting the interests of the skilled tradesman, the memorial proposed handicraft councils to advise the authorities on economic policy, occupational courts to arbitrate industrial disputes, guilds which all craftsmen would have to join, and rigid requirements of training and skill for those seeking the master's title. "The Association of Handicraftsmen believes in the justice of its cause. In this belief it hopes for the good will of the German governments. The Association of Handicraftsmen demands only order and legal regulation of its rights. It knows that the labor of the artisan is also included within the divine promise."[28]

To be sure, not all handicraftsmen favored corporative industrial control. "There is still a difference of opinion between the south and the north of Germany," explained master mason F. Wagner from Stuttgart. "In our parts, people disagree completely with the view which prevails in the north regarding the question of industrial freedom and industrial regulation. That has been the case for a long time. Along the Baltic and the North Sea the so-called guild system has assumed a stricter form than in the south, especially along the borders of France." The liberals of course also ques-

---

[28] *Denkschrift des Deutschen Handwerkerbundes betr.: den Erlass einer allgemeinen Deutschen Handwerker-Ordnung* (Bückeburg, 1864), p. 17. Cf. *ibid.*, pp. 6, 8, 10, "Anlage A. Grundzüge zu einer allgemeinen Handwerkerordnung"; *Verhandlungen des 1860 abgehaltenen Preusz. Landes-Handwerkertages*, pp. 35, 75; *Verhandlungen des deutschen Handwerkertags 1862*, pp. 47, 82-83, 131, 145-146, 165, 168, 197-198, 202-212; *Der zweite deutsche Handwerkertag 1863*, pp. 10, 12-13, 18, 133, 141-150; *Der dritte deutsche Handwerkertag zu Cöln vom 26. bis 28. September 1864* (Aachen, 1864), pp. 49, 179-183; "Der deutsche Handwerkertag in Weimar vom 5. bis 8. September 1862," *Berliner Revue*, xxx (1862), 421; "Der zweite deutsche Handwerkertag zu Frankfurt a. M.," *ibid.*, xxxv (1863), 177-185.

tioned the right of the artisan movement to speak in the name of the class of independent tradesmen. A committee of the Prussian legislature, for example, maintained that the State Convention of Handicraftsmen represented at most a third of the artisans of the kingdom. For only 6,372 craftsmen in Pomerania had signed a petition against the liberalization of economic legislation, although there were some 33,000 master tradesmen and skilled mechanics in the province. It pointed out, moreover, that in the Rhineland and Westphalia most artisans were not members of a guild, while in Berlin only a small majority belonged. "It is in no way proven that even most artisan corporations agree with the views and proposals of the Convention of Handicraftsmen."

But this reasoning was specious. The evidence supports the contention of the German Association of Handicraftsmen that the majority of skilled tradesmen, journeymen as well as masters, including the many who were too impoverished, apathetic, or discouraged to attend meetings and compose manifestoes, shared the views of the minority which actively participated in the artisan movement. This was certainly true of northern Germany. The petitions regarding legislative proposals to relax industrial regulation which assemblies of handicraftsmen submitted to the Prussian legislature are a case in point. Twenty-two out of twenty-nine demanded "unaltered maintenance of the industrial legislation, particularly that of February 9, 1849," or urged the lawmakers "not to vote for industrial freedom." Even farther south many tradesmen found it hard to accept the abrogation of economic restrictions. The Dresden chamber of commerce complained that the new liberal industrial law "has not been regarded by most guilds with that unprejudiced view which it deserved. . . . An attempt to regain obsolete rights has frequently been apparent." And in Baden a report from the business community expressed satisfaction at the establishment of freedom of enterprise, "although it was unavoidable that some interests were thereby temporarily injured, as is inevitable in the inauguration of all great measures. . . . Competition is now naturally much more severe and intense. It is much more difficult to hold one's own than was formerly the case."

The artisan movement was in any event a more genuine and spontaneous expression of the underlying social attitudes of the urban masses of Central Europe than either the liberal of the socialist labor organizations. For the sharpest conflict of class interests during the period of national unification was not between the propertied and propertyless or employers and employees. That was still to come. The great struggle raged between the proponents and opponents of industrial capitalism. The defenders of the old economic order, independent skilled tradesmen supported by the conservative landed aristocracy, realized that the odds were against them. "The Association of Handicraftsmen is well aware that it is following a difficult course, that it has to fight against views and opinions which completely dominate the minds of men," read the memorial to the governments of the German Confederation. "But despite all, the Association of Handicraftsmen cannot act otherwise; it must do what it is doing. Fortified by the knowledge of its duty, it cannot shrink from a struggle which for the time being is still uneven." To the artisans the issue was simple. "Why should and must civilized nations be brought to ruin, so that a small number of factory owners can accumulate riches?" asked a speaker at the national meeting of tradesmen in Frankfurt am Main. In the opposing camp were bourgeois wealth, learning, talent, and ambition. "It is a morally just principle," insisted the chamber of commerce in Karlsruhe, "to pronounce that the citizen should not be prevented from using his intellectual endowments and his mental and physical energies for his own profit and to the best of his ability." The differences separating the two sides were too basic to be compromised. The struggle had to

131

go on until one or the other had won a total victory. And there could be no doubt which it would be. The era of conflict which concluded with the achievement of national unification also witnessed the final triumph of industrialism in Central Europe.[29]

[29] *Verhandlungen des deutschen Handwerkertags 1862*, p. 11; Prussia, *Stenographische Berichte über die Verhandlungen der durch die Allerhöchste Verordnung vom 27. Dezember 1860 einberufenen beiden Häuser des Landtages: Haus der Abgeordneten* (7 vols., Berlin, 1861), VI, 1047-1048; Adalbert Hahn, *Die Berliner Revue: Ein Beitrag zur Geschichte der konservativen Partei zwischen 1855 und 1875* (Berlin, 1934), p. 92; *Denkschrift des Deutschen Handwerkerbundes*, pp. 3-4, 16-17; *Preussisches Handelsarchiv* (1864), I, 455, II, 350; *Der zweite deutsche Handwerkertag 1863*, p. 36.

II

THE CLASH OF IDEOLOGIES

FOUR

The Liberal Creed

THEODOR VON BERNHARDI, who always cultivated with great assiduity those in a position of authority, recorded in his diary under January 4, 1863, a conversation with Max Duncker, the confidential adviser of the crown prince of Prussia. Bismarck had come to power four months before, and the constitutional conflict was now moving toward a climax, without prospect of moderation or compromise. Political gossip in Berlin dwelt on the forthcoming session of the legislature, which was about to reconvene. What strategy would the prime minister follow in dealing with the recalcitrant chamber? Would he make partial concessions in order to split the opposition, or would he try his luck in a new election? Perhaps he would even risk all on a coup d'état, although there was always the chance that, realizing the hopelessness of his position, he might resign. But Duncker did not speculate on what course the cabinet was most likely to adopt. To him the test of strength between crown and parliament was more than a struggle for partisan political advantage. It represented a fundamental conflict of class interests: "People on all sides misunderstand the true character of the situation. This is no longer a fight over a few articles of the constitution. It is a struggle involving principles, it has become a class struggle, a struggle of the bourgeoisie against Junkerdom."[1]

Throughout the period of national unification opposing ideologies were stating in universal terms the aspirations of contending social classes. The changes in the

[1] *Aus dem Leben Bernhardis*, v, 7.

structure of society arising out of the growth of industrial capitalism had produced a new configuration of civic ideas and ideals in Central Europe. Within this configuration liberalism was above all the creed of the bourgeoisie. Its imperatives and absolutes were an expression *sub specie aeternitatis* of the outlook of a vigorous middle class hoping to overthrow a hierarchical order of society based on hereditary status and to give free scope to individual ability. Julius Fröbel, the radical firebrand of 1848 turned moderate and respectable, recognized the social foundation of liberal thought in his *Theorie der Politik*: "Liberalism, moreover, which currently plays a dominant role in the life of European peoples and states, is by no means to be understood as the system of popular freedom in general, but as a system in the special interest of quite specific elements of society which are assembled in the commercial and industrial middle class. The liberal state in this conventional sense is the state which represents the interest of this social group. But that does not in any sense mean that it must also represent the interest of all other classes of the population or even only the interest of the true majority of the people." A few years later, on the morrow of the Seven Weeks' War, another disillusioned liberal, the historian Hermann Baumgarten, saw in retrospect middle-class ambition at the root of the constitutional conflict in Prussia: "The bourgeoisie, proudly conscious of its intelligence, its diligence, its wealth, and its almost unanimous will, wanted to win at last the position in public life which, as it firmly believed, was its due."[2]

While parliamentarianism found champions in all strata of society, its most ardent disciples came from the bourgeoisie. "The entire intelligent and propertied middle class with a few exceptions belongs to the democratic

---

[2] H. Baumgarten, "Der deutsche Liberalismus: Eine Selbstkritik," *Preussische Jahrbücher*, xviii (1866), 592. Cf. Julius Fröbel, *Theorie der Politik, als Ergebniss einer erneuerten Prüfung demokratischer Lehrmeinungen* (2 vols., Vienna, 1861-64), i, 258.

constitutional party of our province," noted the reformist schoolmaster Hermann Büttner of Elbing in West Prussia after the Revolution of 1848. The same commitment of urban wealth and education to the ideal of representative government prevailed in other regions of Central Europe. The liberal creed derived its economic support from the manufacturers, bankers, entrepreneurs, businessmen, and merchants who placed at its disposal the financial resources of an expanding industrial capitalism. But its intellectual defenders, its spokesmen and propagandists, generally came from the ranks of the learned professions, from the jurists, civil servants, publicists, newspapermen, scientists, physicians, and teachers who sought to form an alliance between bourgeois affluence and academic learning capable of creating a new social order.

Among the stalwarts of the Prussian Progressive Party which fought Bismarck so bitterly were judges like Benedikt Waldeck and Karl Twesten, lawyers like Hermann Schulze-Delitzsch and Max von Forckenbeck, the engineers Hans Viktor von Unruh and Werner Siemens, the publishers Franz Duncker and Immanuel Guttentag, the physicians Johann Jacoby and Paul Langerhans, the pathologist Rudolf Virchow, and the historian Theodor Mommsen. Publicists formed the vanguard of those liberals who devoted themselves to the propagation of laissez-faire economics: John Prince-Smith, Max Wirth, Victor Böhmert, Julius Faucher, Otto Michaelis, August Lammers, and Arwed Emminghaus. South of the Main in Bavaria the leaders of the liberal movement came largely from the industrial districts of Swabia and Middle Franconia and from the Palatinate. Joseph Völk had a law practice in Augsburg; the journalist Karl Brater had been born in Ansbach; Marquard Barth lived in Eichstätt and Augsburg before settling down in Kaufbeuren as a lawyer; and in Munich the Palatine August Vecchioni waged an uphill struggle in his *Neueste Nachrichten* against traditionalism and particularism.

137

Even in the agrarian east the most vigorous support for the liberal movement came from the business and commercial interests of the towns. The Kantian ethic, to be sure, was a powerful stimulus to progressive ideas in the homeland of the great philosopher, while the appeal of free trade led many of the well-to-do grain growers to free politics as well. Here and there, moreover, some aristocratic frondeur would boldly come out for a parliamentary form of government. This was the case with Baron Leopold von Hoverbeck, who, according to a conservative opponent, was "educated entirely in conformity with Rousseau's *Emile*," and possessed "the greatest talent for the role of deputy in the National Convention and member of the Committee of Public Safety." But the workhorses of constitutionalism in East and West Prussia were the men of means and education from the middle classes of Danzig, Elbing, and Königsberg gathered about Heinrich Rickert, editor of the *Danziger Zeitung*.[3]

The parliamentary representation of the liberal movement reflected its social composition. In the heavily conservative lower house of the Prussian legislature which convened in the fall of 1854 more than 75 per cent of the members on the right were noblemen, while in the center and on the left 80 per cent were of bourgeois origin. By the beginning of the constitutional conflict seven years later the alignment of parties had undergone a complete transformation. Now liberalism had an overwhelming majority. There were only 11 conservatives in

---

[3] *Max Duncker: Politischer Briefwechsel aus seinem Nachlass*, ed. *Johannes Schultze* (Stuttgart and Berlin, 1923), p. 35; Hans Ruider, *Bismarck und die öffentliche Meinung in Bayern, 1862-1866* (Munich, 1924), pp. 9, 13-15; Hermann Wagener, *Erlebtes: Meine Memoiren aus der Zeit von 1848 bis 1866 und von 1873 bis jetzt*, 2nd edn. (2 vols., Berlin, 1884), II, 15; Reinhard Adam, "Der Liberalismus in der Provinz Preussen zur Zeit der neuen Ära und sein Anteil an der Entstehung der Deutschen Fortschrittspartei," *Altpreussische Beiträge: Festschrift zur Hauptversammlung des Gesamtvereins der deutschen Geschichts- und Altertums-Vereine zu Königsberg Pr. vom 4. bis 7. September 1933* (Königsberg, 1933), pp. 164-165, 168-169, 174.

the chamber which sat from May to October 1862: 4 landowners, 6 county commissioners, and 1 jurist, all of them aristocrats. Among the 285 representatives in opposition, on the other hand, only 42 were of noble birth. The largest occupational category was the civil service, comprising about half of the total number. It included 77 judges, 19 administrators and commissioners, 17 civil and military officeholders on inactive status, 15 district and municipal officials, 7 professors, 6 clergymen, and 3 secondary-school teachers. There were 71 landed property owners and rural magistrates, both aristocratic and bourgeois. The learned professions were represented by 16 lawyers, 6 physicians, 3 journalists, 1 publisher, and 1 preacher. Commerce and manufacture accounted for 26 members, 14 of them merchants, 7 industrialists, and 5 owners of handicraft establishments. Finally, a small group of 11 enjoyed independent means.

The occupational background of the 168 liberal deputies in the first parliament of the German Empire elected in March 1871 was strikingly similar. About three-fourths belonged to the National Liberal Party, which was ready to collaborate with Bismarck in the work of political and economic consolidation, while the others who would not compromise their constitutional principles formed the Progressive Party. But both factions drew their leadership from the ranks of the bourgeoisie. Among their legislative representatives were 37 officials of the higher civil service, 21 members of the lower bureaucracy, 22 landowners and agriculturists, 12 merchants, 7 factory owners, 5 industrial managers and administrators, 24 lawyers, 14 professors, 8 writers, 5 clergymen and teachers, 3 physicians and engineers, and 10 rentiers and pensioners. Throughout the period of national unification the great majority of liberal politicians thus belonged by descent as well as occupation to the middle class.[4]

4 L. Berger, *Der alte Harkort: Ein westfälisches Lebens- und Zeitbild*, 4th edn. (Leipzig, 1902), p. 511; Adalbert Hess, *Das Parlament das Bismarck widerstrebte: Zur Politik und sozialen Zusammensetzung*

139

The world of ideas in which they moved mirrored their station in society. Liberalism was convinced that the accumulated wrongs of centuries of autocratic oppression were about to be made good in a coming era of civic freedom and social justice. In his *Einleitung in die Geschichte des neunzehnten Jahrhunderts* Georg Gottfried Gervinus hailed the new golden age which was opening for his generation:

Individualism, the self-awareness of the personality, has become so powerful in men that it will modify political concepts and institutions; it will dissolve the closed corporations, the states within the state; it will eliminate all caste and class differences. The striving for the equality of all relations, for the freedom of man toward man, is necessarily involved in this self-awareness of the personality. . . . The emancipation of all the oppressed and suffering, such is the call of the century. The might of these ideas has triumphed over powerful interests and deep-rooted conditions in the abolition of servile dues and obligations in Europe, and the emancipation of the slaves of the West Indies. This is the great movement of our time.

The defenders of the old order remained blind to the dawning of the new day, but they were doomed to defeat in any event, argued the liberals. Their overthrow was only a matter of time. "The struggle against a decayed generation, which specterlike has possession of all the important positions in the state, is like a struggle against the dead," observed the popular author Gustav Freytag. The forces of freedom were bound to prevail.

In the new world which liberalism hoped to create, wars among nations would become an impossibility. The spread of popular education would reveal to all man-

des preussischen Abgeordnetenhauses der Konfliktszeit (1862–1866) (Cologne and Opladen, 1964) , pp. 24, 53, 65-69; Joachim H. Knoll, *Führungsauslese in Liberalismus und Demokratie: Zur politischen Geistesgeschichte der letzten hundert Jahre* (Stuttgart, 1957) , p. 172.

140

kind the evils of militarism, while the progress of industrialization would lead to an increasing economic interdependence of the peoples of the earth. Hermann
Schulze-Delitzsch was sure that the growth of political
liberty would eliminate the evils of international conflict:

> As wealth and education spread among the masses, they
> will be less inclined to risk in combat their goods and
> lives, their laboriously acquired possessions of property
> and culture. . . . Warmongering does not originate with
> the peoples, as is acknowledged more and more, but in
> the lust for power of dynasties which involve the former
> in a tragic fratricidal struggle under the false pretense of
> national honor and national interest. In such a struggle
> victory is generally more disastrous than defeat. For it is
> still true that the subjugation of other peoples, the as-
> sertion of a preponderant position in foreign affairs which
> can only be maintained by a large war machine, has
> brought the dominant people nothing but its own enslave-
> ment, the loss of its internal freedom.

Victor Böhmert, on the other hand, emphasized the
emergence of a world-wide economy as the best guarantee of peace:

> The striving forward, the striving for improvement of our
> position with the help of free competition in all areas of
> knowledge and creativity, drives mankind by virtue of an
> inner physical necessity, of that *vis interna rerum*, farther
> and farther, from region to region, from country to coun-
> try, from people to people. This inner physical necessity,
> the law of human development, must with the help of an
> international division of labor cause us to take an interest
> in the favored position, the climate, and the culture of
> foreign countries, in their economic progress, and gener-
> ally in the entire development and ripening of other
> states and peoples. Finally, it must lead us, with the grow-
> ing strength of an international consciousness, to a soli-
> darity of the interests of peoples and to a community

141

under the law of nations. But in this economic association of peoples free labor, free exchange, and free trade are the indispensable foundations of the power of each state. They form the strong roots of the tree which branches out over lands and seas, and in whose shadow the nations should henceforth lead their economic existence side by side in friendly competition, so that through the peaceful exchange of their goods and ideas they can enjoy the fruits which they have honestly earned with their brains and hands.[5]

Amity among the peoples of the earth, however, could be established only on the basis of national self-determination. The underlying harmony of the political and economic interests of all mankind could not prevail until there were no longer conquerors and conquered, oppressors and oppressed. The liberals were therefore in theory on the side of all nationalities attempting to gain independence or unity. But where alien political aspirations implied a diminution of German power and prestige, they were of two minds. The struggle to re-create a free Poland, for example, forced them to make a difficult choice between their profession of faith and the appeal of self-interest. The more radical among them agreed with Arnold Schloenbach that "the Polish people want only what we ourselves want, national freedom and independence, and we will never deserve and gain these great blessings if we do not wish them for every other people, and that means also the Polish people." But the patriotic Nationalverein, alarmed at the prospect of territorial losses on the eastern frontier, spoke for the many who insisted that "under no circumstances are we to contemplate a voluntary surrender of

---

[5] Victor Böhmert, *Freiheit der Arbeit!: Beiträge zur Reform der Gewerbegesetze* (Bremen, 1858), pp. 160-161. Cf. G. G. Gervinus, *Einleitung in die Geschichte des neunzehnten Jahrhunderts* (Leipzig, 1853), pp. 168-169, 173-174; Hermann Oncken, *Rudolf von Bennigsen: Ein deutscher liberaler Politiker* (2 vols., Stuttgart, 1910), I, 604; Hermann Schulze-Delitzsch, *Schriften und Reden*, ed. F. Thorwart (5 vols., Berlin, 1909-13), I, 582.

Prussian soil." The *Preussische Jahrbücher*, moreover, always frightened at the thought of bloodshed and revolution, speculated that the repression of the national movement in Poland might restrain the hotheads of Hungary. And was it not obvious that the establishment of an independent Magyar state would create a check to German influence in Eastern Europe?

Yet liberals of various complexions could unite in support of the struggle for the unification of the Italian Peninsula. Not only was there no major conflict of interest between Germany and Italy, not only would the triumph of nationalism south of the Alps stimulate it in the north as well, but the politics of Cavour could win the unqualified endorsement of bourgeois parliamentarianism. Here was a statesman who did not hesitate to exploit the forces of revolution, but then knew how to tame and emasculate them. Here was a believer in middle-of-the-road constitutional government who resolutely opposed Garibaldian foolhardiness and radicalism. He had shown courage in fighting clerical obscurantism, yet he had also learned that industrial capitalism was the foundation on which national greatness must be built. Above all, he was the exponent of the *juste-milieu* between autocracy and mob rule. Many years later Victor Böhmert recalled that "at that time Cavour was an ideal for us young people." And on February 6, 1861, a week before the capitulation of Gaeta crowned the lifework of the Sardinian statesman, the lower chamber of the legislature in Berlin voted to assert in its address to the crown that "we consider it neither in the Prussian nor the German interest to oppose the progressive consolidation of Italy."[6]

6 Prussia, *Verhandlungen des Landtages: Haus der Abgeordneten* (1861), I, 130-132. Cf. *Frankfurter Reform*, April 15, 1863; "Deutschland und der polnische Aufstand," *Wochenschrift des Nationalvereins*, April 10, 1863, p. 1299; [Max Duncker], "Politische Correspondenz," *Preussische Jahrbücher*, VII (1861), 372, 482; Otto Westphal, *Welt- und Staatsauffassung des deutschen Liberalismus: Eine Untersuchung über*

The supreme devotion of the liberals, however, was reserved for the unification of their own country. They were agreed that the German Confederation in its existent form could not meet the essential needs of a vital and ambitious nation. The states which commanded large resources of wealth and population dominated the world, while Germany, torn by historic rivalries and jealousies, was being deprived of her place in the sun by hardhearted neighbors. "Europe has no sympathy with Germany," brooded Karl Mathy, "and the German may console himself with the knowledge that the condition of his great common fatherland could be much worse than it is. The fate of the poet in Schiller's division of the world has long been assigned to him in the French dictum: Aux Français la terre, aux Anglais la mer, aux Allemands l'air." But it was not only injured pride which aroused a sense of national purpose among the advocates of constitutionalism. "The political desultoriness of Germany paralyzed the spirit of industrial enterprise in the nation," complained the *Deutsche Vierteljahrs-Schrift.* "Who wants to establish or modernize factories when in view of our national weakness a war threatens us at any moment? How are our industrialists to win foreign markets for their wares as long as Germans abroad are left to their own resources without vigorous state support in their fatherland? No fleet collects for German industrialists the unpaid claims which they may happen to have in Mexico. And if they want to send their products to a London exhibition, then it costs them the greatest effort to procure from the governments permission for German industry to appear there as a national unit."

Still, the liberals were convinced that the era of particularism in Central Europe was coming to a close. All signs pointed to a growing national consciousness. Hein-

die Preussischen Jahrbücher und den konstitutionellen Liberalismus in Deutschland von 1858 bis 1863 (Munich and Berlin, 1919), p. 320; H. Oncken, *Bennigsen*, I, 316, n. 2.

144

rich von Sybel, charting the course of history from his professorial chair in Munich, assured Grand Duke Frederick of Baden that "from whichever side and in whichever direction I scrutinize our German life on the basis of the historical factors of the last hundred years, the computation always produces the same result. With every decade our nation has advanced in regard to the active patriotism of its people and the natural development of its conditions. It cannot possibly miss the goal. In the near future the call will resound irresistibly from one frontier to the other: Deutschland über alles." And Johannes Miquel, in transition from the socialism of his youth to liberal orthodoxy, maintained that the growing integration of the economy and legislation of Central Europe would lead to political unity. Writing in the spring of 1857 to Karl Marx, he pronounced the German Confederation doomed: "While the period of reaction has made Germany an economic totality, while every day general lawmaking encroaches by means of treaties farther on the independence of the individual state, while extensions of authority by the federal diet and 'internal constitutional developments' make this people every day more accustomed to a central administration, the petty, vulgar, self-centered, and greedy behavior of the small states disgusts everybody more and more, the 'hereditary' princely house becomes every day more burdensome, and the realization penetrates every cottage 'that we must begin to clean up, first at home and then in Frankfurt.' "[7]

The liberals were in agreement, moreover, that the united fatherland of the future must be governed by a parliamentary system in which the authority of the crown was restrained by popular representation. But

[7] Wilhelm Mommsen, *Johannes Miquel* (Stuttgart, 1928) , p. 67. Cf. [K. Mathy], "Deutsche Interessen," p. 3; "Die Stellung der Industrie im heutigen Wirthschaftsleben," *Deutsche Vierteljahrs-Schrift*, xxv (1862) , no. 2, p. 106; *Grossherzog Friedrich I. von Baden und die deutsche Politik von 1854-1871: Briefwechsel, Denkschriften, Tagebücher*, ed. Hermann Oncken (2 vols., Berlin and Leipzig, 1927) , I, 276, n. 2.

how should this popular representation be constituted, and what ought to be the extent of its competence? Here there were sharp differences. The moderates maintained that Germany was not ready for a government responsible to the legislature, because the tradition of monarchical leadership was too powerful in Central Europe. "Parliamentary life among us is still a weak, delicate plant which needs to be cared for and nursed," concluded Theodor von Bernhardi. "It does no good to pretend that our situation is already like that in England, for instance, and to talk and act accordingly. That leads only to a reaction, first in a conservative, then in a democratic sense." To middle-of-the-road constitutionalists any civic reform leading to the preponderance of the masses jeopardized the foundations of the state. The historian Johann Gustav Droysen felt that "the absolutism of democracy is just as unbearable as that of the court party. . . . In our days flattery of the people is about as dangerous as flattery of the princes." More dangerous, most moderates would have insisted. The proletariat lacked the means and education essential for the judicious exercise of political power. Once unleashed, it would turn against those who had foolishly hoped to use it for their ends. Gustav Mevissen, musing darkly in the aftermath of the Revolution of 1848, warned that "the rule of the masses has begun in Europe, although they have not been trained to rule. They have freed themselves from the burdens, partly imaginary, partly real, which oppressed them, and violent revolutions rapidly following one another have placed the reins of power in their hands. These masses must still acquire the education needed for government; they must still acquire the measure of self-control necessary for the achievement of social purposes."

The right wing of the liberal movement, therefore, sought to oppose political and social egalitarianism by a circumspect reform of the established order. "It is our wish to calm tempers and prevent revolution through the establishment of a liberal and national regime," explained Sybel at the onset of the Prussian constitutional conflict. The moderates saw in unyielding ideological consistency a vice which weakened the resistance of the bourgeoisie against mob rule. Karl Twesten condemned the "abstract radicals" who "for the sake of principle are not willing to say anything but no—*fiat iustitia, pereat mundus.*" The collaboration of the nobility, on the other hand, was indispensable for that program of cautious improvement which alone could save the existent social system. The *Preussische Jahrbücher,* a leading advocate of the *juste-milieu,* insisted that the moderate liberals "want to educate the feudal party for service to the state. . . . We subscribe to the opinion that Prussia possesses and needs a landed aristocracy. We do not believe that the interests and resources of the bourgeoisie and of the small landowners are sufficient to establish a healthy and full political life in our country or to nourish it in a regular and effective manner." Max Duncker, who believed that "all pages of history preach the lesson of the golden mean," assured the crown prince of Prussia that the middle-of-the-road parliamentarians "want the harmony of classes, not the subjugation of one by another; not only the subjection of the opponent to reform, but also his good will for it. They want absolutism neither from above nor from below; they want political influence exercised by the propertied, not the propertyless classes; they want no dictatorship, whether it be based on an army of soldiers or on an excited and aroused army of the multitude." This was the voice of the upper bourgeoisie of Central Europe, espousing the ideological middle ground from which it could oppose both aristocratic prerogative and proletarian impertinence.[8]

[8] *Aus dem Leben Bernhardis,* III, 260; Johann Gustav Droysen, *Briefwechsel,* ed. Rudolf Hübner (2 vols., Berlin and Leipzig, 1929), II, 813, 881; J. Hansen, *Mevissen,* II, 488; *Deutscher Liberalismus im Zeitalter Bismarcks: Eine politische Briefsammlung,* ed. Julius Heyderhoff and Paul Wentzcke (2 vols., Bonn and Leipzig, 1925-26), I, 98, 186; [Max

The democrats who formed the left wing of liberalism differed from the moderates in their theoretical commitment to popular sovereignty and their readiness to adopt aggressive tactics in the struggle for a parliamentary form of government. Some of them had once had republican sympathies, although the great majority had always been willing to accept a monarchical state in which the king reigned more than he ruled. They were also more favorable or at least more conciliatory toward the political aspirations of the lower classes. Since they taught that the voice of the people was the voice of God, they supported in principle both manhood suffrage and unrestricted eligibility for public office. Even an act of insurrection was in their eyes justifiable, as long as it represented an expression of the general will. During the Revolution of 1848 they had preached constitutionalism to the masses, advocated passive resistance against royal authority and, after all else failed, sanctioned an armed uprising against the dynastic order. But they were Jacobins in a land without *sans-culottes*, and during the years of reaction they paid a heavy price for their miscalculations in prison, exile, or obscurity. With the revival of the liberal movement in the late 1850's, they began to return to the political scene, but now their mood was cautious and subdued. The reckless idealism of the prerevolutionary era had given way to a calculating prudence which weighed advantage against risk, principle against expediency. The difference between the moderate and radical wings of parliamentarianism had become more a matter of theory and temperament than of everyday practice.

For one thing, the democrats were now ready to renounce their earlier republican leanings. Even Johann Jacoby, who in 1848 had exclaimed in the presence of

---

Duncker], "Politische Correspondenz," *Preussische Jahrbücher,* vii (1861), 488, viii (1861), 521; O. Westphal, *Welt- und Staatsauffassung des Liberalismus,* p. 320; *Duncker: Politischer Briefwechsel,* ed. J. Schultze, p. xvii; H. O. Meisner, *Der preussische Kronprinz,* p. 179.

Frederick William IV of Prussia that "it is the misfortune of kings that they do not want to hear the truth," stated publicly ten years later that "now there is not a single person in our country, in the entire democratic party, who so much as dreams of wanting, much less of striving for, a form of government other than monarchical for Prussia as she is." The controversial suffrage issue was treated with discreet equivocation. The Progressive Party, which included the left-wing liberals of Prussia, announced at the time of its formation that it "considered the question of the general and equal suffrage open." Hermann Schulze-Delitzsch condemned the use of force in the struggle for constitutional government. Lower-class unrest would only play into the hands of the enemy. "No respectable workingman will at this moment allow himself to be drawn into it. I myself would intervene against it, for a greater service to the reaction could not be rendered." He warned that "impatience and rashness would now be the biggest mistake." Only through law and order could victory be won. "Our task now is to rally all liberal elements ever more closely about us, and to bind the propertied classes ever more closely to us."

Similarly, while the political opponents of Baron Leopold von Hoverbeck felt that they could "foretell all his actions with almost mathematical certainty through the aid of Rousseau's *contrat social*," the program of reform which he advanced sounded more like Constant or Guizot:

> It is now the dominant view of democracy that its efforts must no longer be directed toward the achievement at all costs of the freest form of the state, but toward the promotion of the peaceful development of strength in the people. Democracy therefore demands now from the government only that it offer no improper resistance to the growth of popular strength. . . . Freedom of press and religion will suffice for the expression of the warranted forces of popular strength. Self-government in a limited

sphere will for a long time to come be an adequate school in which to exercise the independence and civic vigor of the people.

Even the most temperate of liberals could endorse such modest demands, while the old revolutionary war-horse Arnold Ruge sighed that "the democratic republican party as such has completely disappeared."[9]

In the secondary states of central and southern Germany there arose still another form of liberalism, reflecting the radical but particularist outlook of the petty bourgeoisie below the Main. Here the small independent landowners, shopkeepers, merchants, professional men, and white-collar workers tended to regard with suspicion the big-power politics pursued in Berlin and Vienna. They believed in an individualistic federal republic like that of neighboring Switzerland, where the proud spirit of localism could flourish in a union of free and equal communities. Opposed to autocracy, clericalism, jingoism, centralizing bureaucracy, and restrictive economic regulation, they sought to realize a Jeffersonian ideal in the social milieu of Central Europe. Their basic demands were expressed in the program adopted on September 25, 1865, by representatives of the People's Party of Württemberg:

(1) Democratic foundation of the constitution and administration of the German states, general and direct suffrage, parliamentary rule; self-government of the people in municipal and county organizations; popular education, separation of church and school; freedom of the press, of assembly, and of association; removal of the still existent

[9] *Arnold Ruges Briefwechsel und Tagebuchblätter aus den Jahren 1825–80*, ed. Paul Nerrlich (2 vols., Berlin, 1886) , II, 264. Cf. Veit Valentin, *Geschichte der deutschen Revolution von 1848–49* (2 vols., Berlin, 1930-31) , II, 266; Johann Jacoby *Gesammelte Schriften und Reden*, 2nd edn. (2 vols., Hamburg, 1877) , II, 98; Ludolf Parisius, *Deutschlands politische Parteien und das Ministerium Bismarck* (Berlin, 1878) , pp. 38-39; H. Schulze-Delitzsch, *Schriften und Reden*, IV, 223-224; H. Wagener, *Erlebtes*, II, 15; Ludolf Parisius, *Leopold Freiherr von Hoverbeck* (2 vols., Berlin, 1897-1900) , I, 150.

legal discriminations imposed on the working class and of the obstacles to free economic development; reform of the military system, universal conscription. (2) Federative association of the individual states with a central authority and parliament superior to the state governments. Neither a Prussian nor an Austrian head of state! (3) Mutual recognition of the principles of nationality and of the right of self-determination, of freedom and justice in dealing with other nations.

While the two Great Powers of Central Europe drifted closer to armed conflict, the petty bourgeois radicals of the secondary states continued to invoke the slogans and strike the poses of 1848. Gustav von Struve, who had fought for the democratic cause in Baden during the revolution and in America during the Civil War, returned home in the 1860's to demand the "re-establishment of the legal basis of 1848 and 1849, and accordingly a German parliament and a unitary central authority." The republican hero of two continents, whom the socialist August Bebel remembered as "a haggard, tall-looking figure with a falsetto voice and a remarkably red nose," accused reactionary statesmen of treason, called for arming the citizenry, urged the convocation of a national assembly chosen by manhood suffrage, and insisted on the promulgation of the constitution which the Frankfurt Parliament had drafted fourteen years before. The radical German People's Party was confident that the formation of a popular militia would suffice to frustrate the enemies of freedom. Once the common people acquired weapons, they would know how to defend their rights and liberties. "Let no household be without arms, no factory without muskets and pikes for all workers! . . . Let every young man arm himself at his own expense, and for this purpose let him, in the name of God, give up beer and tobacco for a month!"

There was a charmingly ingenuous flavor about this small-town radicalism which hoped to overthrow the established order with the purity of its ideals. "Do you then not realize that world history is not made in Württemberg and in Nassau?" asked the Lassallean *Social-Demokrat*. It was a legitimate question. The dogmas and phrases inspiring a revolution in the 1840's were unsuited to the age of *Realpolitik* which had opened in the 1850's. On the eve of the Seven Weeks' War, when the fratricidal struggle which they had so anxiously sought to avoid appeared inevitable, some of the democrats in the secondary states sensed at last the hopelessness of their position. "Where are you, youth of the Forties, who never thought about anything except the glory and freedom of the fatherland, least of all about yourself, where are you today?" lamented the *Deutsches Wochenblatt* in Mannheim. "As for us forty-eighters, more and more isolated, who are the only ones in Germany still struggling for complete and true freedom, our heart almost breaks when we see ourselves so often without new blood, without young people ready for sacrifice." Three months later the Prussian victory at Sadowa destroyed the basis of petty bourgeois federalist democracy in Central Europe.[10]

The liberals were in greater agreement on economics than on politics. While their differences regarding the basis and authority of constitutional government were often irreconcilable, they all believed that the civic rights of man included the liberation of his productive energies. And since political and economic liberty were inseparable, any threat to the freedom of the citizen constituted ipso facto an obstacle to his pursuit of material well-being. "Once the independence of individuality is removed through legal as well as administrative prescription, then not only must spiritual development be naturally retarded, but also the de-

---

[10] *Europäischer Geschichtskalender*, ed. H. Schulthess, (1865) , p. 109; G. Struve, *Diesseits und jenseits*, I, 129-130; August Bebel, *Aus meinem Leben* (3 vols., Stuttgart, 1910-14) , I, 147; "Krieg oder Friede?," *Deutsches Wochenblatt*, May 13, 1866, p. 154; "Politische Uebersicht," *ibid.*, April 8, 1866, p. 116; *Social-Demokrat*, September 26, 1865.

velopment of labor in the fields of industry, commerce, art, and culture," claimed the publicist and lawyer Siegfried Weiss. By the same token, an enhancement of the economic vitality of the nation was bound to prepare the way for its liberalization and unification. After the political failure of 1848 Mevissen sought consolation in the thought that "material interests form the only basis on which a better future may be built." And ten years later the journal of the middle-of-the-road Nationalverein maintained that "every so-called material advance in the German question, every common law, every common German regulation of bills of exchange, commerce, legal procedure, and rules of court, every common regulation of coinage, weights, and measures, every further step toward a more intimate economic union will be and must be welcome to us. We see in it not only the momentary satisfaction of a particular, urgent national need, but also a powerful instrument for further unification."

The economic boom of the mid-century reinforced the conviction of the liberals that the passing of the old order was only a question of time. A political system which had originated in the preindustrial era would sooner or later be forced to adjust to the changing conditions created by the growth of capitalism. John Prince-Smith, the high priest of laissez-faire economics, taught the inevitability of civic reform with all the assurance of a scientist expounding immutable laws of nature:

Our governmental institutions and governmental attitudes are at present still derived from that period of economic isolation and weakness, that is to say, from the period before the introduction of steam engines, railroads, steamships, and the electric telegraph, before the general application of machinery and factory production on a large scale. They are no longer suited to the newly emerging economic life, to the movement of goods growing like an avalanche. In practice they are being driven back on all fronts; they must make daily concessions to the imperative need for economic liberation. The tariff duties separating states are being riddled, the guild barriers are falling, the system of monopoly is declining, freedom of movement is spreading. The economic seed is everywhere breaking through the sod of the old state; the old inveterate attitudes are being forced into a new environment. The traditional national antagonism is changing into a force for national unity.[11]

A sense that history was on their side, that they had been chosen to participate in the predestined revival of their country inspired the liberals. They felt themselves involved in an epic struggle which demanded endurance and sacrifice, but whose outcome was not in doubt. In the forefront of that struggle stood the middle class, committed by its position in society to the cause of a free and united fatherland. The liberals invited all men of good will to assist in the creation of a new order, but they considered the bourgeoisie particularly suited to the task of national regeneration. August Ludwig von Rochau, whose *Grundsätze der Realpolitik* reflected the disenchantment of a generation embittered by the failure of 1848, expounded that "the middle class is and remains the most indispensable and valuable material for the construction of the German state." Baron Karl von Bruck, a successful businessman whose services to Austria had been rewarded with a patent of nobility and the ministry of finance, urged his emperor to liberalize the government in accordance with the wishes of the bourgeoisie, the true defender of the national interest. "It combines, far more than any other class of society, those common objectives of welfare and culture

[11] *Die Verhandlungen des Vierten Congresses deutscher Volkswirthe zu Stuttgart am 9., 10., 11. und 12. September 1861* (Stuttgart, 1861), p. 36. Cf. S. Weiss, *An die deutsche Nation*, p. 28; J. Hansen, *Mevissen*, I, 616; M., "Die nationale Partei und ihr Verhalten innerhalb der Einzelstaaten," *Wochenschrift des Nationalvereins*, November 29 and December 6, 1861, p. 682.

which . . . constitute in their entirety a unifying, powerful, socially dynamic force firmly opposed to separatism within the boundaries of the state, while the principal particularities and traditional divisions find support primarily in the attitudes and interests of the varied landed aristocracy." The *Deutsche Vierteljahrs-Schrift* argued in the same vein that since the economic ties of the business world transcended local boundaries, the industrialists were of necessity disposed to favor civic reform: "They are precisely those who have been chosen above all to demonstrate to the nation, through the connection of their enterprises, the economic interdependence of the German lands in a financial and governmental sense, and thereby to force into the background political tendencies which endanger both governmental and economic relationships." The Silesian politician and textile manufacturer Leonor Reichenheim stressed in addition the spiritual significance of capitalism: "The calling of industry is not only to pursue material interests, not only to strive for material success. It has a higher mission to fulfill, the mission of acting solely as the pioneer of liberalism in the moral as well as political sense, and this mission it will fulfill."

The most eloquent idealization of the bourgeoisie came from Schulze-Delitzsch, who saw in the business community the patriciate of a new social order. On September 18, 1863, at a banquet in Chemnitz, "the Manchester of Saxony," he portrayed before a large middle-class gathering the grand destiny awaiting the German entrepreneur:

> Industrial and spiritual interests are thus one. The former depend for their stability on the progress of the nation, since their success is possible only in a free state among free citizens. A people which is politically unfree, which is alien to humane endeavor suffers an industrial decline. German industry is beyond a doubt closely associated with the national struggle. To be sure, despite the political reaction of past decades which placed obstacles in its path,

it has demonstrated its robust vitality. But it needs the entire national energy for its full development if it is to withstand victoriously the great competition on the world market. The German industrialists have so far shown that they identify themselves with the ideals of the people and do not subscribe to imperialistic endeavors. . . . The seed of the aristocracy of the future lies in the industrialists, as soon as they seek their salvation in the nation. Even though now the Junkers rule, they are without roots in the people; their future is the grave. A toast to the industry of Chemnitz![12]

Yet the middle class could fulfill its historic calling only in a society which was economically as well as politically free. Any restriction imposed on individual ability in the struggle for material advantage represented a violation of what the liberal Nassau politician Karl Braun called "the natural laws of economics which no lawmaker, no schemer, no agitator has yet trampled underfoot with impunity." The true function of government, he explained, was "nothing other than legal protection for person and property in domestic affairs, and the development of power in foreign policy which is beneficial to individuals and to society as a whole." The conclusion he drew was that the state should abandon ownership of the railway, telegraph, and postal systems, the construction of highways and canals, the administration of mining, forestry, and medical services, the furtherance of education, and the promotion of agriculture and industry.

Most liberals were not as rigid in their adherence to laissez faire, but by and large they shared Prince-Smith's

[12] H. Schulze-Delitzsch, *Schriften und Reden*, II, 213-214. Cf. [August Ludwig von Rochau], *Grundsätze der Realpolitik, angewendet auf die staatlichen Zustände Deutschlands*, 2nd edn. (2 vols., Stuttgart and Heidelberg, 1859-69), I, 157; K. v. Bruck, *Aufgaben Oesterreichs*, pp. 38-39; "Die Stellung der Industrie," p. 125; Prussia, *Stenographische Berichte über die Verhandlungen der durch die Allerhöchste Verordnung vom 22. December 1862 einberufenen beiden Häuser des Landtages: Haus der Abgeordneten* (5 vols., Berlin, 1863), I, 24-25.

belief that "it is commerce, naturally under complete freedom of competition, which performs the function of an economic police force, as it were, and which induces every man through either the reward of a profitable enterprise or the penalty of impoverishment to apply his resources of labor and capital in such a way that they make the greatest possible contribution to the general welfare under the given natural conditions." For example, Paul, a simple artisan who is the protagonist of Victor Böhmert's *Briefe zweier Handwerker*, defends economic liberalism with all the rhetorical zeal of the Manchester school:

> All men will more or less compete with one another to the extent that they seek to achieve the broadest possible satisfaction of their needs, to reach a higher level of well-being, and in general to improve their position. He who knows how to achieve this in the area of his occupation by doubling his exertions and employing legal means deserves only our recognition and respect. The paths which lead to the goal are different, and equally different are the results which individuals attain. Yet this incessant struggle of the human spirit, this universal unfolding of human energy and activity will be apparent in every occupation. The mass of inventions which have thereby been directly produced, perfected, and disseminated and the so obviously greater well-being of mankind are gratifying proof of the blessed results of competition.

And what of the man who could not achieve success through competition? Here the liberals were inclined to share the scriptural view that we have the poor always with us. Thrift, sobriety, hard work, and rugged self-reliance would do much to improve the lot of the laboring population, but economic inequality and economic privation could never be completely vanquished. "Nothing is more natural, just, and desirable," agreed the Nationalverein, "than that the working classes should strive to better their economic condition, provided only that they confine themselves to the proper means for this end and that their demands remain within the limits of possibility. These limits are determined above all by the total amount of production, which down to the present day has been and probably will also remain in the future much too small to provide for the entire population or even for a majority that carefree existence and life of pleasure which would be desirable for all the world. The earth is too poor and the labor of man too barren for the fulfillment of such wishes."

Poverty, moreover, was not an unmitigated evil, since it provided a stimulus to human industriousness and enterprise. Without it mankind might sink into a lotus-eating indolence. Karl Braun elaborated on this theme, contending that "the inequality of property is by no means a misfortune. On the contrary, I affirm that the equality of property and its immutability would be the greatest misfortune which could befall the world. For if every man had exactly as much property as every other, and each one knew that he could not increase this property, then anybody devoting himself to work would be a fool. For the inclination toward *dolce far niente* is a tendency deeply implanted in hearts of all of us, and we can overcome it only for compelling reasons, whether it be the inducement of hunger or the ethical motives of family, community, and state." The progress of humanity thus depended on the threat of privation and on the response to that threat.[13]

If unrestrained competition was a manifestation of civic liberty, then corporative regulation of manufacture

[13] Germany, *Stenographische Berichte über die Verhandlungen des Reichstages des Norddeutschen Bundes: I. Legislatur-Periode, Session 1869* (3 vols., Berlin, 1869), I, 121, 123; Carl Braun, "Staats- und Gemeinde-Steuern, im Zusammenhange mit Staats-, Heeres-, Kommunal- und Agrarverfassung," *Vierteljahrschrift für Volkswirthschaft und Kulturgeschichte*, IV (1866), no. 2, pp. 7, 17, 22-23; *Verhandlungen des Vierten Congresses deutscher Volkswirthe 1861*, p. 33; Carl Victor Boehmert, *Briefe zweier Handwerker: Ein Beitrag zur Lösung gewerblicher und socialer Fragen* (Dresden and Döbeln, 1854), p. 60; "Die Fortschrittsparthei und der Socialismus," *Wochen-Blatt des National-Vereins*, April 6, 1865, p. 7.

represented an invasion of the inalienable rights of the citizen. Liberals of all shades of opinion were accordingly unanimous in their advocacy of industrial freedom. Victor Böhmert was the most vocal among them on this question, but the sedate *Preussische Jahrbücher* also paid homage to "the principle of industrial freedom, that mighty palladium of the welfare of the people." Rudolf von Bennigsen, head of the Nationalverein, condemned the "suppression of economic liberty" and deplored the "restricted freedom of labor and the laborer." The democrats of East and West Prussia promised that they would "support a revision of industrial legislation, so that restraining regulations which bring to mind the obsolete guild system cease, and the free movement of all industrial energies is permitted." Gustav von Struve spoke for the radicals of the south in advocating a law that "every person regardless of sex, origin, and citizenship has the right to practice an occupation throughout the entire territory of the country, subject to those provisions which may be promulgated with respect to certain occupations out of regard for the health and security of the citizens." Even August Ludwig von Rochau, although primarily concerned with principles of politics, taught the doctrine of free enterprise: "The first, the most pressing and imperative demand of economic interest is that every material energy be employed as intensively as possible. The economic interest of society is indifferent to the contract of apprenticeship and the master's examination. It asks only for proficiency, however and wherever that proficiency may have been acquired."[14]

Freedom of movement was the logical corollary of freedom of industry, and the same postulates which demonstrated the reasonableness of one could be em-

14 [A. L. v. Rochau], *Grundsätze der Realpolitik*, I, 97. Cf. [Karl Neumann], "Politische Correspondenz," *Preussische Jahrbücher*, III (1859), 107; O. Westphal, *Welt-und Staatsauffassung des Liberalismus*, p. 319; H. Oncken, *Bennigsen*, I, 361; L. Parisius, *Deutschlands politische Parteien*, p. 33; G. Struve, *Diesseits und jenseits*, I, 97.

ployed to prove the desirability of the other. A.E.F. Schäffle described freedom of movement as "the practical supplement of industrial freedom, the 'inseparable sister' of the latter." He saw in it a vital juridical principle "which renders possible and facilitates in fact a natural circulation of the blood and the natural equalization of energy in the total national economy demanded by the entire development of our time, which assures the broadest scope to every economic energy, and which counteracts local unemployment, the material and moral decay of the population, and the overburdening of the budget of the community." Wilhelm Adolf Lette, the reformist Prussian economist and politician, eulogized "the most valuable of all fundamental rights, the freedom of movement. . . . Let us not talk about a united German fatherland as long as one state or, worse still, one community still shuts its doors against another, as long as an able-bodied German who wants to support himself honestly outside his place of birth can still be driven from land to land and be separated from his family."

Professor Franz Löher of the University of Munich considered freedom of movement across state boundaries one of the most important rights of the German people. "Uncounted forces endowed with skill and vigor which have in the past lain quiescent or been lost through emigration will become mobile and will find in Germany herself a place to settle profitably. A thousand resources which lie fallow in this or that region or are little-known will be utilized through the inflow of other German energies." The *National-Zeitung* of Berlin stressed the growth of national loyalty as well as the increase in material welfare which freedom of movement would stimulate: "Through freedom of movement we shall first of all create for the German a fatherland in the matters which are closest to him. We shall retain the strength and ability which grow so abundantly in our soil, and shall attract from other nations the strength and ability which can and want to contribute in our commonwealth to our welfare, honor, and might. Through freedom of movement we shall create public spirit and national sentiment, welfare and contentment." An important economic reform which promised to enhance both ideals and profits seemed beyond exception.[15]

The arguments for the freedom of movement of the individual could in turn be enlisted to support the freedom of movement of credit. Was not the unrestricted flow of capital as important for the flowering of the national economy as the unrestricted flow of labor? And would not free enterprise produce the same beneficial results in the world of finance as in industry and commerce? The logic of the liberal program of economic reform was all of a piece, the rationale of each proposal supporting and reinforcing the demand for every other. The indefatigable Karl Braun pointed out that "freedom of movement [and] the liberation of labor, of capital, of landed property, of credit, and of commerce from all those fetters which feudalism, the police state, and the lack of economic judgment have imposed upon them are closely connected with one another." He accordingly advocated repeal of the usury laws, poking fun at those who believed that "we can by means of 'laws,' that is, by means of commandments or prohibitions manufactured in a constitutional law factory make bread bigger, tastier, and cheaper, or the interest rate lower, or the trades prosperous, or the freight costs everywhere uniformly cheap."

In northern Germany the *Preussische Jahrbücher* insisted that the only defenders of credit restrictions were

[15] A.E.F. Schäffle, "Vorschläge zu einer gemeinsamen Ordnung der Gewerbebefugnisse und Heimathrechtsverhältnisse in Deutschland nach den Grundsätzen der Gewerbefreiheit und der Freizügigkeit," *Deutsche Vierteljahrs-Schrift*, XXII (1859) , no. 1, p. 239; *Bericht über die Verhandlungen des sechsten Congresses deutscher Volkswirthe zu Dresden am 14. 15. 16. 17. September 1863* (Berlin, 1863) , p. 5; [Franz Löher], *Recht und Pflicht der Bundes-Staaten zwischen Preussen und Oestreich: Zur Bundesreform auf Grund des Bundesrechts* (Munich, 1862) , pp. 176-177; H. Rosenberg, *Die nationalpolitische Publizistik*, I, 426; *National-Zeitung*, October 10, 1863.

"some reactionary politicians of half juridical, half-theological complexion, who do not want to stray so far from canon law." To the south the *Deutsche Vierteljahrs-Schrift* maintained that the attempt to control the rate of interest by legislative enactment was harmful, because "only through the uniform freedom of the credit industry is the healthy and natural circulation of capital through the economic life of the nation assured." As for Austria, no less a personage than Baron Bruck advocated the revocation of the usury laws of the empire. Convinced that only a policy of rigorous modernization could save the state from decline, the reformist minister of finance advocated "the so urgently needed abolition of the barriers which impede the free movement of the forces of capital and labor, barriers like the ossified system of guilds and privileges, the obsolete usury law with its fixed rate of interest, and the shackling monopolistic system in the sale of alcohol which prevails in several crownlands."[16]

What is striking about this liberal program of economic reform is its close resemblance to the demands of the business community stated in the annual reports of the chambers of commerce. The same emphasis on the emancipation of middle-class acquisitive talents from the tutelage of the state is apparent in both. Both maintain that the natural laws of economics operating within a system of unrestrained competition will assure to society a volume of production and a level of well-being impossible under a regime of corporative regulation or governmental supervision. What industrialists and financiers believed to be true on the basis of everyday experience, liberal publicists and parliamentarians proved to be in accord with the eternal truths of human nature

[16] K. v. Bruck, *Aufgaben Oesterreichs*, p. 43. Cf. Carl Braun, "Studien über Freizügigkeit," *Vierteljahrschrift für Volkswirthschaft und Culturgeschichte*, I (1863), no. 3, pp. 65, 84; C. Braun, "Staats- und Gemeinde-Steuern," p. 18; [A. Lammers], "Die wirthschaftliche Reformbewegung in Deutschland," *Preussische Jahrbücher*, VI (1860), 580; A.E.F. Schäffle, "Vorschläge zu einer gemeinsamen Ordnung," p. 259.

and the social order. Practice and theory found themselves in agreement on the fundamental validity of the teachings of laissez faire: freedom of industry, freedom of movement, freedom of credit.

Even with regard to reforms of secondary importance there was a remarkable concurrence of opinion. While the businessmen of Düsseldorf asked that "the way . . . be prepared as soon as possible for a uniform system of patent legislation for all Germany to meet a general need," A.E.F. Schäffle demanded a common regulation of "the patent laws, because only in this fashion will the reward for inventions be secure and their application to the common good become uniform." The complaint of the Magdeburg chamber of commerce concerning the "petty obstacles" created by river tolls on the Elbe was an echo of the indignant article in the *Preussische Jahrbücher* attacking the narrow-minded fiscal policy of the minor states: "The most irrational system of taxation and the privileges of the small princes are to be maintained at the expense of German commerce, and with the revenues derived from the Elbe tolls they are building in Schwerin a palace which surpasses Windsor and Versailles." Here as elsewhere the liberal attack against particularistic and bureaucratic obstacles to free enterprise expressed the needs of industrial capitalism *sub specie aeternitatis*.[17]

In dealing with the lower classes, on the other hand, bourgeois constitutionalists were generally uneasy. There could be no bond of sympathy between the well-to-do liberal champions of a parliamentary system of government and the brutalized proletariat of Central Europe. To be sure, the masses were an integral element of the sovereign people whose rights the advocates of reform were asserting, but they could also be willful and un-

---

[17] *Preussische Handelsarchiv* (1862), III (Jahresberichte der Handelskammern und kaufmännischen Korporationen des preussischen Staats für (1861), 257, 348; A.E.F. Schäffle, "Vorschläge zu einer gemeinsamen Ordnung," p. 259; [R. Zwicker], "Die Elbzölle," *Preussische Jahrbücher*, III (1859), 448.

predictable. It was so difficult to communicate with them, to teach and to guide them. "I really do not know what to make of the masses and above all of the fourth estate," confessed the venerable scholar and politician Friedrich Christoph Dahlmann. Most liberals shared his perplexity. There were even some who frankly expressed their contempt for the uneducated and ill-bred. "The people is in general little or nothing," affirmed the historian Johann Gustav Droysen. "Under the best of circumstances it is a cloud of dust filling the air and obscuring the view, until a gentle rain settles the whirling mass into the thick and sticky form which we commonly call mud."

Still, the mob could not simply be ignored. It had the strength of numbers, yet was swayed by rabble-rousers and demagogues. "Napoleon is the master of France because he has the soldier and the *ouvrier* in hand," warned the *Preussische Jahrbücher*. The masses could ravage and destroy; to arouse them was to invite self-destruction. Wilhelm Löwe-Calbe, who had spent a decade in exile for his democratic convictions, warned the government of Prussia against enlisting the aid of the proletariat in the constitutional conflict: "Consider carefully that you could thereby easily suffer the fate of the sorcerer's apprentice described by Goethe, the sorcerer's apprentice who could not rid himself of the spirits again when he wanted to be rid of them." And Schulze-Delitzsch invoked "the profound myth of antiquity concerning the sphinx" to make the same point: "We may well describe the social question as the modern sphinx of our time. . . . Now there is in human nature, in all of us as we are, in large and small, in the eminent and the humble, a dim boundary line where the bestial and the human meet, and woe to him . . . who wantonly and with a frivolous hand touches this boundary line! He unleashes the beast which will tear him to pieces with its lion's claws!"[18]

[18] Prussia, *Stenographische Berichte über die Verhandlungen der durch die Allerhöchste Verordnung vom 29. Dezember 1864 einberu-*

While the wild beast of anarchy lurked in all men, it was particularly ferocious in impoverished villages and urban slums. Liberalism therefore hesitated to extend to the propertyless masses a franchise which might be used to support radical economic experiments or an autocratic regime built on bread and circuses. The moderates openly announced their opposition to manhood suffrage, contending that the lower classes lacked the intellectual training and financial independence to vote in keeping with the higher interests of the state. The ballot should be restricted to those whose property guaranteed their loyalty to the social order. Johannes Miquel advocated a limitation of the franchise "according to the existent level of education and the other conditions," grumbling that "universal suffrage forces us to wage a difficult struggle against the stupidity of the masses." The former radical Julius Fröbel, enlisting his literary talents in the service of the Austrian government, denounced "democratic absolutism with its *suffrage universel.*" The defenders of a broad franchise, he insisted, were in effect recommending "a daily breakfast of warm lion's milk, and for this purpose the purchase of a harmless and healthy lioness. The realization of the idea would present its difficulties." The most magisterial condemnation of manhood suffrage, however, came from Heinrich von Sybel, who based his attack against popular rule on the lessons of history itself:

> As far as my historical experience extends, the introduction of the general, direct, and equal franchise has always been the beginning of the end for any form of parliamentarianism. . . . The general, direct, and equal franchise can produce desirable results only when all is well not merely in the state but also in society; when an equality

fenen beiden Häuser des Landtages: Haus der Abgeordneten (8 vols., Berlin, 1865) , I, 156, 185. Cf. Anton Springer, *Friedrich Christoph Dahlmann* (2 vols., Leipzig, 1870-72) , II, 391; J. G. Droysen, *Briefwechsel*, II, 188; [Wilhelm Wehrenpfennig], "Politische Correspondenz," *Preussische Jahrbücher*, X (1862) , 502; O. Westphal, *Welt- und Staatsauffassung des Liberalismus*, p. 321.

in social relations among individual men complements these general political rights; when all men have an equal measure of intellectual training, social well-being, and moral strength of character; when all men are alert and free and godly and joyous; when conditions on this sad and sinful earth are such as pious minds imagine in their vision of the millennium, such as in the vision portrayed by an old father of the church where tigers and wolves feed on bran and play with sheep and lambs. . . . I, who have devoted my life to the historical investigation of human affairs, am the last to deny the constant progress of historical development. I am the last to doubt that step by step, with every generation, with every century we are drawing closer to this goal which is infinitely distant. But . . . no mistake seems to me more disastrous than to declare by some law that this condition has in principle already been achieved, and that individual laws are now to be fashioned and formed in keeping with this mistake.[19]

The left wing of liberalism, however, could not openly accept Sybel's contention that the introduction of manhood suffrage should wait until "the political tigers and the social wolves live together in peace with the lambs and sheep of our human society." It was too deeply committed to the doctrine of popular sovereignty. Whatever its mental reservations, in principle it had to favor the enfranchisement of the masses. Yet even the radicals of the secondary states, the most consistent proponents of an unrestricted ballot, had their moments of doubt. Karl Blind, the fiery insurrectionist from Baden, for instance, warned that "general suffrage without the previous destruction of tyranny has never yet led to reforms, but has often served to consolidate princely despotism." Among the democrats of the north opinions

---

[19] Germany, *Stenographische Berichte über die Verhandlungen des Reichstages des Norddeutschen Bundes im Jahre 1867* (2 vols., Berlin, 1867) , I, 427. Cf. Hans Herzfeld, *Johannes von Miquel: Sein Anteil am Ausbau des Deutschen Reiches bis zur Jahrhundertwende* (2 vols., Detmold, 1938) , I, 25, 51; Julius Fröbel, *Ein Lebenslauf: Aufzeichnungen, Erinnerungen und Bekenntnisse* (2 vols., Stuttgart, 1890-91) , II, 187, 277.

were sharply divided. Some like Hoverbeck and Schulze-Delitzsch favored an outright endorsement of a broad franchise, but many of the others felt serious misgivings. Benedikt Waldeck, for twenty years a leader of the left, worried that the lower classes might use the vote to tamper with the established order of society. "The general suffrage is a political, not a social demand; now is obviously not the time to strive for it." Johann Jacoby, although supporting a program which included the popular franchise, pointed out reassuringly that "there is not a word here about improper pressure, not a word about a fixed deadline or a stipulated condition." And the embittered old forty-eighter Franz Ziegler asserted bluntly: "We men of the Progressive Party fear nothing as much as the equal, general, and direct suffrage, because it would reduce our numbers frightfully." The democrats finally decided that since the question of the franchise could not be settled in the near future anyway, given the existing political conditions, it would be best to leave the matter open.[20]

The equivocal attitude of the liberals toward manhood suffrage derived from their fear of its consequences. In France the enfranchisement of the lower classes had led to the plebiscitary autocracy of Napoleon III, while east of the Rhine both Bismarck and Lassalle were suspected of planning to exploit it for the destruction of middle-class parliamentarianism. The proletariat would therefore have to learn to resist the blandishments of demagogues before it could make intelligent use of the right to vote. It would have to learn that its standard of living could not be improved by governmental fiat or socialistic sleight of hand. "For the economic position of the wageworker or the average level of wages is quite

[20] *Neue Frankfurter Zeitung*, June 8, 1863; L. Parisius, *Hoverbeck*, I, 209; Walter Gagel, *Die Wahlrechtsfrage in der Geschichte der deutschen liberalen Parteien, 1848-1918* (Düsseldorf, 1958), pp. 32-33; Wilhelm Biermann, *Franz Leo Benedikt Waldeck: Ein Streiter für Freiheit und Recht* (Paderborn, 1928), p. 296; J. Jacoby, *Schriften und Reden*, II, 99; L. Dehio, "Die preussische Demokratie," p. 258.

simply the quotient of the wage fund divided by the number of workers," explained Prince-Smith. "Except for a decimation of the workers, this quotient can be enlarged only by an increase in the wage fund. The wage fund in turn is part of the production created by labor and capital. It therefore increases only with the enlargement or the more efficient use of capital, that is, with the general rise in the income of the nation for which we must simply wait, however slowly it may proceed." The functioning of the wage mechanism was as logical and ineluctable as a mathematical formula: "The man without financial reserves receives for his labor a price which is determined in the market just like the price of every market commodity. He looks for the person who values his work most highly and is willing to give him the most money for it. The buyer naturally does not want to give more for it than others who seek work are ready to accept for an equally good performance. If therefore the price obtained for labor does not suffice for a comfortable existence, then it is not the buyers but the sellers of labor who have depressed the price. The notion that the capitalist can arbitrarily dictate the price of labor . . . is fundamentally false."[21]

While not all liberals were as mechanistic in their economic views, they agreed by and large that the wage of the workingman was determined by the impersonal law of supply and demand, which not even the best-intentioned of employers could alter. It followed that labor strikes must fail to achieve any lasting improvement in the position of the proletariat. There were, to be sure, some dissenting views. The Swabian moderate Robert von Mohl conceded reluctantly that "in many cases a threat and, if necessary, the execution of a general work stoppage is the only weapon with which the workers can protect themselves against the injustice, harshness, and abuse of authority by employers." And

[21] John Prince-Smith, "Die sogenannte Arbeiterfräge," *Vierteljahrschrift für Volkswirthschaft und Kulturgeschichte*, II (1864), no. 4, pp. 195-196, 203-204.

the radical Arnold Schloenbach actually insisted that the strike movement had "its great moral and political significance," because it was "the first positive action of the workers, the first proof of their strength and power in dealing with the hitherto predominant power of money, police, and the masters 'by the grace of God.' " But the authentic voice of middle-class constitutionalism was heard in the contention of the liberal industrialist Friedrich Harkort "that we cannot unilaterally raise the wages of labor, that supply and demand decide." Indeed, according to a report of the Berlin police, the opposition deputies Leonor Reichenheim, John Prince-Smith, and Julius Faucher wanted to urge the factory owners of the kingdom to blacklist striking workers. For liberalism saw the only ultimate solution of the labor problem in the moral perfectibility of mankind. "The social question," maintained Schulze-Delitzsch, "which is more to us than merely a question of the belly, which involves the possibility of a full development and participation in life, coincides with the cultural question. Only through the rising level of civilization, through the constant progress of humanity in education and morality by which it struggles upward from imperfect to ever more perfect conditions do we gradually approach its solution." The improvement of society depended ultimately on the improvement of the individual.[22]

The emphasis on self-perfection as the goal of civic experience made it difficult for liberalism to accept the attempt to better the lot of the proletariat by political action. An independent labor movement was bound to aggravate class differences and to exalt material gain at the expense of moral value. It would militate against the ethical calling of mankind, just as the strike move-

[22] Robert von Mohl, *Staatsrecht, Völkerrecht und Politik* (3 vols., Graz, 1962), III, 571-572; *Allgemeine deutsche Arbeiter-Zeitung*, July 23, 1865; Prussia, *Verhandlungen des Landtages: Haus der Abgeordneten* (1865), I, 158; Rolf Weber, *Kleinbürgerliche Demokraten in der deutschen Einheitsbewegung, 1863-1866* (Berlin, 1962), p. 185; H. Schulze-Delitzsch, *Schriften und Reden*, IV, 666.

ment challenged the logic of the laws of economics. A division between bourgeois and workingman, moreover, would be exploited by the forces of reaction to maintain the established order. Yet the social question could only be solved under a parliamentary form of government. Franz Ziegler saw in Lassalle's efforts to organize the lower classes nothing more than a pandering appeal to the ignorant and greedy mob:

> Our fatherland, all of Germany, and many other nations besides are struggling at this moment for the most sacred rights of man. The fight is far from being over; the entire earth watches it in suspense. Yet here come the workers and say: "What do we care about honor, freedom, self-government! The belly! Help us, O state! He who does not want to provide for our belly cannot become deputy! . . ." I believe in the ultimate victory of justice, even in relief for the socially oppressed. But I must give this up too, for even your workers are not defending ideality but their interests. . . . I see the belly of the bourgeois in a struggle with the belly of the worker, not a struggle of heart against heart, idea against idea.

The Berlin democrat Adolph Streckfuss, on the other hand, argued during the constitutional conflict that agitation by the proletariat for an improvement in its economic condition would be inopportune rather than unjustified. "The entire labor movement is precisely at this time a serious mistake." Resistance to unconstitutional authority should remain the first duty of the citizen. "All our efforts must be concentrated on this one point. All other questions, however important they may be, must be put aside until the present crisis has been overcome!" And Leopold Sonnemann, the progressive publisher of the *Neue Frankfurter Zeitung*, who at first believed that organizations of workingmen should avoid involvement in questions of politics, gradually came to feel "that the laboring class is not only fighting for its material interests, but that it also has a heart for the great questions which stir the fatherland, and that it has been summoned always to be in the fore-front whenever men must defend the freedom and might of the fatherland." Political action on the part of the proletariat was thus acceptable to some liberals, but only insofar as it coincided with their own efforts and objectives.[23]

What could then the worker do to overcome the poverty which was his lot under the existing order? Prince-Smith, always the unbending champion of laissez faire, had a simple answer: "In dealing with more general economic hardships, the conscientious economist thus has only the one old advice: 'Work and save!' " Victor Böhmert reminded the lower classes of employers who had kept their factories open in hard times "for the humanitarian purpose of not reducing their workers to hunger and misery," while the journal of the National-verein maintained that "the educated and well-to-do middle class . . . has freed the urban worker as far as it could from police pressure and guild coercion; it has to the full extent of its power removed from his path the obstacles to industrial independence, and has con-quered for him every civic right which he possesses to-day." The view of most German manufacturers and journalists, according to the philosopher Friedrich Albert Lange, was that the working class must always remain in a subordinate position. "Yet it can gradually improve its position somewhat, and every man can rise to be an entrepreneur if he has courage and intelligence."

But the ability of the proletariat to overcome privation was limited by governmental restriction and its own ignorance. Many liberals accordingly sought the solution of the social question in the economic emancipation and educational improvement of the lower classes. Once the

[23] F. Lassalle, *Briefe und Schriften*, v, 104, 162; *Volks-Zeitung*, October 22, 1862; *Verhandlungen des ersten Vereinstages der deutschen Arbeiter-vereine*, p. 27; *Flugblatt vom ständigen Ausschusse des Vereinstags deutscher Arbeitervereine*, August 13, 1865.

worker was permitted to employ his full energies for the satisfaction of his material needs, once he acquired the knowledge needed to survive in the rough-and-tumble of unrestrained competition, he would recognize the advantages of free enterprise. Gustav von Struve demanded nothing for the laborer except noninterference by the government: "I do not want any state help for the working class, which must always be accompanied by state tutelage. I only want the state to remove the restraints which it has artificially fashioned for the worker." The German People's Party, speaking for the radicals of the secondary states, demanded thoroughgoing reform of the system of popular education: "We must seek to achieve through legislation an improvement in the elementary school, the establishment of continuation schools, and free instruction in these schools." Freedom and learning were the answer to the riddle of "the modern sphinx of our time."

The self-improvement of the lower classes within a free economy, however, would have to be based on a program of cooperative self-help. Unrestrained competition between the small shopkeeper and the factory owner was obviously uneven competition, yet an invitation to the state to arbitrate between them must mean the end of free enterprise. The only way out of the dilemma acceptable to liberal orthodoxy was the voluntary association of those with limited resources to produce the capital necessary for survival in the economic struggle. Self-help was a golden mean between the stultifying corporative dogmas of conservatism and the unnatural egalitarianism of the socialists. Not only that; it could be instrumental in the moral regeneration of the masses. "Self-help and self-responsibility," preached Gustav Schmoller in the *Preussische Jahrbücher*, "are thus the only remedy for our time, provided that we thereby express the principle that only such changes are of enduring benefit which transform the inner self, the thoughts and the wishes of the working class." Max Wirth, moreover, was convinced that a rugged self-reliance was native to the German character: "Nothing demonstrates more clearly that the Teutons and no other race are the bearers of the new epoch of culture than a comparison of the economic movement of Germany with the socialistic endeavors of France. . . . We must point out the one great difference, namely, that the French socialists also want to place the private economy under the tutelage of the state, so that the establishment of their system would have further increased the despotism of centralization, while social endeavors in Germany build their projects on the foundation of self-help and self-responsibility, the two pillars of German nationality."[24]

The training of the proletariat for survival under free competition became the primary objective of the labor organizations over which liberalism exerted an influence. The most important of these were the workingmen's educational societies, some formed by mill hands and handicraft artisans, but most of them established on the initiative of middle-class reformers. In September 1865, after they had been united in the Assembly of German Workingmen's Societies, the executive committee reported that, of the 2,100 marks received in voluntary contributions during the fiscal year, some 1,500 had come from the Nationalverein and another 500 from the Nürnberg industrialist Theodor von Cramer-Klett. The number of workers' associations receiving communications from the assembly had totaled 186 with about 41,000 members, although only 106 with 23,600 members had actually returned the questionnaires sent to

[24] Max Wirth, *Die deutsche Nationaleinheit in ihrer volkswirthschaftlichen, geistigen und politischen Entwickelung an der Hand der Geschichte beleuchtet* (Frankfurt am Main, 1859), p. 454. Cf. J. Prince-Smith, "Arbeiterfrage," p. 193; C. V. Boehmert, *Briefe zweier Handwerker*, p. 27; "Die Fortschrittsparthei und der Socialismus," p. 6; Fr. A. Lange, *Die Arbeiterfrage in ihrer Bedeutung für Gegenwart und Zukunft* (Duisburg, 1865), p. 137; G. Struve, *Diesseits und jenseits*, I, 124; *Europäischer Geschichtskalender*, ed. H. Schulthess (1868), p. 170; Gustav Schmoller, "Die Arbeiterfrage," *Preussische Jahrbücher*, XIV (1864), 421.

them. In the course of the next three years the affiliated organizations declined to 99 and the membership to 13,000. As for the purpose of the workingmen's educational societies, it was defined in the resolution adopted by a nearly unanimous vote at the initial meeting of the assembly in June 1863. The primary duty of labor was "to pursue the spiritual, political, civic, and economic improvement of the working class in harmony with itself, in harmony with all who strive for the freedom and greatness of the German fatherland, and in harmony and cooperation with all who work for the uplift of mankind."

This purpose could be achieved first of all through the moral and intellectual instruction of the lower classes. The Assembly of German Workingmen's Societies urged its members "to broaden their knowledge in spiritual, business, and economic questions, and to cultivate and fortify their moral and civic character." They should "(1) provide an opportunity for additional school training by appointing an instructional staff and arranging lessons; (2) keep workers from harmful company and inspire in them a sense for a higher way of life through social gatherings, to the extent that local conditions and material means make it possible; (3) employ all means to achieve a higher moral standing in civic society through the moderate leadership and conduct of the labor organizations." The subjects of instruction by which the ignorant laborer would be transformed into an educated and intelligent citizen included "German language, arithmetic, drawing, bookkeeping, singing, and gymnastics, where no suitable gymnastic society exists. French and English may be recommended." It was also important to provide lectures on history, especially of Germany, on geography, and on jurisprudence. And if circumstances allowed, the worker should be initiated into economics, the natural sciences, hygiene, pedagogy, and stenography.

174

The progress of the proletariat was also to be encouraged by the liberation of its economic capacities, since "a lasting improvement in the position of the workers is inconceivable without the general introduction of industrial freedom and freedom of movement." The establishment of old-age and disability insurance would afford a measure of security for the laboring classes. "A reduction in the workday is urgently needed in the interest of the workingmen as well as of the employers." Finally, the formation of savings, credit, consumer, and warehouse cooperatives was sure to prove "one of the best means for advancing the material welfare and the civic independence of the workers." The program of the Assembly of German Workmen's Societies thus sought to solve the social question in harmony with the liberal imperatives of self-improvement and self-help.[25]

The first meeting of the assembly concluded with a cheer for "the father of the German labor movement," Hermann Schulze-Delitzsch. For he more than any other liberal leader had dedicated himself to the civic and material improvement of the lower classes under a parliamentary system of government. Where most bourgeois politicians muttered darkly about the dangers of mob rule, he came out unequivocally against all privilege based on social or economic status. Not even the specter of equal manhood suffrage frightened him. In a series of lectures before an audience of Berlin workingmen, he outlined a bold program of reform designed to achieve the emancipation of the proletariat within the existing order of society:

> We demand first of all, as we have already said, equality before the law. No individual, no social class should be

[25] R. Weber, *Kleinbürgerliche Demokraten*, p. 25; *Verhandlungen des ersten Vereinstages der deutschen Arbeitervereine*, pp. 5, 12-13, 17, 21-25; *Verhandlungen des zweiten Vereinstags deutscher Arbeitervereine*, pp. 7-8, 21-22; *Jahresbericht für den dritten Vereinstag der deutschen Arbeitervereine*, pp. 4-6, 14; Erich Eyck, *Der Vereinstag deutscher Arbeitervereine, 1863-1868: Ein Beitrag zur Entstehungsgeschichte der deutschen Arbeiterbewegung* (Berlin, 1904), p. 88.

favored above another, should be endowed with rights and privileges which make it more difficult for the others, especially for the less-well-to-do, to work their way up, to get ahead. Such rights and privileges exclude the gifted and intelligent from the position which is their due, and put rank, birth, and fortuitous wealth in the place of talent and merit. This is the first demand, and here we can properly advance the general and equal franchise as a consequence of this demand. Then, gentlemen, we demand in addition as equal, just, and unoppressive an assessment of state taxes as possible. . . . We also include as a chief demand the improvement of the public school, the most important institution for the education of the worker, without which the lasting amelioration of the laboring class itself can never be successfully achieved.

Schulze-Delitzsch believed, however, that in the end the alleviation of destitution depended on economic rather than political improvement. State intervention must mean state tutelage, and the tyranny of government could be as stultifying as the tyranny of caste or hierarchy. An effective program to raise the standard of living, he maintained, should be based on the principle of voluntary self-help. The Revolution of 1848 had stimulated his concern for the welfare of the lower classes, and soon thereafter he began to organize cooperative societies which were to provide the small shopkeeper and skilled artisan with the financial means to withstand the competitive pressure of big business. Credit unions proved the most successful of the enterprises he helped establish, but before long he was also engaged in the formation of cooperatives for the purchase of raw materials, the maintenance of warehouses, the ownership of retail stores, and even the management and operation of workshops. In 1854 the number of societies submitting financial statements to him was only 4, but by 1859 it had risen to 80, by 1864 to 455, and as of 1869 it stood at 735. The membership during those years climbed from 1,019 to 18,676, 135,013, and 304,772, while the volume of credit advanced to borrowers increased from 163,152 marks to 12,394,308, 144,442,485, and 544,806,327 marks. Liberal publicists like August Lammers hailed these achievements as evidence that the solution of the social question lay in the collective activity of free men determined to defend their interests. "The German credit unions therefore no longer need to fear comparison in regard to economic significance as well as moral worth with the banking system which has in recent times developed so widely and splendidly. . . . The solid foundation on which the German credit unions rest becomes fully apparent with the results of each year."[26]

Yet Schulze-Delitzsch himself acknowledged that his program of cooperative self-help could do no more than palliate the economic inequalities arising out of class differences. He was incapable of conceiving a social system in which wealth and status did not predominate. The propertied and the propertyless were divided by an impassable gulf inherent in the human condition which no amount of good will could bridge. All that men might hope for was to maintain an uneasy equilibrium among opposing classes within an eternally static order of society. Manhood suffrage was a pro forma juridical right, a legal corollary of the abolition of serfdom and slavery. "Ever since free labor and earning a livelihood ceased to be considered factors excluding the worker from the higher human and civic aspirations, . . . the course of development necessarily had to lead in the direction of the general and equal franchise." The political emancipation of the masses, moreover, would have a prophylactic effect in maintaining civic tranquillity. "Only by granting complete equality of rights will you have the weapon with which to oppose effectively the socialistic leveling of the outward fortunes of life, which

[26] [A. Lammers], "Ein Blick auf die deutsche Genossenschaftsbewegung," *Preussische Jahrbücher,* VI (1860) , 416-417. Cf. *Verhandlungen des ersten Vereinstages der deutschen Arbeitervereine,* p. 37; H. Schulze-Delitzsch, *Schriften und Reden,* I, 170, II, 111-112.

nature did not want and which will never be realized."
But there was no possibility that the enfranchisement of
the masses would lead to an egalitarian transformation
of society. Schulze-Delitzsch remained convinced "that
great social interests like an important social position
will automatically prevail, and that the general suffrage
without property requirement is perhaps the most suitable means to establish these interests, to the extent that
they are justified. The man who occupies an important
position, who stands at the head of an important industrial establishment, the man who by his intelligence
surpasses a great part of his fellow citizens, the proprietor of a large estate, . . . you will not deprive him of
his altogether justifiable influence over many of his fellow citizens, whatever system of voting you establish.
Those are powers in life which assert themselves of their
own accord."

The principle of self-help on which the cooperative
movement was founded could not lead to the social
emancipation of the lower classes either. "Instead of
complaining about the encroachments of the factory
and of commerce and about the predominance of capital," exhorted Schulze-Delitzsch, "you yourselves should
rather master the advantages of factory and mercantile
operation, and make capital your servant." It may have
been sound advice for the independent shopkeepers and
master craftsmen of small provincial towns like that in
which he had grown up. For the propertyless proletariat,
however, for the workingman who had no resources except his own two hands, it was a will-o'-the-wisp. The
figures for participation in the cooperative movement
reveal that it was helpful to the little businessman and
would-be entrepreneur rather than the factory hand or
artisan journeyman. At the time of the Seven Weeks'
War the credit unions, whose chief function was to extend loans to small-scale manufacturers and merchants,
had a sizable membership of 193,712 but those societies
which were supposed to assist primarily the laboring

masses lagged far behind. There were 14,083 persons in consumer cooperatives, 572 in organizations for the purchase of raw materials, 150 in warehouse associations, and 27 in producer cooperatives.

Even some of the established handicraftsmen and storekeepers found it difficult to borrow funds at interest and commission rates ranging from at least 6 per cent in Magdeburg and Norden to more than 13 per cent in Königsberg. Gustav Schmoller, analyzing the decline of the artisan class, estimated that "half to two-thirds of the people in the credit unions are not entered in the list of handicraftsmen. There are even many small merchants, smaller and bigger factory owners, men of private means, and other persons who are participants, and among the handicraftsmen themselves not everyone who is a member of a credit union is thereby necessarily helped." The conservative *Historisch-politische Blätter für das katholische Deutschland* gibed that "the most favorable result of the Schulze-Delitzsch societies can be nothing other than the elevation of a handful of half and three-quarters bourgeois to full bourgeois." The remark was not altogether unjust.[27]

For at no time during the period of national unification did liberalism really come to grips with the social question. While still struggling to achieve power by the overthrow of the conservative agrarian aristocracy, it suddenly found itself confronted with the emergence of the fourth estate as a force in society. It lacked the security and confidence to evolve a program of reform capable of winning the support of the lower classes. All it had to fall back on were the ideals of individual freedom and collective self-help, ideals harmonizing with the experience of the bourgeoisie, but meaningless in

[27] H. Schulze-Delitzsch, *Schriften und Reden*, I, 56, IV, 415, 582, 632, V, 132; Ernst Friedrich Goldschmidt, *Die deutsche Handwerkerbewegung bis zum Sieg der Gewerbefreiheit* (Munich, 1916), pp. 100-101; G. Schmoller, *Geschichte der Kleingewerbe*, p. 666; [Edmund Jörg], "Zur Kritik von Lösungen der socialen Frage: Schulze-Delitzsch," *Historisch-politische Blätter für das katholische Deutschland*, LV (1865), 207-208.

the context of the proletarian struggle for economic improvement. The middle-class creed of laissez faire, understandable in view of the historic role of the state as protector of a hierarchical civic order, was incapable of inspiring the laboring masses, which feared that their own unaided efforts could never prevail against status and wealth. Despite the universality of its rhetoric, liberalism remained the ideology of a bourgeoisie eager to end the domination of a hereditary landed caste, but threatened in turn by demands for the social and political emancipation of the working class it had helped create.

FIVE

Conservatism and the Old Order

SHORTLY after the establishment of the German Empire the nationalist historian Heinrich von Treitschke published a caustic portrait of the typical landed aristocrat stubbornly refusing to accept the new order in politics and society:

> There he sits in his village, listens to the pastor declaim against the new paganism, and complains about the insubordinate hired hands and the annoying self-assertion of his peasants. He measures with the yardstick of his village experiences all the developments of a frightful time. As a peer of the realm he looks down disdainfully upon the youthful forces of modern world commerce, which he barely knows from hearsay. When he comes to the capital, he lives in good middle-class fashion in a furnished room, and yet fancies that he must "make his appearance" as a support of the crown. In the upper chamber of the legislature he is then immediately received into the circle of his cousins and compeers. So he enters into the spirit of obstinate partisan opinion and incorrigible arrogance.[1]

The portrait, like much of what Treitschke wrote, has wit, but it also displays his characteristic impatience with the complexities of motivation and conduct. It oversimplifies. The nobility of the lands beyond the Elbe was indeed provincial, observing the world from the narrow viewpoint of a country squire. But its claim to prerogative rested as much on its function in society as on hereditary status or historic right. The Junkers

---

[1] Heinrich von Treitschke, "Das Zweikammersystem und das Herrenhaus," *Preussische Jahrbücher*, XXXI (1873), 230.

were no ornamental court aristocracy. They became leaders in the improvement of agriculture, hard pressed at times by the competition of bourgeois landowners, but generally successful in applying new methods of management and technology to husbandry. Active participation in farming, moreover, helped maintain their domination over the masses of the countryside. And the growing demand for foodstuffs at home and abroad provided them with a profitable market for their produce. Despite the rise of industrialism, they thus continued to play a vital role in the economy of the nation. Furthermore, their hold on the bureaucracy had hardly diminished since the beginning of the century. The upper and middle levels of government administration, from the posts of cabinet minister and provincial governor to county commissioner and legation secretary, were filled with members of patrician families whose services to the state were generally of a high order. Gifted commoners, to be sure, could also climb the bureaucratic ladder to high executive positions. Yet custom combined with prejudice to give the nobleman an advantage which he often justified by the effective performance of duty. Finally, the tradition of leadership in the armed forces reinforced the claim of the aristocracy to a privileged position in society. The Prussian officer corps remained its preserve throughout the nineteenth century, especially in the higher ranks, although the preponderance of the Junkers began to diminish after the achievement of national unification. The nobility, in other words, was more than a landed caste exercising authority by virtue of an inherited prerogative. Its status derived to a large extent from the important function which it performed in the economy and administration of the state.

Conservatism was the dominant ideology of this nobility. Landowners and bureaucrats of patrician origin, Bredows, Alvenslebens, Bodelschwinghs, Itzenplitzes, Arnims, and Eulenburgs, led the right wing of the Prussian legislature. During the period of reaction they dominated parliamentary life so completely that the house elected in 1855 came to be popularly known as "the chamber of county commissioners." When the tide turned a few years later, the decimated conservative faction still consisted largely of aristocratic landed proprietors and civil servants. For most legitimist politicians continued to maintain close contacts with agriculture or state administration. They saw in politics an avocation rather than a full-time career. Leopold von Gerlach and Edwin von Manteuffel served as generals in the army, Ernst Ludwig von Gerlach and Hans Hugo von Kleist-Retzow held positions in the bureaucracy, Alexander von Below-Hohendorf and Moritz von Blanckenburg led the life of gentlemen-farmers, and Prince Adolf von Hohenlohe-Ingelfingen and Count Eduard von Bethusy-Huc moved in the exclusive circles of the grand aristocracy. The efforts of these amateur politicians, however, were supported by an important group of middle-class publicists who enlisted their talents in the service of conservatism. A Junker who had been rusticating for years on his estate in some remote corner of Brandenburg or Pomerania was bound to feel out of place in the world of party politics. He had of necessity to rely on the help of such men as the journalist Hermann Wagener, the philosopher Friedrich Julius Stahl, the sociologist Wilhelm Heinrich Riehl, the historian Heinrich Leo, and the economist Johann Carl Glaser. The nobility like the bourgeoisie, that is to say, recruited its spokesmen from intellectuals of plebeian background who sought psychological as well as material fulfillment in an identification with one of the great class interests of society.

The period of national unification was a time of trial for the conservatives. Believing that the ultimate justification of political and social interests was a right established by tradition, they saw about them the disintegration of a historic order based on prescription. It was their misfortune to live in an age when inherited certi-

183

tudes and pieties seemed to crumble all at once. In international affairs the community of legitimate monarchical interests embodied in the Holy Alliance was being sacrificed for the stratagems of an amoral *Realpolitik*. The result, they feared, would be a diminution in the authority of every throne. "All European alliances are broken," despaired Edwin von Manteuffel. "The system on which the European balance rested has been violently shaken or has, properly speaking, already collapsed. Revolutionary tendencies have gained power in all states. The movements against the old Europe and the old dynasties which began with the year 1789 find support in a great part of mankind. . . . These crises must lead to a great European war or to socialist revolutions which will overthrow the present dynasties." The only hope for a restoration of stability founded on justice in international relations lay in a return to the principle of dynastic legitimacy embodied in the Holy Alliance.

Liberalism, the eternal subverter of the established order, according to the traditionalists, misrepresented the objectives of this solemn covenant concluded by the crowned heads of Europe. It spread the lie that legitimate rulers whose authority derived from the divine will had formed a conspiracy against the rights and liberties of their subjects. Nothing could be farther from the truth, Leopold von Gerlach insisted:

> The kings of the earth perceived the nearness of the Lord; they realized that the old system of politics no longer sufficed; they concluded the Holy Alliance. What nonsense has been uttered about this truly magnificent document. It is supposed to be an association of princes against peoples, designed to take away and diminish their freedom; it is supposed to be a trick by Russia to carry out her plans against Turkey and Asia. But it contains nothing of all this. The princes declare that they derive their power from God, and that they want to rule in

accordance with God's commandments. It was precisely this, however, which the revolutionaries did not like. There should no longer be any authority instituted by God. Men wanted to establish it by themselves, to control it by themselves, and so forth. The subjects wanted to be rulers, and the rulers should become subjects. . . . You cannot and must not disavow the principles of the Holy Alliance. They are nothing other than that authority comes from God, and that the princes must accordingly govern as agents commissioned by God.

The conservatives saw the great threat to traditional monarchical institutions in the Caesarian regime of Napoleon III founded on the false doctrine of popular sovereignty. "It must be said to the credit of our party," Leopold von Gerlach boasted, "that it has always held fast to the basic truths: 1. The Holy Alliance against the revolution; 2. Identity of Bonaparte with the revolution." The French emperor, "a stinking *aventurier*," symbolized the triumph of opportunism over principle. Not only had he usurped the authority which belonged to the legitimate dynasty of his nation, but he sought to justify this usurpation by invoking the will of the people. In dealing with foreign states he displayed the same indifference to established rights as in governing his own country. For political like personal morality was all of a piece; a violation of any part inevitably weakened the entire fabric. Bonapartism as a system of government was by its very nature a danger to every authority derived from historically validated tradition. It was "the revolution incarnate." Gerlach, to whom all political questions were ultimately moral questions, urged Bismarck to resist the force of evil in public life: "Just hold fast to the belief that Bonaparte is our only important adversary. Everything else is secondary. . . . Believe me, Bonapartism is the archenemy of Christianity, and that will become even more apparent this time than during its first appearance." He could not conceive of a reason of state transcending the commandments of the Decalogue.[2]

The abominable doctrines of Bonapartism were already spreading beyond the borders of France to the Italian Peninsula, where the establishment of a united nation was being achieved at the expense of legitimate dynasties. To the liberals of Central Europe the formation of the Kingdom of Italy represented a triumph of the popular will over princely despotism, but to the conservatives it was an act of iniquity. They saw in Victor Emmanuel II the "robber king," while Cavour was "in his principles a minister of the Confederation of the Rhine like Montgelas, for example." Ernst Ludwig von Gerlach insisted that "I would rather be doorkeeper for a democratic minister than dirty my hands by an alliance with Cavourian politics." The conservative Prussian People's Association bitterly opposed diplomatic recognition of the Italian state. "This kingdom was created . . . by a land-hungry conqueror with the help of a robber chieftain and his barricade heroes, with treason, falsehood, deceit, revolution, and insurrection. . . . Italy is now the most wretched country in the world. There no man is any longer sure of his life and property. There treason, robbery, murder, and perfidy rule everywhere." Even William I of Prussia, although grudgingly accepting the new regime south of the Alps, could not overcome a deep-seated instinctive hostility toward the usurper of established thrones. General Hans Lothar von Schweinitz noted in his memoirs that when in the fall of 1862 the crown prince set out on a tour of the Mediterranean, the old king expressed the hope that his son would not visit the Italian court: "He has not been able to avoid the recognition of Victor Emmanuel

[2] Rudolf Stadelmann, *Das Jahr 1865 und das Problem von Bismarcks deutscher Politik* (Munich and Berlin, 1933), p. 80; *Denkwürdigkeiten aus dem Leben Leopold von Gerlachs, Generals der Infanterie und General-Adjutanten König Friedrich Wilhelms IV.* (2 vols., Berlin, 1891-92), II, 650, 724; *Briefe des Generals Leopold von Gerlach an Otto von Bismarck*, ed. Horst Kohl (Stuttgart and Berlin, 1912), pp. 44, 167, 199, 230.

any longer, but to enter into a personal relationship with him is another matter."

The conservatives refused to make their peace with the Kingdom of Italy. To have done so would have meant to accept not only "the revolutionary act of violence and the general franchise as the new bases of the European law of nations, . . . but . . . also the continuation of the insurrection against the state of legality in Europe." Their hero was the youthful Francis II, last ruler of the Two Sicilies, whose brief reign was one unbroken succession of disasters. His hopeless resistance against the forces of revolution in his kingdom won him the respect of the defenders of the old order in the German Confederation. Prince Alfred Windischgrätz considered him the "only one who still plays a decent role in the world," while Prince Emil Sayn-Wittgenstein saw in him "the only fighter for honesty and loyalty, the last champion of the self-denying monarchical principle in Europe." A committee of prominent noblemen, among them Count Karl Goertz, Count Alfred Erbach-Fürstenau, and Count Eberhard Stolberg-Wernigerode, presented the deposed king with a silver shield as a token of its admiration.[3]

The hapless Bourbon himself felt certain that with his defeat the entire structure of political traditions and loyalties in Europe would begin to crumble. Writing to the king of Prussia from besieged Gaeta, he acknowledged that his military position was desperate. Yet he would not surrender. "A conviction more powerful than my interests sustains me here nevertheless. It is that I am defending on the ramparts of this fortress the law of

---

[3] *Ernst Ludwig von Gerlach: Aufzeichnungen aus seinem Leben und Wirken, 1795-1877,* ed. Jakob von Gerlach (2 vols., Schwerin, 1903), II, 279; *Briefe des Generals von Gerlach an Bismarck,* ed. H. Kohl, p. 230; Gustav Adolf Rein, *Die Revolution in der Politik Bismarcks* (Göttingen, 1957), p. 147, n. 52; L. Parisius, *Hoverbeck,* II/I, 83, n. 11; *Denkwürdigkeiten des Botschafters General v. Schweinitz* (2 vols., Berlin, 1927), I, 147; *Neue Preussische Zeitung,* April 4, 1862; Heinz Gollwitzer, *Die Standesherren: Die politische und gesellschaftliche Stellung der Mediatisierten, 1815-1918,* 2nd edn. (Göttingen, 1964), pp. 219-220.

nations, the dignity of sovereigns, the independence of peoples. And if the political considerations which today paralyze the arm of the conservative Great Powers of Europe cause me to fall without help, I am sure at least that the world will do justice to my efforts, and perhaps some day it will regret the destruction of this bulwark of legitimate monarchies." He was right, for Italian unification was only the initial stage of a historic process which ultimately overturned all the great thrones of the Continent. Almost sixty years later, during the November days of 1918, the widow of Francis II, a Bavarian princess, heard shooting in the streets of revolutionary Munich, and stray bullets struck her home. The old woman suddenly remembered the other great tragedy of her life. "That reminds me of Gaeta," she exclaimed. The principle of popular sovereignty which had triumphed in the creation of the Kingdom of Italy led logically to the downfall of the whole system of monarchical legitimacy in Europe.[4]

Alarmed by the revolutionary means employed in the achievement of Italian unification, the conservatives were all the more resolved to oppose the abolition of prescriptive rights in Central Europe. Their economic and social position, moreover, facilitated their acceptance of the German Confederation. Noble landowners, unlike bourgeois industrialists and bankers, suffered no material disadvantage from the existence of thirty-odd state boundaries. On the contrary, they enjoyed a privileged status in the army and bureaucracy which would be threatened by a centralized parliamentary regime. It was thus natural that rural aristocrats should defend the status quo, although many of them were ready to concede that moderate change within the framework of established class relationships was desirable. To oppose all reform, argued Baron Ernst von Dörnberg in a mem-

---

[4] *Die auswärtige Politik Preussens, 1858-1871* (10 vols., Oldenburg and Berlin, 1932-45), II/II, 196, n. 1; Kurd von Schlözer, *Petersburger Briefe, 1857-1862*, ed. Leopold von Schlözer (Stuttgart, Berlin, and Leipzig, 1923), p. 195, n. 2.

orandum which he submitted to Francis Joseph of Austria, would allow the national movement to fall under the domination of the forces of revolution:

> Germany urgently needs a greater centralization of her national energies and a fresh animation of the national spirit as well as a heartfelt sympathy between people and governments so that she will not always seem to be threatened in her most important interests and even in her existence. If therefore under these circumstances legitimate authority does not remain at the head of the reform movement which the general clear recognition of threatening danger has inspired in the entire German people from one boundary of Germany to the other, if legitimate authority does not gain control of the leadership of this movement in order to direct it toward a goal consistent with the interests of legitimacy and of the conservative principle, then either a revolution will become unavoidable in Germany or, in the event that foreign intervention should anticipate this development, the dissolution of the national bond is almost certainly to be feared.[5]

It followed that the established order should properly undertake the task of national reform. The fulfillment of this task, however, presupposed the continuing collaboration between Austria and Prussia in which the conservatives saw the basis of civic stability in Central Europe. Not only the Austrians, who occupied the leading position in the German Confederation, but the Prussian legitimists as well favored the maintenance of the dualistic political system established at the Congress of Vienna. Hermann Wagener, before he became an apologist for the Bismarckian policy of blood and iron, argued in the legislature in Berlin during the early 1860's that a German federal state with a Prussian head must be "harmful and repugnant to the true interests

---

[5] *Quellen zur deutschen Politik Österreichs, 1859-1866*, ed. Heinrich von Srbik (5 vols., Oldenburg and Berlin, 1934-38), III, 135.

of Germany." National unity could be achieved only by "agreement and unity with and through the princes. . . . An Austrian Empire which has endured for many centuries is . . . deeply rooted in Germany and in the sympathies and interests of the German people." The great Leopold Ranke, although believing that the tradition of Protestantism and a military devotion to duty formed the historic principle of the Hohenzollern kingdom, asserted that its interaction with the Catholic Habsburg monarchy "is a basic element of German life and, properly understood, strengthens both states." The conservative publicist Philipp von Nathusius urged the nation to hold fast to the conviction that the true unity of Germany lay in harmony between Austria and Prussia. Their dissension would lead to the intervention of foreign states and the devastation of Central Europe. But the most eloquent defense of the Austro-Prussian dualism came from Ernst Ludwig von Gerlach, whose article "War and Federal Reform" appeared in the *Neue Preussische Zeitung* only a month before the outbreak of the Seven Weeks' War:

> The justified mission of Prussia to develop her power in Germany is opposed by the equally justified mission of Austria to maintain her power in Germany. This dualism is the vital fundamental characteristic and the real basis of the constitution of Germany. It has matured and gained strength more and more during the last three hundred years, and after the glorious liberation of Germany in 1815 it was sealed by solemn treaties. It has given Germany fifty years of peace, of flourishing prosperity, and, as almost never before, of freedom from foreign intervention. Germany is no longer Germany if Prussia is absent or if Austria is absent. . . . The German Confederation has great defects, but I do not destroy my family or my fatherland because they have defects.[6]

[6] *Neue Preussische Zeitung*, May 8, 1866. Cf. Prussia, *Verhandlungen des Landtages: Haus der Abgeordneten* (1861), I, 307-308; Leopold von Ranke, *Neue Briefe*, ed. Bernhard Hoeft and Hans Herzfeld (Hamburg, 1949), p. 345; *Volksblatt für Stadt und Land*, September 30, 1863; H. Rosenberg, *Die nationalpolitische Publizistik*, II, 676-677.

The conservatives could subordinate state interests to a universal moral order because their political loyalties were traditional rather than national in character. They rejected as impious the doctrine that territorial boundaries should express ethnic or cultural divisions regardless of historically established rights. "The principle of nationality . . . is not justified . . . ," maintained Wagener, "but is lawless, unrighteous, and unchristian, seeking to dissolve and disintegrate the Christian community of peoples, and simply to lead the peoples back to the natural pagan basis of blood and descent. . . . We have . . . no right to tear a province away from another state because its inhabitants speak the same language we do and are of the same descent as we are." Ranke opposed intervention in Schleswig-Holstein in behalf of the German population: "By recognizing and defending the principle of nationality there, we are opening the doors wide for it in Posen, for example." General Eduard von Treitschke, a legitimist of the old school, was dismayed by his son's advocacy of Prussian annexation of the duchies. "Heinrich has become a Jesuit," he grumbled. "For him the end, which in my opinion is most reprehensible and pernicious, justifies the means."

Even Leopold von Gerlach, the confidant of Frederick William IV of Prussia, condemned the "vice of patriotism" in the name of a civic morality which embraced all mankind: "Why do I detest patriotism, 'the dearly beloved fatherland,' and things of that sort? Partly because of the hypocrisy and emptiness, but there is also something wrong with them. Loyalty to the king and love for our fellow man, which can just as well be extended to Russians, Englishmen, and Frenchmen, are quite enough." And his brother Ernst Ludwig invoked Saint Luke to prove the superiority of religious over national piety: "If any man hate not his father (hence also his fatherland), he cannot be my disciple." He warned a sinful world against "the abominable heresy that God's holy commandments do not also apply to the areas of politics, diplomacy, and war,

191

and that these areas have no higher law than patriotic egoism. *Justitia fundamentum regnorum.*" To the conservatives the teachings of Christianity offered the same unchanging answer for all problems of human experience.[7]

The false doctrines which were threatening the legitimate order in international affairs were also undermining established authority in domestic politics. Originating in the French Revolution, a period of moral chaos, they endangered the foundations of society by preaching a godless individualism. Hermann Wagener felt certain regarding the destructive consequence of unrestrained freedom:

> It should not surprise us that in Prussia as in France the same causes had the same effects; that with the postulation of the virtuous, rational citizen, state and church lost their justification as well as their purpose; that with the establishment of the individual as the sole authorized being and of egoism as the moving principle, the atomization and disintegration of society began; that with the absolute mobility of property, its perpetual duties began to seem intolerable burdens, fell into general disfavor, and were sacrificed to the sword of vengeance of the fanatical innovators; that with the unrestricted quest of gain, a war of all against all broke out, a desperate and destructive struggle which can end everywhere only in the complete social and political subjugation of the less powerful, in the modern masterless slavery. . . . But what is the might of evil? It is the mighty lie, the unconquered doctrine, the doctrine, born of the womb of the French people and in the pangs of the first revolution, which is circulating through Europe. It is the doctrine which, denying both the grace and the provi-

---

[7] *Neue Preussische Zeitung,* May 20, 1864, May 8, 1866; *Aus dem Leben Bernhardis,* IV, 91; *Heinrich von Treitschkes Briefe,* ed. Max Cornicelius, 2nd edn. (3 vols., Leipzig, 1913-20), II, 399, n. 1; *Ernst Ludwig von Gerlach: Aufzeichnungen,* ed. J. v. Gerlach, II, 297, 310; *Denkwürdigkeiten aus dem Leben Leopold von Gerlachs,* II, 240-241.

dence of God, trampled on history and justice, and tried to build state and society on the virtue of sinful man.[8]

Liberalism was the embodiment of that overweening pride which was prepared to destroy the vital fabric of society to make it conform to some doctrinaire ideal of constitutional perfection. It strove to impose on the nation alien political theories and institutions unsuited to the historical milieu of Central Europe. "With French rights of man and American forms of state you may indeed satisfy German newspapers, but not German nationality," contended Friedrich Julius Stahl. Representative government was by its nature weak, since it was forced to rely on ephemeral parliamentary coalitions reflecting the endless shifts of public opinion. An article in the *Jahrbücher für Gesellschafts- und Staatswissenschaften* concluded that "the final result of constitutionalism is the terrorism of majorities, not civic freedom." True liberty could not survive amid the rough-and-tumble of party politics, explained the *Berliner Revue*, because "public opinion is eternally inconstant, and the interests of the 'educated' are eternally fluctuating. Whoever wanted to follow these shifts in the government of the state would within a few years destroy the state and the freedom of the people. The history of the government of Louis Philippe provides instruction enough for the man who wants to be instructed."

The ultimate weakness of the parliamentary system, according to the conservatives, was the inability of the industrialists and bankers whose interests it represented to conceive of a political authority with higher ideals and powers than a business enterprise. "As far as capitalism is concerned, the state is a large industrial establishment, a sort of joint-stock association calculated to produce the highest net profit possible," Johann Carl Glaser expounded. "The state officials are the managers, and the head of state is the president of the firm, whether he

[8] Hermann Wagener, *Die kleine aber mächtige Partei* (Berlin, 1885), pp. 6-8.

directs it in a republic simply as the agent of the stock-holders, or in a monarchy as the principal of the business, on the analogy of a limited-liability company. In any case, he is responsible to the stockholders for his management of the business, or he must provide a security in the form of responsible ministers."[9]

The conservatives acknowledged that the moneyed interests, which generally supported a moderate constitutionalism, sought nothing more drastic than a prudent reform of the established order. But they saw the danger that a middle-of-the-road regime might prove the Trojan horse by which the democrats could eventually overthrow the existing political and social system. The acrimonious "Prussian Letters" which appeared in the *Berliner Revue*, while perceiving the difference between right-wing and left-wing liberalism, maintained that the latter would inevitably use the former for its own ends:

> Democracy, through liberalism and in association with it, wants to destroy the old Prussian army and the last remnants of the old Prussian system of society in which the corporative spirit of the handicrafts still plays an important role. On both of these points liberalism has only vague ideas about possible partial changes and reforms. Democracy wants an actual so-called people's army which is responsible to the people and commands itself, as it were, but which in any case protects the "liberties of the people" against attacks from above. Democracy, furthermore, wants a revolution in society, in property as well as personal relationships, a revolution which in any case can only be brought about by raising to the highest degree the tension between the

[9] Johann Carl Glaser, "Die Arbeiterfrage und die Parteien," *Jahrbücher für Gesellschafts- und Staatswissenschaften*, v (1866), 114. Cf. Hans von Arnim, "Friedrich Julius Stahl," in *Deutscher Aufstieg: Bilder aus der Vergangenheit und Gegenwart der rechtsstehenden Parteien*, ed. Hans v. Arnim and George v. Below (Berlin, 1925), p. 61; "Parlamentsgedanken eines Politikers a. D.," *Jahrbücher für Gesellschafts- und Staatswissenschaften*, v (1866), 484. "Das Haus der Abgeordneten," *Berliner Revue*, xx (1860), 436.

few great property owners and the millions of the propertyless, and by bringing about a breach, the outcome of which will then be a leveling of social differences carried out by the state. Liberalism, on the other hand, shrinks back from these two goals of democracy. It only wants an army which is not basically aristocratic, and a society in which capital rules, protected by a well-situated lawgiving minority chosen in elections with a property qualification for voting.

To the anonymous author a parliamentary system in any form was incompatible with the traditional order of society, since it justified and appeased the bourgeois hunger for power. To submit to it would mean the rule of mammon.[10]

The conservatives believed that the agitation for political and social change originated not with the proletariat but with the middle class, which employed the rhetoric of civic reform merely to advance its own interests. They therefore regarded bourgeois liberals with a contempt aggravated by fear. The prime minister of Prussia during the 1850's, Baron Otto von Manteuffel, spoke of his dislike for "the so-called educated class." Clemens Theodor Perthes, professor of law and political science at Bonn, ridiculed "the members of the legislature, the newspaper editors, and the clubbists," who waged war against royal authority in "dressing gown and slippers." Hermann Wagener insisted that "what threatens the monarchical principal is not the broad mass of the population, which is always monarchical out of need and instinct, but the oligarchs of moneyed capital as well as the 'Catilinarian creatures' whom they have on their leash, namely, men of letters and enlightened notables of bureaucratism favorable to change." But the most detailed description of the enemies of legitimate government appeared in an article of the *Berliner Revue* dealing with the Prussian legislature:

10 v. X., "Preussische Briefe," p. 417.

First of all, let us ask who formed and still forms that new bourgeoisie which stands apart from the mass of the people as a new nobility, so to speak. The answer is provided by the membership list of the lower house of the legislature, in France as well as in Italy, in Germany as well as in Prussia. In first place ahead of everyone else are those who have acquired a higher academic education by attending a secondary school and a university, but who have remained virtually strangers to the actual realities of life, in other words, men of that abstract education which is instructive about everything and nothing. In this category should be included the judicial officials, the administrative officials, to a considerable extent the clergy, the physicians, the scholars, the teachers at the higher levels, the lawyers, and similar people. In this bourgeoisie, furthermore, are generally to be classed all those who have acquired a modern scholarly education and whose spiritual sensitivity has been diminished to the extent that their intellect has been trained, in other words, the engineers, the higher technicians, the men of letters, especially the Reformed Jews of the press, and others of that sort. Finally, there are also the bigger merchants, manufacturers, artificers, managers, noble landowners who have given up the old traditions, and others of that sort. Naturally, not all members of the mentioned occupations belong to the new bourgeoisie. We only wanted to assert that its members are chiefly to be found here.[11]

The selfish yet impractical political views of the bourgeoisie reflected a barren formalism divorced from the living spirit of the nation. "Wherever it gains control of the government," the article continued, "it has nothing more urgent to do than make new constitutions and

[11] "Das Haus der Abgeordneten," p. 434. Cf. *Preussens auswärtige Politik*, ed. H. v. Poschinger, I, 141; *Denkwürdigkeiten aus dem Leben des Grafen von Roon*, II, 147; Wolfgang Saile, *Hermann Wagener und sein Verhältnis zu Bismarck: Ein Beitrag zur Geschichte des konservativen Sozialismus* (Tübingen, 1958), p. 142.

forge new laws. In this it is inexhaustible, as inexhaustible as in the countinghouses." Its objective is "absolute equality of men, that is, of the 'educated.' For 'uneducated people,' for the crown, for the aristocracy there is no room in its constitutions. Old rubbish which must be removed! The goal is a democratic republican constitution, but, mark it well, a representative constitution. For the bourgeoisie does not like to deal with the 'people' themselves. The small burghers, the handicraftsmen, the peasants, the workers are nothing but the raw material with which experiments are to be made." The very way of life of the middle class predisposed it to a narrow doctrinairism. "It creates new laws in order to destroy the organic associations of the people. But it does not go beyond this negative activity, indeed, it cannot do so in view of its essential character. It knows how to deal on the stock exchange, in money changing, in administration, in police work. It excels in literature; it has almost sole possession of the press. But it is incapable of conceiving positive ideas in politics. It therefore also provides the form of government which is most hateful to the people."[12]

The answer to middle-class liberalism, however, was not to be found in royal absolutism. The conservatives taught that the despotic rule of the crown could be as dangerous as the parliamentary system of the bourgeoisie. Each threatened to undermine those natural relations among classes of the community which had developed in the course of time. Big government, whether monarchical or republican, was inevitably bad government. Its symptoms were always the same: growth of centralization, expansion of bureaucratism, increase in police power, decline of local self-rule, and suppression of hereditary rights and obligations. The final result was bound to be the subversion of the true freedom of the people as defined not by a paper constitution, but by tradition and history. Ernst Ludwig von Gerlach could

[12] "Das Haus der Abgeordneten," pp. 434-435.

thus insist that "absolutism is also revolution," since it meant the destruction of the just balance of power in the state. His brother Leopold argued that only a corporative organization of society supported by a system of self-government "can establish freedom and oppose the absolutism of a Caesar and of a sovereign people." Indeed, Bismarck conjectured that the friend and mentor of Frederick William IV sang at vespers in his home the old church hymn:

> Verlasse Dich auf Fürsten nicht,
> Sie sind wie eine Wiege.
> Wer heute Hosiannah spricht,
> Ruft morgen crucifige.

Hermann Wagener agitated for the "limitation and restriction of the bureaucracy." An article in the *Berliner Revue* describing "Our Task" epitomized this traditionalist opposition to the concentration of governmental power: "Our hope is directed toward the introduction of self-government in all circles which are capable of it, and we seek to make more and more groups of the population capable of it."

What the conservatives wanted was a state in which the prerogatives of noblemen restrained the authority of the crown, and a hierarchical organization of society ensured the dominant position of the landed aristocracy. In short, they wanted a state governed in keeping with the motto of the Order of the Black Eagle, *suum cuique*, to each his own. The most explicit statement of their political objectives appeared in the program adopted by the Prussian People's Association at the time of its establishment on September 20, 1861:

I. Unity of our German fatherland, yet not in the fashion of the "Kingdom of Italy" with fire and sword, but through the union of its princes and peoples, and through adherence to authority and justice. No disavowal of our Prussian fatherland and its glorious history; no descent into the filth of a German republic; no spoliation of crowns and swindle about nationalities.

II. No break with the past in the internal affairs of our state; no destruction of the Christian foundation and of the historically proven principles of our constitution; no derangement of the center of gravity of our position in Europe by weakening the army; no parliamentary regime and no constitutional responsibility of the ministers; personal kingship by the grace of God and not by the grace of a constitution; church marriage, Christian school, Christian authority; no abetment of the demoralization which is steadily gaining ground and of the disregard for the divine and the human order.

III. Protection and respect for honest labor, for every form of property, right, and class; no favoritism and exclusive rule of moneyed capital; no abandonment of the handicrafts and landed property to the false teachings and usurious tricks of our times. Freedom through the participation of the subject in legislation, and through the autonomy and self-government of the corporations and communities; freedom through adherence to the order which protects us. No resort to bureaucratic absolutism and to social bondage as the result of an unrestrained and licentious anarchy; no resort to an imitation of the political and social practices which led France to Caesarism. Development of our constitution in the spirit of German freedom, in love and loyalty to king and fatherland.

Here were all the major themes of the conservative political ideology: maintenance of the established order in Central Europe, devotion to a particularistic state patriotism incompatible with the principle of nationality, affirmation of the Christian basis of civic institutions, rejection of the parliamentary system of government, local self-administration expressing a corporative or-

199

ganization of the community, and opposition to a bureaucratic, centralizing absolutism.[13]

In economics as in politics conservatism defended a traditional order against disruptive forces arising out of industrialization. It rejected the contention that the production and distribution of wealth should be governed by immutable laws founded on a basic human quest for advantage. In his pursuits of material gain man was subject to the same restraints imposed by religion and history which properly determined his conduct in civil affairs. Yet the individualistic doctrines threatening to overthrow legitimate political authority were also undermining established forms of employment in agriculture and industry. "Economic liberalism . . . ignores as a matter of principle the social and political factors in society," a conservative manifesto circulating among the members of the Prussian legislature maintained. "It wants to produce the largest volume of goods for the present moment, unconcerned about the stability of production, unconcerned whether the higher moral goods of humanity vanish as a result, indeed, unconcerned even whether productive human energy be prematurely worn out and destroyed. The effects of these doctrines could not be anything other than most pernicious." The advocates of laissez-faire economics were for the most part publicists and academics blind to the everyday realities of life. "They all basically hold the position which the social consequences of the first French revolution have prepared," explained an anonymous "H. K.," probably the journalist Hermann Keipp. "They are all basically animated by a more or less conscious aversion to historic right. And finally, the education of all these gentlemen rests basically on a strong and self-satisfied skepticism regarding the efficacy

[13] *Ernst Ludwig von Gerlach: Aufzeichnungen*, ed. J. v. Gerlach, II, 374; *Denkwürdigkeiten aus dem Leben Leopold von Gerlachs*, II, 660; O. v. Bismarck, *Werke*, XV, 37; "Ein Vortrag des Justizraths Wagener," *Berliner Revue*, XXIX (1862), 259; "Unsere Aufgabe," *ibid.*, XVI (1859), 382; *Europäischer Geschichtskalender*, ed. H. Schulthess (1861), pp. 44-45.

of any of the historic forces which still exist as half ruins in the life of modern society, and whose intrinsic validity has still received so little investigation."

The most vigorous attack on liberal economists and their teachings appeared in the "Aphorisms concerning the Labor Movement" which the *Berliner Revue* published: "The life of these prophets contradicts the laws of economics. They move outside the scope of those forces whose rules they establish. They are either civil servants who receive a salary from the state, although free economics will not hear of state help; or they are men of letters who have contracted a wealthy marriage, although strict economics will not hear of the acquisition of capital by marriage; or they are adventurers who have received a donation, although respectable economics abhors the word 'donation.'" These impractical doctrinaires had become the chief exponents of a new economic pseudo science. The theories which they preached sought "to raise economics to a divinity with its own infallible laws and its own sovereign motion, a divinity with whose sway no human hand can interfere unpunished, and from whose verdict no appeal is possible." Yet the substance of this divinity was commonplace. "If you look more closely, you find that it is really nothing but a few bales of cotton, a few hides, bristles, sugar loaves, sacks of grain, barrels of oil. But these prosaic things are concealed by obfuscation about supply and demand, about capital and labor, about product and commodity, until the crowd falls down in worship before the economic humbug, like the medieval visionary who in his contemplation of the antithesis between spirit and matter, between *voluntas exterior* and *voluntas interior*, forgot the actual human condition." The imperatives of laissez faire were only rationalizations for the exploitation of the poor by the rich. "And now they preach to us the obligations which we owe the divinity of economics. You must quietly allow yourself to be crushed when the mighty goddess steps on you.

You must not grumble when she causes you to go hungry, for you may be sure that you are starving according to the rules, in keeping with the law of supply and demand. Yes, when the iron foot of the divinity kicks you and thousands of others into the abyss of poverty, you must go submissively to your destruction. . . . There is only one power in heaven and on earth, and that is economics."[14]

The conservatives urged the nation to rise against the juggernaut of laissez faire. The program of liberal economic reform, they argued, was a stratagem by which big business hoped to ruin the independent tradesman. Industrial freedom was particularly dangerous, because it left the artisan masses defenseless against the machinations of capitalism. Established authority should therefore defend the traditionalist handicraftsman against industrialists and bankers, who generally favored a parliamentary form of government. A statement of legitimist principles submitted to the lawmakers in Berlin maintained that the task of conservatism was "to see to it that hereafter production is not raised to morbid heights which endanger the producers, as happened under unrestricted industrial freedom. The skilled artisan, tradesman, and manufacturer should rather receive guarantees for the security of his existence and occupation, to the extent that changed conditions of commerce permit it, or at least his existence and occupation should not be jeopardized by unrestrained and improper competition." For the *Berliner Revue* there was no doubt that in the struggle against free enterprise the small shop owner had justice on his side: "It is a question of competition between capital, which does the work through mass production and with the cheapest labor, and the certified and reliable master craftsmen, who offer a moral guarantee of their work, and who have besides assumed in the

---

[14] "Aphorismen zur Arbeiterbewegung," *Berliner Revue*, XXXVII (1864), 289-290. Cf. *Die deutschen Parteiprogramme*, ed. Felix Salomon (2 vols., Leipzig and Berlin, 1907), I, 34; H. K., "Der volkswirthschaftliche Congress zu Frankfurt a. M.," *Berliner Revue*, XIX (1859), 145.

interest of society the task of always training new workers for the job." The *Neue Preussische Zeitung* offered support to the artisan movement in its efforts to maintain corporative regulation of production: "May the handicraftsmen for their part not tire in the future of upholding and defending the old discipline and propriety. It is uncomfortable to swim against the current, but it is often very meritorious."

The conservatives, moreover, opposed freedom of movement as part and parcel of the system of free enterprise. They opposed it for the same reason that the liberals favored it, because it was essential for the growth of industrialism. Some of them, to be sure, were simply suspicious of innovation in general. For example, Leopold von Gerlach reported that his brother Ernst Ludwig "has frequently said that he does not know what is to become of the states under general freedom of religion, general freedom of trade, and the constantly growing ease of communication." But others were more sophisticated. An article in the *Berliner Revue* attacking the teachings of Schulze-Delitzsch insisted that freedom of movement condemned the laborer to the "life of an industrial nomad." Far from improving the economic situation of the proletariat, "it is only capable of cheating the worker out of what is often the only happiness in his life, the happiness derived from home and family." The publicist Moritz von Lavergne-Peguilhen contended in a similar vein that "unlimited freedom of movement has substantially furthered the centralization of industry. . . . It is not necessary that the workers always follow the movements of industry, which are often capricious, which are often occasioned by the change in residence of a few capitalists. Industry will not infrequently do well to go in search of the workers." An anonymous "S. S.," writing in the *Neue Preussische Zeitung* on "The Serious Harm to the Prussian People Caused by the Liberal Majorities," maintained furthermore that the influx of new residents was imposing a heavy burden on local government: "The new freedom of movement oppresses and taxes the respectable proprietors through the arrival of tramps who frequently move into individual communities in significant numbers. The building of new schools is one of the usual unavoidable consequences of this free access." In short, neither the honest worker nor the solid man of property but only the industrialist derived benefit from the mobility of population, which depressed wages and inflated profits.

No liberal demand aroused greater indignation among the conservatives than the agitation for repeal of the usury laws. In advocating continued control of interest rates, they combined an affirmation of the spiritual basis of economic life with a defense of the material interests of agriculture, the perpetual borrower. Denunciations of the grossness of moneylending and the cupidity of Jews were also used to embellish the argument for the regulation of credit. The petition which the Prussian People's Association composed for presentation to the upper house of the legislature breathed this antiliberal and anticapitalistic spirit of agrarian traditionalism:

> In the name of the Christian foundations of the state, in the name of the morals and of the concepts of justice of our people, in the interest of landed property, which nourishes and maintains the state, and finally, in the interest of all who still have not and do not want to fall under the sway of the speculating moneyed economy, the undersigned hope and ask that it may please the honorable house to protect our fatherland by its vote against this new pernicious gift of "progress"! Our religion as well as the Holy Scriptures brand usury as well as the usurer. The old Mosaic law itself forbade the Jews to take interest among themselves, because their lawgiver well knew that otherwise there would be no limit to interest for his people. Only in dealing with the foreigners was it allowed! Should Christian law hand over the Christian inhabitants of the land to speculating Jewry as if they were "foreigners"? . . . [Repeal of the usury

laws] will ruin the land not only morally, but materially as well. Landed property will lose its value, its profitability. It supports and nourishes the state. When the interest rate is reasonable, the industrious and honest proprietor can pay his interest and his taxes, and feed his family. When the interest rate is arbitrarily raised through speculation and avarice, his entire property becomes insecure. The farmer must raise the price of bread which the poor pay, the houseowner must raise his rents, only in order to satisfy the demands for interest on the part of his mortgagees. And despite all that, the final result will be foreclosure. But the upshot of the matter is that those who have already seized control of capital will now also seize control of all landed property, and that the former owners will then be nothing more than managers, and will work for money. Whoever asserts that good mortgages will always be available at a reasonable interest rate, and that the competition generated by the removal of restrictions on the interest rate will actually reduce it, does not know human nature and the tendency of our time. This tendency is characterized by a longing for riches, for a life of idle pleasure, for more luxury. And if those who possess money get the chance to raise their interest arbitrarily without having to turn a hand in the process, they will do it. For selfishness will always prevail over the love for our fellow man. That unfortunately is human nature.[15]

The conservative hostility to economic liberalism arose basically from the realization that a hierarchical social system dominated by the landed nobility could not survive under industrial capitalism. The advance

---

[15] Hugo Müller, *Der Preussische Volks-Verein* (Berlin, 1914), pp. 60, 123-124. Cf. *Parteiprogramme*, ed. F. Salomon, I, 36; [Moritz von Lavergne-Peguilhen], "Die Doctrin und das Gewerbe," *Berliner Revue*, I (1855), 273; *ibid.*, XVI (1859), 413; "Wir nehmen die Verantwortlichkeit, gebt uns die Freiheit!," *ibid.*, XXXIII (1863), 26; A. Hahn, *Die Berliner Revue*, pp. 35-36, 68; *Neue Preussische Zeitung*, April 24, 1868, April 7, 1870; *Denkwürdigkeiten aus dem Leben Leopold von Gerlachs*, II, 750.

of the factory system must in the long run undermine the status of an aristocratic caste which derived its wealth from farming. The circumstances of their society thus compelled the defenders of the old order to favor husbandry over manufacture, to extol the countryside at the expense of the city. The prejudices of the village squire merely reinforced the necessarily anticapitalistic ideology of an agrarian patriciate threatened by the growth of a business economy.

The arguments which the conservatives adduced in support of the rural interest were varied, but they all agreed that the security of the state depended on the well-being of agriculture. Ernst Ludwig von Gerlach complained that the liberal legislation of the reform era early in the century "had nothing more to say regarding landed property than that it produces rye and wheat, and that it feeds cattle. People had at that time completely forgotten about its political significance, and that justice and authority rest on landed property." Otto von Manteuffel contended that farming was the basis of the military strength of Prussia: "This capacity for self-defense is in our country dependent above all on the prosperity of agriculture, because in the event of war landed property has to endure by far the greatest sacrifices, and it must be able to bear them. It will thus be important on the one hand that we give support and direction to landed property and its organization, and on the other hand that we promote the business of landed property, namely agriculture, with every conceivable energy and strength." The *Berliner Revue* saw in husbandry the ultimate source of national wealth: "Only through the accumulated capital of the original inhabitants of the land, the farmers, does an indigenous industry become possible. People should never forget that. People who pride themselves on their ownership of capital should not consider it a chief task to encroach upon the rights of those who patiently struggle against the elements in order to gather the nourishing fruits from their plots of earth. People should not burden them more than others with the taxes imposed by the state. The stream stops flowing when the springs dry up." Whatever their reasoning, the conservatives were unanimous that agriculture had to be protected against the rapacity of the banker and industrialist.

More than that, capitalism was a threat to the form of society which had become rooted in the agrarian economy. It was a threat to the class differences defining a man's rights and obligations, since it preached a divisive individualism inconsistent with the corporative ideal. Under a liberal system of government the mutual regard between strong and weak, between rich and poor would be replaced by the tyranny of the cash nexus. To defend the hierarchical structure of society was thus of utmost importance. "The party of legitimacy wants the natural organization of the people," expounded Friedrich Julius Stahl. "It wants an organization in keeping with the natural foundations, needs, and purposes of society, in keeping with the powers which determine society, in other words, in keeping with property, occupation, and walk of life. This is in opposition to the aggregativeness of the revolution. It wants estates of the realm. . . . It wants corporative bodies, unifying associations of the estates of the realm, of the communities, counties, provinces. And it wants the autonomy (self-government) of these corporative bodies. . . . That is organization of society, while the reverse is leveling." The decline of an organic social system must mean the atomization of the community, the end of civic self-discipline, and the coming of a ruinous class war. The maintenance of historically confirmed corporative differentiations, on the other hand, would preserve the legitimate form of authority and distribution of property. Leopold von Gerlach contended that "revolution has power only where almost every organic body has disintegrated, that is, among arrogant, hungry men of letters and among atomized factory workers. As soon as revolution encounters an organic body, even if it is corroded and weak, an organic body like an estate of the realm or a corporative association, it is forced to retreat." The uncorrupted forces in national life should therefore be rallied against the bourgeois doctrine of individualism.[16] These uncorrupted forces could be found above all in the countryside. Here respect for the established order still prevailed, safe against the subversive doctrines flourishing in an urban environment. The conservatives idealized the village as the abode of those homely virtues which had made the nation great. "The poisonous drink of discontent and distrust which poisons peoples and drives kings to madness is mixed not there, but in the cities," maintained "v. X." in the *Berliner Revue*. For one thing, the nobility could exercise a salutary influence over the rural masses. It could perform its historic function, which according to Stahl consisted in serving as "the organic bond of the nation between fatherland and state, between past and present." But even without prodding from the great landowners, the peasantry was naturally favorable to established authority, for the countryman's way of life fostered loyalty to the familiar and enduring. Hermann Wagener assured Bismarck that "the masses always want a strong government, and the population of the countryside would basically prefer to have absolutism once more." And in his works of pseudo sociology Wilhelm Heinrich Riehl presented an analysis of the role of the peasant in society which was pure legitimist sentimentalism:

> There is an unconquerable conservative force within the German nation, a hard core which withstands all change, and that is our peasantry. It is truly a unique social class, and no other people can offer a counterpart to it. The

[16] Prussia, *Stenographische Berichte über die Verhandlungen der durch die Allerhöchste Verordnung von 13. November 1852 einberufenen Kammern: Zweite Kammer* (3 vols., Berlin, 1853), I, 192; *Unter Friedrich Wilhelm IV.: Denkwürdigkeiten des Ministerpräsidenten Otto Freiherrn v. Manteuffel*, ed. Heinrich v. Poschinger (3 vols., Berlin, 1901), III, 107; "Zur Arbeiterfrage" (Part 1), p. 399; Friedrich Julius Stahl, *Die gegenwärtigen Parteien in Staat und Kirche* (Berlin, 1863), pp. 310-11; *Denkwürdigkeiten aus dem Leben Leopold von Gerlachs*, I, 639.

conservatism of the man of education may be a matter of theoretical conviction, but the conservatism of the peasant is a way of life with him. In the social crises of our time the peasant has played a more important role than most people realize, for he has formed a natural barrier against the spread of the French doctrine of revolution among the lower classes of society. . . . In our fatherland the peasant has a political significance which he enjoys in no other country of Europe. The peasant is the future of the German nation. The inward refreshment and rejuvenation of the life of our people can come only from the peasant class.

While such conservative reflections on the mentality of the villager were illusive, the economic position and social status of the rural masses did tend to make them indifferent to the teachings of liberalism.

But even in the city there were forces ready to defend the old order. The conflict of interest between industrialist and artisan in particular could be exploited to the advantage of legitimism. "The elements of society which are still healthy and favorable to the monarchy, the elements whose sympathy is of vital importance, are the army, the rural population, and the great mass of the workers in the cities," Wagener maintained. "We can easily calculate what significance should be attached to the sympathies of these classes if we consider that they amount to almost 75 per cent of the entire population." The agriculturist and the tradesman, moreover, had a common enemy in industrial capitalism, which threatened the well-being of both. The *Berliner Revue* pointed out that "the handicrafts are oppressed and persecuted in the same way as the landed nobility, and indeed by the same forces. They are reproached for their defensive and distrustful attitude in the same way as the landed nobility. The scorn and anger of the men of progress in the liberal as well as the democratic camp are directed against the handicraftsmen in the same way as against the landed nobility." There was thus good reason to hope that "at the last hour a league of the aristocracy of the countryside with the preservative and corporative element of the city will come into existence. This league would be the mightiest bulwark of legitimacy in these times."[17]

Still, the price which conservatism was willing to pay for an alliance with the lower classes was modest. In their articles and lectures legitimist intellectuals discoursed at length about the attractions of tory democracy, but the landowners who formed the main support of the old order were rarely able to rise above the dictates of self-interest. They considered the rights of proprietorship no less sacred than did the industrialists. Behind demands for improvement in the position of the proletariat they were inclined to see the cloven hoof of egalitarianism. The gains which city workers wrung from the millowner might encourage insubordination among agricultural laborers and tenant farmers. Once the masses began to question the existing distribution of wealth, they were not likely to draw a distinction between urban and rural forms of ownership. An attack on any part of the system of property rights was a threat to all of society.

Many conservatives felt therefore that to advocate conciliation of the lower classes by extensive economic reform was to recommend a cure more dangerous than the disease. Any innovation which might alter the traditional relationship among social classes was unacceptable to them. Baron Maximilian von Handel, an Austrian diplomat of the old school, felt uneasy about the growing militancy of labor: "The workers' movements which are emerging everywhere seem dangerous to me." The egalitarian doctrines of socialism seemed still more dangerous. Leopold von Gerlach, who despised Napoleon III as an unprincipled careerist, conceded never-

[17] v. X., "Preussische Briefe," pp. 419, 497; Ferdinand Tönnies, "Deutscher Adel im neunzehnten Jahrhundert," *Neue Rundschau,* XXIII (1912), 1060; W. Saile, *Wagener und sein Verhältnis zu Bismarck,* p. 139; W. H. Riehl, *Die bürgerliche Gesellschaft,* p. 41.

theless that "if legitimism, authority from above, the Holy Alliance do not intervene, if they do not have the courage to crush radicalism, socialism, and communism, then Caesarism, which is what I . . . call Bonapartism, must do it." A few weeks before the Paris Commune, General Helmuth von Moltke was writing to his brother Adolph that "the great danger for all countries lies now probably in socialism." An anonymous publicist in the *Berliner Revue* came to the conclusion that even the theories of Schulze-Delitzsch, though false, were preferable to the radicalism of Lassalle: "Let us not delude ourselves; Lassalle is more dangerous than Schulze. With Schulze there is the possibility of limiting the war to two classes of society. Lassalle tears down every barrier. He declares war against all who are not workers." Men like these, haunted by the red specter of radicalism, hesitated to support the economic emancipation of the proletariat for the sake of problematical political advantages.[18]

Distrust of the lower classes led the conservatives to oppose equal manhood suffrage. To be sure, they were critical of the three-class system of voting in Prussia which divided the electorate into categories based on wealth, because it increasingly served the interests of the urban middle class. But they were equally opposed to a franchise assigning the same weight to the propertied and the propertyless. The Pomeranian Junker Adolf von Thadden-Trieglaff proclaimed that "I cannot recognize a basic principle according to which there is one elector for approximately 10,000 pounds of human flesh (including human bones) , and perhaps 40,000 hundredweight of these substances furnish a member of parliament." Baron Adolf Senfft von Pilsach, the ultraroyalist politician, emphasized the disparity between rich and poor: "I cannot consider it just and reasonable that a

---

[18] *Quellen zur deutschen Politik Österreichs*, ed. H. v. Srbik, III, 214; *Denkwürdigkeiten aus dem Leben Leopold von Gerlachs*, II, 510; Helmuth von Moltke, *Briefe, 1825-1891*, ed. Eberhard Kessel (Stuttgart, 1959) , p. 366; "Zur Arbeiterfrage" (Part 2) , *Berliner Revue*, XXXIII (1863) , 331.

simple workingman has as much voice as his employer who hires hundreds or thousands like him, gives them bread, and feeds their families. That employer and worker should be equal in this respect makes no sense. Furthermore, I cannot call it proper that people who first of all do not understand anything about legislation and secondly do not really want to vote at all are designated as voters. I find that to make such people voters is not just, not fair, not reasonable." The conservative bureaucrat Gustav von Diest, pointing out to Bismarck the shortcomings of manhood suffrage, quoted with approval Schiller's *Demetrius*:

> Was ist die Mehrheit? Mehrheit ist der Unsinn:
> Verstand ist stets bei wenigen nur gewesen.
> Bekümmert sich ums Ganze, wer nichts hat?
> Hat der Bettler eine Freiheit, eine Wahl?
> Er muss dem Mächtigen, der ihn bezahlt,
> Um Brot und Stiefel seine Stimm' verkaufen.
> Man soll die Stimmen wägen und nicht zählen;
> Der Staat muss untergeh'n früh oder spät.
> Wo Mehrheit siegt und Unverstand entscheidet.

These political traditionalists believed that the common run of humanity simply lacked the means and the education to exercise the franchise intelligently. Here they were in complete agreement with most of the bourgeois parliamentarians whom they so bitterly opposed.

The disagreement of the legitimists with liberalism lay rather in their advocacy of a system of voting based on occupational categories and corporative institutions. Popular elections might lead to mob rule, while a propertied franchise would soon establish the domination of the middle class. It was thus essential to devise a form of the suffrage which could safeguard existing social distinctions. Leopold von Gerlach favored a plan by which the countryside was sure to outvote the city while the well-to-do citizens exercised a restraining influence over the masses:

Under a new election law we should go back to estates of the realm. 1. Separation of town and country. 2. Separation in the town of freemen and nonfreemen. 3. Separation in the country into large estates where the owner does not manage the property himself, medium-sized farms, and small peasants and day laborers. The ratio of town and country is determined for each province in keeping with the ratio of the population. Freemen, large estate owners, and farmers vote directly; nonfreemen, day laborers, and small peasants vote for electors, not from their own number, but from wherever they want. These electors elect the members of parliament. The freemen elect two thirds of the urban members of parliament; the nonfreemen elect the other third. The electors receive positions in such things as poor relief, as tribunes of the people, etc. In the country the owners of noble estates elect half, farmers a fourth, small peasants a fourth.

While most conservatives were less specific, they all feared that an unrestricted franchise would prove incompatible with stable government. Even Hermann Wagener, the tireless proponent of an alliance with the working class, argued that "the general suffrage must be introduced, since the moneybag cannot outweigh the obligation of each citizen to risk his life for his country. Yet it should not be done in the way which democracy wants, but through a popular representation based on estates of the realm." In the final analysis the political enfranchisement of the masses was no more acceptable to the aristocracy than to the bourgeoisie.[19]

What could then legitimism offer the lower classes of Central Europe? Nothing more than a common struggle

---

[19] Prussia, *Verhandlungen des zum 2. April 1848 zusammenberufenen Vereinigten Landtages,* ed. E. Bleich (Berlin, 1848), p. 99; Prussia, *Stenographische Berichte über die Verhandlungen der durch die Allerhöchste Verordnung vom 28. Juli 1866 einberufenen beiden Häuser des Landtages: Herrenhaus* (2 vols., Berlin, 1867), I, 105; O. v. Bismarck, *Werke,* VII, 216; *Denkwürdigkeiten aus dem Leben Leopold von Gerlachs,* I, 281; *Europäischer Geschichtskalender,* ed. H. Schulthess (1862), 182.

against the spread of industrialization. For the basic purpose of the conservatives was to preserve rather than reform the old order. They were willing to advocate an improvement in the position of the urban proletariat at the expense of big business, but for the peasantry they had little beyond pious platitudes. The *Neue Preussische Zeitung* lamented that "the peasant goes now to the Jew and scratches his name under a promissory note whose contents he does not even understand. He receives money for the moment, but after some time he often loses his house and land." Yet the only remedy it could suggest was resistance to economic liberalism. The idea of diminishing the latifundium in order to strengthen the small farm never occurred to it. Hans Hugo von Kleist-Retzow, the legitimist politician and bureaucrat, was alarmed by the growing impersonalization of class relationships in the countryside. "The old bonds of piety are dissolving more and more," he sighed. "Once the servant and the day laborer turn from God, they will know only the bounds imposed by fear of men and punishment, and they will therefore seek to exceed them through deceit." He urged the landowners to set Sunday aside as a day of rest and prayer for their farm hands. Ernst Ludwig von Gerlach preached that "property is sacred only in connection with the duties which rest on it. As merely a means of enjoyment, it is not sacred but sordid. Communism is right in attacking property without duties." But he contemplated no measures against those proprietors for whom their possessions were "merely a means of enjoyment." That was God's province.

Wealthy conservatives would occasionally offer more practical proof of their concern for the rural population. The Prussian Mortgage Credit and Banking Company, for example, was organized in 1862 as a joint-stock financial institution to advance loans to small landholders as well as to engage in standard banking operations. The chairman of the board of directors was the well-known

214

aristocrat Count Eberhard Stolberg-Wernigerode, although the prosaic details of management were left to the banker Hermann Henckel. The new enterprise, capitalized at 6,000,000 marks, was paying a respectable dividend of 6 per cent a year after its establishment. Ventures of this sort, however, could not provide a solution of the agrarian problem. Not only were they too small and too few, but they extended help to that element of the peasantry which required help least, the well-to-do independent farmer. They were irrelevant to the interests of the broad masses of the countryside, the seasonal laborers, hired hands, skilled workers, part-time farmers, share tenants, and market gardeners. This rural proletariat needed more than easy credit. It needed a revolution in property relationships reducing the power of the nobility, and that was something which legitimism by its nature could never contemplate. The peasant would have to content himself with the sense of security derived from the perpetuation in the village of an old and familiar way of life.[20]

The conservatives could afford greater boldness in dealing with the urban working class. Independent craftsmen organized in trade guilds occupied an important position in that hierarchical social system which legitimist theory considered the safeguard of monarchical authority. To champion their interests was thus ideologically consistent. The price for the support of the artisan masses, moreover, would have to be paid not by the landed nobility, but by bourgeois factory owners in the city. The hostility of the aristocracy toward industrial capitalism fostered its support for the handicrafts in their struggle against free enterprise. The *Berliner Revue* hailed enthusiastically the first meeting of the German Association of Handicraftsmen in Weimar: "In the future history will trace the rebirth of the German

---

[20] *Neue Preussische Zeitung*, April 7, 1870; Herman v. Petersdorff, *Kleist-Retzow: Ein Lebensbild* (Stuttgart and Berlin, 1907), p. 359; *Ernst Ludwig von Gerlach: Aufzeichnungen*, ed. J. v. Gerlach, I, 541; H. Müller, *Der Preussische Volks-Verein*, pp. 59, 82.

burgher class back to that day when the German artisan class resolved to break with the spirit of the times and to regain its lost position in society." Conservative politicians canvassed for votes on a platform proclaiming that "we want above all that the old fame of the German handicrafts for their skill should remain assured through the continuation of master's examinations." And a petition of the Prussian People's Association sought the solution of the social problem in a revival of the industrial councils created in 1849 and government assistance to the laboring classes:

1. Formation of a state industrial council for the consideration of the common interests of the handicraftsmen and workers of the entire country in conjunction with the royal ministry of commerce.

2. The formation of district or local industrial councils is absolutely essential in order to establish the connection of the state industrial council with the handicraftsmen and workers in the entire country, and also in order to take into account everywhere the local needs of the working class whose importance should not be underestimated. . . .

3. In our opinion jurisdiction should then also be conferred on the industrial councils or the industrial courts to be established at the same time in so far as . . . [labor] disputes are concerned. . . .

4. We consider it particularly important to encourage credit for the handicraftsmen by state action, in the same way in which big industry and commerce enjoy it, through an expansion of banking institutions. . . .

5. As far as the workers are concerned, we recommend to the royal government that it establish norms and provide means to be able to help them as far as possible in their efforts to become entrepreneurs on their own.[21]

[21] *Neue Preussische Zeitung*, July 22, 1863. Cf. "Der deutsche Handwerkertag in Weimar," p. 422; L. Parisius, *Deutschlands politische Parteien*, pp. 112-113.

But the conservatives did more than exhort and encourage. They helped organize a vigorous press campaign in defense of the artisan movement. It goes without saying that newspapers and periodicals like the *Neue Preussische Zeitung*, the *Volksblatt für Stadt und Land*, the *Berliner Revue*, and the *Jahrbücher für Gesellschafts- und Staatswissenschaften* condemned industrial freedom. Still, for them the maintenance of the independent tradesman was only one of many political, economic, social, and religious questions which the established order had to consider. The *Deutsche Bürger-Zeitung* was therefore founded, largely through the efforts of Hermann Wagener, to deal above all with the problems of the handicraftsman, and to justify his struggle against the factory system. Furthermore, the *Preussisches Volksblatt*, which expressed the views of the Prussian People's Association, also served as an organ of the Prussian State Convention of Handicraftsmen. The master craftsman in need of credit could turn to one of the lending institutions established under conservative auspices. The most important of these was the joint-stock bank H. Schuster & Co. established in Berlin in 1863 with a capitalization of 3,000,000 marks. Not only were its operations successful enough to yield consistently dividends of 7 per cent, but it provided a model for the more modest credit unions and loan offices which handicraftsmen formed in a number of cities with the help of well-to-do aristocrats. To be sure, borrowed funds could not protect the artisan shop against the progress of mechanization. The tradesman like the peasant was in the grip of economic forces too powerful to be overcome by loans. The old order could offer no basic solution to his problems, because tacitly it recognized that in a world of factories and railroads the return to a preindustrial economy was out of the question. Yet by its concern for the independent craftsman it won support among the artisan masses.[22]

[22] H. Müller, *Der Preussische Volks-Verein*, pp. 43, 64, 82, 117; W.

In dealing with industrial labor, on the other hand, conservatism was of two minds. The unskilled mill hand could not be fitted into the familiar categories of a corporative society. He was the product of a new economic age for which the landed aristocracy had neither sympathy nor understanding. A small group of legitimist intellectuals including Hermann Wagener, Johann Carl Glaser, Hermann Roesler, and Rudolph Meyer, most of them men of middle-class background, appreciated the growing importance of the factory proletariat. Their journal was the *Berliner Revue*, which urged the government to take the lead in improving the economic position of the urban working class. It maintained that "the wages of labor are as a rule determined in such a way that after the expense of the bare necessities of life, the worker does not have enough left to be able to accumulate savings for himself and his family to provide for sickness and misfortune, or even for old age and the period of incapacity." The only solution was a bold policy of social reform. "Let the state therefore begin with the construction of cloth factories in which it will employ heads of families. . . . Let it at the same time build housing for its working-class families, thereby providing an example for the capitalists. . . . We suggest, moreover, that an office of factory inspection be established for every province. The inspectors must know exactly what the branches of manufacture and the living conditions in their province are, and on their inspection trips they must assume the role of arbitrator between workers and employers with regard to wage rates." Hermann Wagener, who proposed to Bismarck a similar program of welfare legislation, favored in addition sickness insurance, old-age pensions, and producer cooperatives. He even defended the right of labor to unionize, although he hastened to explain that it should not be re-

---

Saile, *Wagener und sein Verhältnis zu Bismarck*, pp. 73-74; *Jahrbuch für die amtliche Statistik des preussischen Staats*, II (1867), 91; H. v. Poschinger, *Bankwesen und Bankpolitik*, III, 124; A. Hahn, *Die Berliner Revue*, p. 121.

garded "as a preparation for so-called strikes," but "as a first step and a preparation for corporative associations."[23]

For most conservatives, however, such a course was too radical. They feared that the emancipation of the proletariat meant the unleashing of a monster who would destroy established society in city and country alike. Rudolph Meyer called the legitimist politician Moritz von Blanckenburg an "inveterate Junker who only in church sees in the worker a human being." The characterization was apt. Conservatism was so mistrustful of the masses that at times it could even subordinate the antagonism between aristocracy and bourgeoisie to their common interest in preserving established property relationships. On the floor of the Prussian legislature August von der Heydt, who had served as minister of commerce during the reactionary 1850's, derided the proponents of tory democracy amid loud applause on the right: "They want no strikes, gentlemen, they want the precise opposite of strikes. And as the surest means of achieving the goal, they want to begin by repealing the prohibition against strikes. They promise the worker state support, and overlook that reliance on outside support has everywhere proved to be the most paralyzing obstacle to self-reliance. . . . Do you then believe that the weakening of credit, which inevitably follows strikes, is less dangerous to the other citizens and to the state itself than to the factory owner? On the contrary, . . . urban and rural landed property suffer the most serious disadvantage when capital withdraws because of a disturbance of public order!"

The high priest of legitimism himself, Ernst Ludwig von Gerlach, defended industry against the claims of labor: "Hostility toward the bourgeoisie or toward big

[23] *Neue Preussische Zeitung*, June 5, 1864. Cf. "Zur Arbeiterfrage" (Part 1), p. 399; "Aphorismen zur Arbeiterbewegung," p. 291; W. Saile, *Wagener und sein Verhältnis zu Bismarck*, p. 137; Hans-Joachim Schoeps, "Hermann Wagener: Ein konservativer Sozialist," *Zeitschrift für Religions- und Geistesgeschichte*, VIII (1956), 204-205, 207.

capital or toward industry is just as immoral and un-christian as hostility toward the nobility or the mon-archical principle. . . . To be sure, the factory owner also needs the workers, and as a rule, where conditions are healthy, the interests of the owners and of the work-ers go hand in hand. But the owner is always the su-perior, the governing part, superior through property, superior through intelligence, superior through business acumen. And this superiority is protection for the work-ers themselves, protection which they need against pri-vation and want and against their own ignorance and corruptibility." Could any liberal economist have af-firmed the proprietary rights of capital with greater conviction?

Their way of thinking about public affairs made it impossible for the conservatives to reach an accommoda-tion with the masses of Central Europe. They regarded class relationships in religious and traditionalist rather than economic and legal terms. While the proletariat sought a means of escape from its impoverishment, le-gitimism preached and exhorted. It saw the salvation of society not in the satisfaction of material needs, but in sound moral principles. Leopold von Gerlach considered the labor question of secondary importance: "If liberal-ism with its doctrine which weakens authority had been overcome, if people had faith like a grain of mustard seed, then soon there would no longer be any talk about all this stuff." His brother Ernst Ludwig was equally dogmatic: "The future of this century and the fate and civilization of the world do not depend on the labor question, but on the great question . . . whether there is a living God, . . . whether God's revelations . . . are truth or falsehood, whether church, marriage, au-thority, and oath are holy institutions of God . . . or human precepts subject to the autonomy of the hu-man spirit and the wish of carnal man for the satisfac-tion of his appetites. These are the highest social as well as political questions, to which the labor question must be completely subordinated." But the most characteristic expression of the conservative mentality could be heard in the lecture which an obscure Captain von Schmettau delivered before the Conservative Club of Saint Luke's Parish in Berlin: "Schulze-Delitzsch says: 'Help yourself.' Lassalle: 'The state must help you!' The Christian says: 'Trust in God, pray and work, and God will help you.' " Here in all its artless incomprehension was the voice of an aristocratic landed caste confronting the complexities of a new era of industrialism.[24]

The moral fervor and intellectual sophistication of the legitimist ideologues could not alter the fact that they were defending the interests of a social class which wanted above all to preserve a way of life in which it enjoyed a position of privilege. Rustic, parochial, inflexible, and unimaginative, it remained blind to new dynamic forces in the community which had to be grasped before they could be controlled. In his memoirs Hermann Wagener recalled that "the great mass of the conservatives still had absolutely no understanding for questions of this sort. . . . They were often satisfied merely to be able once more to drink their glass of wine and play their game of omber in peace." Here lay their weakness. They were unable to rise above the limitations imposed by tradition and status. Behind all the ringing phrases about legitimate authority and corporative justice stood a rural nobility frightened by the changes in society arising out of industrialization, and resolved to resist those changes at all costs. It would take a leader of extraordinary skill to shake the faith of the conservatives in the old order. And when he appeared, they followed him only with great reluctance, unwilling to accept the passing of a pastoral age in which life had been placid and uncomplicated.[25]

[24] Johann Karl Rodbertus-Jagetzow, *Briefe und socialpolitische Aufsätze*, ed. Rudolph Meyer (2 vols., Berlin, 1882), I, 199, n. 2; Prussia *Verhandlungen des Landtages: Haus der Abgeordneten* (1865), I, 179; *Neue Preussische Zeitung*, September 8, 1865, May 6, 1866; *Denkwürdigkeiten aus dem Leben Leopold von Gerlachs*, I, 485.

[25] H. Wagener, *Erlebtes*, I, 63.

SIX

The Emergence of Socialism

THE period of national unification which coincided with the breakthrough of industrial capitalism in Central Europe also stimulated the growth of class consciousness in the urban proletariat. To be sure, the development of a labor movement was still in its initial stage. Most workingmen remained indifferent to broad questions of politics or economics, and those displaying interest in the problems of their society were usually independent artisans whose way of life was being destroyed by the factory system. Yet here and there could also be found a growing awareness that the old patriarchal world of the master craftsman was gone beyond recall, and that the changed condition of the working class required a new ideology to express its interests. For the first time socialism, spreading beyond isolated coteries of radical theoreticians, began to win a following among the masses. Its early converts came for the most part from the manufacturing regions, but they were not primarily mill hands driven to revolutionary ideas by privation. As a rule they were skilled operatives with a higher level of income and education than the common run of industrial labor. Having broken with the tradition of the trade guild, they now found themselves threatened by the rise of large-scale enterprise. In the Rhineland, for example, the ribbonmakers of Barmen and Ronsdorf, under increasing pressure to work at the looms of factory owners rather than in their own shops, began to question the entire system of social values prevailing under capitalism. The cutlers of Solingen, famous throughout Europe for their metalworking craftsmanship, joined the socialist movement by the hundreds.

The radical stronghold of the Saxon textile district was not industrialized Chemnitz, but small towns like Glauchau and Meerane where household manufacture was still common. In Hamburg tailors, shoemakers, joiners, and cigar makers predominated among those attracted to socialism. It was the workers occupying a favorable position within the labor force, particularly if that position was jeopardized by capitalistic entrepreneurship, who were most disposed to reject established economic relationships.

These lower-class adherents of socialism were unsophisticated in their approach to ideology. What made them opponents of the established order was not the logic of doctrine, but a deep resentment of social injustice. Julius Vahlteich, who had become active in the labor movement during the early 1860's, recalled forty years later that "our knowledge in the field of economics was small. We knew nothing about constant and variable capital, and we were not initiated in the profoundest mysteries of capital formation. But we knew very well that capital and the capitalists were our enemies, and we also knew that we could overcome them only through the development of power, that is, through organization. We knew nothing about relative surplus value or a hundred other economic categories, . . . but we were quite firm in the conviction that we would be cheated and robbed by the entrepreneurs, and that the laws were made for the purpose of sanctioning this sort of conduct."

The youthful labor movement, however, made up in enthusiasm what it lacked in sophistication. It believed that the establishment of a new society in which man no longer exploited man was only a matter of time and dedication. Sooner or later the masses would realize that neither the liberals nor the conservatives but only they themselves could create a better world for mankind. And once they became conscious of their grand destiny, nothing would stand in their way. "Do you then not hear that around us only the most sacred, the most

223

important social questions, the questions of our existence or nonexistence are being discussed in all circles?" asked the address to "Workers! German Brothers!" issued by a committee seeking to convoke a national labor congress. "What would the world say, if you were to remain silent in the face of all these facts?" As yet most workers did not care what the world said, but a small minority was prepared to seek the solution to social problems outside the framework of the established order.[1]

While the nucleus of a socialist movement had thus come into existence by the early 1860's, there was still no leadership capable of providing it with direction and purpose. The influence of Marx and Engels, the best-known German critics of the capitalistic system, was limited by their personal situation as well as their theoretical position. A long exile in Great Britain had made it impossible for them to acquire the knowledge of men and circumstances in Central Europe indispensable to an effective party organizer. The two were at all events temperamentally unsuited to the rough-and-tumble of factional politics. They lacked the suppleness and extroversion of the successful manipulators of men. Their strong point lay in the formulation of doctrine, not in the rhetoric of mass agitation. Most important of all, they had concluded that the objective conditions necessary for the establishment of socialism were wanting in the German Confederation. Only some unexpected upheaval could weaken the established order sufficiently to make its overthrow possible. Therefore, instead of frittering away their energies in the chores of party administration, which seemed in any case futile, they preferred to await a providential catastrophe.

[1] A. Thun, *Industrie am Niederrhein*, II, 204-205; F. Mehring, *Geschichte der deutschen Sozialdemokratie*, 103-104, 201-202; Roger Morgan, *The German Social Democrats and the First International, 1864-1872* (Cambridge, 1965), pp. 3-4; Julius Vahlteich, "Das Leipziger Zentralkomitee und Ferdinand Lassalle," *Die Gründung der deutschen Sozialdemokratie: Eine Festschrift der Leipziger Arbeiter zum 23. Mai 1903* (Leipzig, 1903), p. 20; *Volks-Zeitung*, October 22, 1862.

After the defeat of the revolution in 1849 they had remained confident for a time that "the workers and peasants who now suffer under the rule of the saber . . . will see to it that in the next insurrection they and not the petty bourgeois take the helm." The failure of the next insurrection to materialize was disappointing, but then the economic crisis of 1857 aroused new expectations. Hard times might rekindle the revolutionary zeal of the masses. "Chronic pressure is necessary for a while to heat the populations," Engels argued. "The proletariat will then fight better, in better *connaissance de cause* and with greater accord." It was another false hope. The depression passed without exciting social disturbance, and nine more frustrating years elapsed before the Austro-Prussian conflict once again raised the prospect of unrest among the lower classes. Even the bourgeoisie must realize by now that if a revolution did not take place, Central Europe would go through a civil war from which it could not recover for fifty years or more, maintained Marx, while Engels expected an uprising in Berlin and mutinies in the mobilizing Hohenzollern armies. The outcome of the war destroyed their illusions. It was clear that the achievement of national unification had strengthened the established order and that there was little sense in waiting for its inner inconsistencies to produce a collapse. The two impatient exiles, realizing that the victory of Prussia had completely altered the political situation in Central Europe, hastened to adapt their strategy to the new realities. Even before the Preliminary Peace of Nikolsburg, Engels was writing that "in my opinion we can thus do nothing but simply accept the fact without giving it our approval, and use as far as we can the greater facilities which must in any event be offered now for the national organization and association of the German proletariat." He and Marx were at last ready to test their theories in the crucible of party politics.

But prior to the Seven Weeks' War they had not considered the formation of a socialist movement in Central

225

Europe a feasible goal. Disunity and particularism would make the task of party organization exceedingly difficult, they feared. "The working class needs for the full development of its political activity a much greater field than the separate states of today's splintered Germany offer," argued Engels. "The existence of many states will be an obstacle to progress for the proletariat." Besides, the masses were not yet ready for radical ideas. Their enfranchisement would probably play into the hands of the reaction. Marx pointed to the exploitation of manhood suffrage by the Second Empire in France, and Engels insisted that "as long as the rural proletariat is not drawn into the movement, . . . the general direct franchise is for the proletariat not a weapon but a snare." The only practicable strategy was a united front with the democratic bourgeoisie, the same strategy which had been pursued with such meager results in the 1840's. "It is thus in the interest of the workers to support the bourgeoisie in its struggle against all reactionary elements, so long as it remains true to itself," Engels explained. "Every gain which the bourgeoisie extorts from the reaction is under this condition of ultimate advantage to the working class." Yet a program of collaboration with middle-class reformism, though sanctioned by the Marxian dialectic, had little appeal for workingmen seeking to oppose social injustice by collective action. It presented no clear-cut alternative for those who were affiliated with the left wing of liberalism through the Assembly of German Workingmen's Societies, while for those who were impatient for an outright attack on capitalism it offered only stratagem and caution. Its following was therefore small to the point of nonexistence, and the labor leader Bernhard Becker could gibe that "the Marxian clique . . . consists of three persons, namely, the master Marx, his secretary Engels, and his agent Liebknecht." There were others, to be sure, but not many.[2]

2 Friedrich Engels, "Die deutsche Reichsverfassungs-Campagne: Für Republik zu sterben!," *Neue Rheinische Zeitung: Politisch-ökonomische*

The beginnings of an organized socialist movement in Central Europe go back to the General German Workingmen's Society founded in 1863 by Ferdinand Lassalle. A popular agitator of extraordinary gifts, he had neither the strength nor the weakness of Marx and Engels. Their inferior as a theoretician, he was too restless and flamboyant for the painstaking examination of social problems. He preferred nostrums and panaceas. To Marx, the rigorous dialectician of class relationships, his thinking seemed marred by "disputatiousness," "speculative conception," and "infection with old French liberalism." But abstract reasoning was never Lassalle's strong point. He was above all a man of action with a remarkable talent for swaying people by sheer force of personality. He appeared at his best on the platform before an audience waiting to be captivated by his eloquence. "In my early youth I thought that I was meant to be a dramatic actor," he once told a friend. "But later I realized that I am destined to play in life itself the role which I wanted to portray on the stage." His boundless ambition, stimulated by the insecurity of a sensitive Jew only two generations removed from the ghettos of Poland, drove him to seek fame in some sensational achievement which would attract the attention of the world. Hermann Wagener remembered hearing from Lassalle that "he, Bismarck, and I, that was the order, are the three cleverest men in Prussia." The only question was in what field he should strive to win the recognition he so badly wanted.

Lassalle did not decide to become a tribune of the people until he had failed to win renown in a number of other enterprises. His *Philosophie Herakleitos des Dunklen von Ephesos* demonstrated that he was a gifted

Revue, I (1850) , no. 3, p. 79; K. Marx and F. Engels, *Briefwechsel*, II, 301, III, 387, 401, 406, 418; Karl Marx and Friedrich Engels, *Ausgewählte Briefe* (Berlin, 1953) , pp, 246-247; Friedrich Engels, *Die preussische Militärfrage und die deutsche Arbeiterpartei* (Hamburg, 1865) , pp. 38, 50, 53; *Die Geschichte der Social-demokratischen Partei in Deutschland seit dem Tode Ferdinand Lassalle's* (Berlin, 1865) , pp. 34-35; R. Morgan, *The German Social Democrats*, p. 59.

amateur philosopher, just as *Das System der erworbenen Rechte* earned him a reputation as a gifted amateur jurisprudent, and *Franz von Sickingen* as a gifted amateur playwright. That was not enough for a man in quest of immortality. His political pamphlets on the war in Italy and the constitutional conflict in Prussia evoked more discussion than praise. Only after these disappointments did Lassalle find in the socialist movement a field of endeavor worthy of his ability. He threw himself into it with the zeal of an evangelist, the figure of Luther hovering before him. To his confidante Countess Sophie von Hatzfeldt he wrote that the *Offenes Antwort-Schreiben an das Zentral-Komitee zur Berufung eines allgemeinen deutschen Arbeiter-Kongresses zu Leipzig* "must . . . produce approximately the effect of the theses on the castle church in Wittenberg!" The same reference to the ninety-five theses appeared in letters to his supporters Gustav Lewy and Otto Dammer. He reported, moreover, that when Franz Ziegler warned him of the dangers he was inviting, "I only replied to all this with old Luther: 'Here I stand, I cannot do otherwise; God help me, Amen!' "

Yet not even Luther's fame was enough for Lassalle. He wanted to be more than a religious reformer; he wanted to be a prophet, a messiah. The doctrines which he expounded were graven tables from Mount Sinai, holy and eternal. An account of the reception of the great agitator in Wermelskirchen in the Rhineland which he himself edited described how "everything created the impression as if one were present at the establishment of a new religion." Writing to Countess Hatzfeldt, he suggested that he felt himself engaged in the founding of a great secular faith: "I had the impression constantly that this is how it must have looked at the establishment of new religions." As befitted a redeemer of oppressed humanity, he had no doubts about his infallibility. Following the publication of his *Herr Bastiat-Schulze von Delitzsch,* he assured the working class that "the most famous names of Germany have . . . confirmed to me, if I still needed a confirmation, that I am right in every line and in every syllable." And in his last public speech before the court in Düsseldorf he was the savior going to his crucifixion: "O gentlemen, fifty years after my death people will think differently about this mighty and remarkable cultural movement which I am creating before your eyes, . . . and a grateful posterity, of that I am sure, will ask of my spirit forgiveness for the insults." If at the founding of the General German Workingmen's Society Lassalle hoped to emulate Luther, before long he was identifying himself with even more exalted figures in the history of mankind.[3]

The new religion which Lassalle preached was his own form of socialism. His point of departure was the common contention of contemporary opponents of private ownership that under the capitalistic system the working class was doomed to perpetual impoverishment. Existing disparities in property relationships, he maintained, precluded the social emancipation of the proletariat through a gradual rise in the standard of living. "The iron economic law which determines the wage of labor under the conditions of today, under the rule of supply and demand for labor, is this: that the average wage of labor always remains reduced to the necessary subsistence which is customarily needed in a nation for the maintenance of existence and for propagation. This is the point around which the actual daily wage always oscillates, without ever being able either to rise above or fall below for any length of time." It was thus senseless to seek an improvement in the position of the lower classes through freedom of enterprise. "If the propertied want to talk to you about 'free competition' and that everyone should rely only on his isolated strength, then

[3] K. Marx and F. Engels, *Briefwechsel*, III, 23; F. Lassalle, *Briefe und Schriften*, IV, 340, 355, V, 109-110, VI, 428; H. Wagener, *Erlebtes*, II, 6; "Briefe Lassalles an Dr. Otto Dammer in Leipzig, Vicepräsidenten des Allgemeinen Deutschen Arbeitervereins," ed. Hermann Oncken, *Archiv für die Geschichte des Sozialismus und der Arbeiterbewegung*, II, (1912), 389; F. Lassalle, *Reden und Schriften*, III, 442, IV, 212, 236.

they must first make conditions equal, so that competition will indeed be free," Lassalle taught the workers. "Then the propertied must either first give up their wealth, which would be absurd, and also compete against you with only their muscles and nails! . . . Or, to make competition free, you should at least also be furnished with capital, so that you can really compete with the capitalists. . . . But the entrepreneurs do not want this free competition; they want only unequal, unfree competition with you, the competition of the armed with the unarmed."

What the working class needed above all was protection against laissez-faire capitalism. Yet this protection could not be found in the corporative regulation of industrial production. The factory owner would have to be fought with his own weapons. Lassalle was convinced that "to restore the old association of capital and labor in the middle estate, where it has been lost, even if this were for the moment possible, would in the long run be wasted effort, just as it is impossible to guard this old association, where it still exists in the middle estate, against the power of attraction of big industry. Once the organic power of big industry has been established, it is impossible to protect the still remaining remnants of the middle estate in their old form against it." It would therefore be best to clear away the rubble of a decayed economic order and prepare to meet the demands of a new age of mechanization. "Freedom of movement and industrial freedom are things which are no longer debated in a legislative body, but are decreed as a matter of course."

The cooperative movement which Schulze-Delitzsch had founded could be no more effectual than the guild system in achieving the emancipation of the proletariat. "As for the credit or loan associations and the associations for the purchase of raw materials, they are both similar in that they exist only for the man who conducts a business on his own account, that is, only for the small handicraft establishment. For the working class in the

230

strict sense, for the worker employed in large-scale factory production, . . . both associations do not exist."
But even for the independent artisan they were of little
value. "These associations can . . . only prolong the
death struggle in which the small handicrafts are destined to succumb and make room for big industry. They
can thereby only increase the agonies of this death
struggle and delay in vain the development of our culture." By the same token, benevolent societies organized
on the principle of self-help were only palliatives:

> Is it your purpose to make the misery of individual
> workers more bearable? To counter the thoughtlessness,
> the sickness, the old age, the misfortunes of all sorts by
> which a few individual workers are accidentally or neces-
> sarily forced below even the normal position of the
> working class? In that case sickness, disability, savings,
> and relief funds are entirely proper means. Only then
> it was not worth the trouble to incite a movement
> through all of Germany for such a purpose. It was not
> worth the trouble to initiate a general agitation in the
> entire working class of the nation. We must not let
> mountains labor as if they wanted to give birth so that
> then a little mouse can appear! This highly limited and
> subordinate purpose can rather be left safely to local
> associations and to local organization, which are also able
> to achieve it much more effectively.

Both the conservative and the liberal solutions of the
social question were thus rejected by Lassalle, the one
because it was anachronistic, the other because it was
insufficient. His own program had the advantages of
simplicity, ingenuity, and a specious reasonableness.
Like so much of Lassalle's thinking, it was plausible
rather than convincing:

> To make the working class its own entrepreneur, that is
> the means by which and by which alone . . . that iron
> and cruel law determining the wage of labor can be abro-
> gated! . . . The abolition of the profit of the entrepreneur

231

in the most peaceful, legal, and simple manner, in that the working class through voluntary associations organizes itself as its own entrepreneur, . . . that is the only true improvement in the position of the working class, the only one meeting its just claims, the only one which is not illusionary. But how? Look at the railroads, the machine factories, the shipyards, the cotton spinneries, the calico factories, etc., etc. Look at the millions which are needed for these installations. Then look at your empty pockets, and ask yourselves where you will ever get the vast capital needed for these installations, and how you will therefore ever make possible the operation of big industry on your own account. And surely nothing is more certain, nothing is more settled than that you will never make it possible if you remain confined exclusively and solely and only to your isolated efforts as individuals. Precisely for this reason it is the business and task of the state to make this possible for you, . . . to offer you the means and the opportunity for this self-organization and self-association of yours. . . . Once again then, the free individual association of the workers, but the free individual association made possible by the supporting and furthering hand of the state, that is the only way out of the wilderness open to the working class.

The realization of Lassalle's program thus depended on the willingness of the government to support producer associations organized by the workers which could compete with capitalistic establishments and gradually destroy them. Yet he had no doubt about its practicability. To him all problems arising out of the industrialization of society could be solved by economic sleight of hand, by spells and incantations, while the financial difficulties involved in an attempt to use the resources of the state to replace individual with cooperative ownership would melt away before his eloquence:

Assume for a moment that we had only a hundred million talers for our purpose. . . . The interest on capital is in general 5 per cent. . . . These 5 per cent produce annually 5 million talers, which we could also invest again, if we had those 100 million, for the same purpose, for the establishment of workers' associations. Through the efficacy of interest on interest these annual 5 million would within 14 years have doubled the capital, and we would from then on have 200 million, so that from now on we have 10 million in annual interest which we could use for workers' associations. Assume now that on an average for all occupations approximately 4,000 workers can work on a capital of a million talers. . . . On the basis of the 100 million talers, 400,000 workers could thus form associations. With their families, if we estimate them on an average at 5 persons, that would be a population of 2 million. With 10 million in annual interest, the possibility of freedom and well-being could arise for another 40,000 workers annually and thereby for another 200,000 people, or during the first 14 years, as long as we assume only 5 million annually, for at least again another 20,000 workers with their families annually. And so a way would be found which, within a fixed period of time, would lead all of you out of the wilderness, all the laboring classes of society without exception. . . .

You may ask now: "Where are we to get these hundred million?" Gentlemen, I of course will not and cannot here explain a long financial theory to you. But I must make you cast a fleeting glance at how easy, yes, how ridiculously easy it would be to obtain these hundred million without the poor peasant . . . needing to hand over one pfennig out of his pocket for this purpose. I raise the question: "On what do the banks depend which issue bank notes? On what," I say, "depends the profitability of such an enterprise?" On nothing other than the following:

When a bank, for example, puts a hundred million in its vaults, it can now issue 400 million in bank notes, and this depends simply on the fact established by experience that never will more than a fourth of the bank note holders appear at the same time to exchange their notes for cash. On this simple axiom, on this fact established by experience, all banks throughout Europe which issue bank notes depend. This is a fact of society, a fact lying in the nature of all men. No one has made this fact, neither Peter nor Christopher nor William. It is an elementary law of society, just as there are elementary laws of nature. Whoever takes advantage of this law thus has, in the example given, 300 million for his use which do not belong to him, but of which also no one else is deprived. For to the bank note holders, the true creditors of this institution, the bank notes represent the same service which the silver talers would have performed for them. Besides, we cannot even determine who is the creditor of this bank. I, you, all of us, everyone who for a moment has a taler in his pocket which within the next quarter of an hour already belongs to another man.[4]

To working-class audiences spellbound by Lassalle's oratory his arguments must have sounded irrefutable. But could he himself have believed that the same Prussian state which was fighting popular government tooth and nail would undertake the economic emancipation of the proletariat? He had his doubts, although he managed to suppress them. A man so eager for quick success was forced to fall back on desperate expedients. He had no time to wait for the ripening of insurrectionary sentiment among the masses. "You seem over there, ten years removed from here, to have as yet really no idea at all how little our people are alienated from the monarchy," he had written to Marx in London. Perhaps it would actually be easier to revolutionize the ruling classes than the proletariat. That was why he began to preach to the authorities the duty of the state to undertake drastic social reform: "The bourgeoisie considers the moral purpose of the state to be as follows: it consists exclusively and solely in the protection of the

[4] F. Lassalle, *Reden und Schriften*, III, 246-247, 252-253. Cf. *ibid.*, III, 48-49, 53-58, 69-70, 88, 234, V, 370.

personal freedom of the individual and his property. This is a night watchman idea, . . . because it can conceive of the state itself only in the image of a night watchman whose entire function consists in preventing robbery and burglary." The demeaning ideal of laissez faire, however, was unworthy of a great nation. "The purpose of the state is thus not to protect only the individual's personal freedom and property with which he, according to the idea of the bourgeoisie, allegedly already enters into the state. The purpose of the state is rather precisely to put individuals through this association in a position to reach such goals, such a level of existence as they as individuals could never reach, to enable them to acquire a sum of education, power, and freedom which would be simply inaccessible to all of them as individuals."

Lassalle even hoped to enlist the Hohenzollern dynasty itself in his crusade for a socialist economy:

We are finally at the point where the monarchy, if it cannot yield to a clique, can on the other hand very easily call the people to the stage and rely on them. For this it needs only to realize what the pillar is on which it stands. The people, not the bourgeoisie, pay its taxes! The people, not the bourgeoisie, fight its battles! For this it needs finally only to remember its origin, for every monarchy was originally a popular monarchy. A monarchy like that of Louis Philippe, a monarchy created by the bourgeoisie, could not of course do this. But a monarchy which still stands there kneaded out of its primeval clay, leaning on the pommel of its sword, could do that very easily if it is resolved to pursue truly great, national, and popular goals.

This was the same Lassalle who had privately admitted to a friend that "if the *signatura temporis* really points to Caesarism, then all would be lost for the present."[5]

5 F. Lassalle, *Briefe und Schriften*, VI, 358. Cf. F. Lassalle, *Reden und Schriften*, II, 195-198, III, 217, IV, 159.

There was more guile than naiveté in his summons to the established order to join with him in an assault on the capitalistic system. Basically he agreed with Marx that the state must of necessity maintain the interests of the dominant class in society. It followed that socialism could be established only after political and economic power had shifted from the propertied to the property-less. But Lassalle had characteristically hit upon a simple device which would swiftly and painlessly ensure the victory of the proletariat. "I have referred you not to the present state," he explained to the workers, "but to the state which will be established under the rule of the general and direct franchise. . . . I have demanded nothing more and nothing less than that the future state, the democratic state reborn through the introduction of the direct and general franchise, should through a very easy credit operation provide you with the capital loans which the workers need for the establishment of producer associations!" The political enfranchisement of the masses would compel the government to bring about their economic liberation as well:

> The working class must be organized into an independent political party, and must make the general, equal, and direct suffrage the principal watchword and banner of this party. The representation of the working class in the legislative bodies of Germany, only this can satisfy its legitimate interests in regard to politics. To open a peaceful and legal agitation for it with all legal means is and must be the program of the workingmen's party. . . . When the legislative bodies of Germany are chosen by the general and direct suffrage, then and only then will you be able to induce the state to perform this duty which it has.

He thus expected the salvation of society not from the Prussia of William I and Bismarck, but from the great German democracy of the future built on the enfranchisement of the proletariat.

Yet even here he was not candid. Although publicly advocating no more than "a peaceful and legal agitation," he must have realized that the peasant masses of Central Europe were not likely to cast their votes for socialism. And he was enough of a revolutionist to be tempted by the thought of direct action.

Ehrwürd'ger Herr! Schlecht kennt ihr die Geschichte.
Ihr habt ganz Recht, es ist Vernunft ihr Inhalt,
Doch ihre Form bleibt ewig—die Gewalt!

he had written in his *Franz von Sickingen*. Years later a former follower recalled that "what Lassalle understood by 'suffrage' those can tell you who knew him. 'Every time I say general suffrage, it must be understood by you as revolution and again as revolution,' Lassalle once said in Frankfurt at a social gathering. . . . Lassalle could not after all call for a revolution directly, but all workers who heard him understood it anyway." Not all workers, but those who wanted to understand it. For Lassalle was all things to all men. To those in authority he lectured on the high mission of the state. To those interested in peaceful social reform he offered the expedients of manhood suffrage and producer associations. And to militants he dropped dark hints of conspiracies and insurrections. In the end he himself was probably no longer able to distinguish between the genuine and the spurious in his pronouncements. Wilhelm Liebknecht, whose socialism was based on entirely different political calculations, wrote to Marx that "he plays such a complicated game that he himself will soon not be able to find his way out. But he is honest. And that I say this before you shows you that I had doubts." Three months later Lassalle had found his way out. Death came to him at a time when all his schemes had finally failed.[6]

[6] F. Lassalle, *Reden und Schriften*, I, 224, III, 47, 89, 175-176, 245, IV, 48; *Der Volksstaat*, July 30, 1870; Wilhelm Liebknecht, *Briefwechsel mit Karl Marx und Friedrich Engels*, ed. Georg Eckert (The Hague, 1963) , p. 38.

Did he provoke the fatal duel solely out of disappointed love for the pretty Helene von Dönniges, or was Liebknecht right in the surmise long afterward that Lassalle had committed "indirect suicide"? His achievements must have appeared to him pitifully inadequate in view of his extravagant expectations. In the spring of 1863 he had talked about an association "including 1,000,000 workers in Germany with 150,000 talers annually for purposes of agitation." By the summer of the following year he had managed to enlist some 4,600 workers in his movement. The masses of Central Europe were as yet too brutalized to be interested in a crusade for the betterment of mankind. Only a handful could look beyond the drudgery of everyday toil to ideals of political equality and social justice. The General German Workingmen's Society had 529 members in Barmen, 523 in Ronsdorf, 500 in Solingen, and 489 in Hamburg, but a mere 61 in Augsburg, 46 in Bremen, 13 in Dresden, and 12 in Mainz. Lassalle, who had set out to conquer the world, was crushed by the reports of his lieutenants. In Frankfurt am Main the news was that "the number of members of the General German Workingmen's Society has risen from 40 to 64, and there is the prospect that very soon some 30 new ones will join." From Berlin he learned that "at the meeting of the 18th once again two new members were enrolled, the first ones in four months." In Altona "the number of members of the local group consists for the moment, to be sure, of only seven, but an increase in a very short time can be expected with complete confidence." From Dortmund came an account that "only five men here firmly profess your principles."

Julius Vahlteich, who had at first shared Lassalle's inflated hopes, soon conceded that "the time for a purely political and social agitation among the working class is not yet far enough advanced. The great mass has no taste for the more spiritual, ideal movement." A following of almost five thousand won in the space of fifteen months might have satisfied a man more patient or

realistic than Lassalle. But to him the thought of waiting for years for the gradual spread of his ideas was
unbearable. He needed an immediate success, yet he
seemed to stand still, counting two members here and
five members there. He was forced to admit to himself
that his heroic vision would in all probability never be
realized. He was no Luther, no Franz von Sickingen,
perhaps not even a Schulze-Delitzsch. "Events will, I
fear, unfold slowly, slowly," he wrote Countess Hatzfeldt a month before his death, "and my burning soul
has no joy in these childhood diseases and chronic law-
suits. Politics means immediate, present effectiveness.
Everything else can also be taken care of through scholarship! I will try . . . to exert pressure on events! But
to what extent that will be effective I cannot promise,
and I myself do not expect too much from it! Ah, if I
could withdraw!"[7]

His disappointment did not spring solely from the
failure to make a deeper impression on the working
class. He had also been anxious to win support among
men of means and education who shared his desire to
save the proletariat from eternal poverty. In one of
those boastful speeches which tell more about his hopes
than his accomplishments, he claimed that "my word
on the one hand works with irresistible force on the
great mass of the people, on the other hand it works
with perhaps even greater force within the minority of
the educated on precisely the most educated and the
most intelligent of all." That was wishful thinking. The
fact was that the bourgeoisie remained hostile to him
for reasons inherent partly in his theories, partly in his
tactics. It went without saying that the moderate liberals
with their ideological commitment to laissez-faire economics would reject all socialist criticism of the capi-

---

[7] F. Lassalle, *Briefe und Schriften*, IV, 370. Cf. *ibid.*, V, 111, 202, 228,
n. 1, 309, 351; J. B. von Schweitzer, *Politische Aufsätze und Reden*, ed.
Fr. Mehring (Berlin, 1912), pp. 23-24; H. Oncken, *Lassalle*, pp. 393-
394; F. Mehring, *Die deutsche Sozialdemokratie*, pp. 54-55; B. Becker,
Arbeiter-Agitation Lassalle's, p. 81.

talistic system. To them Lassalle was the great distorter and falsifier. "To multiply capital by government decree or law," explained the journal of the Nationalverein, "and to make it a sort of common property, to want to place it at everybody's disposal is a foolish fancy. . . . To demand of the state that it help all of its citizens achieve prosperity is about the same as to expect the state to guarantee health to its subjects or supply everybody with an adequate measure of talent." It would have been a waste of time to try to proselytize the rugged individualists professing this philosophy.

But there were the more militant liberals, liberals ready to challenge the authority of the crown and work for the emancipation of the proletariat. With their backing Lassalle would have been able to strengthen the base of his movement. He may indeed have been thinking of an alliance with middle-class radicalism when he stated in January 1863 that "we, bourgeoisie and workers, are the rank and file of one people, and are completely united against our oppressors!" By October, however, he had created an irreparable breach with the democrats of the north as well as the south. To the Progressive Party, fighting for its life in the conflict with Bismarck, he had proclaimed his scorn:

> For us the Prussian constitution thus has . . . no value and no interest, any more than it has a legal existence. For us the struggle of the two parties has no particular interest, for both parties, the reactionaries as well as the Progressives, are equally alien to us. For us the struggle has no particular interest, because the entire object of the struggle, the Prussian constitution, has no such interest for us. On the contrary, the Prussian constitution can arouse no interest in us other than to make it disappear as quickly as possible! . . . And if we exchanged gunshots with Herr von Bismarck, justice would require us to admit even during the volleys that he is a man, but [the Progressives] are old women!

240

And in the same breath he had condemned the federalist ideal of the small-town radicals in central and southern Germany:

> The return to the Frankfurt imperial constitution is not my, is not our position! For us the idea of restoring the Frankfurt imperial constitution is nothing more than a reactionary utopia. For us the Frankfurt imperial constitution was already in 1849, when it was promulgated, nothing more than the last proof of the impotence of federalism. German unity, a unitary sovereign central authority with the retention of 34 distinct separate sovereignties, that is a contradiction in itself. It is no more possible than that a black coat should at the same time be white. Sovereignty, whether it resides with the prince or the people, is by its nature indivisible, as indivisible as the soul of an individual. What we really need, if we are to talk about German unity, is that these 34 independent sovereignties cease and fall together into a single one. This is also the reason why the Frankfurt imperial constitution could not really operate for a single day. It was destroyed not . . . because of its revolutionary character for which the time was not yet ripe, but because of its reactionary character. It was destroyed not because of what it innovated, but because of what it preserved. It was destroyed because of that logical contradiction of a unitary central authority with 34 sovereignties.[8]

Lassalle broke with liberalism, convinced that it could never be persuaded to back his program of social reform. He had been too outspoken in his attack on the capitalistic system, too forthright in his condemnation of private ownership. But there was still more to his calculation. By turning against the bourgeoisie, he might attract confederates in the aristocracy who could win for him a favorable hearing by the government. The idea of an alliance between socialism and conservatism di-

[8] F. Lassalle, *Reden und Schriften*, III, 372-373. Cf. *ibid.*, III, 382-383, IV, 151; "Die Fortschrittsparthei und der Socialismus," p. 7.

rected against their common enemies in the middle class seemed to make sense. Both condemned the self-seeking industrialists who put profits before ideals; both despised liberal parliamentarians as the lackeys of urban wealth; both looked to the state for the enforcement of social justice. Lassalle thus came to believe that the best chance of interesting the Prussian government in producer associations, his open-sesame for the solution of the labor question, lay in supporting the crown in the constitutional conflict. As the authorities became more involved in a test of strength with the legislature, they would become more dependent on the good will of the masses. Gradually they would find themselves compelled to raise their price for the aid of the working class, and in the end they would be its captives. He proposed, in other words, to exploit the struggle between aristocracy and bourgeoisie by playing one off against the other, until manhood suffrage and cooperative proprietorship had achieved the liberation of the proletariat.

The weakness of this plan was that he lacked the mass following which could tempt the conservatives to seek an agreement with him. They recognized that, despite his professions of faith in the monarchy, the differences separating them from him were basically greater than the differences separating them from the liberals. For he wanted more than a reform of the political system; he wanted its overthrow. If he had been able to offer them the support of a large party whose votes could affect the outcome of the constitutional conflict, they might have been willing to risk an alliance with the General German Workingmen's Society. But it hardly seemed sensible to give aid to a dangerous radical for the sake of a few thousand ballots on election day. The *Berliner Revue* had no illusions about Lassalle's ultimate objective:

> Wherever he speaks of the state, he is thinking not of the present state, but of the future state, of the social state of the workers. And one cannot get to that state

without the revolution, without the destruction of the right to ownership and property. If it were only the help of the state of today which Herr Lassalle invokes, an understanding with him would be easy. But precisely on this point we must beware of deception. Lassalle today puts up in silence with the charge that by his demands for state help he is working for the reaction. He would, however, deride the latter, just as today he derides the Progressive Party, if his movement were in full swing, and he and the workers left the old society behind.

The *Neue Preussische Zeitung* was equally hardheaded. After a carping analysis of Lassalle's theories, it concluded that "we are in agreement with them to the extent that they call for criticism and rejection of the institutions and principles of modern unchristian liberalism. But we are his decided opponents whenever and to the extent that his attacks are directed against the foundation of the Christian political and social order itself."

Lassalle made a special effort to ingratiate himself with the conservative spokesman most interested in the labor question. Hermann Wagener, however, was too shrewd not to see the gulf between them. He accepted the socialist leader's compliments, but he knew that "Lassalle was certainly not the man to let himself be used by others. He wanted to rule himself." Nor was Wagener deceived by flights of oratory about the moral mission of the state: "We would indeed be judging [Lassalle] falsely, if we were to assume that the Prussian state *in concreto* and not rather the idea of the state *in abstracto* would have mattered to him." Addressing the Prussian People's Association, he emphasized his disagreement with the egalitarian teachings of socialism: "Our task is not to alter radically, but only to want to cleanse and heal. . . . We should not consider it our goal to want to equalize fully in the communist fashion the position of workers and employers, but our goal should only be to put the worker once again in a position worthy of a human being and in possession of his right as a Christian!" Besides, Lassalle was too much like Wagener himself, ambitious, clever, and opportunistic. The latter was not inclined to encourage a potential competitor. In a private memorandum to Bismarck he warned the prime minister against "a dangerous egoist with the air of a reasonable socialist who, just as the 'reaction' tries to use him, so he for his part tries to use the reaction for his purposes and as a transitional stage." Wagener saw in Lassalle a threat to monarchical government, a threat to private property, and perhaps worst of all, a threat to Wagener.[9]

But there was one conservative who was willing to listen to Lassalle. The constitutional conflict between crown and legislature posed for Bismarck a problem which only audacity could solve. Only some great success in domestic or foreign policy could overawe the liberals who were trying to force his dismissal. And as yet there was little on the international scene which promised to provide him with a major triumph of statecraft. Throughout 1863, therefore, he toyed with schemes of political and social reform designed to win popular support for his struggle against parliamentarianism. In May he invited Lassalle to present his views regarding the labor question, and a secret association began between the two which continued intermittently until early the following year. Their conversations and letters dealt mostly with the strategy to be followed in the contest with the Progressive Party. Lassalle of course advocated the introduction of equal manhood suffrage, assuring the prime minister that "the working class feels instinctively inclined toward a dictatorship, if it can first be justly convinced that this dictatorship is being exercised in its interest." Bismarck, on the other hand, wanted to be sure that the weapon with which he was being asked to arm the workers would not some day be

[9] "Zur Arbeiterfrage" (Part 2), p. 331; *Neue Preussische Zeitung,* May 29, June 5, 1864; H. Wagener, *Erlebtes,* ii, 6, 39-40; W. Saile, *Wagener und sein Verhältnis zu Bismarck,* pp. 142-143.

turned against him. "Why do you not generally vote with the conservative party where you have no prospect of electing your own candidates?" he asked Lassalle. "Our interests are common. You fight from your standpoint, as [we] do from ours, against the efforts of the bourgeoisie to seize power." But Lassalle did not seek to defeat the bourgeoisie only to strengthen the aristocracy. He wanted promises and commitments to the proletariat which Bismarck was not prepared to make. Eventually he concluded that the prime minister "has . . . from the beginning had the wish to carry out wherever possible the social element of the labor movement without the political." They continued to spar and tease, but nothing concrete came or could come of their negotiations.

The strange relationship between the Junker politician and the socialist agitator was in truth more intriguing than important. Each was too discerning not to see through the other. Bismarck, knowing that the position of his ministry was precarious, would have been willing to gamble for high stakes. Lassalle's feeble General German Workingmen's Society, however, was not a prize to tempt him. Many years later he insisted before the Reichstag that "our relationship could not in any way have the nature of a political negotiation. What could Lassalle have offered and given me? He had nothing behind him. . . . His idea which he sought to realize was the German empire, and in this we had a point of contact. Lassalle was ambitious in the grand style, and he was perhaps undecided whether the German empire should end up with the Hohenzollern dynasty or with the Lassalle dynasty." The account was in the main correct, although not entirely candid. At the time of their meetings Bismarck distrusted Lassalle, yet he hoped to use him. He confided to his assistant Robert von Keudell that the latter "is indeed a visionary and his philosophy of life a utopia, but he talks so wittily about it that people like to listen to him. He is the best speaker who has ever been heard. It is his sport to talk before a few thousand workers and become intoxicated with their applause. His opposition to the Progressive Party would be politically welcome. We can therefore let his agitation continue for a while, with the proviso that at the right moment we will intervene." The prime minister felt uncomfortable throughout his brief flirtation with socialism. He soon saw that little would be gained by encouraging a working-class movement which was both radical and weak. Then late in 1863 new developments on the international scene opened to him the opportunity of attaining his ends by a triumph of foreign policy. He turned in relief from projects of social reform to the more congenial statecraft of blood and iron.[10]

For Lassalle, on the other hand, the association with Bismarck had become the last hope of achieving success. He had set out to ensnare the prime minister in an alliance which would ultimately destroy the old order in Central Europe. He ended, driven by ambition and despair, in his own trap. In September 1862 he had greeted the news of the appointment of a new ministry in Berlin with a sneer about "Bismarck-Schönehose" whom he described as "a thoroughly reactionary fellow and Junker from whom only reactionary experiments are to be expected." After they met his opinion of the Prussian statesman improved, but at no time would he acknowledge that in their relationship the latter's position was the stronger. Four months before his death he was still assuring Countess Hatzfeldt that Bismarck "is now acting, intentionally or not, as my agent." In one of their conversations he is even reported to have told the prime minister that "we would only go a short way together, and then would fight against one another all

10 O. v. Bismarck, *Werke*, XI, 606, XIV/II, 640; Gustav Mayer, *Bismarck und Lassalle: Ihr Briefwechsel und ihre Gespräche* (Berlin, 1928), p. 60; Hermann Oncken, "Publizistische Quellen zu den Beziehungen zwischen Bismarck und Lassalle," *Archiv für die Geschichte des Sozialismus und der Arbeiterbewegung*, IV (1914), 97; F. Lassalle, *Briefe und Schriften*, IV, 353; R. v. Keudell, *Fürst und Fürstin Bismarck*, p. 178.

the more bitterly." Yet in fact he was increasingly dependent on Bismarck's good will. As it became obvious
that all his eloquence and charm could not create a
strong political movement, Lassalle recognized that the
only chance of achieving his purpose lay in the support
of the government. As long as his meetings with the
prime minister continued, he could still hope that the
Prussian state would become the instrument for the establishment of socialism. He could still feel important.
He could still prophesy before a court trying him for
subversion: "I proclaim to you then in this solemn place
that perhaps not another year will pass before Herr von
Bismarck plays the role of Robert Peel, and the general
and direct franchise is promulgated!" His listeners, impressed by rumors that he had connections in high
places, half believed his prophecies.

Bismarck's growing involvement in the Schleswig-
Holstein question, therefore, meant for Lassalle the
dwindling of his prospects. Throughout the fall of 1863
he hoped against hope to retain the favor of the prime
minister by pronouncements on foreign policy favorable
to the interests of Prussia. In dealing with the Polish
uprising he argued that "Germany has in many ways
known how to Germanize provinces which had originally been conquered by force, and to transform them
into conquests of German culture. . . . The re-establishment of an independent Poland under the protection
of Germany is the most glorious and legitimate foreign
task of the latter." His position on the conflict with
Denmark, moreover, was bound to meet with Bismarck's
approval: "We cannot possibly fight for the legitimate
right of succession of the Duke of Augustenburg! . . .
We should warn with utmost vigor against the sending
of volunteers and gymnasts to Schleswig-Holstein. . . .
The supporters of the Nationalverein and of the Progressive Party, who are full of enthusiasm for the legitimate right of succession of princes, seem to want to use
Schleswig-Holstein as an opportunity to divert attention

from the domestic situation, and to escape under the guise of patriotism from the solution of a conflict to which they are not equal." He also wrote directly to the prime minister, assuring him that "the growth of my movement among the public is increasing amazingly, in the Rhine Province on the most colossal scale!" More than that, he had found "the desired 'magic formulas,' magic formulas of the most sweeping effect" for gaining a majority in parliament favorable to the government.

It was useless. Bismarck was growing tired of the importunities of the socialist agitator. The demands of international diplomacy now left him little time for schemes of popular enfranchisement or social improvement. Lassalle, sensing that their relationship was drawing to a close, became more urgent. He was pathetically eager to retain the prime minister's interest. He sent him a copy of his *Herr Bastiat-Schulze von Delitzsch*, boasting that "this work will bring about the most thorough destruction of the Progressive Party and of the entire liberal bourgeoisie." The reply was a curt note from Keudell thanking the author for the book and expressing his chief's regret that "he is in no position to receive you in person in the next few days, and that he also cannot arrange for any appointment, because pressing business has accumulated in greater volume than ever." The tone was unmistakable. Lassalle's association with Bismarck had come to an end. He must have realized that the game was up, for he wrote the prime minister a final letter full of injured pride. After expounding his views on foreign and domestic policy, he expressed dignified disappointment that the presentation of his work had inspired nothing more than an impersonal acknowledgment by a secretary whom he did not even know. As for future meetings, "it goes without saying that before I inconvenience his Excellency again, I shall await his initiative."

That was late in February 1864. If Lassalle still entertained the hope that Bismarck might renew their association, the prime minister's silence during the en-suing months disabused him. Now that his ties to the cabinet had been cut, what could he expect to accomplish with a movement whose membership was not even five thousand? As the future began to look hopeless, his resiliency seemed to leave him. He sounded tired in his speech before the court in Düsseldorf, admitting that "it is hard for a man of my age and my habits to go to prison for twelve months or only for twelve days, and in this respect things are no longer the same with me as in my youth." Shortly before his death he was writing to Countess Hatzfeldt: "I wish for nothing with greater longing than to be rid of politics as a whole, and to withdraw to scholarship, friendship, and nature. I am sick and tired of politics! . . . I am too old and too big for children's games!" Before him now stretched the dreary prospect of an existence wasted in thankless party drudgery.[11]

The duel with Janko von Rakowitza saved him from all that. If his lifework had proved a disappointment, he was at least fortunate in his death. His mission as a labor organizer had been accomplished, and anything he might have done thereafter would only have diminished his reputation. He lacked the patience and the selflessness to guide a working-class party through the years of painful growth. His imperious will would sooner or later have alienated his followers and splintered the weak socialist movement. Lassalle alive could expect only disillusionment, but Lassalle dead received a full measure of that recognition for which he had always hungered. The laboring men to whom he had brought hope of salvation mourned in him the great departed prophet, singing of the graveyard in Breslau where "slumbers the one who gave us swords." Marx, who had resented Lassalle's airs and achievements, could

[11] F. Lassalle, *Briefe und Schriften*, IV, 297, 353, 370; H. Oncken, "Publizistische Quellen," p. 97; G. Mayer, *Bismarck und Lassalle*, pp. 81-82, 103-104, 106-108; F. Lassalle, *Reden und Schriften*, III, 443-444, IV, 154, 306-309.

now grieve in an unexpectedly elegiac tone: "He died young, in triumph, like Achilles." He even conceded that "Lassalle, and this remains his immortal accomplishment, awakened the labor movement in Germany once again after its slumber of fifteen years." At the opposite pole Hermann Wagener, freed from the threat of a talented competitor, was equally generous in his praise: "Lassalle was a man of genius, a creative man, . . . and . . . if he made errors and mistakes, they were the errors and mistakes of a great, important man." Long afterward even Bismarck, at the height of his power as chancellor of Germany, paid a condescending tribute to the socialist leader: "I regret that his political position and mine did not allow me to see much of him, but I would have been glad to have a man like that, of such talent and witty disposition, for a neighboring landowner." Death at last brought Lassalle the homage which life had denied him.[12]

It also brought liberation to the General German Workingmen's Society. The socialist movement could not have developed into a vital force in political life without emerging from the shadow of its creator, who had become its incubus. Now that he was gone, it followed its course free from his despotic tutelage. Although torn by factional jealousies and rivalries, it went on preaching to the lower classes the gospel of communal ownership which would end their impoverishment:

> Only the mode of production built on an equality of rights has the power to relieve basically the misery of the workers. Not through gentlemen of the clergy, not through supervision of women and children in the factories, not through factory inspectors, also not solely

---

[12] H. Oncken, *Lassalle*, p. 431; J. B. v. Schweitzer, *Aufsätze und Reden*, p. 33; K. Marx and F. Engels, *Ausgewählte Briefe*, p. 246; Prussia, *Stenographische Berichte über die Verhandlungen der durch die Allerhöchste Verordnung vom 28. Juli 1866 einberufenen beiden Häuser des Landtages: Haus der Abgeordneten* (6 vols., Berlin, 1866-67), II, 1266; O. v. Bismarck, *Werke*, XI, 606-607.

through having the workers participate in the profits of labor and thereby accumulate savings, not through the attempted but impossible creation of a new middle estate lying in the middle between rich and poor, but simply and solely through having the workers rely on the principle of the equality of rights, become themselves the entrepreneurs, and in this way pocket the profits of labor as independent men rather than as wards, can we help the working class basically and effectively. Only one way, the starting point of every improvement, leads to the state credit which is necessary for this, namely, the general and direct suffrage.

This was Lassalle's familiar panacea whose appeal did not diminish with his death. Others could use it to good effect. The membership of the General German Workingmen's Society, which amounted to about 4,600 in the summer of 1864, rose to 9,400 by December 1865, and at the outbreak of the Seven Weeks' War late the following spring it was reported to be 9,200. The socialist movement was demonstrating its capacity to grow without the possessive genius of its founder.[13]

Even Bismarck was impressed. To be sure, he had no intention of entering into a personal relationship with any of the labor leaders. His association with Lassalle had revealed how deep was the gulf separating him from working-class radicalism. But he was prepared to maintain an indirect connection with the socialist movement in the hope of using it for the furtherance of his policies. He planted articles in the *Social-Demokrat*, for example, the organ of the General German Workingmen's Society, whose hostility to bourgeois liberalism reinforced his own position. The *quid pro quo* of this transaction remains a secret, but the prime minister must in all likelihood have offered financial assistance to the chronically impoverished newspaper. More is

---

[13] *Nordstern*, November 12, 1864; H. Oncken, *Lassalle*, pp. 393-394; F. Mehring, *Die deutsche Sozialdemokratie*, pp. 54-55; F. Mehring, *Geschichte der deutschen Sozialdemokratie*, II, 166-167, 182; A. Bebel, *Aus meinem Leben*, II, 41.

known about his dealings with the Lassalleans on the eve of the Seven Weeks' War, when he was feverishly trying to whip up popular support for the conflict with Austria. Early in April 1866 the *Social-Demokrat* received a loan of 7,500 marks from Bismarck, while a month later its editor, Johann Baptist von Schweitzer, was unexpectedly released from prison, where he had been serving a one-year sentence for the incitement of public disorder.

The ostensible reason for this act of clemency was Schweitzer's poor health, although no sooner had he regained his freedom than he launched into a vigorous agitation whose tone was sure to please the authorities in Berlin. He endorsed Bismarck's proposal for a German national assembly elected by manhood suffrage: "They are placing a weapon in our hands. Should we, out of mistrust of our own strength, timidly shrink back from this weapon? . . . If a German parliament is convoked on the basis of a general, equal, and direct franchise with the full qualification of everyone to elect and be elected, if such a parliament is convoked, what should keep us from electing our representatives to this parliament? . . . Our watchword must therefore be: We will vote!" As for the danger of a civil war in Central Europe, he had written while still in prison that the interests of the proletariat harmonized with those of Prussia: "It is entirely clear to the workers that they, if for no other reason than that it is impossible, can have no good grounds for wanting to keep Prussia from destroying the system of petty states, that is, from waging war against Austria, if she has the courage for it." When hostilities began, he argued that "we should never abandon the cause of justice and freedom, not for the general suffrage and not for all the possessions in the world. But we should and we want to abandon Austria, the stupefied Austria of the concordat, or rather her government, just as we would gladly abandon Prussia and her absolutism if Austria had followed a course of concessions

252

to us." And, shortly after the battle of Sadowa, a meeting which the General German Workingmen's Society convened in Hamburg called on the German people to back Prussia because only through her could national unity and a representative assembly based on manhood suffrage be achieved.[14]

The Seven Weeks' War marked a turning point in the development of the labor movement in Central Europe. For one thing, it ended once and for all Bismarck's dealings with socialism. The Lassalleans, to be sure, had generally backed his policies, yet their help had been of no practical effect. The outcome of the hostilities was determined not by public opinion, but by the force of arms. Now that success had made him a national hero, he no longer needed the support of the industrial proletariat. Indeed, a connection with lower-class radicalism might embarrass him in the negotiations with his new liberal allies, whom he needed for the consolidation of his victory. He thus lost interest in projects of social reform which had intrigued him during the constitutional conflict. The General German Workingmen's Society also underwent a change. At first it tried to remain in the good graces of the government. Schweitzer, the most able of Lassalle's successors, endorsed the growth of Prussia at the expense of the secondary states; he supported the formation of the North German Confederation; he even accepted the separation of Austria from Germany as a provisional arrangement. But the increasing commitment of the government to a program of laissez faire destroyed whatever hopes the

14 Adolf Richter, *Bismarck und die Arbeiterfrage im preussischen Verfassungskonflikt* (Stuttgart, 1935) , p. 259; Gustav Mayer, "Der Allgemeine Deutsche Arbeiterverein und die Krisis 1866," *Archiv für Sozialwissenschaft und Sozialpolitik*, LVII (1927) , 170-172, 174-175; Heinz Hümmler, *Opposition gegen Lassalle: Die revolutionäre proletarische Opposition im Allgemeinen Deutschen Arbeiterverein, 1862/63–1866* (Berlin, 1963) , pp. 206-207; J. B. v. Schweitzer, *Aufsätze und Reden*, pp. 116-117, 131-132, 149; Gustav Mayer, "Die Lösung der deutschen Frage im Jahre 1866 und die Arbeiterbewegung," *Festgaben für Wilhelm Lexis zur siebzigsten Wiederkehr seines Geburtstages* (Jena, 1907) , p. 246.

labor movement might have had regarding the new regime. The parliamentary elections of 1867, moreover, revealed that the introduction of manhood suffrage would not of itself alter the established system of property relations. Socialism therefore began to turn from the nostrums of its early years to the essential tasks of organization and propaganda.

The result was an unspectacular but steady growth. Internal conflicts and disappointment with the election results had reduced the membership of the General German Workingmen's Society to only about 2,500 in May 1867. Yet it rose again to 3,400 in November, by August 1868 it stood at 7,200, and in March 1869 it reached 12,000. Then came a decline, but in January 1870 the organization still had between 8,000 and 9,000 followers. Furthermore, the association of trade unions which Schweitzer helped found in September 1868 contained approximately 50,000 members as of May 1869, although by the beginning of the following year the number had fallen to less than half. The voting for the Reichstag of the North German Confederation had also shown that the Lassalleans enjoyed support in the working-class districts of the Rhineland, Saxony, Silesia, and the Hamburg region. In February 1867 they polled some 40,000 votes, but the distribution of the ballots was such that none of their candidates prevailed. In the next election seven months later, however, while their total strength declined, they won three seats, and for the first time socialists entered a legislative body in Germany. Early in 1869, moreover, the General German Workingmen's Society displayed its growing power by a victory in the by-election in Duisburg with an absolute majority over the combined votes of the liberal and the conservative candidate. Even the hapless *Social-Demokrat*, which was in constant financial difficulty, gradually increased its circulation to respectable proportions. In the first two years after its founding in December 1864 the newspaper never had more than 400 subscribers. But in the course of 1867 sales doubled from 600 to 1,200, and by September 1868 Schweitzer was reporting in a letter to Marx that the run would soon be enlarged to 3,400 copies. A year later the figure was more than 4,500. For a publication whose readership came almost entirely from the working class, this was a creditable achievement.[15]

The followers of Lassalle were not the only ones to gain strength from the increasing class consciousness of labor. While the General German Workingmen's Society was trying to effect the liberation of the proletariat in alliance with a conservative and expansionist Prussia, others hoped to attain the same end through a democratic federation of self-governing states in Central Europe. Wilhelm Liebknecht had been a fiery bourgeois forty-eighter whose passionate devotion to freedom led him to favor the destruction of all social distinctions based on private property. August Bebel, on the other hand, was a self-educated and self-made son of the working class who had become important in the labor movement as a leader of the liberal Assembly of German Workingmen's Societies, although he soon found the teachings of Marx more congenial than those of Schulze-Delitzsch. Immediately after the Seven Weeks' War he and Liebknecht helped organize the Saxon People's Party on a platform designed to rally the progressive forces in the secondary states which still hoped to reverse the verdict of Sadowa. It condemned "the war . . . which has been waged solely in the interests of dynastic

15 Gustav Mayer, *Johann Baptist von Schweitzer und die Sozialdemokratie: Ein Beitrag zur Geschichte der deutschen Arbeiterbewegung* (Jena, 1909), pp. 21, 167-169, 193, 199, 201-202, 207, 226, 228, 248-251, 300, 342, 355, n. 1, 363-364, 407; F. Mehring, *Geschichte der deutschen Sozialdemokratie*, II, 200-202, 205-206, 208, 210, 233-234, 241, 255, 263, 270, 280, 286-287; F. Mehring, *Die deutsche Sozialdemokratie*, pp. 77-78, 89; A. Bebel, *Aus meinem Leben*, II, 50, 52, 58, 66, 69, 109-111; *Europäischer Geschichtskalender*, ed. H. Schulthess (1868), p. 89; R. Morgan, *The German Social Democrats*, p. 163; Eduard Bernstein, *Die Geschichte der Berliner Arbeiter-Bewegung: Ein Kapitel zur Geschichte der deutschen Sozialdemokratie* (3 vols., Berlin, 1907-10), I, 168, 174-179, 206; J. B. v. Schweitzer, *Aufsätze und Reden*, p. 232, 277.

and particularistic endeavors," and demanded the convocation of a national parliament "representing all German states including of course German Austria." A free and united fatherland was to be built on "general, direct, and equal suffrage with secret voting in all areas of civic life." There should be "no hereditary central authority, no smaller Germany under Prussian leadership, no Prussia enlarged through annexation, no greater Germany under Austria leadership." Federal democracy in Central Europe would abolish all privileges based on class, birth, and religion. It would separate church and state, promote popular education, introduce freedom of movement and enterprise, establish local self-government, improve the administration of justice, and recognize the right of assembly, association, and free speech. The only plank dealing with the social question spoke of "improvement in the position of the working class," and recommended "furtherance and support for the system of cooperatives, especially of producer cooperatives, so that the opposition of capital and labor can be eliminated."

This was a program calculated to facilitate an alliance between bourgeois reformism and plebeian radicalism. It could attract middle-class democrats, reformers, federalists, particularists, enthusiasts, and visionaries as well as the independent skilled workers who still considered themselves burghers rather than proletarians. The ringing phrases were not enough to change the outcome of the Seven Weeks' War, but they helped elect Bebel and Liebknecht to the parliament of the North German Confederation. Here the two continued to inveigh against the new order, the former insisting that "this confederation is only a greater Prussia surrounded by a number of vassal states whose governments are nothing more than governors general of the Prussian crown," while the latter prophesied that "world history . . . will transcend this north confederation which signifies nothing other than the dismemberment, enthrallment, and enfeeblement of Germany. It will transcend this north

256

German Reichstag which is nothing but the fig leaf of absolutism."

Liebknecht in particular was obsessed by hatred for the new order, which to him was only the tool of a despotic and militaristic Junkerdom. His implacable hostility toward the North German Confederation, however, seemed illogical to Engels, who argued that national unification was a necessary condition for the victory of socialism. "We cannot do Bismarck a greater favor than to let ourselves get mixed up with the Austrians and south German federalists, ultramontanes, and dispossessed princes." His advice was "1. to take a position which is critical rather than simply negative, that is to say, reactionary, toward the events and results of 1866 . . . , and 2. to attack the enemies of Bismarck as much as him, for they too are not worth anything." Marx, on the other hand, showed greater understanding for his willful disciple: "To act altogether correctly would require much more critical disposition and dialectical skill than our Wilhelm possesses. . . . Besides, Prussophobia is the feeling to which he exclusively owes his verve and singleness of purpose." For the time being he was prepared to accept Liebknecht's explanation that "I do not deal here solely with trained communists, but rather with commun[ist] recruits who still have certain prejudices which must be treated with consideration."[16]

His patience was soon rewarded. In September 1868 the Assembly of German Workingmen's Societies meeting in Nürnberg voted under the influence of Bebel and Liebknecht to affiliate with the International Workingmen's Association, the First International. Its resolution affirmed that "the emancipation of the laboring classes

---

[16] W. Liebknecht, *Briefwechsel mit Marx und Engels*, p. 87. Cf. F. Mehring, *Die deutsche Sozialdemokratie*, pp. 225-227; Germany, *Verhandlungen des Reichstages im Jahre 1867*, I, 678; Germany, *Stenographische Berichte über die Verhandlungen des Reichstages des Norddeutschen Bundes: I. Legislatur-Periode, Session 1867* (2 vols., Berlin, 1867), I, 452; K. Marx and F. Engels, *Briefwechsel*, III, 539, 552-553.

must be won by the laboring classes themselves," that "the economic dependence of the man of labor on the monopolists of the tools of labor constitutes the basis of servitude in every form, of social misery, of spiritual degradation and political dependence," and that "the political movement is the indispensable tool for the economic liberation of the working classes." This was too much for the more moderate workers' associations, which promptly seceded, but a majority representing about 6,000 members endorsed the shift to the left. The next step was taken in August of the following year at Eisenach with the formation of the Social Democratic Workingmen's Party, which absorbed the Assembly of German Workingmen's Societies. Its platform stated point-blank that "the Social Democratic Party seeks to abolish the present mode of production (wage system) and to secure for every worker the full product of his work through cooperative labor."

The immediate objectives of the new organization were still temperate enough to encourage a few middle-class reformers to hope that they could retain their connection with proletarian radicalism. There were such familiar demands of federalist democracy as the general and direct suffrage, equality before the law, the establishment of a popular militia to replace standing armies, the separation of church and state, the furtherance of public education, the reform of the judicial system, and the freedom of the press and of association. Some of the bourgeois left-wingers in the secondary states might even have swallowed the proposals for the initiative and the referendum, the prohibition of child labor, the restriction of the employment of women, the progressive income tax, and producer cooperatives supported by the state. But when at its congress in Stuttgart in June 1870 the new party decided to support the position of the First International on landownership by proclaiming that "the economic development of modern society will make it a social necessity to transform arable land into common social property," it cut its last ties to the liberal camp. Its commitment to socialism was now irrevocable.[17]

Although the Social Democratic Workingmen's Party gained strength in the course of the year which elapsed between its founding and the outbreak of the Franco-Prussian War, it was unable to catch up with the General German Workingmen's Society. For one thing, it was still too inexperienced in the techniques of organization and propaganda. But more important, its position on national unification placed it at a disadvantage in relation to the Lassalleans. The latter accepted the North German Confederation, adapting their strategy to the broadened political framework which it provided. The Eisenachers, on the other hand, continued to advocate resistance to the new order because of its subservience to Prussia. They thereby restricted the effectiveness of their agitation to the urban proletariat of the secondary states of central and southern Germany, particularly Saxony and Württemberg. The workers of the big cities of the north and west like Berlin, Hamburg, Cologne, and Elberfeld were not to be won by appeals for a free federation of democratic governments in Central Europe. Through their refusal to accept national unification from the hands of Bismarck, the Social Democrats were sacrificing the propagandistic opportunities offered by a large state for the support of a doomed small-town radicalism. In the long run their doctrinaire scruples were bound to prove costly. The 6,000 members who in 1868 supported the decision of the Assembly of German Workingmen's Societies to affiliate with the First International had become about 10,000 by the time of the formation of the new party a year later. But despite the inflated claims of its leaders, the figure as of the middle of 1870 was still not much more than

---

[17] *Europäischer Geschichtskalender*, ed. H. Schulthess (1868), pp. 92-93 (1870), p. 77; F. Mehring, *Geschichte der deutschen Sozialdemokratie*, II, 243; G. Mayer, *Schweitzer*, p. 236; A. Bebel, *Aus meinem Leben*, II, 93-94.

10,000. While the Lassalleans with the help of successful by-elections eventually gained five seats in the Reichstag, the Eisenachers had no more than two, and even those had been won in the name of the Saxon People's Party. The circulation of the *Volksstaat*, the newspaper of the Social Democrats, rose from 2,000 at the time of its founding in the fall of 1869 to approximately 3,000 by the following summer. Two years earlier Liebknecht had written to Engels: "I have won a position here. My objective is primarily to maintain and fortify it." Now he could contemplate his accomplishments with some satisfaction, although the Social Democratic Workingmen's Party was still no match for the General German Workingmen's Society.[18]

The Franco-Prussian War became the great test of the youthful socialist movement, destroying the illusions of the Lassalleans as well as the Eisenachers. If the former saw at last that a victorious monarchy would never become the instrument for establishing a socialist economy, the latter recognized that opposition to the centralization of state authority was only a blind rejection of political reality. When hostilities began, the German labor movement found itself torn between distrust of Bismarck and fear of Napoleon III. For the General German Workingmen's Society the choice was not difficult, since it had always been ready to support the government whenever in its opinion the interests of the established order coincided with those of the working class. The *Social-Demokrat* promptly asserted that "the German nation and even the revolutionary German proletariat will have to take their stand on the side of the Prussian government. . . . A French reaction which achieves complete domination is even more dangerous for the freedom of Europe than a Prussian reaction." The Social Democratic Workingmen's Party, on the other hand,

---

[18] F. Mehring, *Geschichte der deutschen Sozialdemokratie*, II, 274, 280, 288-289; G. Mayer, *Schweitzer*, p. 342; F. Mehring, *Die deutsche Sozialdemokratie*, pp. 98-99, 288; W. Liebknecht, *Briefwechsel mit Marx und Engels*, p. 89.

became divided on the issue of the war. The executive committee issued a proclamation announcing that "we will help with all our determination to defend the inviolability of German soil against Napoleonic and every other despotism," but in the Reichstag Liebknecht and Bebel could not bring themselves to offer their support to the hated North German Confederation. They refused to vote for war credits, explaining that "as opponents in principle of every dynastic war, as social republicans and members of the International Workingmen's Association, which without regard for nationality opposes all oppressors and seeks to unite all the oppressed in one great fraternal alliance, we cannot declare ourselves either directly or indirectly in favor of the present war."

Marx was of course anxious to reconcile his quarreling followers, but privately he hoped for a Prussian victory. "If the Prussians win, then the centralization of state power [will be] conducive to the centralization of the German working class. German preponderance would furthermore move the center of gravity of the West European labor movement from France to Germany, and we need only to compare the movement in the two countries from 1866 to now to see that the German working class is theoretically and organizationally superior to the French. Its preponderance over the French on the world scene would at the same time be the preponderance of our theory over that of Proudhon." Engels was even more emphatic in his rejection of the position taken by Liebknecht and Bebel. He reasoned that "if Germany is victorious, then French Bonapartism will in any case be finished, the eternal wrangling about the establishment of German unity will finally be over, the German workers will be able to organize on a national scale quite differently than hitherto, and the French workers will surely have a freer field than under Bonapartism, whatever government may follow there. The entire mass of the German people of all classes

261

has perceived that what is at stake above all is the national existence." Besides, he went on, "B[ismarck] is now still doing some of our work, as in 1866, in his way and without wanting to, but he is doing it just the same. He is creating for us a cleaner board than before." Yet there were differences of opinion on this point within the German labor movement. The longer the war continued, the more it divided the socialists by compelling them to take sides in a question for which there was no clear-cut theoretical answer.[19]

Sedan solved their dilemma. The fall of Napoleon III and the proclamation of a republic in France ended the only justification for the war as far as socialism was concerned. Now its primary objective became a peace treaty renouncing territorial expansion and establishing friendly relations with the new regime in Paris. The policy of the government, on the other hand, sought to crown the work of national unification with the spoils of victory. A conflict of the two was inevitable. Early in September 1870 the executive committee of the Social Democratic Workingmen's Party published a manifesto demanding "an honorable peace with the French people." The General German Workingmen's Society needed a little more time to make up its mind, but at the end of November the members of parliament from both parties voted against additional war credits. Bismarck's successes only stiffened their resistance. They disapproved the treaties by which the southern states joined the North German Confederation; they opposed the assumption of the imperial title by the king of Prussia; and they condemned the annexation of Alsace-Lorraine as "a crime against international law" and "a blot on German history." The hostility they aroused through their stand on the war was intensified, moreover, by an indiscreet letter from the French consul in Vienna thanking them "for the noble words which you

---

[19] *Social-Demokrat*, July 17, 1870; *Der Volksstaat*, July 30, 1870; A. Bebel, *Aus meinem Leben*, II, 178-179; K. Marx and F. Engels, *Briefwechsel*, IV, 407, 438-439.

have spoken in the Berlin parliament in the midst of an assembly fanaticized by the spirit of conquest and of intoxication with militarism." Most shocking of all, they dared support the Paris Commune. While the propertied classes shuddered at the red specter, the labor movement openly rejoiced. "We are and we declare ourselves to be jointly and severally for the Commune," proclaimed the *Volksstaat*, "and we are ready to defend its actions at any time and against any man." It was the supreme gesture of defiance toward the new order in Germany.[20]

The socialists paid a high price for their boldness. By opposing military victory and national unification they were scorning the political ideals of a nation exulting in success. They had to be punished. While hostilities were still in progress, the executive committee of the Social Democratic Workingmen's Party was arrested, and after the return of peace Liebknecht and Bebel were sentenced to prison for conspiring to commit treason. More serious was the defeat in the first postwar parliamentary election, held amid celebrations of the great triumph of the new German Empire. The number of socialist votes was respectable, to be sure, more than 100,000, or 3 per cent of the total, about 60,000 for the Lassalleans and 40,000 for the Eisenachers. But of the seven representatives of the labor movement who had sat in the Reichstag before the hostilities, only Bebel was left. Its position on the issues of war and unification, moreover, cost socialism a good part of its following. The membership of the General German Workingmen's Society

20 *Der Volksstaat*, September 11, 1870, June 7, 1871; Germany, *Stenographische Berichte über die Verhandlungen des Reichstages des Norddeutschen Bundes: I. Legislatur-Periode (II. Ausserordentliche Session 1870)* (Berlin, 1870), pp. 32-33, 164, 181-182; *Europäischer Geschichtskalender*, ed. H. Schulthess (1870), pp. 126, 137; Germany, *Stenographische Berichte über die Verhandlungen des Deutschen Reichstages: I. Legislatur-Periode, I. Session 1871* (3 vols., Berlin, 1871), II, 921; Sinclair W. Armstrong, "The Social Democrats and the Unification of Germany, 1863-71," *Journal of Modern History*, XII (1940), 504, 508-509; A. Bebel, *Aus meinem Leben*, II, 199.

fell to below 6,000, while the Lassallean association of trade unions dwindled from about 21,000 to 4,000. The decline of the Eisenachers was also serious, from 10,000 to 6,000. The *Volksstaat* lost some 300 readers in the last months of 1870, although by the following summer its circulation was greater than before the war. Subscriptions to the *Social-Demokrat*, on the other hand, diminished by 40 per cent, and the newspaper was forced to discontinue publication. Nor was the government any longer inclined to regard the socialists as exasperating but harmless visionaries. Bismarck came to the conclusion that "action of the state authority presently in power seems to me the only means of putting a halt to the socialist movement in its present aberration." He was already thinking of repressive measures against the enemies of the established order of society.[21]

Yet by refusing to compromise its orthodoxy, socialism sustained its sense of commitment. Adversity transformed it at last into a mature working-class movement free from vain hopes and wishful illusions. It became tougher, more aggressive. It was ready now to battle for the liberation of the proletariat with the unaided strength of the proletariat. On the morrow of the Franco-Prussian War, Liebknecht, speaking for a militant labor movement, defied the ruling classes of Germany in the tone of an Old Testament prophet:

[21] F. Mehring, *Geschichte der deutschen Sozialdemokratie*, II, 287-289, 297-299, 303-304, 308; *Statistisches Jahrbuch für das Deutsche Reich*, I (1880), 140-141; *Die Reichstags-Wahlen von 1867 bis 1883: Statistik der Wahlen zum konstituierenden und norddeutschen Reichstage, zum Zollparlament, sowie zu den fünf ersten Legislatur-Perioden des deutschen Reichstages*, ed., A. Phillips (Berlin, 1883), pp. 267, 269; *Die Reichstags-Wahlen von 1867 bis 1903: Eine Statistik der Reichstagswahlen nebst den Programmen der Parteien und einem Verzeichnisse der gewählten Abgeordneten*, ed. Fritz Specht and Paul Schwabe, 2nd edn. (Berlin, 1904), pp. 318, 320; A. Bebel, *Aus meinem Leben*, II, 128, 230, 233; G. Mayer, *Schweitzer*, pp. 364, 407-408; *Aktenstücke zur Wirthschaftspolitik des Fürsten Bismarck*, ed. Heinrich von Poschinger (2 vols., Berlin, 1890-91), I, 160-161, 165-167; O. v. Bismarck, *Werke*. VI/c, 7-8.

Success does not change injustice into justice. What you call renown is to us the opposite of renown; what you call honor is to us the opposite of honor. The triumphs of which you boast are to us only the triumphs of barbarity. War, even if it is the most glorious, is a sin against the holy spirit of humanity, a misfortune for the conqueror as well as for the conquered. The word "fatherland" which you utter casts no spell over us. Fatherland in your sense is to us an antiquated notion, a reactionary concept hostile to civilization. Humanity cannot be imprisoned in national boundaries. Our native land is the world. *Ubi bene ibi patria,* where we thrive, that is, where we can be human beings, there is our fatherland. Your fatherland is for us only a place of misery, a prison, a hunting ground in which we are the pursued game.

It was socialism's declaration of war against the triumphant new order in Central Europe.[22]

[22] W. Liebknecht, *Zu Trutz und Schutz: Festrede gehalten zum Stiftungsfest des Crimmitschauer Volksvereins am 22. October 1871,* 4th edn. (Leipzig, 1874), p. 4

THE SYSTEM OF POLITICS

SEVEN

Status and Power

THE political struggles of the mid-century culminating in the achievement of national unification involved only a small minority of the population of Central Europe. The age of mass parties was still to come, and the forms of civic authority continued to be determined by groups in society drawn from the well-to-do classes. There was as yet no instrumentality of government through which the wishes of the proletariat could be expressed or ascertained. Although both advocates and opponents of reform insisted that they represented the popular will, neither of them really knew what the popular will was. Both were inclined to identify their own interests with those of the nation; both were resolved to restrict effective participation in politics to men of property and education. In the second part of his *Grundsätze der Realpolitik*, which appeared in 1869, August Ludwig von Rochau pointed to the class basis of the movement for individual liberty and constitutional rule:

> The civic struggle for freedom in Germany has down to the most recent years been waged exclusively by the middle classes, and to them alone must be credited the gains won in behalf of the people from princely authority and from the bureaucracy. The mass of the people stood aloof from this struggle, devoting to it even the mere interest of a spectator only in certain moments, and particularly in a few cases which affected them directly. For the interests primarily at stake were . . . mostly strange and even incomprehensible to the great multitude. This is true of constitutionalism itself, the most important questions of the constitution, freedom of the

269

press, publicity and oral proceedings in law cases, trials by jury, the independence of judicial officials, the separation of justice from administration, in short, most of the civic goals for which liberalism during the last half century has exerted its greatest efforts. Whatever freedom has been achieved in all these directions, the mass of the people has practically no part in it.[1]

Yet not only the masses were uninterested in questions of political principle. The upper and middle classes also displayed an indifference which was the despair of dedicated party men. During those years of prosperity landowners, bankers, industrialists, and merchants were often too busy making money to trouble about public affairs. Especially among the aristocrats beyond the Elbe it was difficult to arouse more than a cursory interest. Discouraged by the "supineness, laziness, and pusillanimity" he had found in the conservatives of Pomerania, Roon sighed that "the few active and energetic characters . . . are too thinly sown. There is too little salt. The dough remains tasteless, it does not rise, and continues in its sticky inertia." Wagener in his memoirs recalled that most noblemen wanted nothing more than to sip their glass of wine in peace and play a sociable game of cards. "In those days I got to know many gentlemen who did not consider it worth the effort even to open the communications which they received from the lower house of the legislature, and who therefore had no idea of what was being debated." The landed aristocracy was just beginning to adjust to the unfamiliar system of party politics.[2]

The urban bourgeoisie was more active in public affairs, although the liberals who led the struggle against authoritarian government complained that their followers were only lukewarm. Sometimes they lacked the courage to defy the established order. Rudolf Haym,

[1] [A. L. v. Rochau], *Grundsätze der Realpolitik*, II, 22-23.
[2] H. O. Meisner, *Der preussische Kronprinz*, p. 165; H. Wagener, *Erlebtes*, I, 63.

editor of the *Preussische Jahrbücher*, admitted bitterly: "Whoever can, looks for an excuse to back out, saying that after all we cannot prevail, we must let the storm die down, and so forth." Heinrich von Treitschke shared this feeling of exasperation: "It is really my conviction that the great mass of the liberals differs lamentably from its honorable leaders in its greediness, cowardice, and lack of courage to make sacrifices, and I do not see why we should not for once tell our party to its face what its faults are." Yet indifference accounted as much as timidity for the reluctance of the middle class to engage in an out-and-out struggle with the old order. While the constitutional conflict raged in Prussia, the *Grenzboten* noted that "half the fatherland is merrily on the move taking trips, having a good time in bathing resorts and in the fresh mountain air, promenading, singing, drinking, laughing, or holding speeches among political friends." Hans Viktor von Unruh deplored "the lack of firm, steadfast dispositions in the middle classes," concluding that "the well-to-do bourgeois are politically apathetic."

This civic indolence was not confined to Prussia. The liberal journalist Moritz Busch, who eventually entered Bismarck's service, remembered conditions in Saxony: "The people in the small towns and in the country were almost without exception indifferent to all politics, vegetating comfortably in their everyday existence without any idea whatever about the great questions of the day. . . . These circles had become known through festivals of gymnasts and singers with a few national-sounding slogans, and were trained by a mildly liberal local press to declaim a little against the Junkers in Berlin and Beelzebub Bismarck." In larger cities like Leipzig the situation was not much different: "Here there was, to be sure, some party activity. Yet while many well-intentioned and estimable people participated, there was no talent which was in any way above average, and never a particularly energetic will."

271

The leaders of this cozy liberalism "would occasionally manage to organize a pretty little demonstration, a resolution, a protest, or similar fun which was considered important by the party and its newspapers, but which was basically harmless. . . . The vast majority was indifferent. Among the others there was much doctrinaire behavior, much Pickwickianism. The well-attended mass meetings did not reveal much real political interest and activity. . . . People used to feed each other the usual phrases, they shouted bravo, helped adopt a few magnificently adorned resolutions, and then sat down to their evening glass in the belief that they had performed a deed for the fatherland."

The Hanoverian jurist Gottlieb Planck, a founder of the Nationalverein, whose members came from all parts of Germany, was distressed because "precisely among the bourgeoisie, and indeed not only among the lower but also among the higher, not only where the material cares of life weighed so heavily as to paralyze intellectual vigor and interest in general questions, but also where there was no lack of political insight and where outside circumstances did not compel abstention, there appeared that lack of interest in the general welfare, that short-sighted egoism which considers only the momentary material advantage of one's own person, that deplorable weakness of character which trembles before every breath from above, that indolence which rejoices at the political movement, but cannot decide to do its own duty." The civic indifference of the well-to-do classes was partly a product of the absolutist political tradition of Central Europe, but it was partly also a reflection of material success. Expanding economic opportunities absorbed energies and talents which might otherwise have turned to constitutional reform. As Hermann Baumgarten concluded, "a people which is getting richer every day does not make a revolution." The business boom mitigated for the bourgeoisie the social grievances which nourish political militancy.[3]

---

[3] *Deutscher Liberalismus*, ed. J. Heyderhoff and P. Wentzcke, I, 162;

The lower classes regarded public affairs with even greater unconcern, but their apathy did not arise out of a sense of well-being. On the contrary, the widespread response to the artisan movement, the steady growth of socialist agitation, the increasing frequency of labor strikes, all suggest dissatisfaction of the proletariat with its position in society. Handicraftsmen did not as a rule share in the prosperity engendered by industrial expansion, and factory workers could not always be placated by a slow improvement in the standard of living which still left them on the brink of impoverishment. Yet the masses did not look to parliament for the solution of their problems. Theodor von Bernhardi was convinced that "the people will not rise over the great questions in politics—I know men well enough for that—but unfortunately an endless amount of dissatisfaction is occasioned by domestic conditions and local reasons." An ordinance promulgated by the Bismarck ministry which authorized the bureaucracy to ban newspapers considered dangerous to the public welfare failed to arouse popular opposition, but at the same time the decision of a Berlin landlord to evict an innkeeper produced a wave of rioting which continued for days. The Bavarian publicist Edmund Jörg, describing the constitutional conflict in Prussia, assured his readers that the legislature stood alone in its struggle against the crown: "The great mass of the people looks at the quarrel with cool composure also because it does not in any way see in these chambers its own representation."

Even the liberal politicians and their sympathizers, who usually claimed widespread popular support, would admit in moments of privacy or inadvertence that there was a great deal of apathy toward public affairs. In a letter to a friend, Leopold von Hoverbeck spoke of "the

---

Treitschkes Briefe, ed. M. Cornicelius, II, 267; "Deutsche Feste und Kriegsgefahr," *Die Grenzboten*, XXII (1863), no. 3, p. 234; H. Schulze-Delitzsch, *Schriften und Reden*, IV, 257; Moritz Busch, *Tagebuchblätter*, (3 vols., Leipzig, 1899), III, 481-482; [Gottlieb Planck], *Der National-verein: Seine Entstehung und bisherige Wirksamkeit* (Coburg, 1861), pp. 34-35; H. Baumgarten, "Der deutsche Liberalismus," p. 596.

slowness of all education, especially of the lower classes of the population." He regretted "that unfortunately the majority of the voters still knows very little about its rights, yes, that a general suffrage would possibly bring us naked absolutism once again. We who work for the freedom of the people do not therefore stand on a solid foundation, and we cannot therefore count on sweeping successes. We must be satisfied if only conditions in these classes improve, even though it may be very gradually." Baron Karl von Vincke-Olbendorf, a moderate member of the Prussian legislature, reported that "there is almost no talk about politics" in the country. "Among the peasants you can often hear: 'Nothing will come of it; let the king rule alone once again.' " The brilliant jurist Rudolf Jhering conceded: "I have been badly mistaken in this respect. I have considered the people more energetic and resolute. . . . The present time constitutes one of the most bitter disappointments of my life." Bernhardi noted in his diary a conversation with a resident of Silesia regarding the state of public opinion: " 'A lot of people from the middle estate,' as he puts it, handicraftsmen and the like, are thoroughly tired of political activity, and do not want to take any part in the elections. 'Nothing will after all do any good,' they say, and think that it would be better if things were again 'as before,' that is, before the introduction of a parliamentary constitution. . . . Bleak prospects!" The novelist and essayist Karl Frenzel also spoke of "the indolence and weariness of the masses, which ultimately saw in the struggle of the Progressive Party against the ministry only an endless argument without any tangible, positive decision." The liberals and the conservatives were thus engaged in a conflict which involved primarily the well-to-do-classes of society.[4]

[4] *Aus dem Leben Bernhardis*, II, 363, V, 121; *Anhang zu den Gedanken und Erinnerungen von Otto Fürst von Bismarck* (2 vols., Stuttgart and Berlin, 1901) , II, 352-353; Ludwig Dehio, "Die Taktik der Opposition während des Konflikts," *Historische Zeitschrift*, CXL (1929) , 322-323; [Edmund Jörg], "Zeitläufe: Deutschland in den Spannungen des

The indifference to politics was most pronounced among the peasantry. Absorbed in the changeless routine of farming, the countryside remained unmoved by the civic issues stirring the big city. This rural apathy prevailed in all parts of Central Europe. The efforts of the liberals in Württemberg to win popular support could not overcome the lethargy of the villages. "The peasants, it is reported to us, no longer have any interest in public affairs, since the question of extinguishing manorial obligations is settled," explained the *Beobachter* in Stuttgart. In Thuringia the *Gothaisches Tageblatt* lamented that "unfortunately the peasant in general still reads very little. He is almost completely unconcerned about books and larger newspapers, and the villages subscribe even to the smaller local press only very occasionally." The county commissioner Karl Rudolf Friedenthal of Grottkau in Silesia reported: "The military question and the budget question have not penetrated the flesh and blood of the rural population. After all, the rustic feels that in military matters and great questions of state the king is master." But the greatest political backwardness was to be found in the eastern borderlands, where conditions provoked the bitter irony of the *Preussische Jahrbücher*:

Perhaps nowhere in Prussia are there still as naïvely loyal subjects of our king as in Masuria and Lithuania. There the patriarchic outlook of days which have elsewhere long since vanished still lives in its unadulterated purity. In the heads of our Lithuanians no constitutional daybreak has as yet dawned. But the situation is not much different with regard to the political education of the German rural laborers. After all, they are to a not inconsiderable extent only Germanized Lithuanians and Slavs, but even the German residue is terribly backward.

Moments," *Historisch-politische Blätter für das katholische Deutschland*, LVII (1866), 487; L. Parisius, *Hoverbeck*, II/II, 55; *Duncker: Politischer Briefwechsel*, ed. J. Schultze, p. 347; *Rudolf von Jhering in Briefen an seine Freunde* (Leipzig, 1913), pp. 164-165; K., "Correspondenz: Aus Berlin," *Deutsches Museum*, XVI (1866), no. 1, pp. 283-284; H. Rosenberg, *Die nationalpolitische Publizistik*, II, 962.

When such a laborer, a dairyman or even a farm steward, receives a ballot, he probably still turns to his master with the question whether he will be punished if he does not obey this summons. Maintenance of his rights and his interests are concepts which have not yet entered his head. There are no political ideas which are as firmly fixed in him as the military reminiscences, and to vote against the county commissioner, the provincial governor, or, perish the thought, a royal prince are ventures which even under a system of secret voting seem to him disrespectful. . . . The laboring population of the big cities is also recruited from these elements.[5]

Service in the armed forces, however, was only part of an educational process which tended to make the lower classes politically submissive. The entire system of public instruction in Central Europe was designed to leave the determination of affairs of state in the hands of a social elite. The civic obligations of the great mass of the population were fulfilled by the payment of taxes and the bearing of arms. During the 1830's the French philosopher Victor Cousin, surveying education in the German Confederation, described Prussia as "that classic country of barracks and schools, of schools which civilize the people, and of barracks which defend them." But the barracks were more important than the schools. In 1855 the total expenditures of the Prussian government amounted to 335,000,000 marks, of which 91,000,000 went for the army and the navy, and 7,000,000 for public instruction. In 1860 the comparable figures were 392,000,-000, 104,000,000, and 8,000,000 marks, while in 1865 they were 452,000,000, 133,000,000, and 10,000,000 marks. Throughout the period of national unification the ratio of the cost of education to the cost of defense and to the overall cost of government remained by and large unchanged, about 8 per cent for the former and 2 per cent

[5] "Aus Ostpreussen," *Preussische Jahrbücher*, XXI (1868), 238. Cf. *Der Beobachter*, April 1, 1864; *Gothaisches Tageblatt*, January 9, 1864; *Duncker: Politischer Briefwechsel*, ed. J. Schultze, p. 356.

for the latter. Yet the budget for the penal institutions of the kingdom totaled 5,000,000 marks in 1855, 7,000,000 in 1860, and 6,000,000 in 1865, averaging more than 70 per cent of the budget for popular instruction. The idea that the state should use its resources to promote the well-being of the lower classes ran counter to prevailing social theories. In any event, the low level of economic development precluded large-scale public expenditures for mass welfare. The government was of necessity forced to appropriate the greatest part of its income for the basic military and administrative functions of self-preservation.

Even the modest sums available for education were distributed in a fashion calculated to maintain the distinction in the forms of learning accessible to the propertied and the propertyless classes. Of the 10,000,000 marks which the Prussian government set aside for public instruction in 1871, 4,000,000 went to the universities, 2,000,000 to the secondary schools, and 4,000,000 to the primary schools. The bulk of the funds spent for educational purposes thus helped support institutions of higher and middle learning, which provided instruction for about 3 per cent of all pupils in the kingdom. The number of those enrolled in the secondary schools was 98,000, while students in all 22 universities of Germany totaled about 15,000. Attendance in the elementary schools of Prussia alone, on the other hand, amounted to 3,900,000. The distribution of teaching personnel among the three levels of the educational system further revealed the emphasis on the training of an intellectual elite determined by economic affluence. At the time of the Franco-Prussian War there were in Germany as a whole some 1,500 university instructors of various academic ranks, 1 for every 10 students. Comparable figures for the secondary schools are unavailable, but in the late 1830's the Prussian Gymnasia employed 1,000 full-time teachers and 350 assistants for 23,000 pupils, a ratio of 1 to 17. At the same time the middle schools and citizen schools in the cities, "which comprehend that sphere of instruction necessary for educated persons of all classes," had an enrollment of 90,000 and a staff of 3,000, a ratio of 1 to 30. Yet the number of teachers in the public elementary schools was 28,000 for 2,172,000 pupils, a ratio of 1 to 79. Nor did this proportion change significantly in the course of the next thirty years, for the increase in instructional personnel barely kept pace with the increase in classroom attendance.[6]

The system of education then was designed primarily to provide academic training for a small body of students who would ultimately find employment in the bureaucracy, the armed forces, the skilled professions, and important industrial and agricultural enterprises. For the lower classes instruction meant little more than the three R's to help them practice their everyday occupations more efficiently without arousing extravagant expectations. In 1867 Heinrich von Sybel opposed manhood suffrage and direct voting, arguing that the proletariat was too ignorant to make intelligent political decisions:

> Here in Prussia two years ago the state had about 6,000 university students and 44,000 pupils in Gymnasia, Realschulen, and higher citizen schools. If on the basis of these figures you calculate roughly how many people live at present in the Prussian state who have received instruction beyond the lowest level of elementary educa-

[6] V. Cousin, *De l'instruction publique dans quelques pays de l'Allemagne et particulièrement en Prusse*, 3rd edn. (2 vols., Paris, 1840), I, 26; L. Clausnitzer, *Geschichte des preussischen Unterrichtsgesetzes*, 2nd edn. (Berlin, 1891), pp. 260, 276; W. Lexis, *A General View of the History and Organisation of Public Education in the German Empire*, trans. G. J. Tamson (Berlin, 1904), pp. 65-66, 68-70, 95; *Das Unterrichtswesen im Deutschen Reich*, ed. W. Lexis (4 vols., Berlin, 1904), I, 652; Friedrich Paulsen, *Geschichte des gelehrten Unterrichts auf den deutschen Schulen und Universitäten vom Ausgang des Mittelalters bis zur Gegenwart*, 3rd edn. (2 vols., Berlin and Leipzig, 1919-21), II, 697; [H. Berghaus], *Statistik des preussischen Staats*, pp. 229-231, 247; J. Tews, *Ein Jahrhundert preussischer Schulgeschichte: Volksschule und Volksschullehrerstand in Preussen im 19. und 20. Jahrhundert* (Leipzig, 1914), pp. 106, 156, 257.

tion, you will reach the figure of at most one million. The other 18 million . . . have not risen above the level of the scantiest elementary knowledge in their intellectual development, and every one . . . knows . . . that there will be a very similar result if you inquire into the outward conditions of social independence, into property relations. Here too there are few per cent of the population which give their members an outward position raising them above the scantiest level of elementary existence.

It was a realistic appraisal of the weakness of public education and its relationship to economic insecurity.

Conditions elsewhere on the Continent were no better, to be sure. Classroom attendance and popular literacy were as a matter of fact higher in the states of the German Confederation than anywhere else in Europe. During the 1820's the ratio of the children in school to the adult population was 1 to 8 in Prussia, 1 to 12 in Holland, 1 to 16 in England, 1 to 30 in France, and 1 to 700 in Russia. The young English writer and politician E.G.E.L. Bulwer-Lytton hailed Prussia as "that country in which, throughout the whole world, education is the most admirably administered." Yet even there the instruction of the lower classes was too superficial to prepare them for effective participation in public affairs. The classrooms were overcrowded and the teachers underpaid. Critics of the government charged that the salaries of elementary school teachers and even of teachers in the Gymnasia were so low that they were often forced to seek outside employment. The situation was particularly serious in the countryside. During the triennium 1862-64 the population at large expanded 4 per cent, but in urban districts the number of schools grew 7 per cent, male teachers increased 8 per cent and female teachers 14 per cent, and salaries rose 14 per cent. The corresponding percentages for rural districts were 1, 2, 17, and 4. Worst of all, there were many who were receiving no classroom instruction at all. In 1822 they constituted about 25 per cent of all children between the

279

ages of 6 and 14. By 1846 the percentage had dropped to 18, and as of 1864 it amounted on an average to 7. Yet in the eastern districts of the kingdom it remained high: 17 in East and West Prussia, 19 in Posen, and 34 in Pomerania, compared with 4 in Westphalia, 3 in the Rhine Province, and virtually complete school attendance in the Province of Saxony.[7]

The system of elementary education in Central Europe was on the whole successful in achieving its basic purpose of familiarizing the lower classes with the rudiments of reading and writing. According to an estimate published in 1845, while the rate of illiteracy was 93 per cent in Russia and 36 per cent in France, in Prussia it was less than 10 per cent. Some thirty years after Victor Cousin had published his admiring report on public instruction in the German Confederation, 28 per cent of the Frenchmen and 41 per cent of the Frenchwomen getting married still had not mastered the alphabet. It is no wonder that throughout Europe social reformers regarded German educational institutions with respect and envy.

Yet classroom attendance was not of itself an accurate measure of popular literacy. There were those who forgot what they had learned during their few years in school, while others managed to acquire a primary education with little or no formal instruction. Statistics on the reading and writing ability of recruits drafted into the armed forces provide a more reliable gauge of the level of learning of the lower classes. They reveal that as of the early 1840's the Province of Posen had the high-

[7] Germany, *Verhandlungen des Reichstages im Jahre 1867*, I, 428; Friedr. Wienstein, *Die preussische Volksschule in ihrer geschichtlichen Entwicklung* (Paderborn, 1915), p. 53; [Edward George Earle Lytton Bulwer], *England and the English* (2 vols., New York, 1833), I, 153; Prussia, *Verhandlungen des Landtages: Haus der Abgeordneten* (1865), I, 588-589, 593; L. Clausnitzer, *Geschichte des Unterrichtsgesetzes*, p. 243; J. Tews, *Ein Jahrhundert Schulgeschichte*, p. 107; *Mittheilungen des Statistischen Bureau's in Berlin*, I (1848), 47; Goldschmidt, "Schulpflicht und Schulbesuch in Berlin," *Zeitschrift des königlich preussischen Statistischen Bureaus*, VII (1867), 251.

est proportion of illiterate conscripts in the Prussian state, 37 per cent. Then came East and West Prussia with 12 per cent, although many years later during the constitutional conflict the liberal politician Max von Forckenbeck charged that "20 per cent of those selected for military service among us in the Province of Prussia, one of the oldest provinces of 'the state of intelligence,' cannot read and write." For Silesia the percentage was 7, for the Rhine Province 5, for Westphalia and Pomerania 2, and for Brandenburg and the Province of Saxony 1. It was 7 for the state as a whole. In the course of the next thirty years the rate of illiteracy among recruits declined to 14 per cent in Posen, 11 in West Prussia, 7 in East Prussia, 3 in Silesia, 2 in Pomerania, and 1 or less in the other provinces, an over-all average of 3 percent, including the territories annexed in 1866. Of the other states of Germany only Bavaria with 2 per cent and Mecklenburg-Schwerin and the Reuss principalities with 1 per cent each had failed to attain virtually complete literacy.

These data demonstrate a significant improvement in the effectiveness of primary instruction in Central Europe, but they do not measure the degree of education of the entire adult population. The generation which took part in the fateful events of the 1860's had received its schooling in the 1820's, 1830's, and 1840's. Its mastery of the fundamentals of learning cannot therefore be determined by the level of achievement of army conscripts at the mid-century, whose classroom training was generally superior to that received by their parents and grandparents. Of greater significance are the results of the census of 1871, which disclose that of the 9,094,757 male inhabitants of Prussia over 9 years of age, 863,843 could not read or write, a rate close to 10 per cent. This figure may be taken as a fair estimate of the degree of adult illiteracy among men in the kingdom during the previous decade, while for the other parts of Germany the proportion would on the whole be substantially lower.

Familiarity with the alphabet, however, is not a valid criterion of the popular capacity to understand public affairs. Of the 754 recruits drafted into the armed forces of Mecklenburg-Schwerin in 1852, only 21 were illiterate in the strict sense of the word. But 330 read poorly, and 106 were only able to name the letters of words; 215 could not write at all, and 285 did so haltingly; 402 did not know how to do simple arithmetic, and 254 had difficulty with sums. All in all, 381, or 51 per cent, had received a deficient elementary education and could be considered only semiliterate, as compared with the 21, or 3 per cent, who were entirely illiterate. Similar calculations for the 50,191 conscripts inducted into the Prussian army in the same period reveal that 37,733, or 75 per cent, had obtained adequate primary instruction, as determined by a mastery of the rudiments of arithmetic and the ability to write legibly and correctly. Another 10,106, or 20 per cent, were classified as having insufficient school training, that is, they could read only printed matter, and their ability to write was limited. Finally, 2,412, or 5 per cent, were out-and-out illiterates.[8]

Here is the most pertinent statistical information regarding the degree of popular education in the German Confederation. It suggests that the rate of illiteracy was in general low. Although in the rural districts of the east there were many who could not read and write, the proportion for the nation as a whole was well below 10 per cent, the smallest in Europe. More serious was the

[8] [H. Berghaus], *Statistik des preussischen Staats*, pp. 219, 221-222; L. Clausnitzer, *Geschichte des Unterrichtsgesetzes*, pp. 94, 248, 265-266, 308; *Das Volksschulwesen im preussischen Staate*, ed. K. Schneider and E. von Bremen (3 vols., Berlin, 1886-87), II, 390; Prussia, *Verhandlungen des Landtages: Haus der Abgeordneten* (1865), I, 475; *Statistisches Jahrbuch für das Deutsche Reich*, I (1880), 151; F. Wienstein, *Die preussische Volksschule*, p. 83; "Religionsbekenntniss und Schulbildung der Bevölkerung des preussischen Staats," *Zeitschrift des königlich preussischen Statistischen Bureaus*, XIV (1874), 148; *Mittheilungen des Statistischen Bureau's in Berlin*, VI (1853), 219, 221, 223-224.

problem of semiliteracy, a level of learning so low as to preclude the ability to read and write with ease. While a precise calculation of its extent is impossible, the available data suggest that it affected approximately 20 per cent of the adult male population. Whatever the technical distinctions between them, moreover, both semi-literacy and illiteracy implied nonparticipation in public affairs. The man who could barely recognize the letters of the alphabet or sign his name may have had political convictions, but he was in effect deprived of the opportunity to influence state policy. His failure to acquire the basic tools of education condemned him to ignorance of civic issues, to submissiveness and apathy. In other words, one German out of four could not take part in politics because he lacked the minimal learning essential for a comprehension of the problems of government.

Low literacy, furthermore, coincided with economic privation. The inadequacy of education was greatest among those classes of society whose standard of living was depressed: the agricultural workers and marginal farmers beyond the Elbe, and the unskilled laborers and mill hands in the cities. Their instruction usually consisted of a few years in an overcrowded school under a poorly trained and poorly paid teacher. Once they left the classroom there was nothing in their environment to stimulate intellectual curiosity. Their way of life was determined by a stultifying routine in which reading and writing appeared unimportant. The few skills they had acquired in the elementary grades were easily forgotten. In many cases all that remained by the time of adulthood was the ability to decipher simple sentences, write a signature, perhaps do a little addition and subtraction. To such people the great political issues of the mid-century were meaningless.

For that matter, fluency in reading did not always imply a concern for public affairs. There was a wide gap between literacy and political consciousness. While about three-fourths of the adult male population of the German Confederation had received an adequate primary education, the proportion of those interested in the problems of government was considerably smaller. The circulation of newspapers, the best available index of the popular understanding of civic issues, suggests that to the lower classes the conflict of ideologies must have been for the most part incomprehensible. Early in the 1850's Johann Gustav Droysen observed, "The people do not read; at best they read the very local weekly papers." Toward the end of the decade Grand Duke Frederick of Baden, reflecting on the need for reform in the German Confederation, concluded that "the effect of the press can be calculated only for the truly educated part of society, and only this part of the nation is to be considered in the achievement of such important objectives." Even at the height of the constitutional conflict in Prussia, Leopold von Hoverbeck admitted to a friend, "I am very much afraid that this entire notion about our moral successes is only an illusion. Those circles of the population which read newspapers at all and concern themselves to some extent in politics have long ago taken their stand on these questions, and are still loyal to it today (that is, in their hearts, for outside pressure causes many to hide their political convictions, and others even to deny them). All our deliberations, however, have no influence on the great bulk of the population, on the third and partly the second class of voters, because they know nothing about them." The masses of Central Europe were neither liberal nor conservative but simply indifferent. They responded to politics with platitudes and catchwords designed to disguise their lack of inner conviction. They were incapable of commitment to complex civic ideals.

The importance of the press lay therefore not in its appeal to the proletariat, but in the influence it could exert over men of property and education. In an age in which political effectiveness was to a large extent a function of economic affluence, journalism played a

284

significant role in shaping the views of the decisive classes of society. For this reason state authorities often sought to mold the editorial policy of newspapers by threats, promises, penalties, and bribes. In 1859 Guido von Usedom, the Prussian representative at the federal diet, charged that "Austria has assigned 400,000 to 500,000 silver guldens annually to the south German press!!— in order to 'make public opinion,' in her favor, of course. All the papers of south Germany are bribed and paid by Austria." His own government, however, did not hesitate to use the same tactics. The historian Max Duncker, who was press secretary for the ministry of Prince Karl Anton of Hohenzollern, tried to plant articles in the south designed to win support for the policies of Berlin. His sole complaint was that "all the south German newspapers are so well paid by Austria that they do not accept articles favorable to Prussia which are sent to them." He told Bernhardi that he was seeking funds from the minister of finance to help establish a Prussophile journal in Frankfurt am Main. Under Bismarck these efforts were redoubled. Several journalists in the south and even in France began to receive secret subsidies from the prime minister, while within the kingdom the enforcement of the press law and the release of public information were used to manipulate editorial opinion.

The secondary states also tried to influence newspaper policy through the distribution of favors and subventions. In Saxony, for example, the *Dresdner Journal* was the official organ of the government, receiving a substantial annual appropriation from the public treasury. The influential *Leipziger Zeitung* was nominally independent, but a representative of the ministry sat on the board of editors. And then there were the fifty or more *Amtsblätter*, small local papers with an average circulation of less than 2,000, whose existence depended on the official announcements which state and municipal authorities allowed them to carry. It was a cozy arrangement suited to the torpid politics of the minor kingdoms and principalities.[9]

The circulation figures of journals and magazines in the German Confederation support the conclusion that only a small minority of the population could have been familiar with political and economic questions. In Prussia the number of newspapers rose from about 850 in 1824 to 2,100 in 1869, but most of them were of only local interest and importance. The big dailies, about half of them concentrated in Berlin, were largely liberal in their editorial policy. The most widely read was the *Volks-Zeitung*, the organ of the Progressive Party, with sales of about 36,000. Far behind were the *Vossische Zeitung*, the newspaper of the well-to-do bourgeoisie of the capital, with 16,000 to 20,000 subscribers, and the *National-Zeitung*, popular with democratic merchants and businessmen, whose run during the early 1860's was between 6,000 and 9,000. The *Berliner Börsen-Zeitung* and the *Spenersche Zeitung*, although farther to the right, also supported the parliamentary cause. The daily circulation of the liberal Berlin press was about 100,000 copies, while that of the provincial papers advocating political reform was 150,000. In Silesia the *Morgen-Zeitung*, the *Schlesische Zeitung*, and *Breslauer Zeitung* had combined sales of close to 25,000. The *Kölnische Zeitung* with some 14,000 subscribers in 1858 was the best-known newspaper of the Rhineland, while the *Magdeburgische Zeitung* in the Province of Saxony, the *Ostsee-Zeitung* of Stettin in Pomerania, the *Danziger Zeitung* in West Prussia, and the *Königsberger Hartungsche Zeitung* in East Prussia were among the leading provincial journals. In the towns and villages, on the other hand, the local press led a life of drudgery and neglect. Even in a city like Trier the two main

[9] J. G. Droysen, *Briefwechsel*, II, 206; *Friedrich I. von Baden*, ed. H. Oncken, I, 47; L. Parisius, *Hoverbeck*, II/II, 54; *Aus dem Leben Bernhardis*, III, 195, 226-227; Otto Pflanze, *Bismarck and the Development of Germany: The Period of Unification, 1815-1871* (Princeton, 1963), pp. 202-203; Herbert Jordan, *Die öffentliche Meinung in Sachsen, 1864-66* (Kamenz, 1918), pp. 48-50.

newspapers had a total circulation in 1857 of not even 1,300, although there were some 400 subscribers to the popular Cologne and Berlin dailies.[10]

The conservatives had no publication which could compete with the great liberal newspapers like the *Volks-Zeitung* or the *Vossische Zeitung*. Their most important organ by far was the *Neue Preussische Zeitung* of Berlin, whose circulation during the early 1860's fluctuated between 6,000 and 8,000. It was followed by a handful of feeble journals like the *Preussisches Volksblatt* with a run of 3,000 to 5,000, *Der kleine Reaktionär* with 2,000, and the *Volksblatt für Stadt und Land* with 1,600. When the constitutional conflict opened, the supporters of the government controlled fewer than forty newspapers in the entire kingdom. Their efforts to expand the legitimist press, moreover, were on the whole disappointing. In Westphalia the *Neue Westfälische Zeitung* began to appear; for the traditionalists of the Province of Posen there was the *Neues Bromberger Wochenblatt*; in Silesia the *Konservative Provinzial-Zeitung für Schlesien* tried to compete with the liberal *Schlesische Zeitung*; and in the Province of Saxony the *Altmärkisches Intelligenz- und Leseblatt* struggled to win a following among the farmers and artisans. Then came numerous conservative pamphlets and broadsides. An almanac published by the Prussian People's Association sought to "counteract the democratic poison" with anti-parliamentary and anti-Semitic exhortations. The indefatigable Hermann Wagener demonstrated in his voluminous *Staats- und Gesellschafts-Lexikon* that the prejudices of the legitimists could be made to appear as scholarly as those of the liberals. The most important journalistic success of the government, however, was the conversion of the *Norddeutsche Allgemeine Zeitung*

10 W. Sombart, *Die deutsche Volkswirtschaft*, p. 412; Otto Bandmann, *Die deutsche Presse und die Entwicklung der deutschen Frage, 1864-66* (Leipzig, 1910), pp. 186-187, 191; E. N. Anderson, *Social and Political Conflict*, pp. 340-341, 343-344; *Berlin und seine Entwickelung: Städtisches Jahrbuch für Volkswirthschaft und Statistik*, VI (1872), 178.

from a liberal Austrophile organ into Bismarck's mouthpiece. Its editor was August Brass, who had once been an ardent forty-eighter apostrophizing the red banner of revolution with the lines:

> Wir färben echt,
> Wir färben gut,
> Wir färben mit Tyrannenblut.

Now he decided to become a defender of the established order, in return of course for "advantages freeing him from other connections." Yet despite its new reputation as the semi-official spokesman of the ministry, the newspaper failed to attract a wide readership. Its circulation rose from 500 in 1862 to 2,000 in 1863 and perhaps 4,500 in 1864. Many of the new subscriptions, moreover, came from government bureaus which bought it as a public duty and a public expenditure.

All in all, the conservative press printed about 15,000 copies a day in Berlin, and probably another 20,000 in the provinces, a total of at most 40,000. Since the sales of liberal newspapers came to 250,000, the over-all circulation in Prussia was in the neighborhood of 300,000. The actual readership was of course much larger. A reasonable estimate would be that there were some five readers for every copy. The high cost made it difficult for people of average means to subscribe to journals, so that the purchaser of an issue would often share it with friends and neighbors. In large towns, moreover, there were public reading rooms which charged a modest fee for access to the leading newspapers and magazines. Yet even a generous approximation of the ratio of readers to subscribers suggests that out of 19,000,000 inhabitants there could not have been more than about 1,500,000 with an understanding of public affairs derived from the press. The population base includes infants and children, to be sure, but even so it appears that the proportion of adult males who could have been considered well-informed on the basis of newspaper reading was 20 per cent at best. Here too the concentration of knowledge coincided with the concentration of wealth and education.[11]

The role of the press in the other states of the German Confederation was essentially the same. Imparting information regarding public affairs to an educated minority, it sought to sway the political beliefs of the well-to-do. Its following varied from region to region, but nowhere did it achieve a mass circulation. It exercised the greatest influence in the big cities, where civic consciousness was most highly developed. In Hamburg, for example, the *Reform*, catering to a bourgeois readership of respectability and wealth, claimed sales of 24,000, while subscriptions to the *Hamburger Nachrichten* may have been as high as 16,000. Those were impressive figures for a community of 300,000. In Frankfurt am Main with about 100,000 inhabitants, the *Neue Frankfurter Zeitung*, which the young Leopold Sonnemann had founded in 1856, soon gained a reputation as one of the leading liberal organs of western Germany, and reached a circulation of 8,000 on the eve of the Seven Weeks' War. In Saxony, on the other hand, good newspapers were few and impoverished. The most popular journal was the localistic *Dresdner Nachrichten* with a run between 10,000 and 13,000. The long-winded *Leipziger Zeitung*, derided by its critics as "the Saxon book for children," had sales between 5,000 and 7,000. The official *Dresdner Journal* fluctuated from 2,000 to 6,000, depending on the ups and downs of political excitement. There were more distinguished newspapers, to be sure. The *Deutsche Allgemeine Zeitung*, which Karl Biedermann edited in Leipzig, was well known throughout and beyond the kingdom, yet its circulation was

11 Gerhard Ritter, *Die preussischen Konservativen und Bismarcks deutsche Politik, 1858-1871* (Heidelberg, 1913), p. 390; H. Rosenberg, *Die nationalpolitische Publizistik*, II, 553; E. N. Anderson, *Social and Political Conflict*, pp. 343, 345, 360-362; L. Parisius, *Hoverbeck*, II/1, 108-109, 125-126, 144-145; H. Müller, *Der Preussische Volks-Verein*, p. 70; O. Bandmann, *Die deutsche Presse*, p. 189; O. v. Bismarck, *Werke*, XIV/11, 628; G. v. Viebahn, *Statistik Deutschlands*, III, 1175.

only about 2,000. The Prussophile *Constitutionelle Zeitung* in Dresden led an even more precarious existence. In neighboring Thuringia the *Weimarische Zeitung* enjoyed great respect but only 1,200 subscriptions, although the obscure *Dorfzeitung* of Hildburghausen boasted that it had 10,000 readers. Even in Stuttgart, the progressive capital of Württemberg, the important *Schwäbischer Merkur* had a run of at most 10,000.

At the outbreak of the Seven Weeks' War there were 1,525 newspapers in the states of the German Confederation, 473 of them in Austria, which were important enough to circulate by mail as well as local sale. Only 30 appeared more than once a day, 55 had one edition daily, and 210 published six times a week. As of 1862 the annual per capita publication of newspapers was 0.98 for Austria, 3.73 for Prussia, 3.15 for Saxony, 4.49 for Württemberg, 3.66 for Baden, 2.94 for Hanover, and 3.00 for Mecklenburg-Schwerin. Although the rate of literacy was higher in Germany than anywhere else in Europe, the circulation of journals was relatively low. In France, for instance, the annual per capita publication of newspapers was 5.65, in Switzerland 9.85, and in England 20.82. In other words, interest in public affairs as measured by the circulation of the press was not commensurate with the popular ability to read and write. The educated classes were a proportionately smaller minority in Central Europe than in the countries west of the Rhine, and their concern for politics was not as highly developed. The beginnings of industrialization and urbanization were so recent that neither the economic nor the psychological factors stimulating civic consciousness had made their influence widely felt. A deep-rooted tradition of governmental paternalism, moreover, was still a powerful force. In a nation lacking the parliamentary system of the English or the revolutionary history of the French or the cantonal democracy of the Swiss, political passivity was a natural frame of mind. Learning tended to become a means of self-purification and self-perfection rather than an instrument for the betterment of society.[12]

Figures for the circulation of periodicals in the German Confederation confirm the view that even the educated classes of society were to a large extent apolitical. Far and away the most widely read publication was the *Gartenlaube*, which Ernst Keil had founded in 1853 in Leipzig. A family magazine offering entertainment, instruction, and moral uplift, it had sales of 100,000 in 1861, 160,000 in 1863, and 215,000 in 1867. The *Kladderadatsch* of Berlin, a satirical journal which poked fun impartially at public figures and civic movements, was far behind in second place with about 40,000 subscribers. The most popular daily newspaper did not attract such a large reading public, while the best-known political periodicals could only envy and despair. The *Preussische Jahrbücher*, whose contributors included such eminent scholars as Ludwig Häusser, Hermann Baumgarten, Heinrich von Sybel, and Johann Gustav Droysen, had a circulation of less than 1,000. The *Grenzboten* commanded the talents of Gustav Freytag, Theodor Mommsen, Heinrich von Treitschke, and Moritz Busch, but its sales were also in the neighborhood of 1,000. Even such a modest readership proved beyond the reach of the leading conservative magazine of Prussia, the *Berliner Revue*. Despite Hermann Wagener's ability as organizer and publicist, its printing declined from 750 in the middle 1850's to less than 400 at the time of the appointment of the Bismarck ministry.

Although indifference to public affairs characterized in varying degrees all strata of society in Central Eu-

12 Olga Herschel, *Die öffentliche Meinung in Hamburg in ihrer Haltung zu Bismarck, 1864-1866* (Hamburg, 1916), pp. 12-13; O. Bandmann, *Die deutsche Presse*, pp. 182, 184, 186, 188, 190; G. v. Viebahn, *Statistik Deutschlands*, III, 1175; W. Kellner, *Taschenbuch der politischen Statistik*, p. 8; H. Jordan, *Die öffentliche Meinung in Sachsen*, pp. 48-50, 52-53; Konrad Bechstein, "Die öffentliche Meinung in Thüringen und die deutsche Frage, 1864-66" (Part 1) *Zeitschrift des Vereins für thüringische Geschichte und Altertumskunde*, XXXIII (1922-24), 177, 179.

rope, it was most pronounced among the lower classes. More important than illiteracy and semiliteracy was the high price of newspapers. A year's subscription to the *Volks-Zeitung* cost 9 marks, to the *National-Zeitung* 27 marks, to the *Neue Preussische Zeitung* 30 marks, and to the *Neue Frankfurter Zeitung* 17 marks. Even the socialist press, eager to win a following among the urban proletariat, had to compromise with the hard financial realities of publishing. The price of the *Social-Demokrat* was 7 marks, while the *Volksstaat*, which appeared only twice a week, charged 4 marks. In a nation in which some 70 per cent of the working population earned less than 300 marks a year, the high cost of public information reduced the civic interest of the masses.

The most effective barrier of all against popular participation in the political process was the widespread conviction that wealth and learning were indispensable for the proper exercise of citizenship. Even the proletariat generally accepted with resignation the elite theory of politics which deprived it of an equal franchise. The opposition to manhood suffrage derived its strength from the common assumption that the ownership of property was a necessary condition of civic trustworthiness. A belief in the fundamental incapacity of the lower classes thus discouraged efforts to educate the uninformed and impoverished for the responsibilities of popular government.[13]

While the masses acquiesced in their political subordination, the well-to-do considered that subordination a positive good. Liberals as well as conservatives agreed that the exclusion of the proletariat from public affairs by a propertied suffrage was justifiable. Johann Gustav Droysen opposed any pandering to the low instincts of

[13] H. Jordan, *Die öffentliche Meinung in Sachsen*, p. 55; O. Bandmann, *Die deutsche Press*, pp. 183, 185, 190; O. Westphal, *Welt- und Staatsauffassung des Liberalismus*, p. 51; H. Rosenberg, *Die nationalpolitische Publizistik*, II, 545, 553, 958; A. Hahn, *Die Berliner Revue*, p. 38; G. Ritter, *Die preussischen Konservativen*, p. 390; P. Benaerts, *Les origines*, pp. 576-577.

the mob: "Above all, let us have no attempt to influence the so-called people through popular pamphlets, etc. The people are only to be won demagogically, whether the demagogues are political swindlers of the sort who were at the helm in 1848, or clerics, both Catholic and Lutheran. We must direct our activity at a much higher level." August Ludwig von Rochau argued that an unrestricted franchise was in any case a deception, since wealth and education would prevail, whatever the method of voting: "The general suffrage then does not in any way alter the fact that among us the hundreds . . . have much greater weight than the thousands, and that elections even under the freest system will certainly not turn out in the spirit of the great mass, but in the sense of small minorities." Ernst Ludwig von Gerlach insisted that "a man who owns a square mile of landed property is endowed with greater political effectiveness than one who owns only a rod or who has no landed property at all." Even Hermann Wagener, although preaching tory democracy to the legitimists of Prussia, maintained that "the political importance of a name should be graded according to its social and political achievement." He pointed warningly to the example of America, "where people stand at the ballot box with revolvers and daggers."

A limited suffrage was the most effective but not the only device favored by the propertied for preserving the elite character of politics. There was also widespread agreement that indirect voting purified the will of the people and protected it against unwholesome influences. Franz Ziegler, the veteran warrior of democracy, distressed his political friends with a proposal for direct elections: "We quarrel about it every evening, and they are beside themselves that I do not want the middlemen, the electors, the bourgeois, the old snuff-users." And in the conservative camp the publicist Heinrich Eugen Marcard maintained that under an indirect suffrage "the voter always has to choose his elector only out of his im-

293

mediate neighborhood, and therefore personal trust under the circumstances is at least possible. . . . The direct vote, on the other hand, if it is not to be splintered into a hundred pieces and thus often result in election by a very small minority, produces a situation in which the various parties as well as the government put up a few candidates after many upsetting preliminary deliberations and disturbances, candidates who are of necessity completely unknown in person to the great majority of the voters. The latter thus elect not the person but simply the party man."

The secret vote seemed even more dangerous than the direct vote, for it encouraged fraud at the polls and reduced the influence of the educated classes. The prevailing view at a meeting of distinguished liberals in Breslau was that "secret voting is by no means a guarantee of the independence and honesty of the elections. France amply proves that at this moment. Every one knows what sort of ballot he is putting in the box, but no one knows what will come out again." The jurist and politician Georg Beseler felt that public voting was in keeping with "the moral dignity of a free people" and expressed "the Germanic principle of publicity." But the fundamental argument against the secrecy of the suffrage was advanced by Theodor von Bernhardi:

> The proper influence of social position, of education, and of higher insight and intelligence ceases under secret voting, and in its place comes the improper influence of the basest political agitation. For let us make no mistake about it. We will then not be the ones who will lead the great uneducated mass. It will be the worst individuals, the most dangerous elements of civil society who will then gain an entirely incalculable influence. For no man of honor knows the wretched tricks which are required to produce an effect on the masses, and if he did know them, he would not use them. The sense of his own personal dignity does not allow him to do so. . . .

The need for secret voting is at bottom always a sign of unhealthy conditions.

There were finally those who contended that the payment of salaries to members of parliament tended to attract to politics lower-class rabble-rousers driven by ambition and aversion to honest labor. It demeaned the dignity of lawmaking, reducing it to the status of a wage-earning occupation. The denial of remuneration to the legislators, on the other hand, would have the effect of admitting to public life only the selfless, idealistic, and financially independent. The legitimist *Volksblatt für Stadt und Land* opposed "the idea of placing the government of a country in the hands of an assembly elected by counting heads and composed of people paid a daily wage." Bernhardi remarked in a conversation with the liberal jurist Rudolf Gneist that "the daily allowance of three talers which the members of the legislature receive is a misfortune for our country. Thereby the sort of people enter the chamber who certainly do not belong there, and who indeed would not rush to do so, if the 3 talers, which tempt people like that, were not there." Gneist assented with reluctance, but some of Bernhardi's other political acquaintances supported his views unreservedly. Karl von Sänger and Baron Franz von Roggenbach, both of them moderate constitutionalists, pointed out "how dangerous daily allowances are precisely in combination with the general suffrage. If the members of the Reichstag had daily allowances, then the cities would naturally vote as democratically as possible. But in the rural districts it could happen that once again people would be elected who used their free time, the time which is not required for their parliamentary activity, to hire themselves out as houseboys, as happened in 1848." While there may have been differences regarding the most effective means to safeguard elections against demagoguery, the great majority of both liberals and conservatives agreed that direct manhood suffrage was incompatible with civic stability.[14]

This fear of the unreliability of the lower classes was reflected in the voting laws of the states of the German Confederation. In one way or another they all sought to limit the political participation of the proletariat, usually through a propertied and indirect franchise. In Bavaria, where the suffrage was comparatively unrestricted, the qualification for voters as well as deputies was the payment of a direct tax. In Württemberg the district electoral colleges were composed two-thirds of the wealthiest taxpayers and only one-third of elected members. In Baden all citizens of good reputation who paid a direct tax were eligible to vote, but a member of the legislature had to own property worth 17,000 marks or receive a lifetime income from a family estate or earn a yearly salary of 2,600 marks. In Saxony the requirement for membership in a district electoral college was the ownership of real property taxable at 30 marks annually. In Hanover the representatives of urban districts had to derive 900 marks from the possession of land or receive a salary of 2,400 marks or earn 3,000 marks from professional or business activity in the space of three years, while the representatives of rural districts were required to be landowners with an income of 900 marks. In short, the method of election generally imposed property requirements on the voters or the electors or the members of the legislature. The specific qualifications for voting and holding office varied from state to state, but their ultimate effect was everywhere the same. They restricted the influence of the lower classes in public affairs.[15]

[14] J. G. Droysen, *Briefwechsel*, II, 175; [A. L. v. Rochau], *Grundsätze der Realpolitik*, II, 14; Prussia, *Verhandlungen des Landtages: Haus der Abgeordneten* (1866-67), I, 300; *ibid.* (1861), II, 654, 656; L. Dehio, "Die preussische Demokratie," p. 259; *Volksblatt für Stadt und Land*, April 30, 1862, May 5, 1866; H. Rosenberg, *Die nationalpolitische Publizistik*, II, 554; *Aus dem Leben Bernhardis*, III, 70-73, VI, 193,VII, 347-348.

[15] Georg Meyer, *Das parlamentarische Wahlrecht* (Berlin, 1901), pp.

The Prussian system of election was unusual in that it did not require the ownership of property for either voting or holding office. The law of May 30, 1849, stated simply that "every independent Prussian who has completed the 24th year of his life and has not lost possession of his civic rights as the result of valid judicial proceedings is a qualified voter in the community in which he has had his residence or abode for six months, provided that he does not receive poor relief from public funds." Yet in fact even this broad suffrage disfranchised between 10 and 25 per cent of the adult male population. The proportion of eligible voters to all men past their twenty-fourth birthday was 89 per cent in the election of 1849, 75 in 1855, 79 in 1858, and 83 in 1861. Between 400,000 and 1,000,000 persons were thus barred from the polls because they could not meet the requirements of the franchise for reasons of poverty, change in domicile, or transgression of the law. But the most important device for minimizing the political effectiveness of the masses was the method of election under which members of the district electoral colleges were chosen in equal number by three categories of voters, each representing the same amount of wealth as measured by the payment of direct taxes. The result was to ensure the preponderance of the well-to-do. In the Prussian elections between 1849 and 1863 an average of 4.73 per cent of all voters belonged to the first class, 13.26 per cent to the second, and 82.01 per cent to the third. It was an ingenious arrangement for safeguarding the interests of the propertied without disfranchising the propertyless. Manhood suffrage presented no danger to the established social order under a system of voting in which 20 per cent of the

---

122-124, 189-191, 196-197; W. Kellner, *Taschenbuch der politischen Statistik*, pp. 86-87, 90-91; Karl Alexander von Müller, *Bayern im Jahre 1866 und die Berufung des Fürsten Hohenlohe* (Munich and Berlin, 1909) , p. 49; Adolf Rapp, *Die Württemberger und die nationale Frage, 1863-1871* (Stuttgart, 1910) , p. 16.

participants, the elite of birth and property, could override the other 80 per cent.[16]

The restricted or weighted suffrage could be further controlled through public voting, which prevailed in such states as Prussia, Bavaria, and Württemberg. The open franchise enabled the authorities to sway elections by pressures which the lower classes often found hard to resist. Especially in rural districts, where firm political convictions were in any case uncommon, the government played an important role in determining the outcome at the polls. In 1855 Prince William of Prussia, brother of the king and heir to the throne, complained about the blatant coercion of the electorate by the bureaucracy: "I am far from denying the government an influence over the elections, but it must always be legal and honest. But among us downright terrorism was directed against people and institutions. And this must have its evil consequences in the future, because we thereby deliberately breed hypocrisy and untruthfulness, something which until now was unknown in Prussia, particularly in the civil service." Yet when he himself became ruler the situation did not change. In 1864 Kurt von Saucken-Tarputschen, a democratic member of the legislature, charged that "the feudal party is gaining considerable ground among all people who are in any way dependent, and a large part of the peasants is like soft wax to be molded by anyone who has it in his grasp. The people in Berlin have no idea what conditions are like in the country. Without an edict regulating the government of counties and small communities, we will perhaps never instill in our rural population an understanding of the value of the constitution, certainly not for many years. Not until the power of

---

[16] G. Meyer, *Das parlamentarische Wahlrecht*, pp. 188-189, 194-195; Prussia, *Gesetz-Sammlung für die königlichen preussischen Staaten* (1849), p. 206; R. Boeckh, "Statistik der Urwahlen für das preussische Abgeordnetenhaus vom neunzehnten November 1861," *Zeitschrift des königlich preussischen Statistischen Bureaus*, II (1862), 92-93; *Statistisches Handbuch für den preussischen Staat*, IV (1903), 649.

the county commissioner is broken will the peasant learn to think independently." On the other hand, when in 1861 the government used its influence to help bring about a liberal victory, it was the turn of the conservatives to grumble. For example, the Junker politician Moritz von Blanckenburg reported bitterly that "the outcome of the elections in Pomerania is decided entirely by the peasants, who are aroused by the county judges and Jews, and who are most decidedly against us. For one thing, they had been talked into thinking that we were against the king! This was believed all the more easily since the authorities here worked one and all against us." Whatever the policy of the government, the bureaucracy was expected to support it by swaying the electorate in its favor.[17]

Even men in private life whose wealth and position gave them a measure of authority used it to mold public opinion. Usually they were conservative landed aristocrats seeking to persuade their peasants to vote for king and country. There was the estate owner in Lauban county in Silesia, for instance, whose announcement on the eve of the election of 1863 must have made an impression on the rustics over whom he lorded:

To the royal Prussian voters of the manor Meffersdorf, Schwerta, and Volkersdorf. His Majesty our most gracious king and sovereign has commanded that on the 20th of this month the election should take place, and has pronounced that the election will be free only if the choice falls on such persons who will vote in accordance with the disposition and will of his Majesty and his ministers. . . . I have commanded that those voters who act to the contrary shall, if they are workers in the forest or on the estates, be dismissed, and that the same procedure shall be followed in the brickworks, the peat banks, and the factory for ovenware and pottery; that the supervisory

[17] G. Meyer, *Das parlamentarische Wahlrecht*, pp. 532-533, 536-538; *Friedrich I. von Baden*, ed. H. Oncken, I, 39; L. Parisius, *Hoverbeck*, II/II, 19, n. 3; *Denkwürdigkeiten aus dem Leben des Grafen von Roon*, II, 56.

personnel of the forest, the estate, the garden, the mill, the bakery, and the sawmill shall be given notice; that final accounts shall be settled with handicraftsmen who have worked for the estates or for the other branches of the management, as well as with the merchants who sell them anything; furthermore, that those who have rented a dwelling or leased farm or forest land shall be given notice as soon as the contractual obligation ends. I demand of all the above-mentioned voters who have any sort of connection with me that they participate in the election on the 20th of this month. Whoever has not brought to me personally a satisfactory excuse for staying away shall be treated in the same way as those voters who on the 20th of this month give their vote to such electors who . . . will again choose the present members of the legislature or choose such members who will vote in the new lower house against the will of his Majesty and his ministers.

The conservatives, however, were not the only ones to try to control the opinions of the lower classes. Bernhardi noted in his diary that "in the neighborhood of Fraustadt [in Posen] a loyalty address [supporting the government] was adopted, and Heydebrand-Röhrsdorf let himself be chosen to deliver it. But he also wanted to have the signatures of the peasants from his own village. But these were not to be gotten. Röhrsdorf is a very large village in which three estates are located, and which has two mayors. The owners of the other two estates are liberals, and they in turn also talked to the peasants. Finally, only one mayor and another peasant signed." The scholar and publicist Rudolf Haym testified to the success of the liberals of Halle in controlling plebeian votes: "Mommsen was elected here not by his colleagues, but by shoemakers and tailors and by the peasants. More than half of them heard his name for the first time on Sunday, and elected him on Wednesday." The industrialist Karl Dietzsch personally led a group of his workers to the polls in Limburg an der

Lenne in Westphalia to make sure they supported him in the voting for the district electoral college. While the adherents and the opponents of the government charged each other with coercion of the voters, in fact both believed that the masses should be guided in the exercise of the franchise. For how could the man whose life was spent in the drudgery of a menial occupation be expected to master the complexities of public affairs? Since he had to be directed in any case, it was only proper that his superiors should see to it that he did not fall under the influence of intriguers and self-seekers.[18]

A combination of indifference, ignorance, submissiveness, restricted voting, and extralegal pressure reduced popular involvement in the political process. In the fall of 1863 Bernhardi predicted that "participation in the election will be very small this time, for the distrustful caution of the lower classes determines for us that a great number of people will stay at home so as not to have to vote for the men of the government, and yet not arouse the displeasure of the county commissioner. The elections will thus be minority elections." It was a safe prediction, because all elections in Prussia were minority elections. The rate of participation in 1849, when the three-class system of voting was introduced, equalled 31.9 per cent. There are no statistics for 1852, but in 1855, at the height of the reaction, it decreased to 16.1 per cent, the smallest figure of the mid-century. The exertions of the government in behalf of the conservatives made the outcome of the election seem so certain that the vast majority of the voters did not even trouble to go to the polls. The result was an overwhelming victory for the right and "the chamber of county commissioners," although some legitimists like Prince William were repelled by the "downright terrorism" employed

18 *Görlitzer Anzeiger*, October 23, 1863; *Aus dem Leben Bernhardis*, IV, 328; *Ausgewählter Briefwechsel Rudolf Hayms*, ed. Hans Rosenberg (Berlin and Leipzig, 1930), p. 225; Friedrich Zunkel, *Der rheinisch-westfälische Unternehmer, 1834–1879: Ein Beitrag zur Geschichte des deutschen Bürgertums im 19. Jahrhundert* (Cologne and Opladen, 1962), p. 193.

against the opposition. The establishment of the regency, which embarked on a policy of cautious liberalism, revived interest in politics, so that in the elections of 1858 and 1861 the ratio of participants to eligibles was 22.6 and 27.2 per cent. Finally, the constitutional conflict, involving a test of strength between crown and parliament, stimulated the exercise of the franchise, which reached 34.3 per cent in 1862 and 30.9 in 1863. The average for the entire period 1849-63 was 27.2 per cent. In other words, even in times of crisis only about a third of the voters took part in the ballot, while under ordinary political conditions the proportion was closer to a fourth.[19]

Although participation in voting was to a large extent a function of wealth and influence, the rate of abstention among the well-to-do was considerable. In the election of 1861 a voter in the first class paid an average of 168 marks in direct taxes, in the second class 54 marks, and in the third class under 9 marks. The weight assigned to those comprising each class varied accordingly. There were 7.4 eligible voters for every member of a district electoral college chosen in the first class, 19.9 in the second class, and 128.0 in the third class. That is to say, a vote cast in the wealthiest 4.7 per cent of the population counted almost 3 times as much as one in the middle 13.5 per cent, and 17 times as much as one in the bottom 81.8 per cent. Yet despite the fact that men of means determined the outcome of the elections, about half of them did not appear at the polls. The rate of participation in the first class was 55.4 per cent in 1849, 39.6 in 1855, 50.2 in 1858, 55.8 in 1861, 61.0 in 1862, and 57.0 in 1863. The corresponding figures for the second class were 44.7, 27.2, 37.1, 42.4, 48.0, and 44.0 per cent. The mean for all 6 elections was 53.2 per cent

---

[19] *Aus dem Leben Bernhardis*, v, 124-125; R. Boeckh, "Statistik der Urwahlen 1861," p. 112; *Friedrich I. von Baden*, ed. H. Oncken, I, 39; Ernst Engel, "Die Ergebnisse der Urwahlen für das preussische Abgeordnetenhaus vom 28. April 1862 und vom 20. October 1863," *Zeitschrift des königlich preussischen Statistischen Bureaus*, v (1865), 69.

in the first class and 40.6 in the second, although there were wide local variations from these averages. Prosperous and educated Berliners, for instance, never seemed to grow tired of politics. Even in 1855, 73 per cent of the eligibles of the first class and 63 per cent of those of the second class voted in the Prussian capital, while by 1861 the percentages had risen to 80 and 71. In the city of Barmen 68 per cent of the voters of the first class and 56 per cent of the second class went to the polls in 1862, and 70 and 56 per cent in 1863. Yet in Düren county the percentages for the two upper classes in the election of 1861 were 37 and 19, in Solingen county 35 and 15, and in Kreuznach county 32 and 18.

There are no detailed statistics for most of the other states in the German Confederation, but scattered election results support the conclusion that there the political indifference of the propertied was at least equally extensive. Leipzig, the second city of Saxony, had about 80,000 inhabitants, of whom only 7 per cent had the right to take part in the municipal elections. There were 5,600 eligible voters and 3,200 ballots cast in 1864, while a year later the figures were 5,800 and 3,300, a ratio of 57 per cent. In neighboring Thuringia with its eight quaint little principalities, their populations ranging from 286,000 to 45,000, apathy toward politics was even more common. After all, who could take very seriously a legislature debating the destinies of Saxe-Weimar or Reuss-Schleiz-Gera? Not even the citizens of Saxe-Weimar or Reuss-Schleiz-Gera. Participation in the elections of the middle 1860's was so small that in some cases it approached complete abstention. In Jena 272 ballots were cast out of a total of 1,007 eligible voters, and in Apolda there were three wards in which no one went to the polls. In the town of Gera only 155 persons took part in the voting for members of the electoral college. In four wards in Coburg the election of municipal councilmen could not take place during the first round of balloting because the required minimum number of voters, 25 per cent of the eligibles, did not participate. There was a ward in which the third round of balloting still failed to attract the prescribed quorum to the polls. In short, it is clear that concern for public affairs was limited even among men of affluence. There was more interest in the large kingdoms, less in the somnolent duchies and principalities. But nowhere did the well-to-do display a widespread and consistent concern for the problems of government.[20]

Among the masses indifference to politics was understandably greater. In some states they were generally barred from the polls; in others the effectiveness of their franchise was minimized by the various election devices. Even the workingman or peasant familiar enough with public affairs to have civic convictions was often discouraged from voting by the realization that he could not prevail against the combined might of wealth, education, and influence. In Prussia the rate of participation of voters in the third class equaled 28.6 per cent in 1849, 12.7 in 1855, 18.5 in 1858, 23.1 in 1861, 30.5 in 1862, and 27.3 in 1863. The average of 23.5 per cent came to less than half of what it was in the first class and about three-fifths of what it was in the second class. Variations in the degree of civic interest, to be sure, were as common among the poor as among the wealthy. For one thing, an urban environment tended to stimulate the concern for public affairs, so that in the election of 1863 the ratio of participants to eligibles for all three categories of voters was 37.7 per cent in the city and 27.8 per cent in the country. The lower classes of Berlin went to the polls consistently in impressive numbers, 42.7 per cent in 1849, 34.2 in 1855, 39.5 in 1858, and 39.7 in 1861. In Danzig the percentages for the propertyless voters were less stable, but in times of political excite-

---

[20] R. Boeckh, "Statistik der Urwahlen 1861," pp. 86-89, 96, 101, 112; E. Engel, "Ergebnisse der Urwahlen 1862 und 1863," p. 69; W. Köllmann, *Sozialgeschichte der Stadt Barmen*, p. 295; W. Kellner, *Taschenbuch der politischen Statistik*, p. 22; H. Jordan, *Die öffentliche Meinung in Sachsen*, p. 43; "Beiträge zur Statistik," p. 277; K. Bechstein, "Die öffentliche Meinung in Thüringen" (Part 1), p. 170.

ment they became substantial: 32.4 in 1861, 40.3 in 1862, and 35.9 in 1863. In many of the towns of the west, on the other hand, nothing could shake the pervasive apathy. In Bochum county the proportion of the eligibles of the third class taking part in the election of 1861 was 7.1 per cent, in 1862 19.3, and in 1863 13.9; in Iserlohn county the percentages were 7.8, 9.3, and 11.5; in Wetzlar county 6.0, 10.1, and 8.5; and in Recklinghausen county 4.6, 9.3, and 11.1. Such a profound civic lethargy might have been expected in one of the gingerbread principalities of Thuringia, but not in a major power vying for political supremacy in Central Europe.

The most important reason for the indifference of the lower classes toward public affairs was neither poverty, ignorance, rusticity, nor submissiveness. It was the conviction that the issues debated in parliamentary assemblies were irrelevant to the everyday concerns of the little man. When the masses could be persuaded by a skillful leadership that their vital interests were at stake, they streamed to the polls. The Province of Posen, agrarian, impoverished, and backward, provided an illuminating example. Its rate of illiteracy was the highest in the kingdom, and only in Pomerania was the proportion of children not attending elementary school greater. Yet 57.1 per cent of the eligible voters in the Posen district took part in the election of 1861, 72 per cent in the first class, 70 per cent in the second, and 53.4 per cent in the third. In the Bromberg district the over-all percentage was 56.7, while the figures for the three classes were 70, 66, and 54.0 per cent. Nor was it primarily the urban vote which accounted for the high level of participation. In the city of Posen, to be sure, 57.2 per cent of the voters in the third class went to the polls, but even this impressive total was overshadowed by such rural communities as Krotoschin with 66.3, Mogilno with 66.5, Obornik and Inowraclaw with 71.2 each, and Schubin with 71.9 per cent. The decisive factor was the Polish peasantry, resolved to assert its historic identity against the threat of Germanization, which voted in alliance with the aristocracy and the bourgeoisie for its nationality and its religion.

In the Rhine Province, on the other hand, all the conditions favorable to popular involvement in politics existed except the belief that politics mattered. Here was a thriving region, one of the most highly industrialized and urbanized in Prussia, with a rate of male illiteracy of only 5 per cent and a rate of school attendance of 97 per cent. But those who took part in the election of 1861 even in the cities constituted only a small minority of the eligible voters. In Düsseldorf the percentage of participation in the third class was 17.8, in Cologne 16.8, in Barmen 9.7, in Elberfeld 8.5, in Aachen 8.2, and in Krefeld 4.4. The lower classes of the western districts, like the lower classes everywhere in Central Europe, generally considered the great civic issues extraneous to their basic needs. To them public affairs were the province of the well-to-do, in the same way as material affluence or social respectability or higher learning.[21]

During the period of national unification, then, politics was controlled by an elite of wealth and status. This control was maintained by legal prescription, economic pressure, political theory, and deep-seated habit. Although contending party leaders invoked the will of the people for rhetorical purposes, they were by and large reluctant to encourage the democratization of the state. Afraid to entrust the lower classes with the power to decide government policy, they preferred to guide and manipulate them. Men of substance dominated public affairs. In the lower house of the Prussian legislature which was elected in 1849, 68.0 per cent of the members had received a higher education; in 1855 the percentage was 63.2; in 1862 it was 65.5; in 1866, 58.5.

[21] R. Boeckh, "Statistik der Urwahlen 1861," pp. 78-79, 82-83, 86-89, 112-117; E. Engel, "Ergebnisse der Urwahlen 1862 und 1863," pp. 42-43, 50-55, 62-65, 69; W. Gagel, *Wahlrechtsfrage*, pp. 28, 177; "Religionsbekenntniss und Schulbildung," pp. 148-149; Goldschmidt, "Schulpflicht und Schulbesuch in Berlin," p. 251; "Das definitive Resultat der Volkszählung im preussischen Staate am 3. December 1861," *Zeitschrift des königlich preussischen Statistischen Bureaus*, II (1862), 271.

Their occupations reflected even more clearly the preponderance of property and learning. The proportion of agriculturists was 17.4 per cent in 1849, 22.3 in 1855, 23.6 in 1862, and 23.9 in 1866; for civil servants the figures were 16.0, 33.7, 12.9, and 20.5 per cent; for judicial officers 20.9, 16.0, 26.7, and 15.6 per cent; and for merchants and industrialists 6.9, 4.3, 7.2, and 8.1 per cent. None of the deputies, on the other hand, were classified as handicraftsmen, laborers, or clerks in 1849 and 1855. There were 3, or 0.9 per cent, in 1862, but they vanished again after the election of 1866.

The well-to-do also held a commanding position in the district electoral colleges which exercised, as the *Grenzboten* put it, "a mild sort of tutelage over the multitude through the aristocracy of the electors." Among the 448 electors chosen in Cologne in 1861 were 181 merchants, 67 handicraftsmen, 45 civil servants and administrators, 27 persons of independent means, 26 lawyers and notaries, 22 men in military service, 14 clergymen, 12 physicians, 8 grocers, 8 innkeepers, 6 apothecaries, 5 publishers, editors, and booksellers, and 3 technicians and mechanics. While the occupational composition of the electoral colleges differed from region to region, the propertied and educated classes had the upper hand throughout the kingdom. The political struggles of the mid-century were thus waged by dominant minorities distrustful of the broad masses of the population and isolated from them. That was what Jacob Burckhardt had in mind when early in the 1870's he defined for his students in Basel the significance of the constitutional conflict in Prussia: "The acquisitive and reasoning classes sought in fact to gain control of the power of the state through the right of decision over the budget and the term of military service."[22]

22 Jacob Burckhardt, *Gesammelte Werke* (10 vols., Basel, 1955-59), IV, 147. Cf. Gertrud Beushausen, *Zur Strukturanalyse parlamentarischer Repräsentation in Deutschland vor der Gründung des Norddeutschen Bundes* (Doctoral Thesis, University of Hamburg, 1926), pp. 100-101, 104-105; "Das allgemeine und geheime Stimmrecht vor dem Reichstage," *Die Grenzboten*, XXVI (1867), no. 1, p. 446; F. Zunkel, *Der rheinischwestfälische Unternehmer*, p. 193; E. N. Anderson, *Social and Political Conflict*, pp. 301-303.

EIGHT

Civic Organizations

POLITICAL pressure groups in Central Europe reflected the oligarchic character of public life. Since there was no mass electorate, there could be no mass parties. The forms of civic activity were adapted to the interests of a small minority which played the decisive role in affairs of state. A rigid party system had not yet emerged. While ideology provided a criterion for the separation of liberals from conservatives, within each camp there was a constant process of alignment and realignment, especially before election time. Old combinations disintegrated and new ones arose through the decision of a few influential politicians. The very names of the legislative alliances suggest the extent to which they were built around personalities: "the Bethmann-Hollweg faction," "the Count Pückler faction," "the Mathis faction," "the Vincke faction," "the Bockum-Dolffs faction," and "the Grabow faction."

The activities of these rudimentary party organizations reflected a system of elite politics. Their leaders would deliberate from time to time on the strategy to be pursued in parliament; they would issue an occasional manifesto to the country; as election time approached they established closer contact with local sympathizers; they might even address the members of the district electoral colleges, who were generally the more substantial citizens of the community. But there was as yet no party structure, no bureaucratic apparatus, no binding program, and no group discipline. Above all, there was no attempt to enlist the support of the lower classes. Each faction hoped that the propertyless would unite with the propertied to support candidates for the legislature who

308

approved its policies. But the politicians had no intention of appealing to the masses directly. To rouse the mob for the sake of partisan advantage was to open the gates to anarchy. Theodor von Bernhardi expressed a sense of shock, because at a meeting of liberal notables in Breslau the historian Richard Röpell had argued that "we must seek to exert influence below;—stirring up the masses is absolutely necessary;—'we must agitate.' " Describing this impropriety in his diary, he added an incredulous "*(ipsissima verba)*." The proud assertion of self-sufficiency which Baron Georg von Vincke made before the Prussian legislature characterized the attitude of the parliamentary grandees: "Never in my life have I sought the position of a representative. I have not issued a single declaration to my voters. I have never received from them an address expressing confidence or no confidence. I have always refused to permit it. . . . I believe that with respect to my voters I am thus in a completely independent position."[1]

A more systematic organization of political activity began in the early 1860's. The rule of the notables came to be challenged by an incipient party system based on principle and interest rather than personality. The rationalization of the civic function, although still in its initial stage, represented a departure from the cozily haphazard conglomeration of factions characteristic of the previous decade. The pioneer in this development was the Progressive Party, which arose in response to middle-class demands for a more resolute liberal movement in Prussia. Its program was not made up of the usual rhetorical generalities. It declared unequivocally that "the existence and the greatness of Prussia depend on a firm unification of Germany, which cannot be conceived without a strong central authority in the hands of Prussia and without a common German popular representation." It advanced proposals for far-reaching do-

[1] Prussia, *Verhandlungen des Landtages: Haus der Abgeordneten* (1861), III, 1440. Cf. *Aus dem Leben Bernhardis*, III, 7.

mestic reforms including judicial independence, ministerial responsibility, local self-government, religious
equality, advancement of popular education, introduction of civil marriage, relaxation of industrial regula-
lation, frugality in military expenditure, and reform of
the upper house of the legislature. It concluded with an
appeal to the voters for support at the polls: "We now
call on all those sharing our views to elect men who will
carry these principles . . . deep in their hearts, men
whose character and outward position in life give assurance that they will acknowledge these principles in
the legislature openly and without regard for any sort
of consideration."

To coordinate its efforts the Progressive Party established a permanent central election committee of sixteen
members, among them Hans Viktor von Unruh, Theodor Mommsen, Rudolf Virchow, Karl Twesten, Max
von Forckenbeck, Leopold von Hoverbeck, and Hermann Schulze-Delitzsch. Its function was to impose discipline on the political process, to rationalize and channel
the energies devoted to public affairs:

> We should not delay until the electors have been chosen.
> We must see to it in time, and especially in the country-
> side, that contacts are established, individuals are aroused,
> and candidates are named, in order that we may get elec-
> tors who belong decidedly and unreservedly to the liberal
> party. We have established an office . . . , and we ask
> both the individuals who undertake to campaign in our
> behalf and the election clubs and committees to get in
> touch with us . . . , to concert with us on questions of
> organization, on the procurement and dissemination of
> literature, as well as on the nomination and support of
> candidates in the individual election districts, to send us
> information about the state of affairs and especially about
> the election maneuvers of our opponents, and finally, to
> support us with suggestions and with the choice of suita-
> ble candidates.

The party, furthermore, published election pamphlets appealing to the lower classes: "To the Rural Voters"; "Get a Better Law on County Government!: A Word to the Rural Voters"; "Handicraftsmen in City and Country!"; "Elect Pro-German Deputies!"; "Voters in City and Country!"; "German Voters of the Province of Posen!"; and "To the Prussian Handicraftsmen: An Answer to Many Inquiries." Some of its deputies in the legislature even began to justify their views to the voters. Kurt von Saucken-Tarputschen, for example, reported that he had addressed three mass meetings of his constituents. "Participation in the proceedings was very large, and the mood of those present was excellent." More than that, "under the fresh impression of the knavery in Berlin, I immediately arranged for confidential discussions among the most radical men in my election district regarding the possibility of a refusal to pay taxes." It was a new style in politics.

The growing militancy of the liberals forced the conservatives into a more rigorous organization of their party. During the placid 1850's they had treated public affairs with an aristocratic casualness. Whatever political decisions were necessary, they had felt, could be reached in informal discussion sealed with a gentleman's word. Even a clear-cut statement of objectives seemed to them a needless encumbrance. Why engage in the haggling which the formulation of a program entailed? "The gentlemen rely on inspirations," old Field Marshal Friedrich zu Dohna used to observe.

The decline in conservative fortunes caused the party to change its approach to politics. At the beginning of the 1860's a permanent central election committee was formed including Count Eberhard Stolberg-Wernigerode, Alexander von Below-Hohendorf, Moritz von Blanckenburg, and the ubiquitous Hermann Wagener. It established contact with the legitimists in the provinces, encouraged the organization of local election campaigns, urged cooperation with handicraftsmen opposed

311

to industrial freedom, and called for a vigorous effort to familiarize the voters with the teachings of conservatism. Economic pressure was to reinforce political indoctrination:

> In the country it will especially be the duty of the landowners to try to let no one who is accessible to their authority stay away from the polls. It goes without saying that in a similar fashion every reasonable and legally permissible influence must be exercised over subordinates and those with whom business connections are maintained. It is in general reasonable and necessary that the conservatives decide, as their opponents have done, to make use of their social position in the community and to grant the advantage of their patronage as far as possible only to tradesmen who have similar views. An open acknowledgment and pronouncement of this principle will not be without effect.

At first the committee hesitated to formulate a party program, afraid of jeopardizing unity among its followers. But it soon overcame its scruples, and a convention of the conservatives meeting in Berlin approved the statement of objectives it had drafted. This statement advocated the achievement of political unity in the German Confederation through agreement among the princes rather than "with fire and sword." There was to be no "spoliation of crowns," no "swindle about nationalities." Prussia, moreover, should retain her identity as a leading power with a "glorious history." As for domestic policy, Christianity was to remain the foundation of the state, maintained in marriage, school, and civil authority. Both reduction of the army and ministerial responsibility were condemned. The program finally denounced the "rule of moneyed capital," defended handicraftsmen and farmers against the "usurious tricks of our times," asserted the autonomy of corporative organizations and communities, rejected bureaucratic absolutism as incompatible with "the spirit of German freedom," and called for love and loyalty to king and country. The liberals, trying to spur their followers on to greater efforts, overstated the achievements of the conservatives: "The feudal party boasts that it has extended a powerful organization over all parts of the country; it has committees or trusted agents in almost every county to carry on its election campaign; it mobilizes all the local influences and all the private interests which are at its command." It was an exaggerated tribute to the attempt of the legitimists at political rationalization.[2]

The transition to a system of mass parties, however, was only in its beginning. The attitudes and practices of factional politics continued to prevail throughout the period of national unification. Before the election of 1861 the moderate liberals of Prussia published a lengthy report on the legislative accomplishments of the previous two years which scorned the popularization of civic issues: "This report presents at the same time the credentials of the liberal party for the forthcoming elections. It must first of all carry on the work which has been begun. It must also, if the progressive development of the times imposes new problems on the process of legislation, achieve their solution in the same spirit in which it has acted since the first beginnings of our constitutional life. It therefore has no reason to put its leading principles down in a program. The formulation of these principles in short sentences open to misunderstanding provokes dissensions which it is better to avoid." Farther to the left the faction led by Florens Heinrich von Bockum-Dolffs managed in 1862 to gain about a hundred seats in the legislature without establishing a central election committee. The Progressive Party of Bavaria was built on the talents of a small group of skilled politicians, among them Karl Brater, Joseph Völk, and Marquard Barth. As for the civic

---

[2] L. Parisius, *Deutschlands politische Parteien*, pp. 37-38, 40-44, 46-47; L. Parisius, *Hoverbeck*, II/II, 19, n. 3; H. Wagener, *Erlebtes*, I, 63; H. Müller, *Der Preussische Volks-Verein*, pp. 22-25.

organizations of Saxony, Moritz Busch's diary ridiculed their frailty: "We had a Progressive Party, but only a barely noticeable progress in matters which went beyond the interests of the ministry. We had a few hundred members of the Nationalverein, whose leaders, mostly lawyers or at least jurists, would occasionally manage to arrange a pretty little demonstration, . . . and who considered the organization an end in itself. Finally, we had a legislature in regard to whose deliberations it was as a rule best to imitate the smile with which Minister von Beust used to face it."[3]

The social composition of the leadership of the parties, moreover, did not change during the 1860's. A meeting of the liberal notables of Westphalia held in Hamm early in the decade appointed a provincial election committee of 23 members including 5 industrialists, 5 lawyers, 3 merchants, 3 judicial officers, 1 landowner, 1 physician, and 1 school principal. Among the 60 members of the liberal election committee in Halle were 11 merchants, 10 industrialists, 5 professors, 5 municipal officials, 4 landowners, 3 judicial officers, 2 city councillors, 1 banker, and 1 lawyer. In Breslau the liberal election committee consisted of 3 merchants, 1 banker, 1 lawyer, 1 editor, 1 accountant, 1 bricklayer, and 1 master furrier. The liberal election committee of the Königsberg district contained 6 landowners, 4 merchants, 2 city councillors, 2 professors, 2 physicians, 1 banker, and 1 lawyer out of a membership of 23.

The conservatives also felt the influence of wealth and status, although occasionally they would assume an egalitarian pose. In Berlin, where they were as a rule heavily outvoted, their election committee prepared a list of 17 acceptable candidates for the legislature which

[3] M. Busch, *Tagebuchblätter*, III, 481-482. Cf. [Moritz Veit], "Die Legislaturperiode des Hauses der Abgeordneten 1859-1861: Ein Rechenschaftsbericht," *Preussische Jahrbücher*, VIII (1861), 402; O. Westphal, *Welt- und Staatsauffassung des Liberalismus*, p. 320; L. Parisius, *Deutschlands politische Parteien*, p. 62; L. Parisius, *Hoverbeck*, II/1, 108; H. Ruider, *Bismarck und die öffentliche Meinung*, p. 13.

included 7 artisans and only 2 noblemen. The purpose was to show that the party did not pursue "selfish or, worse still, feudal aims," but supported "respectable and patriotic citizens of Berlin instead of specimens of the year 1848 brought in from the outside." Yet handicraftsmen who entered into an alliance with legitimism soon discovered that they were generally ignored by the aristocracy, which wanted only their votes. The class predilections of the conservatives were reflected in the names of the 34 men whose election in 1863 the party leadership recommended with special urgency. First came the veterans of traditionalist politics, Hermann Wagener, Moritz von Blanckenburg, and Ernst Ludwig von Gerlach, followed by a long list of highborn notables: Prince von Hohenlohe, Count von Pückler, Baron von Hertefeldt, General von Brandt, Judge von Brauchitsch, Privy Councilor von Olfers, and County Commissioner von Seydewitz. There were 20 noblemen and 14 commoners on the list, but even the latter were almost without exception men of high position: Mayor Strosser, Professor Glaser, State Attorney Wendt, Privy Councilor Elwanger, and Consistory Director Nöldechen. The presence of Master Guildsman Neuhaus in this company could not disguise the fact that conservatism was the ideological instrument of privilege and property.[4]

The activities of parliamentary parties were reinforced by civic organizations whose aims ostensibly transcended factional differences, but which were in fact intimately involved in partisan politics. The most important of these was the Nationalverein, founded in 1859, when the successes of the unification movement in the Italian Peninsula stimulated nationalism in the German Confederation. In response to "the dangerous condition of Europe and Germany at this moment, and the need to subordinate political party demands to the great common task of German unification," it advanced

[4] E. N. Anderson, *Social and Political Conflict*, pp. 298-301, 356, 366-367; H. Müller, *Der Preussische Volks-Verein*, pp. 40-41.

a program advocating the establishment of a liberal and united German state under the leadership of Prussia:

1. We perceive in the present political situation of the world great dangers for the independence of our German fatherland, dangers which have been increased rather than decreased by the peace concluded between Austria and France.

2. These dangers have their ultimate cause in the defective common constitution of Germany, and they can be removed only through a prompt alteration of this constitution.

3. For this purpose it is necessary that the German federal diet be replaced by a stable, strong, and permanent central government of Germany, and that a German national assembly be convoked.

4. Under present circumstances the most effective steps for the achievement of this goal can come only from Prussia. We should therefore strive to bring it about that Prussia assumes the initiative in this matter.

5. Should Germany in the immediate future once again be directly threatened from abroad, then, until the final establishment of the German central government, the command of the German military forces and the diplomatic representation of Germany abroad are to be assigned to Prussia.

6. It is the duty of every German to support the Prussian government to the best of his ability, insofar as its endeavors are based on the principle that the tasks of the Prussian state coincide essentially with the needs and tasks of Germany, and insofar as it directs its activity toward the introduction of a strong and free common constitution for Germany.

7. We expect of all German friends of the fatherland, whether they belong to the democratic or the constitutional [right-wing liberal] party, that they will place national independence and unity above the demands of the party, and that they will work together harmoniously and

perseveringly for the achievement of a strong constitution for Germany.

This was essentially the program of the Prussophile *kleindeutsch* liberals who ten years before had gained a majority in the Frankfurt Parliament only to be disowned by Frederick William IV. Now they hoped to redress that defeat with a more efficient organization and a more vigorous ruler. They asserted repeatedly that "the German people will never give up its claim to federal unity which . . . has found its lawful expression in the imperial constitution of 1849." Nor had their aversion to illegality and violence abated since the days of the revolution. Bismarck, trying to discredit parliamentarianism, claimed that they "seek the overthrow of the institutions existing in Germany, and until the achievement of this goal, they seek at least to encroach on the independence of the German governments by intimidating them through demonstrations in which they hope for the ultimate participation of the masses." But that was a red herring. The Nationalverein feared the involvement of the lower classes in politics even more than he did. Its journal explicitly repudiated the use of force in achieving the unity and freedom of Germany:

> [The national party] does not follow a revolutionary unitary policy; it does not want to level; it accepts what exists and seeks to reform it. A violent revolution from below as well as a conquest from above would in like fashion make our program and its execution impossible. The national party is therefore resolutely opposed both to the revolutionary party which wants to construct a new Germany out of a general overturn, declaring that only this road to Germany unity is conceivable, and to the specifically Prussian party which would like to treat Germany like an artichoke to be consumed by old Prussia leaf by leaf.

It preferred the tactic of exhortation: "Reform must be sought and moral pressure . . . must be applied to the

317

governments through the press, through organizations, through the legislatures, through all the means of legal agitation which have until now been much too little employed and developed in Germany." The use of violence might intensify class antagonism and encourage social unrest. It might transform a Fabian campaign for political reform into a revolutionary movement threatening established property relations. And to liberal bourgeois nationalists even the decrepit German Confederation was preferable to an egalitarian red republic.[5]

Although the Nationalverein spoke of "the need to subordinate political party demands to the great common task of German unification," it was in fact deeply involved in the partisan struggles of state politics. For how could national and domestic reform be separated? Besides, its social composition inclined the Nationalverein toward the middle-class liberals who were fighting for a parliamentary form of government. The same men who sought to restrict princely authority advocated national unification; the same parties which opposed aristocratic privilege preached loyalty to the common fatherland. The Nationalverein therefore upheld constitutionalism, while most constitutionalists tended to support the Nationalverein. An organization demanding "liberation of the political and economic energies of the people restrained by false principles of government" was bound to appeal to the liberal politicians in the state legislatures.

The connection between the Nationalverein and party politics was particularly close in Prussia. The former greeted the formation of the Progressive Party with loud jubilation: "It is, so far as we know, the first time that in Berlin a number of well-known men of politics come before the Prussian people with an election manifesto at the head of which stands the great German national

---

[5] [G. Planck], *Der Nationalverein*, pp. 60, 93-94; Rudolf Schwab, *Der deutsche Nationalverein: Seine Entstehung und sein Wirken* (Frauenfeld, 1902), pp. 46-48, 76-77, 91-92, 94, 96, 101, 103; O. v. Bismarck, *Werke*, V, 314; M., "Die nationale Partei," p. 687.

question. . . . Therefore we extend with joy a welcome to the first attempt of our political friends in Berlin . . . to arouse the spirit of the people." Speaking in turn for the Prussian liberals, Schulze-Delitzsch attested that the "Progressive Party is the best recruiter, the executive committee of the Nationalverein in Prussia, and the movement led by us has contributed significantly to the spread of the organization. All important members of the legislature from our party have joined the National-verein, and only members of the Nationalverein are to be found in the central committee of the party." But the participation of the Nationalverein in state politics was not limited to the exchange of civilities with the opposition parties. In Pillau the members formed an election committee and decided to recommend nominees for the district electoral college. A conference representing branches in East and West Prussia, Pomerania, and Posen endorsed the program of the Progressive Party. In Osterburg and Stendal counties the Nationalverein was primarily responsible for the great victory of the liberals at the polls. In Breslau and Görlitz it campaigned vigorously for the candidates of the left. Its claim of nonpartisanship was only a pose which neither friends nor enemies took very seriously. The National-verein was as firmly committed to parliamentarianism as any of the bourgeois reformist parties in Central Europe.[6]

Its identification with the liberal middle class was apparent in economics no less than in politics. The same civic philosophy which led it to oppose traditional institutions of government led it to oppose traditional restraints on manufacture. The Nationalverein favored repeal of corporative regulations of production, arguing that "Prussia, in order to fulfill her German mission, must be free of all feudal and medieval fetters. Only a bourgeois state can win the German bourgeoisie." The

<hr>

[6] *Wochenschrift des Nationalvereins,* May 1, 1860, p. 1; *ibid.,* June 21, 1861, p. 494; H. Schulze-Delitzsch, *Schriften und Reden,* IV, 59-60; E. N. Anderson, *Social and Political Conflict,* pp. 306-307, 326, n. 81.

introduction of industrial freedom, moreover, would be an important step toward the integration of the material interests of the German Confederation. That was why the program adopted by the members in Cologne demanded "revision of industrial legislation on the basis of industrial freedom, with the strictest possible limitation of the practice of requiring licenses." That was why the *Wochenschrift des Nationalvereins* reported with satisfaction that "industrial freedom advances from all directions toward the Prussian borders from which the government of [former prime minister] Manteuffel expelled it." The prevailing view was that the restriction of business initiative was a natural consequence of the bureaucratic officiousness with which the nation was governed. Free enterprise could not contribute to the creation of a new Germany, as long as paternalistic supervision by the state hampered the growth of the economy. "We enjoy . . . the dubious benefit of tutelage, of a system of meddlesome government which hinders us in the development of our commercial and industrial investments. Capital has no confidence in the stability and strength of a confederation which rests only on the community of dynastic interests without ever being able or even only wanting to do anything useful for the material interests of the people."[7]

In its attitude toward the lower classes, moreover, the Nationalverein clearly reflected bourgeois social biases. Although hoping to enlist the support of the masses, it could not overcome a secret fear of their undisciplined strength. Some of its adherents did sense the growing political importance of the proletariat. Rudolf von Bennigsen warned that "the Nationalverein must guard very carefully against underestimating the incipient labor movement. It could soon achieve such scope and organization that under certain conditions it might exercise a

---

[7] Sch., "Unsere materiellen Interessen," *Wochenschrift des Nationalvereins*, May 31, 1861, p. 469. Cf. *ibid.*, November 29, 1861, p. 678; M., "Die nationale Partei," p. 688; L. Parisius, *Deutschlands politische Parteien*, p. 44.

dangerous influence. But with a healthy development it will have an equally practical and useful effect." Georg Fein, the radical forty-eighter who had become a leader of the German workingmen's societies in Switzerland, pointed out to his friends in the Nationalverein that laborers who joined the organization would be "less exposed to the danger of being dominated by purely negative and destructive tendencies, of being taken in tow by truly wicked demagogues, and of letting themselves be incited against the upper classes." The industrialist Theodor Müllensiefen even insisted that without the support of the masses national unification could never be achieved: "People of rank will not wake up from their sleep until they hear *allons enfants de la patrie.* . . . I realize indeed what the objections are, but without the working classes a united Germany remains after all a dream. Are we then to reject them?" But most of the members agreed with August Ludwig von Rochau, who scornfully dismissed a suggestion that the *Wochenschrift des Nationalvereins,* which he edited, should appeal to the lower classes: "In my opinion this proposal is nonsense. For first of all, there is in the entire Nationalverein perhaps not a single man who can write for those classes with drastic effect. Secondly, it is not those classes which make politics and history in Germany. Thirdly, the small burgher and the farmer are different in each German province with regard to their customs, their prejudices, their education, and their interest."

At times the Nationalverein displayed a paternalistic concern for the welfare of the masses, but it carefully barred them from membership. The executive committee resolved that "the labor movement is to be furthered by the Nationalverein, not directly and officially, to be sure, but indirectly through its members and leaders in the interest of a healthy development which will maintain a harmonious association with the national movement." The organization published an occasional popular pamphlet like Friedrich Henneberg's "German

Distress and Help Described for the Free German Farmer by a Friend of the Fatherland," which had a modest printing of 4,500 copies. It appropriated 4,100 marks to send twelve workers to the London world's fair of 1862 under the chaperonage of the liberal economist Max Wirth. It gave cautious approval to the *Allgemeine deutsche Arbeiter-Zeitung*, a labor newspaper with a circulation of 800 which its secretary Fedor Streit edited in Coburg.

The annual dues, however, remained 3 marks, an amount large enough to discourage the propertyless from participation. All efforts to reduce the dues or at least to allow payment in monthly installments failed. A yearly subscription to the *Wochenschrift des Nationalvereins*, furthermore, cost 4 marks, so that Streit was forced to admit: "We should nevertheless not conceal from each other that the *Wochenschrift* can be intended above all only for those strata of the German people which have reached the level of education of our middle class." Even Schulze-Delitzsch acquiesced in the exclusion of the proletariat. His advice to workers seeking admission was to turn to more suitable organizations: "You will do much better to contribute to funds which will secure for you progress, well-being, and, in the educational societies, a higher degree of education, than to those of the Nationalverein. Since education and uplift of the German working class are among the finest and greatest national tasks, you will advance the national cause a thousand times better in this fashion than if you bring many talers to our treasury. You are in spirit the true honorary members of our organization, even if you do not offer us a single pfennig." For the Nationalverein the lower classes were too unreliable to be entrusted with public affairs.[8]

[8] Hermann Oncken, "Der Nationalverein und die Anfänge der deutschen Arbeiterbewegung 1862-63," *Archiv für die Geschichte des Sozialismus und der Arbeiterbewegung*, II (1912), 121, 125-127; R. Weber, *Kleinbürgerliche Demokraten*, pp. 49, 52-53; Paul Herrmann, *Die Entstehung des Deutschen Nationalvereins und die Gründung*

The organization, then, was essentially a pressure group of the well-to-do. Even one of its founders, the Thuringian lawyer Hugo Fries, expressed regret that it was so narrowly limited to men of substance: "Is this a national society as we had intended? We did not want to found an association of political notables through which we could influence the people, but the organization was to include the people directly, and in this we have failed." The membership remained small and exclusive: 5,000 in 1860, 15,000 in 1861, and some 25,000 in 1862, followed by a decline to 23,000 in 1863, 21,000 at the most in 1864, 11,000 in 1865, and 5,000 in 1866. The circulation of the *Wochenschrift des Nationalvereins* and of its successor the *Wochenblatt des Nationalvereins* was even more restricted: 5,000 copies in 1860 and 1861, 6,000 in 1862, 2,000 in 1864 and 3,000 in 1865.

Prussia provided the largest number of members, 3,073 out of 5,803 in September 1860. There were significant differences, however, between the industrial west and the agrarian east: 683 in Westphalia and 587 in the Rhine Province, but 248 in Pomerania, 177 in West Prussia, 64 in Silesia, and 63 in Posen. The only one of the secondary states in which the organization had a substantial following was Baden, with a membership of 433. In Hanover the figure was 194, in Bavaria 193, in Saxony 124, in Nassau 109, in Württemberg 45, and in Hesse-Darmstadt 32. The greatest support for the Nationalverein outside Prussia came from the municipal republics and minor principalities, whose political weakness aroused longing for a strong united fatherland. In Saxe-Coburg-Gotha 282 persons belonged, in Bremen 191, in Hamburg 163, in Saxe-Meiningen 111, and in

seiner Wochenschrift (Leipzig, 1932), pp. 159-162; "Aus den Briefen Rudolf v. Bennigsens," ed. Hermann Oncken, *Deutsche Revue*, XXX (1905), no. 3, pp. 85-86; H. Oncken, *Bennigsen*, I, 470; R. Schwab, *Der Nationalverein*, p. 81; Richard Le Mang, *Der deutsche Nationalverein* (Berlin, [1909]), p. 51; H. Schulze-Delitzsch, *Schriften und Reden*, III, 222, n. 1, 224, n. 1.

Frankfurt am Main 98. Indeed, an analysis of the geographic distribution of the members as of October 1865 reveals that the largest proportional participation was to be found in Bremen with 0.59 per cent of the population, followed by Frankfurt am Main with 0.37, Lübeck with 0.33, Hamburg with 0.24, and the Reuss principalities with 0.20 per cent. Of the larger states the percentage for Hesse-Darmstadt was 0.16, for Nassau 0.10, for Hanover 0.06, for Baden 0.05, and for Prussia 0.04. In last place were Schleswig-Holstein with 0.03, Saxony with 0.02, the Mecklenburgs with 0.015, and Bavaria and Württemberg with 0.005 per cent each.

The size of the Nationalverein was limited in part by the hostile attitude of most of the governments. Its advocacy of Prussian hegemony, moreover, aroused popular disapproval in many parts of Central Europe. Max Duncker reported in the summer of 1860 that "the organization found . . . sympathy only where the ideas on which it is based were already powerful twelve years ago. Its sole important new acquisition was Hanover, in return for which, however, Saxony seems to be as good as completely lost. In Baden the organization has found some sympathy, but not until the Baden government itself had opened the way for it. In Württemberg, Hesse-Darmstadt, and Bavaria it has remained completely without influence." But the most important reason for the small membership was the exclusion of the lower classes.

The barriers were not insurmountable, to be sure. In Carwitz in Pomerania some 9 peasants joined, while the villages of Schlawin and Notzkow had over 12 members each. There were 35 handicraftsmen in the Königsberg branch out of a total membership of 294. Even industrial workers, like the 55 factory employees in Stromberg who made a contribution, would occasionally display interest in the Nationalverein. The best gauge of its social composition, however, is an analysis based on data provided by the *Wochenschrift des National-*

vereins regarding the occupations of those attending local meetings or subscribing to the organization's special funds for the national cause. Of the 588 men for whom information is available, 133 were lawyers and notaries, 75 merchants, 56 professors and teachers, 54 judicial officers, 37 industrialists, 36 municipal officials, 32 physicians, 25 landed proprietors and rentiers, 24 editors and journalists, 20 booksellers, 20 apothecaries, and 19 master craftsmen and handworkers. Gottlieb Planck explained in his official history of the National-verein that "admittedly a real mass accession did not occur anywhere. But for the time being we did not strive for it at all. What we primarily sought to achieve was to gain firm footholds throughout Germany, and to attract everywhere the politically independent, active, and influential men." The organization hoped to attain its ends by enlisting the support of the propertied and educated who dominated politics.[9]

The attempt to unite the well-to-do classes behind a program of national unification and representative government alarmed the defenders of the status quo. In Prussia it led to the founding of the Prussian People's Association, the propaganda organization of the Conservative Party. The association was formed at a great gathering of legitimists, representing a coalition of aristocratic landowners and master artisans, which took place in Berlin on September 20, 1861. There were over 1,200 participants from all parts of the kingdom, some of them attracted by the assurance that all sympathizers "of whatever class and influence" would be "most heartily welcome," and encouraged by a promise that food

---

9 R. Weber, *Kleinbürgerliche Demokraten*, pp. 27-28; H. Oncken, *Bennigsen*, I, 455, 469, 608, 649; [G. Planck], *Der Nationalverein*, pp. 36-37, 43; E. N. Anderson, *Social and Political Conflict*, pp. 330, 334-335; H. Rosenberg, *Die nationalpolitische Publizistik*, II, 966; K. Bechstein, "Die öffentliche Meinung in Thüringen" (Part 1), p. 163; Walter Grube, *Die Neue Ära und der Nationalverein: Ein Beitrag zur Geschichte Preussens und der Einheitsbewegung* (Marburg, 1933), p. 166; Lenore O'Boyle, "The German *Nationalverein*," *Journal of Central European Affairs* XVI (1957), pp. 334-335.

and lodging would be provided for "friends from out-side the city who are without means." The conservative central election committee which was responsible for organizing the meeting, moreover, called on its sup-porters in the provinces "who are blessed by God with greater wealth . . . to reimburse the poorer political friends in their circle of acquaintances for the round trip." Among those present at the convention were representatives of the Mennonites in the Marienburg district of West Prussia, delegates sent by the peasants of Westphalia, conservative handicraftsmen, pietistic clergymen, and loyal village mayors. But the leading personalities were men like the former Provincial Gov-ernors von Meding and von Kleist-Retzow, Generals von Maliszewski and von Winterfeld, Counts von War-tensleben and von Finckenstein, Barons von Waldow-Reitzenstein and von Senfft-Pilsach, Ernst Ludwig von Gerlach, Moritz von Blanckenburg, and of course Her-mann Wagener.

The deliberations were opened by Count Eberhard Stolberg-Wernigerode in the name of the Holy Trinity, and they concluded with the singing of "Nun danket alle Gott." The main speakers, among them Kleist-Retzow, Wagener, and Blanckenburg, thundered against red republicanism, moneyed capital, and heartless usury. The upholsterer Bachmann from Frankfurt an der Oder prophesied amid laughter and applause that "if we do not stick close together, we will within a short time see persons sitting at the ministers' table who are not native to Germany, but who are descended from the Orient!" The statement of principles approved by the assembly became the platform of the Conservative Party. It ad-vocated the unification of Germany in a form maintain-ing the authority of the princes and the sovereignty of the states; it upheld the prerogative of the crown, the influence of the church, and the power of the army; and it championed the interests of artisans and landowners against laissez-faire capitalism. Here was a program calculated to win popular support for the preservation of the established order.[10]

The *Neue Preussische Zeitung* hailed the Prussian People's Association as "an anti-Nationalverein . . . whose most essential task it is to destroy that organization and its works." Yet in fact the activities of the association were directed toward the spread of conservative loyalties within Prussia. It published pamphlets preaching devotion to the crown like "A Word regarding the Next Elections to the Legislature"; "Whom Should We Elect?"; "What We Want, What They Want: A Comparison and Illumination of the Election Programs of Both Parties"; "Who Should Govern in Prussia?"; and "To the Voters of All Parties." It sought to weld into a single political force the various independent legitimist associations such as the Patriotic Alliance, Men of the Loyal Order with God for King and Fatherland, the Monarchic Constitutional Election Society, the Conservative Constitutional Election Society, and the Christian Conservative Election Society. It even distributed "Advice for the Conservative Election Campaign in City and Country." In the small towns and villages its followers should first of all come to an understanding with the clergymen, mayors, and landowners. It would then be the duty of the latter to make clear to the voters the dangers created "by the growing proletariat, the breaking up of estates, the rising bureaucratization, the injury to church and school through their separation, which liberalism favors, by the equalization of the proletariat with the taxpayers, of the propertyless with the peasants by the representation of their rural interests solely through county judges, and the growing predominance of the cities." The members were to reinforce among the people that "old Prussian feeling," "national pride," and "the old love for the royal house of the Hohenzollerns." On election day they should note "in silence" any ir-

---

[10] H. Müller, *Der Preussische Volks-Verein*, pp. 24-27; L. Parisius, *Deutschlands politische Parteien*, pp. 41-42; L. Parisius, *Hoverbeck*, I, 217.

regularities at the polls, and "if the result was favorable to the opponents," they were to challenge the legality of the proceedings.

After the constitutional conflict began, moreover, the executive committee urged its adherents to send deputations to Berlin expressing loyalty to the crown:

> We recommend that the members of these deputations should be chosen as far as possible, in keeping with their high purpose, through careful selection from all classes, without even any restriction to members of the People's Association, and especially that handicraftsmen and farmers should not be left out. It is naturally inadvisable to compose the addresses in one and the same form, and we therefore ask you to see to it that they have a suitable style, as short and pithy as possible. But we only suggest the following points on which a special emphasis should be placed. . . . Our loyalty, our life, our devotion and property for the strong and beloved throne of the Hohenzollerns!

Early in 1863 an address thanking the crown for the efforts to reorganize the army, and condemning the "unpatriotic resolutions and revolutionary encroachments of the misled majority of the country" carried some 500,000 signatures. A year later the king received on the occasion of his birthday a delegation bearing a statement of congratulation and gratitude signed by more than 50,000 supporters of the Prussian People's Association.

In the petitions which it submitted to the government and the legislature the organization advocated the "formation of a state industrial council for the consideration of the common interests of the handicraftsmen and workers of the entire country," opposed repeal of the usury laws, and inveighed against "speculating Jewry." It helped establish financial institutions designed to meet the needs of the master handicraftsman and the peasant proprietor. Prominent members of the association sat on the board of directors of the Prussian Mortgage Credit and Banking Company, which extended loans to landholders, and of H. Schuster & Co., a firm specializing in credit for skilled artisans and small businessmen. The moving spirit behind all these activities was Hermann Wagener, who handled the business details, planned the annual meetings, spoke before countless audiences, and above all directed the publicity campaign. Even Marx was impressed with such inexhaustible energy. After a visit to Germany he wrote Engels that the members of the legislature in Berlin were simple-minded Philistines. "The only figures who at least look respectable in this stable of pygmies are Waldeck on one side, and Wagener and Don Quixote von Blankenburg on the other." This was high praise from a man who was captious about most people, including his own followers.[11]

The Prussian People's Association was essentially a pseudo-popular civic organization serving the interests of the conservative nobility. Since it invited the participation of all classes of society, its followers included artisans, shopkeepers, peasants, and even factory workers, as well as aristocratic landowners and bureaucrats. Early in 1862 the membership numbered 15,000; by the end of the year it had risen to over 26,000; and the following winter it reached the high point, about 50,000. This was twice the size of the Nationalverein in its heyday, although the difference was small considering that the latter sought the support only of the well-to-do. Those who attended the meetings or signed the petitions of the associations, furthermore, did not always act out

11 *Neue Preussische Zeitung*, September 26, 1861, July 22, 1863; H. Müller, *Der Preussische Volks-Verein*, pp. 59-60, 63-64, 70-71, 75, 81-82, 117, 119, 122-124, 126; *Europäischer Geschichtskalender*, ed. H. Schulthess (1862), p. 181, (1864), p. 166; F. Löwenthal, *Der preussische Verfassungsstreit*, p. 136; G. Ritter, *Die preussischen Konservativen*, pp. 39-40; K. Marx and F. Engels, *Briefwechsel*, III, 27.

of conviction. Theodor von Bernhardi noted in his diary a letter from a friend in the army describing some of the methods employed to recruit members:

> The reactionary People's Association is flooding the Rhenish army corps and probably all others as well with invitations to join the association and make an annual contribution of at least 5 talers for the purposes of the reaction. They seek out, moreover, only officers with whom they can count on success because of their names, or because they are subscribers to the *Kreuzzeitung* [*Neue Preussische Zeitung*], or because they advertise their "sound opinions," and "thereby they immediately stigmatize all those who have not been invited," among whom naturally Etzel himself belongs. He wanted to bring the matter up for discussion officially, but at once found opposition because his division commander himself, although entirely of Etzel's opinion, had already signed up out of fear of his friends in Berlin.

How much more vulnerable to this kind of pressure were tradesmen and farmers? Many of them had to listen willy-nilly to legitimist orators declaiming against "the modern rule of money" which "enslaves men," or preaching that "the sole remedy . . . is to be found only in the strengthening of the Christian elements in church and state."

While the Prussian People's Association sought a following among the lower classes, its policies like those of the Nationalverein were determined by men of means. Here and there some handicraftsman with a talent for popular oratory would be commissioned to win conservative votes among the artisan masses. The shoemakers Kaffka and Panse, the goldsmith Neuhaus, and the upholsterer Wohlgemuth, for example, won the approbation of the Junkers for their services to legitimism. Kaffka eventually put away his last and his awl to become a director of H. Schuster & Co., while Panse's posthumous reward was the eulogy in Wagener's memoirs of "a man wise and skilled, energetic and careful, and at the same time upright and reliable, a born parliamentarian, equally expert in presiding and in debating, in short, a man who in a republic like America would have had the stuff to become president." But these were exceptions. The leadership of the association in the provinces was by and large made up of landowners, clergymen, county commissioners, and higher civil servants. The fact that some 20 per cent of the members of an organization claiming to represent artisans and peasants resided in Berlin, moreover, suggests its close connection with the aristocratic bureaucrats, politicians, and army officers in the capital.

The executive committee of the Prussian People's Association consisted at first of thirteen noblemen and one commoner, but this was too much even for a staunch conservative like the historian Heinrich Leo, who expostulated with Wagener: "We must strongly deplore that while our party is being strongly attacked by its opponents as a feudal or Junker party, the obvious wisdom of not having only noblemen on the executive committee has been so completely disregarded that the executive committee is in fact (with the exception of your person as a non-noble jurist) composed solely of noblemen, and thereby acquires the appearance of being a board of the nobility with a non-noble syndic." In his reminiscences Wagener asserted that such remonstrances "had the telling effect of immediately supplementing the executive committee, which by the way had been the intention from the very beginning, with non-noble elements from all classes of the population including the handicraftsmen." But either he was embellishing the truth or his memory had failed him. For the executive committee even after its reconstruction in December 1861 contained seven aristocrats and four commoners, the latter consisting of two great landowners, the mayor of Herford, and Wagener himself. Despite the rhetoric about enlisting all classes of society in the struggle against godless liberalism, the men who directed the association had no intention of giving the propertyless a voice in their organization. They merely wanted popular support without popular control.[12] The legitimists of Prussia were not the only adversaries of the Nationalverein. In other parts of Central Europe there was also opposition to projects of federal reorganization which implied the expulsion of Austria from Germany. The *grossdeutsch* movement was a conglomerate of diverse sects and factions held together by the conviction that a solution of the national problem could not be achieved without the Habsburg monarchy. Its conservative adherents believed that an alteration of the settlement of 1815 meant opening the floodgates of revolution. The clericals of the south and west were determined to resist any program of civic reform which might shift the religious balance in favor of Protestantism. Many liberals saw in the Hohenzollern state the embodiment of militarism and Junkerdom. The radicals below the Main with their dreams of a popular cantonal democracy rejected centralized authority as a matter of principle. And throughout Germany there were governments, resolved to maintain their sovereignty, which encouraged particularistic societies and parties. To weld all these groups with their incompatible allegiances into a unified political movement was a formidable task. Only the growing aggressiveness of Prussian policy persuaded the Hofburg in the early 1860's to make the attempt.

The leading statesmen in Vienna, Anton von Schmerling and Johann Bernhard von Rechberg, felt that the moment was propitious for the formation of a *grossdeutsch* civic organization extending throughout the German Confederation. Their chief agent in this venture was Julius Fröbel, a disenchanted Thuringian

[12] H. Müller, *Der Preussische Volks-Verein*, pp. 27, 33-35, 40, 47, 55, 60, 67-68, 70, 85-86; *Aus dem Leben Bernhardis*, IV, 329-330; *Neue Preussische Zeitung*, May 6, 1866; L. Parisius, *Deutschlands politische Parteien*, p. 41; H. Wagener, *Erlebtes*, I, 22, 79, 85.

democrat who in 1848 had been sentenced to the gallows by the Habsburg authorities for his revolutionary activities. Taking advantage of the growing disillusionment of the liberals with Berlin, the Austrian government sought to win their sympathy by advancing a plan for a federal representative assembly composed of delegates chosen by the state legislatures. It began to compete with the Prussians for popularity, moreover, by encouraging its citizens to participate in the sharpshooting meet in Frankfurt am Main, by sending representatives to attend gatherings of business and church groups, by arranging for the convention of German jurists to take place in Vienna, and even by inviting the devoutly Protestant Gustavus Adolphus Society to hold its convention in the imperial capital. In the meantime Fröbel was touring the secondary states to drum up support for the project of a *grossdeutsch* political association. While he found a warm welcome in Bavaria and won important converts in Württemberg, the response in Hesse-Kassel and Hanover was disappointing. He also got in touch with the Austrophiles in Leipzig and with the handful of sympathizers in Berlin. But in Oldenburg, Bremen, and Hamburg prospects were so bleak that he did not trouble to visit the North Sea coast. The results of the Hofburg's diplomatic offensive were on the whole only fair.

They were enough, however, to alarm its opponents. Count Albrecht von Bernstorff, head of the Prussian foreign office, inveighed against Austrian perfidy:

The *grossdeutsch* agitation began everywhere with the cry that Austria should not allow herself to be forced out of Germany. It is apparent to all how this agitation was initiated and carried on with small expedients as well as with big demonstrations, and how in one part of Germany it was finally shaped into "compelling" public opinion. In the sending of Tirolese to the sharpshooting meet in Frankfurt at the expense of the Austrian government, in the trips of Austrian officials to economic meetings, commercial conventions, and church gatherings, in the arrangements for the convention of the jurists in Vienna and the official trips and speeches of the imperial minister of state we can see nothing but a chain of agitation devices aiming at the same goal. The German national tendencies of Austria are everywhere pushed to the foreground. . . . While the festivities of fraternal love were going on, while the conciliatory speeches and exhortations of prominent personalities were being heard, the unleashing of the south German and especially of the Austrian press gave license to all animosities and charges against Prussia. The Viennese newspapers did the most incredible things before the eyes of the Austrian government, and in this connection we only need to recall the articles in the *Botschafter*, the *Donauzeitung*, the *Vaterland*, and the *Presse*, which in their invectives against the Prussian government regarding internal questions often made the point of view of the most radical opposition their own. There is no doubt that this agitation with its wide ramification has indeed led to the creation of a "compelling" public opinion in the south of Germany favorable to Austria.

But his fears were exaggerated. The inner inconsistencies of the *grossdeutsch* movement assured its ineffectualness.

This became apparent at the convention held in Frankfurt am Main on October 28 and 29, 1862, to form a national pro-Austrian organization. Among the 500 participants could be found conservatives, clericals, liberals, and even democrats, all of them imbued with distrust of Prussia. The social distinction of the gathering was impressive. No other civic group could boast of so many former ministers, high bureaucrats, prominent aristocrats, and respected scholars. They represented all parts of Germany from Schleswig to Styria except the northeast, the heart of the Hohenzollern monarchy. The largest contingent came from Bavaria. The Austrian delegation, despite Schmerling's efforts, consisted of only a few zealous supporters of the cabinet's policy. The presence of some members from Hanover, Hesse-Darmstadt, and Nassau, moreover, was the result of prodding by their governments or by Habsburg diplomats. The Prussian *grossdeutsch* sympathizers had been reluctant to come. August Reichensperger, the leader of the Catholic faction in the Prussian legislature, refused to endorse the meeting for fear of losing political influence in Berlin. "I have never hesitated to declare myself a *Grossdeutscher* from the speaker's platform," he explained. "But I am convinced that I would permanently reduce my effectiveness here, however small it may be, if I were to comply with the wish of Herr von Lerchenfeld [a sponsor of the convention]. My position is, apart from this, exceedingly delicate because of the *suspicion légitime* which rightly rests on the ultramontanes." The only prominent Rhinelander to appear in Frankfurt was Joseph Bachem, publisher of the *Kölnische Blätter*.

The outcome of the meeting was the establishment of the Reformverein. Its bylaws announced that the "aim of the organization is first of all to promote as much as possible the reform of the German constitution. The foremost principle is the maintenance of the complete integrity of Germany, and opposition to those efforts the aim or consequence of which would be the exclusion of any part of Germany." To achieve this goal the members approved a program of political reorganization in Central Europe: "(1) The reform of the constitution of the German Confederation is an urgent and pressing need, so that a position of power in foreign affairs as well as welfare and civil freedom in internal affairs can be promoted more vigorously than they have been. (2) This reform must make it possible for all German states to remain in the entire community. (3) It finds its realization in the creation of a vigorous federal executive authority with a national representation. . . . Reform is to be achieved only through agreement and on the basis of the existing federal constitution." Finally, in order to further the economic integration of the Habsburg monarchy with the other German states, the convention voted that "we should work toward the admission of all of Austria to the Zollverein," and that "a revision of the Zollverein tariff is to be effected only by negotiation with Austria." From the point of view of the statesmen in Vienna this platform was unexceptionable.[13]

Yet in fact it was an unsatisfactory compromise. The liberals resented the defeat of their motion that the federal representative assembly should be elected by the voters of the nation rather than by the state legislatures, while the militant Austrophiles and clericals were disappointed by the rejection of the proposal for a guarantee of the Austrian Empire. The leaders of the Reformverein, Baron Gustav von Lerchenfeld, Heinrich von Gagern, Oskar von Wydenbrugk, and Julius Fröbel himself, favored extensive reform of the German Confederation. But the local branches were often tools of particularism, confessionalism, or conservatism. Many of the progressives in the secondary states and even in the Habsburg monarchy, convinced that the *grossdeutsch* movement was only a stalking-horse for the Hofburg, refused to join. Others waged an unsuccessful struggle within the organization for a more determined stand on national unification. Not that their proposals were revolutionary. According to one of them, the Swabian economist and politician A.E.F. Schäffle, "the *grossdeutsch* party cannot and does not want to make propaganda and retain influence through ideologies which inflame the masses. It wants and can offer only the sober measure of progress possible under the given conditions." These liberals maintained that, in order to win popular confidence,

---

[13] Egmont Zechlin, *Bismarck und die Grundlegung der deutschen Grossmacht*, 2nd edn. (Stuttgart, 1960), pp. 372-373; *Die auswärtige Politik Preussens*, II/II, 756-757; Erich Zimmermann, *Der Deutsche Reformverein*, (Pforzheim, 1929), pp. 13-15, 39-40; *Europäischer Geschichtskalender*, ed. H. Schulthess (1862), pp. 100-101.

the federal representative assembly must be invested with constitutional authority, it must meet at regular intervals, have a decisive voice in lawmaking, and be strong enough to resist the pressure of special interests. But even such modest demands were too much for the majority. In his memoirs Schäffle recalled that "the overwhelming mass of the members of the executive committee were excellent men, but also, as I found out more and more, they were frequently conservative particularists to whom a thorough reform of the German Confederation through the establishment of a national representation endowed with effective constitutional powers was not very important."

Unable to reconcile its adherents, the Reformverein remained politically epicene, neither liberal nor conservative. Although cultivated by the governments of the secondary states as an instrument of particularism, it never won a substantial popular following. There are no figures for the total membership, but it was clearly smaller than that of the Nationalverein. The main centers of the *grossdeutsch* movement were Bavaria, Württemberg, Hanover, Hesse-Darmstadt, Hesse-Kassel, and Nassau. Yet the Munich branch, the largest in the Wittelsbach kingdom, had only 1,600 members. The second largest, the Würzburg branch, whose influence extended over all of Lower Franconia, had 1,200. In the city of Hanover there were at most 1,500, while the figure for the entire state of Hesse-Darmstadt was under 500. In Württemberg the organization was torn by the hostility between the Catholic conservative and the nationalist progressive faction. In Saxony the situation was even less promising. Baron Josef von Werner, the Austrian minister in Dresden, reported to his government that "no obstacle will be placed here in the way of Count von der Decken's recruitment for a *grossdeutsch organization*. But Baron Beust [the Saxon prime minister] anticipates little success for it, except in some aristocratic circles, because in contrast to the *klein-*

deutsch organization, it has only negation to offer, nothing positive." The bitterest disappointment for the leaders of the Reformverein, however, was the Habsburg monarchy itself. All efforts of the Viennese cabinet to arouse public interest proved a complete waste. "Among the people the German question hardly exists here," Fröbel sighed.

The governments of the secondary states did what they could to encourage participation. Karl Friedrich von Savigny, the Prussian representative at the diet of the German Confederation, charged that at times they even subsidized "*grossdeutsch* democracy," hoping to find in it "a very useful counterpoison" against "the influence of tendencies toward the Nationalverein." But nothing helped. The circulation of the *Wochenblatt des Deutschen Reformvereins* early in 1863 was less than 1,000. Baron von Lerchenfeld, chairman of the executive committee, described the fundamental weakness of the organization:

> Austria still has great prejudices and very great mistrust against her in Germany, she has few entirely reliable friends, and she has powerful and above all active and enterprising opponents. Through my relationship with the organizations and with the press, I am probably far more than many others in the position to know and judge public opinion in this question. The weakness of the *grossdeutsch* cause lies essentially in the fact that we still move only in the realm of nebulous hopes, not of palpable promises. It is this which keeps alive the old abominable mistrust and continually provides grounds for the inexhaustible suspicions of our opponents, who are so immoderate.

Sickly and distraught, the Reformverein began to decline within a year after its founding. Inner contradictions doomed it long before the Seven Weeks' War decided the question of hegemony in Central Europe.[14]

14 *Europäischer Geschichtskalender*, ed. H. Schulthess (1862), pp.

Involvement in politics was not limited to organizations whose avowed purpose was to influence public policy. In a country where government discouraged civic nonconformance, the advocacy of reform frequently assumed the guise of scholarly, professional, economic, or even musical and athletic associations. Meetings of philologists, historians, theologians, naturalists, jurists, physicians, teachers, farmers, singers, gymnasts, and sharpshooters began to perform a quasi-political function. They might include toasts to the brotherhood of all Germans, speeches proclaiming loyalty to the fatherland, the unfurling of the black, red, and gold flag, and the singing of "Deutschland, Deutschland über Alles." At a banquet celebrating the convention of German jurists Johann Caspar Bluntschli, professor of law in Heidelberg, emphasized the national importance of such gatherings:

All these phenomena which we have for several years been finding once again in Germany in the most diverse branches of life, all these organizations of singers, gymnasts, sharpshooters, economists, jurists, etc. have a political significance. They are symptoms of a political life which exists and grows in the nation. I would like to compare all these organizations to brooks which flow toward a great river, brooks which continually grow bigger until the river embraces them and carries them away. That is how an electric current of unification flows through the heart and the mind of the German nation, a current which sweeps all of us along and which also takes with it him who does not want to go.

100-101; E. Zimmermann, *Der Reformverein*, pp. 9-10, 51, 55-58, 60-61, 70; E. Zechlin, *Bismarck*, pp. 372-373; [A.E.F. Schäffle], "Die Bundesreform und die grossdeutsche Versammlung in Frankfurt," *Deutsche Vierteljahrs-Schrift*, XXVI (1863), no. 1, p. 64; Albert Eberhard Friedrich Schäffle, *Aus meinem Leben* (2 vols., Berlin, 1905), I, 109-110, 113-114; H. v. Srbik, *Deutsche Einheit*, III, 432; *Quellen zur deutschen Politik Österreichs*, ed. H. v. Srbik, II, 335, III, 148; *Die auswärtige Politik Preussens*, VI, 508; E. Marcks, *Aufstieg des Reiches*, I, 461-462.

Not everyone shared his enthusiasm. King William I of Prussia made it a point to leave a concert of the Berlin choral societies for the benefit of a German fleet just before the singing of Ernst Moritz Arndt's "Des Deutschen Vaterland." His son, the crown prince, decided to decline the honorary presidency of the assembly of gymnasts so that, among other things, he would not have to witness a display of the nationalist tricolor. There were thousands of others, however, whose interest in public affairs was stimulated by the half-fraternal, half-civic associations of the 1860's. Long afterward, recalling the miracle of the Seven Weeks' War, Victor Böhmert wrote that "these great events . . . were indeed achieved mainly thanks to the Prussian army and to King William and to the statecraft of his great minister. But numerous political, economic, and benevolent organizations of patriotic German men and women had successfully prepared public opinion in Germany for this turn in German destiny."[15]

Böhmert was in a position to know. He had played a leading role in the most important of these organizations, the Congress of German Economists. In May 1857, while still a young newspaperman in his twenties, he had on his own initiative published in the *Bremer Handelsblatt*, which he edited, a call for the establishment of a national economic association:

> It is time that all friends of economic progress acted more vigorously within their own camp and concluded a serious alliance with the power of public opinion and popular belief which no statesman and lawgiver can in the long run resist! . . . It is important first of all to found economic organizations in the larger cities of Germany, and then to hold in various places periodic meetings and an annual congress of German economists. But in addition influence should be exercised through pamphlets,

15 V. Böhmert, *Rückblicke eines Siebzigers*, p. 34. Cf. J. C. Bluntschli, *Denkwürdiges aus meinem Leben* (3 vols., Nördlingen, 1884), III, 55; E. Zechlin, *Bismarck*, pp. 263-264.

through lithographed newsletters and connections with the main organs of the press, through remonstrances to the governments, and generally through all honest and open means of writing and of speech, with the help of proposals, opinions, motions, complaints, and petitions. A peaceful propaganda will thus be organized extending over all of Germany. The program is not limited merely to changes in the tariff. It reads: reform in the economic life of the nation and clarification of economic questions! We do not want to represent a single class and its special interests. Only the man who realizes that his interests coincide at the same time with those of the entire nation should be welcome to us with his justified wishes. The governments have every reason to favor our work, for how often do also their well-intentioned improvements miscarry because of the ignorance of the masses! What they need is an improvement in finances, and our endeavor should be to increase the wealth and well-being of the people and thereby to promote contentment in the state.

This call was reprinted in several newspapers, attracting favorable attention among progressive publicists, businessmen, and politicians. The following September, at a convention of the International Congress of Charity in Frankfurt am Main, the German members met separately to discuss the propagation of sound principles of economics. The result was an "Appeal for the Establishment of Economic Societies," bearing the signatures of a number of prominent liberals, among them Karl Mittermaier, Wilhelm Adolf Lette, Karl Theodor Welcker, Hermann Schulze-Delitzsch, and Max Wirth. A year later, in September 1858, the first meeting of the Congress of German Economists opened in Gotha with a membership of about 110. Thereafter the organization held annual conferences, each in a different city. The attendance grew to 150 in Frankfurt am Main in 1859, almost 200 in Cologne in 1860, and over 300 in Stuttgart in 1861, the largest figure prior to the Seven Weeks'

War. The significance of these gatherings, however, lay not in the number but in the influence of the participants. They formed the elite of German liberalism. The *Berliner Revue*, hostile to laissez-faire doctrine, scoffed at the 1862 convention in Weimar: "Except for the contingent which the Progressive Party of the Prussian lower house had supplied, hardly a dozen of the better-known notables among the Progressives had appeared at the congress, which was made up in its majority of newspaper reporters and stenographers, of the Weimar bureaucracy, and a few students, Englishmen, and North Americans." Yet in fact the Congress of German Economists had great importance, for its members included civil servants, lawyers, journalists, academics, merchants, industrialists, and financiers who were leading the attack on the established order in Central Europe. Even the reformist *Preussische Jahrbücher* spoke of it as "an association which was basically a great public conspiracy against existing state institutions."

Not all of those present at the meetings were equally interested in questions of trade or manufacture. But the heterogeneous composition of the organization merely underlined the close connection between political and economic liberalism. The congress attracted leaders of the Nationalverein: Rudolf von Bennigsen, Fedor Streit, Hugo Fries, and Gottlieb Planck. Among the members who belonged to the parliamentary opposition in Prussia were Hermann Schulze-Delitzsch, Max von Forckenbeck, Leonor Reichenheim, and Ludolf Parisius. Well-known legislators from the secondary states also attended: Karl Braun of Nassau, A.E.F. Schäffle of Württemberg, and Karl Brater and Marquard Barth of Bavaria. The free traders were led by John Prince-Smith, Otto Michaelis, and Julius Faucher. Several important newspapermen participated, among them Leopold Sonnemann of the *Neue Frankfurter Zeitung*, Victor Böhmert of the *Bremer Handelsblatt*, August Lammers of the *Weser-Zeitung*, and August Vecchioni of the *Neueste Nach-*

richten in Munich. There was a miscellaneous group of patriotic publicists like Gustav Freytag, Karl Biedermann, Max Wirth, and Arwed Emminghaus. Even the eminent philosopher Ludwig Feuerbach appeared at one of the sessions. An association with such a membership was more than a congress of economists. In his opening address to the 1863 convention in Dresden, Wilhelm Adolf Lette, chairman of the executive committee, asserted that "our labors also serve . . . the highest goals of the nation, its unity and freedom." Here lay the ultimate purpose of the organization.[16]

Despite its denials of class predisposition, the Congress of German Economists represented essentially the liberal bourgeoisie. Karl Braun, who was elected president year after year, insisted: "We . . . have arisen through our own choice . . . out of all classes of the people. We count among us members from all strata of the population. We are gathered to represent not only some but all classes, and among them especially the great mass which is as a rule unable to speak for lack of a special corporative representation, and which is called 'the consumers.' " Yet in almost the same breath he conceded that "the economic congress also has opponents. On one side it has to endure the struggle with the feudalists and with various minor caste spirits, with the antiquated guilds, etc., with which the former seek to combine. On the other side it has to endure the struggle with the communists, socialists, and the other utopians who negate the basis of all economic development, property."

The policies advocated by the organization revealed its commitment to economic liberalism. It favored in-

---

16 V. Böhmert, *Rückblicke eines Siebzigers*, pp. 16-18; Victor Böhmert, "Die Entstehung des volkswirtschaftlichen Kongresses vor 25 Jahren (Zur Erinnerung an Schulze-Delitzsch und Huber, Lette und Prince-Smith) ," *Vierteljahrschrift für Volkswirtschaft, Politik und Kulturgeschichte*, XXI (1884) , no. 1, pp. 202-203, 205-206; Ludolf Grambow, *Die deutsche Freihandelspartei zur Zeit ihrer Blüte* (Jena, 1903) , p. 15, n. 2; "Der deutsche Handwerkertag," p. 419; [A. Lammers], "Die wirthschaftliche Reformbewegung," p. 567; *Verhandlungen des sechsten Congresses deutscher Volkswirthe 1863*, p. 4.

dustrial freedom, freedom of movement, repeal of usury laws, founding of cooperative societies, and reform of tariff legislation. Its aim was "to remove all obstacles which stand in the way of German production, which stand in the way of economic development and movement in Germany." The members were spurred on by the conviction that ineluctable laws of economics were on their side. "Do you then first ask the dyer whether the chemist is right in his assertions?" expounded Prince-Smith. "Do you ask the locomotive fireman whether the mechanic's computation of the size and strength of a boiler is correct? And why not? Is it not because chemistry, physics, and statics are based on experience? So is economics, just as completely. Or is it because in practice the principles of the technicians prove true every time? This is also to an equally high degree the case with the principle of economics. It is admittedly only seldom applied, and almost never in its pure form. But where it was applied, its blessed results have always and without exception become apparent." To the congress the liberation of the national economy was not only desirable, but in the long run inevitable.

Laissez faire in economics could not be divorced from laissez faire in politics. The members recognized that the freedom they sought was all of a piece, so that its victory in any one area of civic life depended ultimately on its victory in all. They therefore subscribed to the liberal program of national unification and representative government. Böhmert recalled that at the time of the first meeting in 1858 "the political union of the German tribes was . . . in the hearts of the great majority of the participants in the congress, even if it was not yet on their lips." But before long they became more outspoken. In 1861 a speaker boasted that "our congress is actually the first and oldest among these national organizations, which after all owe their beginning to the purified aftereffects of the great national movement of the year 1848 as well as to the fully justified and indestructible desire of the German tribes for union." In 1865 the welcoming address at the beginning of the session stated point-blank that "the discipline of economics cannot help but deal with politics, for the prosperity of the people depends on the excellence of state laws, on easy movement in commerce, on the relations of states to one another, etc., and our science cannot therefore avoid considering these things."

The Congress of German Economists looked to Prussia for the achievement of unity and freedom. Despite its professions of impartiality, the authorities in Vienna became convinced that "the congress follows not a general but a one-sided course." They therefore decided to leave it to "the inevitable and self-destructive excesses of party spirit." Replying in the name of the executive committee, Lette insisted indignantly that "this reproach itself rests on a predisposed and very one-sided view and is entirely unjustified." After Sadowa, however, he was jubilant at the Austrian defeat:

We too detest those organizations of the year 1815 by means of which a Metternich in league with a Talleyrand and Castlereagh succeeded in fettering the intellectual and political development of Germany for half a century under a pressure which was intolerable to a self-confident people, and under Habsburg influence. For no other goal and right has our congress incessantly and successfully worked up to now within its province, in the great economic sphere of life of the nation. Through it the realization was strengthened and fortified that political freedom rests on the simultaneous liberation of the economic forces, that the national welfare rests essentially on this, but that on the other hand harmful discord, petty particularistic self-seeking, and lamentable narrow-mindedness stand in the way of the economic as well as the intellectual progress of the nation. And these evils have their root and found their expression not only in the constitution of the German Confederation of 1815, but also in the constitution of the Zollverein, that unique, greatest, and most blessed achievement of the German spirit since 1815.

The Hofburg's charges of partisanship had not been "entirely unjustified" after all.[17] Regional economic societies founded under the auspices of the congress helped spread its influence throughout Germany. There was one for the northwest embracing Hanover, Oldenburg, and Bremen; another for East and West Prussia with headquarters in Danzig; a third in Dresden for Saxony; and a fourth in Frankfurt am Main for the southwest. There were affiliated municipal organizations, moreover, in Berlin, Wiesbaden, and even Munich, a stronghold of particularism in economics as well as politics. By the beginning of 1862 Lette could boast that "the congress now already constitutes a great central point and unifying force for the economic societies and organizations which have in the meantime arisen, . . . and which are gradually disseminating the more liberal economic views and principles across the entire great German fatherland." Its doctrines were also propagated by several periodicals and newspapers, not only the *Vierteljahrschrift für Volkswirthschaft und Kulturgeschichte*, which served as the unofficial journal of the congress, but also the *Volkswirthschaftliche Monatsschrift*, the *Arbeitgeber*, and especially the *Bremer*

[17] *Verhandlungen des Vierten Congresses deutscher Volkswirthe 1861,* pp. 11, 20-31, 29; *Zweite Versammlung des Congresses deutscher Volkswirthe 1859,* p. 3; V. Böhmert, *Rückblicke eines Siebzigers,* p. 21; *Bericht über die Verhandlungen des achten Kongresses deutscher Volkswirthe zu Nürnberg am 28., 29., 30. und 31. August 1865* (Berlin, 1865), p. 4; Eugen Franz, *Der Entscheidungskampf um die wirtschaftspolitische Führung Deutschlands (1856–1867)* (Munich, 1933), p. 75; Eugen Franz, "Die Entstehungsgeschichte des preussisch-französischen Handelsvertrags vom 29. März 1862," *Vierteljahrschrift für Sozial- und Wirtschaftsgeschichte,* XXV (1932), 12, n. 2; *Dritte Versammlung des Congresses deutscher Volkswirthe zu Köln vom 10. bis 14. September 1860: Stenographischer Bericht* (Frankfurt am Main, 1860-61), p. 3; "Bericht über die auf Veranlassung der ständigen Deputation des volkswirthschaftlichen Congresses am 4. August 1866 abgehaltene Versammlung zu Braunschweig," *Vierteljahrschrift für Volkswirthschaft und Kulturgeschichte,* IV (1866), no. 2, p. 181.

Handelsblatt. In addition, the anonymous generosity of some of the members provided a fund of 2,400 marks to be awarded for the best works of popularization in the field of economics. Schulze-Delitzsch's *Kapitel zu einem deutschen Arbeiterkatechismus* won first prize.

Yet basically the Congress of German Economists proposed to attain its ends not by appealing to the masses, but by converting men of substance. Two months before its first meeting in 1858 Karl Brater had written, "It would be very pleasing to me if I could contribute to it that this convention was attended by people from Bavaria, and indeed by such men who, in view of their civic position, have an opportunity to disseminate the impressions and experiences gained there within the broader circle of the direct participants. . . . The impulse emanating from the convention could have a very beneficial effect on our country if it is received and transmitted by the right men. I consider these right men to be preferably the intelligent and influential members of our 'chambers of industry and commerce.' " A year later Otto Michaelis announced that "I can recognize as the economic consciousness of the people only the conviction of that part of the educated classes which takes the trouble to consider and study economic questions."

With time the congress became almost as deeply involved in politics as in economics. Many of the participants in the session of 1859 in Frankfurt am Main remained in the federal capital to attend the founding convention of the Nationalverein. Thereafter the connection between the two organizations remained close. The Northwest German Economic Society provided a convenient meeting place for the liberal politicians of the North Sea coast. The Economic Society for East and West Prussia not only debated the policies of the legislative parties; in 1862 it decided to take an active part in the election campaign. Indeed, the program of the Progressive Party originated in a statement of objectives drafted at a conference of the society's executive committee. Liberals from all areas of public life met in the Congress of German Economists, deliberated, argued, exchanged ideas, and concerted plans. According to the Schleswig patriot Karl Philipp Francke, "Schulze-Delitzsch even hopes to see a German parliament born out of the economic congress." Such an expectation was unrealistic. But Böhmert's summation many years later that "the economic movement had not insignificantly sharpened the sense for practical politics" was too diffident. The economic movement had played a major role in preparing educated public opinion in Germany for the new order which was born on the battlefields of Sadowa and Sedan.[18]

The program of the Congress of German Economists however, could not meet the everyday needs of the business community. It was both too theoretical and too radical for that. The reformist politicians and militant publicists who were declared enemies of the status quo found in it a useful instrument for the propagation of liberal ideas. But merchants, industrialists, and bankers required a less controversial organization through which to influence public policy. While they generally accepted the laissez-faire doctrines of the congress, they preferred to advance their practical demands through the chambers of commerce, which had semiofficial status. Even during the conservative 1850's the latter had discreetly kept the government authorities informed of middle-

[18] *Dritte Versammlung des Congresses deutscher Volkswirthe 1860*, pp. 3, 6; *Verhandlungen des Vierten Congresses deutscher Volkswirthe 1861*, pp. 12, 18; *Die Verhandlungen des Fünften Congresses deutscher Volkswirthe zu Weimar am 8., 9., 10. und 11. September 1862* (Weimar, 1862), p. 225; W. A. Lette, *Der volkswirthschaftliche Kongress und der Zollverein* (Berlin, 1862), p. 5; H. Waentig, "Die gewerbepolitischen Anschauungen," p. 31; H. Schulze-Delitzsch, *Schriften und Reden*, v, 186; V. Böhmert, "Entstehung des volkswirtschaftlichen Kongresses," pp. 34, 210; *Zweite Versammlung des Congresses deutscher Volkswirthe 1859*, p. 11; H. Oncken, *Bennigsen*, I, 343-344; V. Böhmert, *Rückblicke eines Siebzigers*, p. 32; E. N. Anderson, *Social and Political Conflict*, pp. 306-307; R. Adam, "Der Liberalismus in der Provinz Preussen," pp. 164-165, 168-171; *Duncker: Politischer Briefwechsel*, ed. J. Schultze, p. 159.

class dissatisfaction with particularism in economics. After the revival of the national movement they had become more assertive and better organized. In the spring of 1858 a meeting of the executive committees of eleven Prussian chambers of commerce was held in Berlin to discuss uniform business procedures. It was decided to invite all the commercial societies of the kingdom to future conferences dealing with common problems of trade and manufacture. This was the background of the Prussian Commercial Association which came into existence two years later at a convention attended by delegates from forty-three chambers of commerce. The sessions, over which the well-known statesman and banker David Hansemann presided, considered mostly technical questions of coinage, transit duties, railroad rates, river navigation, fire insurance, protection of trade marks, and taxation of joint-stock companies. But the members also touched on broader issues of economic policy, voting unanimously in favor of "a revision of industrial legislation" and "the removal of the legal restrictions on interest rates."

The step from a state to a national representation of mercantile and manufacturing interests was obvious. It came, however, not in Prussia but in Baden. The chambers of commerce of the grand duchy had begun convening annually in 1834, until the Revolution of 1848 interrupted the meetings for more than a decade. It was at the conference of 1860, which resumed the yearly sessions, that Theodor Frey, chairman of the trade organization in the small town of Eberbach, moved: "Let the assembly of representatives of the Baden Commercial Association seize the initiative and issue a summons to a general consultation of German merchants and industrialists." In supporting his proposal, he pointed to the economic disadvantages arising out of national fragmentation:

It is only too true that in the political sphere as well as in commercial and social relations the German fatherland is still far from no longer suffering under the burden of disunion and division. For just as the lack of unity weakens political power, so it must to the same extent also have a paralyzing effect on commerce, industry, business, and social life. This fact confronts us most palpably where we have to compete in world trade and world commerce against other states of Europe, which are complete single states under uniform laws and conditions and under the same protection.

The association approved the motion by unanimous vote, and the Heidelberg chamber of commerce was instructed to convoke an assembly representing the business interests of all of Germany.

A year later, on May 13, 1861, the first convention of the German Commercial Association opened in the aula of the University of Heidelberg. The 195 delegates, representing 85 business organizations including 6 in Austria, marched in solemn procession behind a black, red, and gold flag to the great hall. The purpose of the assembly, as defined in the first article of the bylaws, seemed uncontroversial: "The General German Commercial Association declares itself to be and forms an organ of the entire German commercial and manufacturing class in order to express the collective view of the latter regarding generally important questions of trade in regularly recurring meetings of its representatives." Yet it was clear to many observers that an economic organization was being founded which would of necessity strengthen the forces of national unification. A report of the Breslau chamber of commerce asserted that "this collective organ of the German commercial and industrial interests . . . inevitably contributes its modest share to the slowly but confidently developing process of federal unification in Germany." And in the pages of the *Sächsische Industrie-Zeitung* an enraptured versifier sang of the high patriotic mission before the new association of businessmen:

Was einst verkündet Sänger und Propheten,
Reift jetzt zur That—ein einig Reich ersteht;
Drum gilt es, jeden Eigennutz ertödten,
Der wie ein Reif durch junge Blüthen geht.
Engherzigkeit, der alten Zwietracht Schande
Sei abgethan mit Zopf und Todtem Wust:
Gemeinsinn nur, zum theuern Vaterlande
Die Liebe schwelle fortan jede Brust!

In diesem Geiste kämpft, ihr Wackern alle,
Versammelt an des Neckar grünen Strand!
Helft bauen Deutscher Einheit Ruhmeshalle!
Fest um die Stämme schlingt das Bruderband!
Zeigt, Männer, unsers Handels tiefe Wunden,
Legt alle Schäden der Zerklüftung bloss!
So streut ihr Samen für die künft'gen Stunden—
Was ihr begonnen, wächst zum Riesen gross.

Ist erst der Sieg, den ihr erstrebt, errungen,
Bedeutsam, wie kein Sieg in blut'ger Schlacht;
Hat Deutschland, selbstbewusst und kraftdurchdrungen,
Den ersten Schritt zur Einigung vollbracht;
Dann wird es dankbar euer Wirken segnen;
Indem es Lorbeer um die Stirn euch flicht,—
Wo Einheit sich und Bürgersinn begegnen,
Fehlt auch das Volkswohl, fehlt die Freiheit nicht![19]

The German Commercial Association held two more
conventions prior to the Seven Weeks' War, in Munich
in 1862 and in Frankfurt am Main in 1865. There were
close to 400 participants from 189 cities at the former,

---

[19] Eduard Kauffer, "Zur Begrüssung des Deutschen Handelstages zu
Heidelberg am 13. Mai 1861," *Sächsische Industrie-Zeitung*, May 10,
1861, p. 219. Cf. *Der Deutsche Handelstag, 1861-1911*, ed. Deutscher
Handelstag (2 vols., Berlin, 1911-13), I, 1-3, 9, 14; *Verhandlungen des
Handelstages in Berlin, vom 20. Februar bis 2. März 1860* (Berlin,
1860), pp. 27, 80, 82; Fr. Schupp and K. A. Wettstein, *Die Entstehungsgeschichte des ersten Allgemeinen Deutschen Handelstages 1861: Zum
50jährigen Jubiläum des Handelstages* (Karlsruhe, 1911), p. 6; *Preussisches Handelsarchiv* (1862), III (Jahresberichte der Handelskammern
und kaufmännischen Korporationen des preussischen Staats für 1861),
298.

and approximately 225 participants from some 120 cities at the latter. The members included prominent businessmen like the financiers David Hansemann and Hermann von Beckerath, the merchants Hermann Heinrich Meier and Edgar Daniel Ross, and the industrialists Friedrich Hammacher and Johann Classen-Kappelmann. There were state legislators with close ties to trade and manufacture, among them Heinrich Behrend from Prussia, Leo Hänle from Bavaria, Eduard Moll from Baden, Bernhard Eisenstuck from Saxony, and Karl Braun from Nassau. A few well-known economists attended, A.E.F. Schäffle and Adolf Soetbeer, for example. And the tireless laissez-faire publicists flocked wherever there was a chance to preach economic liberalism: Otto Michaelis, Julius Faucher, Max Wirth, and of course Victor Böhmert. The association dealt in the main with questions of commercial and industrial policy, yet it could not help touching on those political issues which affected material interests. It found itself inevitably drawn into the movement for national unification.

The resolutions adopted by the German Commercial Association illustrate the inextricable connection between economic and political reform. Usually they concerned technical measures to facilitate the conduct of business: "the introduction of a comprehensive, uniform system of weights and measures in Germany is becoming an imperative demand"; "the final removal of the exceptional conditions and obstacles which still stand in the way of a complete unity of coinage in Germany is not to be postponed any longer"; or "the draft of a general German commercial code . . . should be introduced immediately . . . in all the German federal states." The achievement of even these moderate demands, however, presupposed a higher degree of national integration, while some of the far-reaching proposals were altogether unrealizable within the framework of the German Confederation. By advocating the establishment of a supreme court to administer a uniform commercial law, by requesting government regulation of railroad rates, and by urging the creation of a national consular representation overseas, the members were in effect espousing change in the system of government. For how else could their program succeed? Indeed, the plan they advanced for the reorganization of the Zollverein revealed their own awareness of the interdependence of business and civic reform: "At the renewal of the Zollverein treaties consideration should be given to the transfer of the law-making power of the Zollverein jointly to the representation of the united governments on one side and to that of the population of the states of the union on the other, so that the concurring resolutions of these two bodies adopted by majority vote shall be introduced as final law in the entire customs area." The political implications of the campaign to promote economic growth led them to support both nationalism and liberalism.[20]

The German Commercial Association remained in theory an organization of businessmen meeting from time to time to discuss practical problems of economics. In fact it became one of the middle-class pressure groups working for the unification of Germany. It sought to rally the merchants and industrialists in the chambers of commerce behind a program of national reform. It sent to the governments of Central Europe resolutions calling for uniform weights and measures, a single coinage system, a common commercial code, and the reorganization of the Zollverein. The executive committee repeatedly conferred with Bismarck, while the president was received by King William himself. In order to promote the conclusion of a trade treaty with Russia, the organization even proposed "to send deputies to St. Petersburg who would act in the matter independently of the efforts of the royal [Prussian] government and

20 *Verhandlungen des ersten deutschen Handelstags zu Heidelberg, vom 13. bis 18. Mai 1861* (Berlin, 1861), pp. 25, 31, 109-110; *Verhandlungen des Dritten Handelstages 1865*, pp. 124, 127.

would have to prepare the terrain by awakening and encouraging public opinion."

The purpose of its lithographed newsletter *Deutscher Handelstag* was not merely to publish communications and reports to the members, but "to give these reports or independent articles such a form, and to add to them, if the opportunity presents itself, such information affecting our interests that also the press, to which the newsletter . . . is to be made available, will gladly make use of them." The first issue of the newsletter contained an appeal to the members for help in gaining the support of newspapers:

> While special importance has already been assigned . . . to the task of winning as active a participation by the press in behalf of our goals as possible, we also want in addition to enlist your kind help in this matter. You will oblige us especially by giving us as soon as possible the names of those newspapers in your district which you consider suitable and disposed to accept now and then some articles or communications from this newsletter. A copy is then to be sent from here regularly to these newspapers. This, however, will in no way make it superfluous that you yourselves should continue to maintain the connection with the newspapers which may be at your disposal, and that you should seek to exercise your influence for the acceptance of reports or reviews which seem especially important to you.

The organization hoped to sway the well-to-do decisive classes of society. As for its effectiveness, the Cologne chamber of commerce felt that "it is leading German unity out of the realm of ideals to a solid, practical basis." This was an exaggeration. But the German Commercial Association was among the many civic groups preparing the way for the realization of national unity in Central Europe.[21]

There were also various professional and academic so-

---

[21] *Verhandlungen des zweiten deutschen Handelstages zu München, vom 14. bis 18. October 1862* (Berlin, 1862) , pp. 3-4; *Deutscher Handels-*

cieties which engaged in politics under the guise of scholarly deliberation. The Association of German Jurists, for example, concluded that the establishment of a common legal system in the German Confederation was an impossibility without a common governmental authority. It supported efforts to achieve a uniform code of law by negotiation among the states: "Since the majority of the German governments declares itself willing to accept the introduction of common legislation regarding civil and credit law, the Association of Jurists expresses its conviction that the successful promotion of this aim is sure to earn the general thanks of the fatherland." But it went on to argue that attainment of the objective required "a common institution recognized by the governments and the legislatures of the individual states, even if its authority is limited solely to this national task. . . . The German Association of Jurists also expresses the same wish concerning common penal legislation." Johann Caspar Bluntschli, who was a president of the organization, asserted amid the applause of the members that "if we want common legislation, and we do want it, then we will also have to create a common organ in which both of those powers, peoples and governments, will be together and will work together. Without it we will not get anywhere." And during the convention in Vienna, he boldly declared, in reply to a toast by Schmerling: "The existing federal system of law is most decidedly in conflict with the justified expectations of the nation, and it needs thorough improvement in the direction of a unified representation of the nation and in the direction of a unified development of power!" What civic organization could have been more clearly committed to political ends?[22]

---

tag (1865) , no. 1, pp. 2-3, no. 8, p. 3; *Der Deutsche Handelstag,* ed. Deutscher Handelstag, I, 23, 27, 130-131, II, 341-342; *Aktenstücke zur Wirthschaftspolitik,* ed. H. v. Poschinger, I, 53; *Preussisches Handelsarchiv* (1861) , III (Jahresberichte der Handelskammern und kaufmännischen Korporationen des preussischen Staats für 1860) , 382.

22 *Europäischer Geschichtskalender,* ed. H. Schulthess (1861) , pp.

Even sport clubs served as instruments of the movement for unity and freedom. The Nationalverein supported societies of gymnasts and sharpshooters, hoping to gain for liberalism a semi-military corps of loyal followers. Fedor Streit helped plan the first national gymnastic meet, convinced that "the organization of the festivities must be of such a sort that they do not simply become specifically athletic, but assume a general patriotic significance." According to Schulze-Delitzsch, "you, the German Society of Sharpshooters and the German Society of Gymnasts, you are the preparliament which leads us to the real German parliament." Prominent members of the Progressive Party like Max von Forckenbeck and Leopold von Hoverbeck endorsed appeals for funds to support athletic organizations. Moritz Busch, still under the spell of parliamentarian ideals, hailed a meeting of gymnasts as "the festival of the emerging unity of the Germans." Who could resist such blandishments? The members of the sport clubs contributed to patriotic causes. They proclaimed their resolve to "rise with a single cry: Long live Germania!" They presented *tableaux vivants* of "Andreas Hofer," "The Death of Körner," "The Exhorting Germania," "Emperor Barbarossa in the Kyffhäuser Being Summoned by Germany," and "Germania in Chains." Long afterward one of them recalled wistfully that "in those days we hoped to gain German unity by gymnastics and singing."[23]

Yet participation in these organizations was not large, considering the high mission they hoped to accomplish. During the years between the Italian War of 1859 and the Danish War of 1864 the number of gymnastic so-

---

74-75; J. C. Bluntschli, *Denkwürdiges aus meinem Leben*, II, 296-297; *Verhandlungen des Congresses deutscher Abgeordneter in Weimar am 28. und 29. September 1862* (Weimar, 1862), p. 9.

[23] Wilhelm Mommsen, "Zur Beurteilung der deutschen Einheitsbewegung," *Historische Zeitschrift*, CXXXVIII (1928), 535. Cf. E. N. Anderson, *Social and Political Conflict*, pp. 312, 314, 338-339; E. Zechlin, *Bismarck*, pp. 265-266; R. Le Mang, *Der Nationalverein*, p. 68; L. Parisius, *Hoverbeck*, II/I, 55; M. Busch, *Tagebuchblätter*, III, 375; K. Bechstein, "Die öffentliche Meinung in Thüringen" (Part 1), pp. 171-172.

cieties in the German Confederation increased from barely 100 to almost 2,000. On December 6, 1863, as hostilities over Schleswig-Holstein were becoming imminent, Gustav Freytag reported that "the number of gymnasts who want to enlist [in volunteer units] is estimated by their leaders at 30,000." A force of such size could not expect to play a major role either politically or militarily. The membership of the sharpshooting societies was even smaller. At the time of the national meet in Frankfurt am Main in 1862 it totaled only about 11,000. Its social composition, moreover, was largely bourgeois. Duke Ernest II of Saxe-Coburg-Gotha, who had been honorary president of the German Society of Sharpshooters, explained that "in general a good and well-to-do part of the populations was represented in the sharpshooting societies, . . . people who mostly occupied a respected position in their circle and not infrequently had influence over community and state representative assemblies." Among the gymnasts, who admitted industrial and rural workers to their clubs, there was a lower-class radical faction with a substantial following in the south and southwest, in the Palatinate, Thuringia, and Oldenburg, and in the region around Frankfurt am Main. But by and large control remained in the hands of men of means who were more interested in political unification than social reform. They saw to it that the athletic associations remained faithful allies of middle-class liberalism and nationalism.[24]

On August 9, 1861, Baron Arthur Mohrenheim, a Russian diplomat stationed in Berlin, noted dryly that "tomorrow the national festival in honor of the gymnasts from all of Germany begins here. Six thousand of them have arrived, it is said! The black, red, and yellow banners already bedeck the main streets

[24] G. Mayer, *Schweitzer*, p. 51; *Deutscher Liberalismus*, ed. J. Heyderhoff and P. Wentzcke, I, 198; Ernest II, *Aus meinem Leben und aus meiner Zeit*, 4th edn. (3 vols., Berlin, 1888-89), III, 226, 236; R. Weber, *Kleinbürgerliche Demokraten*, pp. 38-39, 41-42.

today. We have muscular unity, after so many other forms! Strange nation, which makes gymnastic ideology and preaches doctrine in a bathing suit." In a country where the instrumentalities of civic action were imperfectly developed, ideology was forced to assume non-ideological forms. Germany during the period of national unification was only beginning to emerge from an era of individualistic politics based on coteries and personalities. Party structure had not yet become systematized, so that interest in public affairs was often channeled into organizations which were ostensibly nonpartisan or even nonpolitical. These organizations had interlocking directorates and overlapping memberships. The same liberals who supported the Progressive Party joined the Nationalverein, attended the sessions of the Congress of German Economists, and addressed the meetings of gymnasts and sharpshooters. The same conservatives who upheld the royal prerogative led the Prussian People's Association, formed the Patriotic Alliance, and contributed to the Christian Conservative Election Society. The same Austrophiles who defended the historic mission of the Habsburgs organized the Reformverein, memorialized the politicians of the secondary states, and sought to sway the German Commercial Association. The total number of members in the various political and quasi-political associations was small, no more than a few hundred thousand. But they exercised a powerful influence over public affairs on the basis of property, status, and education. They constituted the decisive classes of society. The others paid taxes, bore arms, worked, obeyed, fought, and died. The age of the masses had not yet arrived.[25]

[25] *Die auswärtige Politik Preussens*, II/II, 434, n. 5.

NINE

Public Opinion

IT IS hard to tell what most men thought about the great issues of unity and freedom during the period of national unification. To subsume the attitudes of the broad masses under those of the well-to-do strata of society is common though questionable. The polemical literature of the mid-century does help demarcate opposing currents of political opinion. But whose political opinion? Books and pamphlets are written by people who have a high level of education. Newspapers and journals are read by a public interested in civic problems. Does the cultured minority, however, reflect the views of the great body of the poor, ignorant, and apathetic? There is no direct way of making sure. The illiterate and semiliterate published no creeds, kept no diaries, composed no memoirs, and left no letters. Their feelings can only be surmised from what contemporary observers outside their own class said about them. This inability to express their views contributed to their ineffectualness in public affairs. Since they did not speak, they were not heard. The great majority of the inhabitants of the German Confederation appears to have had few civic convictions, and those it did have were too amorphous to influence government policy. Heinrich von Sybel's description of conditions in Schleswig-Holstein could have been applied to any of the other states: "A large mass of the people was politically inactive. On the order of the authorities it too would furnish recruits and pay taxes without opposition. But its real concern, nevertheless, was solely its family, its field, its flocks. When a political demonstration was to be organized or a patriotic resolution adopted, then it appeared at the urging of its trusted leaders. . . . But these classes of the population were politically quite inert, and ultimately they followed the instigations of the intellectually animated and politically energetic minority which acted over their heads." Even this account exaggerated the interest of the lower classes in civic issues. Workers and peasants did not as a rule participate in demonstrations or vote for resolutions, despite the exhortations of party leaders. They remained indifferent to problems lying beyond the narrow limits of a harsh everyday existence.[1]

Vocal public opinion was thus determined by groups in the community which understood questions of government policy and adopted a coherent attitude toward them. These groups were drawn largely from the well-to-do, but they also included the more successful and better educated among the lower classes. Their members read newspapers, attended civic meetings, signed petitions, and cast ballots. Although greatly outnumbered by the politically indifferent masses, they represented the economically dominant elements in society: landowners, businessmen, administrators, publicists, jurists, professional men, white-collar workers, master artisans, skilled technicians, and independent farmers. There was a wide spectrum of interest in civic questions corresponding to the wide range in the distribution of property and education in Central Europe. It began with the party stalwart whose life revolved around the conflict of ideologies, and ended with the poverty-stricken landless peasant or mill hand to whom the problems of parliamentary government and national unification were incomprehensible. In between were those who displayed active interest in politics without total commitment, those who were sympathizers in thought more than in deed, those who were half drawn and half pushed into support of a legislative program, and those who had

---

[1] Heinrich von Sybel, *Die Begründung des Deutschen Reiches durch Wilhelm I.* (7 vols., Munich and Leipzig, 1890-94), IV, 84-85.

only vague ideas regarding public affairs. Somewhere in this spectrum a line could be drawn separating vocal from tacit public opinion. On one side stood men who expressed their views forcibly enough to gain the attention of the authorities. On the other were the impoverished, uneducated, incoherent, and mute. This distinction between the articulate and the inarticulate strata of society is important for an understanding of the system of politics in the German Confederation.

The proportion of the population whose attitudes and beliefs made up vocal public opinion was small. It could not have exceeded the 20 per cent of adult males who read newspapers and periodicals. Since comprehension of political principles presupposes familiarity with civic issues, the readership of the press must have included all those who could express a logically consistent view regarding affairs of state. It delimited their number, however, without fixing it. Not every reader of the *Volks-Zeitung* or of the *Neue Preussische Zeitung* publicized his convictions by attending a rally, signing a petition, or casting a vote. The acquisition of information about the problems of government did not always lead to the affirmation of a controversial judgment concerning them. There was a gap between political idea and political deed which many men hesitated to bridge. They may have been too busy, indolent, insecure, or timid. Yet without an open avowal of their opinions they could exercise an influence over government policy no greater than that of the uninformed masses. Vocal public opinion, in other words, was determined by those who were ready to manifest their feelings in some act of civic self-assertion. The state may not have followed the course dictated by expressions of popular belief, but it considered and respected them. It was the ability to attract the notice of the authorities which differentiated between the politically effectual and ineffectual classes of society.

The mass meeting was one act of civic self-assertion reflecting vocal public opinion. Here loyal party men

361

gathered to hear speeches and adopt resolutions proclaiming their political convictions. As the conflict of ideologies became more intense, partisan rallies began to multiply. In Prussia many conservative assemblies, moreover, sent delegations to assure the monarch of their unwavering support. In October 1862 Bismarck reported to the crown prince that "these manifestations of faithful constancy have done the king's heart good and have had a favorable effect on his Majesty's state of health, which had been weakened by cares." Late the following summer Heinrich von Sybel claimed that in the course of the preceding twelve months between 600 and 800 political meetings had been held in the Rhine Province alone. In response to the appeal of a committee representing nationalist members of the state legislatures, 269 patriotic gatherings took place during Easter 1864 in all parts of the German Confederation except Austria and a few of the minor principalities. They approved a statement which "formulated once again the fundamental rights of the duchies [of Schleswig and Holstein], and declared null and void any violation of those rights through an illegal decision." A nation only two generations removed from the age of enlightened despotism was speaking out on the issues of liberty and union.

Participation in mass meetings, however, was limited and vacillating. Only about 1,200 people attended the convention of conservatives in Berlin which established the Prussian People's Association. The numerous political rallies in the Rhineland which followed the appointment of the Bismarck ministry diminished considerably in the course of the succeeding year. By September 1863 Sybel conceded in a letter to Hermann Baumgarten that public interest in the constitutional conflict was flagging: "You will not be surprised that these things [petitions and meetings] are completely exhausted here." The 269 patriotic gatherings in behalf of Schleswig-Holstein during Easter 1864 attracted some 250,000 participants. Yet August Metz, the Hessian propagandist for the Nationalverein who helped organize this demonstration, was not satisfied: "Can you say, when you read from the report of the committee that 250,000 people took part in the meetings for Schleswig-Holstein, and when you divide these 250,000 people into 40 million Germans, can you say that that has been such an enormous display of activity?" All in all, the number of those attending political meetings in the early 1860's could hardly have exceeded 2,000,000, and it may well have been no more than 1,000,000.[2]

Signatures on the petitions submitted to crown and parliament in Prussia during their struggle support this approximation. The liberals, claiming to represent the will of the people, frequently boasted of the public approval they enjoyed. On January 14, 1863, at the opening of a new session of the legislature, the presiding officer of the lower house, Wilhelm Grabow, asserted that "in this conflict, which has become ever more acute, the country has taken a stand at the side of its elected representatives to the complete satisfaction of the latter. That is undeniably demonstrated by . . . the addresses of agreement and thanks which have already reached them and the lower house, and which are still arriving daily, addresses from abroad, from various regions of Germany, and from the election districts of Prussia. Until now there have been 194 of them bearing 221,951 signatures, partly of members of electoral colleges, partly of independent voters acting together with them." By the time the session ended late in May, the number of addresses favorable to the parliamentary cause had risen to 318 with 359,222 signatures, while only 9 addresses with 4,031 signatures voiced disapprobation.

[2] *Kaiser Friedrich III.: Tagebücher von 1848–1866*, ed. Heinrich Otto Meisner (Leipzig, 1929), p. 506; *Deutscher Liberalismus*, ed. J. Heyderhoff and P. Wentzcke, I, 171; *Verhandlungen der Mitglieder deutscher Landesvertretungen in Frankfurt a. M., Sonntag den 1. October 1865* (Frankfurt am Main, 1865), pp. 20, 66; H. Müller, *Der Preussische Volks-Verein*, p. 26.

But the cabinet refused to be impressed. Addressing the legislature, Bismarck insisted that in fact public opinion supported the crown: "The second fact on the basis of which you assert that the people are on your side is the 300,000 and I don't know how many signatures which the addresses of agreement presented to the lower house have had. I do not even want to attach importance to the fact that addresses with an opposite view have received a greater number of signatures. It doesn't matter. We do not live under a regime of general suffrage, but under the rule of the king and of the laws." The prime minister's claim of popular approval was more than bravado. He was speaking with the knowledge that a mass petition endorsing the reorganization of the army and urging the maintenance of royal authority had been signed by about half a million people. At the height of the constitutional conflict, then, the signatures on both liberal and conservative political addresses totaled in the neighborhood of 900,000. This estimate is in keeping with information concerning attendance at political meetings, although in both sets of figures there is the danger of distortion through duplication. A faithful party follower might attend several rallies and sign numerous petitions in the course of a year, thereby exaggerating the degree of interest in public affairs.[3]

Statistics regarding participation in elections the ultimate act of civic self-assertion short of revolution, support the calculation that vocal public opinion was determined by between 1,000,000 and 2,000,000 people. In Prussia, where the franchise was the most generous and the ideological conflict the most bitter, the number of voters appearing at the polls ranged from about 500,000 to 1,000,000. There were 1,037,924 in 1849, before the excitement generated by the revolution subsided. The figures for 1852 remain unpublished, but in 1855, with

[3] Prussia, *Verhandlungen des Landtages: Haus der Abgeordneten* (1863), I, 5, II, 1318-1319; O. v. Bismarck, *Werke*, x, 161; F. Löwenthal, *Der preussische Verfassungsstreit*, p. 136.

the reaction firmly in the saddle, only 466,953 ballots were cast. The change in government policy initiated by the regency in 1858 aroused new interest in public affairs, attracting 703,013 persons to the polls. As the struggle between crown and parliament intensified, exercise of the suffrage rose to 916,260 in 1861, 1,182,501 in 1862, and 1,097,453 in 1863. Finally, in 1866, while the Prussian armies were resolving the domestic as well as the foreign crisis on the field of battle, 1,144,867 citizens elected a new legislature.[4]

Within the minority involved in the struggle for a parliamentary form of government, the division of views regarding the source of political authority coincided by and large with social position and economic interest. After the Prussian election of 1862 a newspaper dispatch from Pomerania reported that in the electoral college in Anklam those voting conservative included " (1) all noble landowners, (2) all clergymen, (3) all army men, (4) all country schoolmasters, (5) a number of inspectors and royal and noble foresters, some so-called little people from the country, and very few peasants. For the candidates of the liberal party voted: (1) all judges and lawyers, (2) all merchants and factory owners, (3) all Jews, (4) almost all bourgeois landowners and peasant proprietors, (5) almost all handicraftsmen, innkeepers, city officials, and generally the electors from the cities with hardly any exceptions worth mentioning." The pattern of voting differed from district to district, for the political affiliations of the artisans and peasants varied with local conditions. It is clear, however, that the foundation on which liberalism rested was bourgeois wealth and intelligence. The conservative bureaucrat Laurenz Hannibal Fischer, who in 1848 had been driven from his post in Oldenburg, sneered at "ambitious men

4 R. Boeckh, "Statistik der Urwahlen 1861," p. 112; E. Engel, Ergebnisse der Urwahlen 1862 und 1863," p. 69; "Die Hauptresultate der Urwahlen für das preussische Abgeordnetenhaus vom 25. September 1866," *Zeitschrift des königlich preussischen Statistischen Bureaus*, VII (1867), 238-239.

of the well-to-do middle class who, conscious of their riches, are certainly not in agreement with the egalitarian principle of the [communists and democrats]. Still, they resent it very much that the princes and the civil service do not place them in a position within the gradations of formal courtesy to which the level of their riches would entitle them." He classified them as adherents of the party of "aristocratic republicans." In his bitterness against the bourgeoisie he exaggerated its vanity and its radicalism. Yet there can be no doubt that the opposition to the established order derived its strength largely from men whose social authority was not commensurate with their economic status.

Conservatism, on the other hand, found support above all in the landed aristocracy. It appealed to the interests of a hierarchical agrarian order threatened by the rise of industrialism. There was nothing veiled about its defense of an authoritarian political system based on rural forms of proprietorship. Friedrich Julius Stahl openly affirmed the social values of a corporative organization of the community:

> The party of legitimacy wants . . . estates of the realm. Whether the estates are to be in the old form, nobility, burghers, peasants, whether there is to be a hereditary or a landed aristocracy, on these points there are within the party itself various opinions. But . . . at all events, there are to be occupational classes with special rights and a special participation in the representative body of the country. At all events, landed property is to be the basis of the most important political rights. At all events, there is to be a differentiation between city and country in all institutions. . . . True aristocracy . . . is not restricted to counts and barons. It runs through all human society: the farmer before the cottager, the master before the journeyman, the freeman of the city before the resident, the clergyman before the parishioner. The foundation and essence of such a true aristocracy is that people are to be considered not only as individuals, so that they are

all equal, but as representatives of a cause, a property, an occupation, and that is the extent to which they have rights and powers.

Yet Stahl's "eternal law" of aristocracy, despite his insistence that it transcended class boundaries, safeguarded counts and barons more than the farmer, the master, the freeman, or the clergyman. A theory of state proclaiming that landed property was the basis of the most important political rights could offer no more than paternalistic solicitude to the urban worker and the propertyless peasant. Its principal concern was the protection of the privileged position of a landowning aristocracy jeopardized by the emergence of capitalistic forms of wealth. The anonymous conservative publicist who asserted the primacy of agriculture over manufacture was only reflecting the fundamental economic bias of legitimism: "Industry has in the course of the years become a many-headed monster. There is a racing and chasing after profit, after the treasures of the earth, so that the quiet observer almost loses his senses contemplating it. But only through the accumulated capital of the original inhabitants of the land, the farmers, does an indigenous industry become possible. People should never forget that." This traditionalist idealization of agriculture, however, did not imply the political and social emancipation of the peasant masses. The Jeffersonian vision of civic virtue based on a class of free and prosperous farmers was alien to the nobility of Central Europe. What the latter sought was a hierarchical, corporative order of society in which the rhetoric of patriotism and tradition masked the reality of aristocratic domination.[5]

The constitutional conflict in Prussia was essentially a test of strength between the interests of the industrial

[5] *Königsberger Hartungsche Zeitung,* May 16, 1862; Laurenz Hannibal Fischer, *Der teutsche Adel in der Vorzeit, Gegenwart und Zukunft vom Standpunkte des Bürgerthums betrachtet* (2 vols., Frankfurt am Main, 1852), I, 237; F. J. Stahl, *Die gegenwärtigen Parteien,* pp. 310-311; "Zur Arbeiterfrage" (Part 1), p. 399.

bourgeoisie and the landed aristocracy. Yet each side found important allies among other classes which were drawn into the struggle by ideology, tradition, self-seeking, or constraint. Academics, jurists, and members of the learned professions were generally in sympathy with the liberal cause. Army officers, Protestant clergymen, and the upper ranks of the bureaucracy tended to support conservatism. The steadfastness of political conviction among the voters, however, varied with their economic status and educational level. The greater the wealth and schooling of a social group, the more constant and predictable its party affiliation. The conservative *Berliner Revue* identified as enemies of the established order "those who have acquired a higher academic education," including judicial and administrative officials, physicians, scholars, lawyers, engineers, and men of letters, as well as merchants and manufacturers. The liberal *Königsberger Hartungsche Zeitung* suggested that the opponents of parliamentary government were primarily aristocratic landowners, ecclesiastics, military men, country schoolteachers, civil servants, and rural administrators. But the lower classes could not be categorized with the same degree of precision. They saw little difference between the doctrines of constitutionalism and legitimism, since neither represented their fundamental interests. To them the conflict between king and legislature was irrelevant. They voted not on the basis of principle, but out of expediency, caprice, or fear. They were combatants in a war of ideologies they neither espoused nor understood.[6]

The artisans, for example, trimmed and vacillated in their political allegiance. Most of them voted for the candidates of the right, especially after the formation of the Prussian People's Association on a platform demanding "no abandonment of the handicrafts . . . to the false teachings and usurious tricks of our times." In the fall

[6] "Das Haus der Abgeordneten," p. 434; *Königsberger Hartungsche Zeitung,* May 16, 1862.

of 1861, while the question of army reform was intensi-
fying party antagonisms, master shoemaker Panse maintained that an alliance with legitimism would serve
the needs of the handicraft trades. "Our endeavours are
. . . conservative, and I hope that at the next election
we will stand firmly by the landowners, and the landowners, the conservatives in general, will stand by us."
It was more than a pious civility. Guildsmen flocked to
the Prussian People's Association; they affirmed a community of interest between urban and rural advocates
of the corporative principle; they inveighed against the
liberal press and against "Jews and the partners of
Jews"; they campaigned for legitimist candidates; they
even formed a central election committee in Berlin
which supported the program and shared the office of
the election committee of the Conservative Party. Hermann Wagener, defending the collaboration of aristocrats with artisans, explained before the legislature that
"we have very real interests in common with the class
of handicraftsmen. That is the sort of entirely reliable,
durable political alliance which will not dissipate. We
have the same interest as the class of handicraftsmen,
and therefore we maintain the interest of the class of
handicraftsmen as our own." Independent tradesmen
and small shopkeepers constituted the bulk of the following which conservatism found in the cities.

Yet there were also many artisans backing the liberals.
Heinrich Leo, who had hoped to win the support of
the handicraftsmen of Halle for the Conservative Party,
discovered that his efforts were useless. "Unfortunately
we cannot influence the handicraft circles directly," he
wrote in September 1861. "For these people, who have
up to now been largely dependent on the judgment and
leadership of the liberal circles, are to a very large degree
distrustful, and are at the moment filled with fear that
they may be misused by the reaction. Our conservative
master handicraftsmen, who are in the midst of the local
handicraft associations, have themselves asked us in the

369

strongest terms never to try to influence the handicraft organizations directly, because we would otherwise spoil the entire mood, which is at present promising." Two months later he reported dejectedly that the artisans would in all probability side with the liberals in the forthcoming election. The handicraftsmen of Breslau and Minden voted for candidates championing parliament against the crown. A motion of master carpenter Piest of Stettin committing his guild to the support of legitimist nominees for the legislature won the approval of only a small minority. Of the 41 tradesmen attending a meeting in Thorn to organize a conservative artisan association, no more than 17 professed sympathy for the "Junker party." As master mason Pesche of Breslau put it, "we have in the class of handicraftsmen enough democrats whose feelings are honest and righteous, and who cherish a warm regard for the class of handicraftsmen."

There was thus no clear-cut pattern of voting among the artisans. Those who had made the transition from independent craftsman to petty businessman tended to align with liberalism, especially in the big cities. The less successful tradesmen of town and village, unable to adjust to the new industrial order, usually favored conservatism. But in neither group was civic allegiance firm and unyielding. The basic factor in the party affiliation of the handicraft workers was economic rather than ideological. Panse explained that "it is a fact that our comrades belong to all political movements. But it is also a fact that at least 9/10 stand fast on the basis of the law of February 9, [1849,] and want to maintain what was granted at that time." The legitimists, who could logically pose as defenders of corporative rights, attracted most of the artisan votes. But where the constitutionalists were willing to sacrifice principle to expediency, they too succeeded in winning a following among the skilled trades. "The day before yesterday the bulk of our handicraftsmen finally decided to go with the liberals," Leo glumly informed Wagener, "if the candidates of the latter would promise them to speak for the retention of the examinations for master artisans (to these narrow limits have the local handicrafstmen restricted their interest). These candidates naturally will not fail to create for them the illusion of promising everything which is being demanded with a few phrases which they do not properly understand and from which it will be easy to wriggle out again."

The artisan masses thought about public affairs in nonpolitical terms. The problems of constitutional government seemed less important to them than the survival of the handicraft occupations in an industrialized economy. The liberal *National-Zeitung* complained of their readiness to subordinate politics to economics:

A large part of our handicraftsmen believes that it can combine the uncombinable; it believes that it can reconcile fire and water. If you were to ask them whether they are adherents of the reaction, whether they are men of the [*Neue Preussische Zeitung*], they would consider the question most insulting, and would rebuff the importunate questioner with blunt firmness. But they would just as unreservedly take a position on the side of that very reaction as soon as the same questioner wanted to know perhaps whether they are for industrial freedom or not. Industrial freedom, they believe, rests on an entirely different basis from political freedom, and yet their own experience could teach them how closely the two of them are connected.

Most handicraftsmen remained unconcerned about the constitutional conflict, because they saw in it a political struggle whose outcome was irrelevant to the needs of the little man. Their ultimate allegiance belonged to a doomed social system which neither crown nor parliament could save.[7]

[7] *Europäischer Geschichtskalender*, ed. H. Schulthess (1861), p. 45; *Neue Preussische Zeitung*, September 25, 1861; H. Müller, *Der Preussische Volks-Verein*, pp. 24, 29-30, 33-34, 39-40, 46-47, 52; Prussia, *Verhandlungen des Landtages: Haus der Abgeordneten* (1861), II,

The civic loyalities of the peasantry were even more pliable. The masses of the countryside had no memories of a golden age of guild regulation to inspire them. They had no collective sense of resentment against the factory system to unite them. For them life had always meant submission to the will of the upper classes. In 1860 the constitutionalist Theodor von Bernhardi concluded that "the farmer, moreover, has no interest in liberal legislation. . . . The peasant wants 'that conditions should for once be different in the country.' And as long as government authority in his district remains in the hands of the same county commissioner who has disciplined and tormented him for so long, the old system is for him still untouched and in full control." Yet in 1861 the legitimist Moritz von Blanckenburg complained that the Pomeranian villagers voted under the influence of anticonservative judges and officials against the candidates of the right. The average rustic was in truth neither liberal nor conservative. Experience had taught him to bow to the wishes of those in power, especially concerning political questions, to which he was in any event indifferent. His outlook was typified by the village mayor who hoped to protect himself against all contingencies by signing one petition in favor of parliament and another in favor of the crown. There were independent farmers, to be sure, prosperous enough to resist pressure from above and educated enough to have civic convictions. Yet they were in a minority. Kurt von Saucken-Tarputschen, a stalwart of the Progressive Party, compared a substantial part of the peasantry to soft wax molded by whoever happened to have it in his grasp.

The political submissiveness of the rural population was of greater advantage to the conservatives than to the liberals. Since aristocratic landowners occupied a

1108; H. Wagener, *Die kleine aber mächtige Partei*, pp. 43-44; E. N. Anderson, *Social and Political Conflict*, p. 435; *Verhandlungen des deutschen Handwerkertags 1862*, pp. 165-166; *National-Zeitung*, August 11, 1860.

dominant position in the countryside, they could exercise considerable influence over the votes of the farms and villages. A visit to East Prussia during the constitutional conflict reassured Roon that the tradition of obedience still prevailed among the rustics. "The appearance of the headstrong minister of war in this region evokes not only curiosity," he wrote his wife, "but also to some extent the respect which is due to the government. . . . It is no trick to make this raw mass confused. But when you show it the strong hand, then it is and becomes just as docile and obedient as you could only wish." Bismarck was even more positive: "If I, for example, could send here in Prussia 100 workers from my estate to the ballot box, then they would outvote every other opinion in the village to the point of destroying it." The invasion of agriculture by bourgeois wealth helped restrain the power of the nobility east of the Elbe. Bernhardi noted the case of a conservative landowner unable to persuade the peasants of his village to subscribe to an address of loyalty to the crown because the two neighboring estates were owned by liberals who frustrated his efforts. Yet the countryside represented a reservoir of support for the established order which under vigorous leadership could be mobilized against the forces of reform in the city.[8]

The division of vocal public opinion between liberalism and conservatism, moreover, was closer than the results of elections indicated. While the representation of the opposing parties in the Prussian legislature fluctuated widely, these shifts in parliamentary strength reflected relatively small changes in the mood of the electorate. There are no figures for the membership of the various factions in the chamber chosen in 1849, but the government could count on a substantial majority

[8] *Aus dem Leben Bernhardis*, III, 275, IV, 328; *Denkwürdigkeiten aus dem Leben des Grafen von Roon*, II, 56, 375; E. N. Anderson, *Social and Political Conflict*, p. 437; L. Parisius, *Hoverbeck*, II/II, 19, n. 3; W. von Hassell, *Geschichte des Königreichs Hannover* (2 vols., Bremen and Leipzig, 1898–1901) , II/II, 247.

for its policy of creeping reaction. In 1852 the conservatives outnumbered the liberals 196 to 78, and in 1855 they succeeded in increasing their lead to 236 against 57. But legislative fortunes were completely reversed at the next election in 1858, when the liberals gained the upper hand by a margin of 210 to 57. They won a still more impressive endorsement in 1861 with 256 seats against only 15; in 1862 they achieved their greatest success, 285 to 11; and in 1863 they scored another clear-cut though less one-sided victory, 258 to 36. In 1866, finally, the diplomatic and military triumphs of Bismarckian statecraft established an uneasy balance, 172 liberals against 136 conservatives.

The outcome of the elections did not depend on the degree of participation. It is true that the great conservative victories of the early 1850's were achieved when there were only about half a million voters, while the even greater liberal victories ten years later came when there were close to a million. But the swing of the electorate to the right in 1849 and in 1866, when the number of ballots was the third and second highest of the entire period, 1,037,924 and 1,144,867, demonstrates that the successes of legitimism were not due basically to the abstention of the constitutionalists. Nor did government influence play a decisive role. During the elections of 1852 and 1855, to be sure, Minister of the Interior Ferdinand von Westphalen exerted every pressure, semilegal, extralegal, and illegal, to secure a favorable result. Yet in 1861 efforts by the cabinet of Prince Karl Anton of Hohenzollern to ensure a compliant majority failed, while the Hohenlohe ministry in 1862 and the Bismarck ministry in 1863 were even less successful.[9]

[9] Gerhard Schilfert, *Sieg und Niederlage des demokratischen Wahlrechts in der deutschen Revolution 1848–49* (Berlin, 1952), pp. 315-316, 408; A. Hess, *Das Parlament das Bismarck widerstrebte*, p. 24; E. N. Anderson, *Social and Political Conflict*, p. 412; W. Gagel, *Wahlrechtsfrage*, p. 176; R. Boeckh, "Statistik der Urwahlen 1861," p. 112; E. Engel, "Ergebnisse der Urwahlen 1862 und 1863," p. 69; "Hauptresultate der Urwahlen 1866," pp. 238-239.

What determined the outcome of the elections were proportionally minor shifts in vocal public opinion. Since there was a delicate equilibrium between popular support of liberalism and conservatism, even a small fluctuation in one direction or the other became magnified in the party composition of the legislature. In 1849 well-to-do urban voters were frightened by widespread radical insurrections into backing the candidates of the right. In 1852 and 1855 the reaction seemed so firmly entrenched that many liberals saw no point in even casting a ballot. But their improved prospects in 1858, when the establishment of the regency was taken to presage a period of civic reform, attracted enough waverers to give them a majority. The elections of 1861, 1862, and 1863 were won by the militants of middle-class parliamentarianism, who saw in the issue of army reform the matrix of constitutional government. In 1866, however, the electorate, responding to a successful war waged in the name of national unification, expressed confidence in the ministry by choosing almost as many conservatives as liberals. In each case victory at the polls was determined by no more than a few hundred thousand voters out of more than three million eligibles.

The election of 1863, the only one for which there is a detailed analysis of the party preferences of the participants, illustrates the narrow margin separating victory from defeat during the constitutional conflict. The achievement of the liberals was impressive enough, to be sure. They got 535,595 votes or 48.79 per cent of the total, compared with 335,633 votes or 30.57 per cent for the conservatives. The remaining ballots were divided between the Polish and the Catholic faction or were doubtful. The advantage of the liberals over the conservatives, moreover, was approximately the same in each of the three classes of voters: 50.50 per cent to 30.59 in the first, 50.09 to 29.03 in the second, and 48.27 to 30.96 in the third. In the cities their preponderance was overwhelming: 65.17 per cent to 21.77 in the first class, 67.00 to 20.87 in the second, and 67.67 to 19.39 in the third, for an over-all lead of 67.39 to 19.80 per cent. Yet even in the rural districts the liberals were on the whole ahead of the conservatives, 37.36 per cent to 37.19, as a result of their superior strength in the first class, 43.89 per cent to 34.56, and in the second class, 41.13 per cent to 33.36. Only in the third class did they fall behind, 35.50 to 38.58 per cent. This triumph enabled the parties upholding parliament to gain 258 seats, while the supporters of the government won only 36.

A closer examination of the election results, however, reduces the dimensions of the success achieved by the opposition. While it could count on the backing of 74 per cent of the members of the lower house, its share of the popular vote came to only 49 per cent. The difference between the liberals and the conservatives was no more than 199,962 ballots in a total of 1,097,453. The distribution of the strength of the opposing sides clearly favored the former, since there were on an average 2,193 votes for each liberal member of the legislature, and 9,083 for each conservative. Yet the disparity in the over-all public support of the two groups was only 18 per cent of the vote. As significant as the outcome of the election was the large number of nonparticipants, who exceeded the combined liberal and conservative voters 2,451,612 to 871,228. However big the majority which a party won in the legislature, it represented in fact only a minority of the entire electorate. To have spoken of a popular mandate under such circumstances was an act of faith. Bernhardi could find comfort in the thought that while "the new lower house was chosen through minority elections, . . . the adherents of the government constitute in this minority again only a minority." Bismarck, on the other hand, derided the opposition for its lack of mass support: "It has been . . . drawn to your attention that participation in the elections was small. I shall leave it open whether there were 27 or 34 per cent. . . . The majority of these 27 or 34 per cent elects the members of the electoral colleges. . . . All of the electors thus represent the majority of the previously mentioned 27 or 34 per cent. If I were to make a high estimate of this majority, it could be 20 to 25 per cent of the entire sum. This is represented by all of the electors. You, gentlemen, were chosen by a vote of the majority of the electors, and thus with certainty by half of 20 to 25 per cent + 1, perhaps even + 3." They were both right.[10]

The results of the election of 1863, moreover, reveal the submissiveness with which plebeian voters followed the lead of the political and economic elite of their community. In the cities the liberals actually won a higher proportion of the ballots in the third class, 67.67 per cent, than in the first, 65.17 per cent, or the second, 67.00 per cent. Deviation from the prevailing party allegiance, in other words, was somewhat more common among the upper than the lower strata of society. Men of independent means could afford to defy the dominant urban loyalty to parliamentarianism. But for the lower classes nonconformance might prove dangerous. Those vulnerable to financial reprisal, storekeepers, shopmen, mill hands, and servants, usually bowed to the civic conventions of their environment. The pliability of the masses was even more apparent in the rural districts. There the conservatives failed to win a majority among the well-to-do voters, because the legitimist proprietors of large estates were outnumbered by professional men, bourgeois landowners, small-town businessmen, and progressive aristocrats. The liberals had the upper hand in the first class, 43.89 per cent to 34.56, and in the second class, 41.13 per cent to 33.36. In the third class, however, the advantage was with the conservatives, 38.58 per cent to 35.50. The peasant population east of the Elbe voted by and large in accordance with the wishes of the Junkers.

10 "Hauptresultate der Urwahlen 1866," pp. 241-242; E. N. Anderson, *Social and Political Conflict*, pp. 412-413; E. Engel, "Ergebnisse der Urwahlen 1862 und 1863," p. 69; *Aus dem Leben Bernhardis*, v, 125; O. v. Bismarck, *Werke*, x, 160-161.

The provincial distribution of the rural vote in the third class illustrates the extent to which noble proprietors of the latifundia were able to enforce political conformity among their rustics. In the Rhine Province and Westphalia, where independent farmers dominated the civic life of the villages, the liberals were ahead 60.43 per cent to 20.41 in the former, and 48.69 to 29.86 in the latter. They also led in the Province of Saxony, which had become Prussian less than fifty years before, 51.07 to 36.53. But on the other side of the Elbe the conservatives were stronger by far: 62.36 to 32.05 in Pomerania, 57.17 to 39.72 in Brandenburg, 54.66 to 35.52 in Silesia, and 15.09 to 11.31 in Posen, although here the Polish vote predominated with 72.70 per cent. Only in East and West Prussia, where the economics of Adam Smith combined with the philosophy of Immanuel Kant to win a substantial following for liberalism even among the great landowners, did the constitutionalists have the advantage, 35.38 per cent to 30.66.

The superiority of the opposition parties in the legislature was thus due in large part to the relatively greater participation in the elections of urban voters, the bulwark of liberalism. There were more than twice as many eligibles in rural districts as in cities, 2,441,366 to 1,107,699, but only about one and a half times as many participants, 680,017 to 417,741. The rate of abstention, moreover, was highest among those groups in society whose civic loyalties were most pliable, 43.0 per cent in the first class, 56.0 in the second, and 72.7 in the third. The conservatives, therefore, had a greater reserve of potential strength than the liberals. The number of nonvoters in the country was 1,761,349, while in the city it was only 689,958. The journal of the Statistical Bureau in Berlin found that "in almost all provinces participation has been smallest in those districts which are thinly populated, in which the urban element is little represented or not all, especially in those which are also neither in the immediate vicinity of larger

378

cities nor distinguished by a certain affluence." But if the established order could mobilize the politically apathetic peasant masses, it would have little difficulty in defeating parliamentarianism. The problem before the legitimists was to attract enough lower-class rural voters to the polls to alter the party composition of the legislature.

They never solved that problem. The election of 1866, which established an equilibrium between liberalism and conservatism, was decided not by an increase in the number of voters, but by a moderate shift of vocal public opinion to the right. Throughout the constitutional conflict, however, Bismarck continued to ponder schemes for enlisting mass support. He remained convinced that the proletariat, especially in the countryside, could be trusted to defend the rights of the crown:

> At the moment of decision the masses will stand on the side of kingship, regardless of whether the latter happens to follow a liberal or a conservative tendency. . . . May I indeed express it as a conviction based on long experience that the artificial system of indirect and class elections is much more dangerous [than the direct and general suffrage], because it prevents contact between the highest authority and the healthy elements which constitute the core and the mass of the people. In a country with monarchical traditions and loyal sentiments the general suffrage, by eliminating the influences of the liberal bourgeois classes, will also lead to monarchical elections.

While the constitutionalists disputed this contention, their aversion to an equal franchise suggests that they had misgivings about the political leanings of the lower classes. An article in the liberal *Breslauer Zeitung*, for that matter, openly conceded that the abolition of the three-class system of voting would strengthen the position of the government: "For even if in principle we also declare ourselves for the general direct suffrage, yet we have no doubt that in view of the large number of

379

rural workers who are under feudal influence, . . . a ministerial majority in the lower house of the legislature could very easily be 'manufactured' through the general and direct suffrage." The absence of civic consciousness among the lower classes meant in any case that election results reflected minority preferences rather than popular convictions.[11]

Thus the struggle for a parliamentary form of government did not arise out of the political beliefs of the masses of Central Europe. Neither liberalism nor conservatism could claim a mandate from the people. They were both groping for an adjustment between an oligarchical party system and their need for a mass following. The forms of civic organization were still adapted to the interests of dominant minorities which exercised a decisive influence over public affairs. The proletarian voter was only a mercenary in the great conflict of ideologies. His allegiance could be cajoled, intimidated, coerced, or bought. And then there was the largest group of all, those who did not vote because they did not care. To them the process of politics was so far removed from the central concerns of life that they simply ignored it. The issue of the role of representative institutions in public life was decided by a relatively small number of people drawn from the propertied and educated strata of society. The importance of this decision is not diminished by the fact that it was a minority decision. Yet claims of widespread popular support for one party or the other can be dismissed as factional rhetoric. The truth is that the masses were neither constitutionalist nor legitimist but indifferent.

The question of national unification like the question of parliamentary government attracted the attention of only a minority of the population. Men of means interested in public affairs generally agreed that the German

[11] "Hauptresultate der Urwahlen 1866," p. 242; E. Engel, "Ergebnisse der Urwahlen 1862 und 1863," p. 69; R. Boeckh, "Statistik der Urwahlen 1861," p. 113; O. v. Bismarck, *Werke*, v, 429, 457; *Breslauer Zeitung*, April 26, 1865.

Confederation should be reformed in the direction of greater centralization, although the extent of this change and the means for achieving it remained the subject of debate. To the lower classes, however, nationalism usually meant little more than patriotic speeches and colorful parades. For every proletarian toast to the great common fatherland there was another proletarian toast to Prussia, Bavaria, or Schwarzburg-Sondershausen. For every declaration of solidarity with the brothers on the other side of the border there was an affirmation of faithfulness to the prince in the state capital. Among the masses, nationalistic sentiments intermixed illogically but inextricably with particularistic loyalties, so that an effective popular movement for federal reorganization was impossible. The zealous advocates of national unification came by and large from the well-to-do groups in the community, especially those whose economic interests suffered from political division.

This fact was the basis of a long critical article in which Friedrich Engels, toward the end of his life, sought to explain the establishment of the German Empire in terms of class interest:

> We see from this how the longing for a unitary "fatherland" had a very material background. It was no longer the nebulous desire of members of the *Burschenschaften* at the Wartburg Festival . . . to restore the romantic imperial glory of the Middle Ages. . . . Nor was it any longer the much more down-to-earth call for unity of the lawyers and other bourgeois ideologues of the Hambach Festival, who thought they loved freedom and unity for their own sake, and who did not at all perceive that the transformation of Germany into a Switzerland, into a republic of cantons . . . was just as impossible as the Hohenstaufen empire of those students. No, it was the demand of the practical merchant and industrialist, arising out of a direct business need, for the clearing away of all the historically transmitted rubbish of the petty states which stood in the way of the free develop-

381

ment of trade and manufacture. It was the desire for the removal of all the superfluous friction which the German businessman first had to overcome at home if he wanted to enter the world market, and which all his competitors were spared. German unity had become an economic necessity. And the people who now demanded it knew what they wanted.[12]

Economic determinists were not the only ones to recognize the connection between patriotic ideals and material needs. There were many discerning observers of diverse ideologies who noted that the middle class was the mainstay of the movement for federal reorganization. In Austria Baron Karl von Bruck found that the bourgeoisie more than any other class of society favored the centralization of the Habsburg monarchy and its close association with the other states of the German Confederation. "First of all, a highly important fact should be confirmed," he reported to the emperor. "While in the old privileged classes of the individual provinces separatistic desires have taken root, the idea of the state in its entirety has undoubtedly the most and the richest soil in the urban and rural middle class. Similarly, those exclusive circles also feel the least sympathy for the closer connection of Austria with Germany, if not a decided aversion to it, while the middle classes everywhere entertain the warmest and most sincere wishes for it, because they quite correctly perceive in it the strengthening of their own interests as well as the lasting guarantee of the internal peace and the powerful position of Austria." By enlisting middle-class national aspirations, the finance minister proposed to retain for his government the leading role in a reconstructed federal union.

Elsewhere in the south the bourgeoisie could also be found on the side of political integration. Its material

---

[12] Friedrich Engels, "Gewalt und Oekonomie bei der Herstellung des neuen Deutschen Reichs," *Die Neue Zeit*, XIV (1895–96), no. 1, p. 681.

needs tied it to northern and eastern markets, encouraging a sense of national community which transcended state boundaries. In Württemberg the Central Office for Manufacture and Trade, speaking for the business interests of the kingdom, pointed out that "the movement of Württemberg's trade is in the main toward the North Sea. Württemberg, Baden, and the industrial trading regions of Bavaria are connected with the North Sea through favorable means of communication. The mentioned states . . . will depend on that movement for the sale of their industrial products. A separation from the customs union with Prussia . . . would create the most harmful disturbances in trade." Differences of opinion concerning national unification coincided by and large with differences in economic and social status. After the Seven Weeks' War the Swabian statesman and scholar Gustav Rümelin identified the groups supporting opposed views regarding the best course for the government of Württemberg to follow:

We have at present two great, main schools of thought in the country. The one agitates vigorously for direct and complete entry into the north German federal state. To it belong the great majority of all educated people, the *Schwäb[ischer] Merkur*, the old [moderate] liberals, the men of Gotha [middle-of-the-road Prussophile constitutionalists] and the supporters of the Nationalverein, the Protestant clergy, and the pious, to whom a south German federal state with two-thirds Catholics would be an abomination. On the opposite side, against Prussian leadership and for the separate south German position, are three very different parties: 1. the dynasty with the court, ministry, privy council, the *Staatsanzeiger*, etc.; 2. the democrats, whose goal and ideal is a south German Swiss Confederation with cantons, and who hope to put an end to the dynasties through parliament, rights of man, and arming of the people. Their organ is the *Beobachter* together with the popular societies which have been organized in the entire country; 3. the Catholics and ultra-

383

montanes, who have a horror of the preponderance of Protestantism in the north German federal state. Their organ is the *Deutsches Volksblatt*.

In Bavaria there was the same interrelationship between national sentiment and social position. Industrialists, merchants, financiers, and professional men, especially in the Protestant districts of Franconia, Swabia, and the Palatinate, were ready to subordinate particularistic loyalties to a new federal union led by Prussia. In Hesse-Darmstadt, Ludwig Bamberger began his long career as a liberal politician by enlisting middle-class support in his first election campaign, waged in behalf of greater unity with the north. "The core of the well-to-do merchant class and of industry stood on my side," he recalled afterward. "In the rural part of the election district, which includes almost a hundred towns and villages, the line of demarcation was simple: Protestant or Catholic. A large number of distinguished men from all classes entered the service of our election campaign, which was conducted day and night with a mechanism calculated to the finest degree." This influential following helped him win a hard-fought victory over an opponent backed by the ministry, the clericals, and the democrats. When Czar Alexander II warned that in the event of war between France and the North German Confederation the southern states might side with the former, General Hans Lothar von Schweinitz, the Prussian military attaché in St. Petersburg, assured him that "this would now no longer be possible. For even if in south Germany the majority is not for us, yet men of intelligence are, and we would . . . immediately encourage them through strong support." The Franco-Prussian War soon proved him right.[13]

[13] K. v. Bruck, *Aufgaben Oesterreichs*, pp. 35-36; Helmut Böhme, *Deutschlands Weg zur Grossmacht: Studien zum Verhältnis von Wirtschaft und Staat während der Reichgründungszeit, 1848-1881* (Cologne and Berlin, 1966, p. 40; *Duncker: Politischer Briefwechsel*, ed. J. Schultze, p. 430; Erich Brandenburg, *Die Reichsgründung*, 2nd edn.

The social basis of nationalism was equally apparent in the states of central Germany, Heinrich von Treitschke reported from Saxony that the party favorable to unification under Prussia was "especially represented among the Leipzig merchants, writers, and professors." Moritz Busch elaborated:

A large part of the world of the bureaucracy was in all respects ready to do most obediently what it was told in Dresden, and it displayed Saxon patriotism. . . . The officers were always rigidly Saxon. Dresden was a city of officials and servants, except for a few independent men among whom some were very able, full of respect for the great statesman [Beust] who directed the destinies of the country, and also full of hate for Prussia and her Cavour. . . . In all of Lusatia and in Freiberg and Zwickau there were similar conditions. In Chemnitz, Glauchau, Plauen, and other great factory cities there were more liberals and nationalists, more good will toward Prussia. . . . The situation was somewhat better still in Leipzig, where many non-Saxons had settled, and where the mercantile spirit sees many things more practically than elsewhere. Here, besides a not very strong "Patriotic Society" with a purely Dresden view of the world, and besides a gang of Prussophobes acting out of red democratic or other unclean reasons, there were Prussophiles of a commercial, of a Nationalverein, and even of a unitarian variety in rather large numbers.

Political developments in Saxony after the Seven Weeks' War confirmed this analysis. The state convention which resolved to form a "liberal national" party favoring a new federal union led by Prussia represented essentially the urban bourgeoisie. Among the 121 delegates from Leipzig were 87 merchants and manufacturers and 29 members of the learned professions. And in Chemnitz

---

(2 vols., Leipzig, 1923), II, 290; Ludwig Bamberger, *Gesammelte Schriften* (5 vols., Berlin, 1913), IV, 14; *Briefwechsel des Botschafters General v. Schweinitz* (Berlin, 1928), p. 63.

a "general election committee" formed to win support for the North German Confederation included "the most influential and important industrialists" of the city.

Even among the minuscule states of Thuringia the pattern of attitudes toward political consolidation was the same. In Saxe-Weimar the industrial town of Apolda was more sympathetic to the policies of Berlin than the surrounding countryside. On the eve of hostilities in 1866 its factory owners played a leading part in organizing a mass meeting of the Prussophiles. In Reuss-Greiz, according to a government official, the population, "especially the merchant class," favored Prussia. Once the war came to an end, moreover, the division of opinion in the principality re-emphasized the dependence of politics on economics. "The bureaucracy trembles at an annexation," wrote a correspondent for the *Blätter von der Saale*, "knowing well that its power and arbitrary rule would then be over. . . . The officer corps, a large part of which was formerly in the Prussian service, is quite satisfied with the imminent reorganization of the military system." But the most enthusiastic support for national unity came from the bourgeoisie. "The merchant class, which is very strongly represented here, rejoices, because it sees well enough that only advantages can accrue to it through a closer connection to Prussia." As for the rest of the population, "which until now was systematically kept in a state of dreadful stupidity by those above," it "reviles Caroline [the regent] because of the connection to Austria, but fears that under Prussian rule its dear sons would be transferred to distant regions where they could not possibly find green potato dumplings of the customary excellence." So great was the dependence of Thuringian businessmen on Prussian markets that many of them hoped for incorporation into the Hohenzollern kingdom.[14]

[14] *Treitschkes Briefe*, ed. M. Cornicelius, II, 46; M. Busch, *Tagebuchblätter*, III, 485; H. Jordan, *Die öffentliche Meinung in Sachsen*, pp. 186-187, 243; Konrad Bechstein, "Die öffentliche Meinung in

Even in the secondary states of the north, which were politically more robust and economically more viable, the middle class felt constricted by the ties of particularism. The merchants, manufacturers, bankers, and professional men of Hanover were ready to promote national unification at the expense of dynastic prerogative. After the Seven Weeks' War they found it easy to adjust to annexation by Prussia. Johannes Miquel assured his countrymen that "the direct participation in the vigorous life of a great state, the mighty advancement of commerce and communication, and the effect of the new sturdy national upswing in all directions which we are approaching, they will, once the first difficulties of the transition are overcome, soon let us feel how much better situated we are than in the small state, whose government, always in conflict with the needs of the people, had taught the people to forget respect for the dynasty and every true feeling for the country." There was little sense in trying to conciliate the die-hard particularists, he argued, for they would consider a federal union with Prussia as objectionable as outright incorporation. "Let us have no illusions on this point. What the particularistic masses find repugnant in the unitary state they find just as repugnant in the federal state. It is universal conscription and the feared increase in the taxation system. But to the national part of the people, especially the industrial bourgeoisie, much in the unitary state is welcome which it would lack in the federal state." He reported to the foreign office in Berlin that "the peasant thinks only of the higher tax of which he has been made fearful. If this fear is not realized, he will be satisfied. The townsman is now already rather generally Prussian, and will soon become completely so if he is treated in the right way." Industrialization and urbanization could in the long run be trusted to reinforce acceptance of the new order in Hanover.

Thüringen und die deutsche Frage 1864-66" (Part 2), *Zeitschrift des Vereins für thüringische Geschichte und Altertumskunde* XXXIV (1926), 92, 105, 138; *Blätter von der Saale*, August 24, 1866.

The choice before the merchant patriciate of Hamburg was more difficult. Here the bourgeoisie was the political and economic master of a city which had grown wealthy as a center of world commerce. Why then exchange a profitable independence for the problematical advantages of a national union ruled from Berlin? The government of the municipal republic would have preferred to remain part of the loose-knit German Confederation, but the outbreak of hostilities in 1866 confronted it with a hard decision. While it feared the ambition of Prussia, it also surmised the weakness of Austria. Its policy therefore sought to appease the one without alienating the other. Only after Sadowa did it finally decide to accept what it could not prevent. By becoming a member of the North German Confederation, the proud Hanseatic state lost its sovereignty, but many of the burghers recognized that in the age of industrialization free cities had become an anachronism. "If the idea of a 'north Elbian republic' did not unfortunately belong to the realm of utopia," wrote the publicist Wilhelm Marr, "if Hamburg could acquire a hinterland, we would be the most zealous defenders of our 'independence,' of our 'sovereign right.' But the times of the Genoas and Venices are over. The railroad, the telegraph, the needle gun, and the rifle cannon make them impossible!" There was nothing to do but seek consolation in the expanded economic opportunities which a united fatherland was sure to offer.[15]

This comfort was denied to the aristocracy, whose social status rested on landownership and service to the state. Enjoying a privileged position within the political milieu of particularism, it was inclined to regard national unification as a threat to sacred tradition. Most noblemen would have been willing to accept a moderate reform of the German Confederation which respected

[15] *Zeitung für Norddeutschland*, August 20, 1866; W. Mommsen, *Miquel*, pp. 364, n. 1, 396; Wilhelm Marr, *Selbstständigkeit und Hoheitsrecht der freien Stadt Hamburg sind ein Anachronismus geworden* (Hamburg, 1866), pp. 52-53.

the separate identity of the member states. But they considered the outright abrogation of historic rights in the name of nationhood unjustified. Since Vienna generally defended the established system of decentralization, it could count on substantial support among the upper classes. Pro-Austrian sympathies were especially strong below the Main. Before the Seven Weeks' War the patrician upper house of the Bavarian legislature thundered against Pomeranian Cavourism and Napoleonism. Nor did the outcome of the hostilities intimidate the highborn opponents of centralism. Marquard Barth in Munich concluded regretfully that an attempt to draw the Wittelsbach kingdom into the North German Confederation could not prevail "against such powers as court, bureaucracy, nobility, and clergy, not to mention the ultrademocrats." The Prussian chargé d'affaires in Stuttgart found similar conditions: "The conservative party of this country consists mostly of people who are tied to Austria through traditional family alliances or material interests. The more difficult it is to dissolve these connections in a short time, the more readily they embellish them by clinging to the phrase, which has until now also been so widespread in other conservative circles, that Austria is the protector of conservative interests, and they oppose with all their might any approach to Prussia." Still worse, "there is . . . a not insignificant number of people here, especially among the higher and highest classes of society, whose gaze is directed toward France, and who make no secret of the fact that, should the situation arise, they are ready to buy their fictitious independence through French help."[16]

Farther north the fear of Napoleon III outweighed the dislike for Bismarck, but aristocratic leanings toward particularism were also obvious. The Austrian envoy reported from Dresden that in Beust's opinion the *gross-*

[16] *Die auswärtige Politik Preussens*, VIII, 436. Cf. *ibid.*, VIII, 408; K. A. v. Müller, *Bayern im Jahre 1866*, p. 85; *Deutscher Liberalismus*, ed. J. Heyderhoff and P. Wentzcke, I, 427.

deutsch movement could expect little success in Saxony except among some circles of the nobility. In the upper house of the legislature of Hesse-Darmstadt a motion calling for the entry of the state into the North German Confederation found only one supporter. During the debate, moreover, a member of the princely Ysenburg family declared defiantly that he would much rather vote for the dissolution of the confederation than for participation in it. After the Prussian annexation of their country, more than a hundred members of the Hanoverian aristocracy signed a declaration deploring the "disregard of the rights of the hereditary royal house." At the courts of the small principalities there was also profound resentment of Hohenzollern ambitions. Prince Günther of Schwarzburg-Rudolstadt insisted that he would "prefer to go to my grave than to put on the Prussian uniform." Even the Mecklenburgs, which had sided with Berlin during the Seven Weeks' War, could not reconcile themselves to the curtailment of their sovereignty. The Prussian minister Karl Albert von Kamptz discovered that courtiers, ministers, noblemen, and civil servants considered the new order a calamity which Providence had inflicted on the land. "Among most people I found no trace of a really political understanding of things," he informed his government. "Everywhere, from the bureaucrat's wife to the great landowner, there is self-interest, which is represented as identical with the interest of the country." The ruling classes of Central Europe tended to regard the achievement of national unification at the cost of particularistic autonomy as a dangerous innovation.[17]

These aristocratic misgivings were reflected in the attitude of most conservative theoreticians toward na-

[17] *Quellen zur deutschen Politik Österreichs*, ed. H. v. Srbik, II, 335; H. v. Sybel, *Begründung des Reiches*, VI, 214; *Europäischer Geschichtskalender*, ed. H. Schulthess (1866), p. 204; Heinrich von Poschinger, *Fürst Bismarck und der Bundesrat* (5 vols., Stuttgart and Leipzig, 1897-1901), I, 105; Otto Becker, *Bismarcks Ringen um Deutschlands Gestaltung* (Heidelberg, 1958), p. 462.

tionalism. The Prussian legitimists did not favor the aggrandizement of their country in defiance of Austria. To them there was no conflict between reason of state and the principle of confederacy. They hoped to safeguard the interests of all members of the German Confederation by close collaboration between Berlin and Vienna. To the end of his life Leopold von Gerlach maintained that "through the Punctation of Olmütz the greatest misfortune which could befall us, a war with Austria, was averted. In this war victory itself would have been ruinous. Prussia would have been forced into the same role in Germany which Sardinia now plays in Italy. And every alliance with the revolution and its heirs leads to an inevitable demoralization." His brother Ernst Ludwig remained unmoved by the enthusiasm with which so many of his countrymen greeted the North German Confederation. "The profound immorality, at best the uncertainty and confusion in judging the misdeeds of 1866 which lie clearly before us come from the fact that we do not know what is state, people, king, nationality," he wrote in his diary. "These misunderstood words become transformed in our hands into substances of nature or idols to which divine and human right cannot be applied, but which must be judged like *monstra* or leviathans in keeping with their own strange properties." And Hermann Wagener taught, at least prior to the Seven Weeks' War, that "every solution on the basis of the principle of nationality, which . . . in the hand of Bonapartism is [a] . . . powerful weapon against the legitimate political order of Europe, is inadmissible. . . . Before the Christian view of the world nationality must move to the background, and justice and morality to the foreground." Beneath this emphasis on the sanctity of established rights was the fear that the destruction of a particularistic political system might undermine a hierarchical social order. There were some noblemen, to be sure, who out of patriotic idealism favored a thoroughgoing reform of

391

the German Confederation. But they were a minority.[18]

The attitude of the lower classes toward national unification was more ambiguous. Their basic interests were not at stake in the conflict between centralism and particularism. While the bourgeoisie hoped to promote industrialization within the broadened framework of a united country, while the aristocracy sought to protect the system of confederal autonomy which had maintained its privileged status, the proletariat could expect from a change in the status quo only a change in the form of its subordination. The establishment of a new federal union would neither alleviate its economic need nor improve its social position. With the passage of time, to be sure, political consolidation was bound to contribute to the material well-being of the masses by expanding the markets for industry and agriculture, by creating new opportunities for employment, by facilitating the large-scale organization of labor, and by raising the general standard of living. For the moment, however, the lower classes could see no vital issue in the struggle to reconstruct the German Confederation. Their view of national unification was determined by upbringing, schooling, habit, and tradition rather than by inner conviction. They tended to cling to the old order in which they had grown up, but their loyalties were neither unequivocal nor inflexible. There was at the mid-century no powerful popular sentiment for a closer union of the states of Central Europe.

The attachment to particularism was strongest among the masses of the south. Here geography, history, religion, and xenophobia had bred a deep-seated distrust of the ideas and institutions on the other side of the Main. The Bavarian politician Wolfgang von Thüngen tried to explain the prejudices of his countrymen to an assembly representing the states of the Zollverein:

[18] *Denkwürdigkeiten aus dem Leben Leopold von Gerlachs*, II, 733; *Ernst Ludwig von Gerlach: Aufzeichnungen*, ed. J. v. Gerlach, II, 297; *Neue Preussische Zeitung*, May 20, 1864.

I cannot indeed conceal from you the fact that the majority of the south German people, the real mass of the people, is obviously unfavorable to any closer connection with Prussia. There is in this quarter a certain mistrust, a fear that through too close a tie injury could be done to our institutions, to our independence. Gentlemen, even if you do not consider these feelings justified, you will still find them understandable if you bear in mind that the south German stocks have always been attached with great constancy to their institutions and in great part also to their dynasties, and if you bear in mind furthermore that precisely the mass of the people, among us just as everywhere, engages in the politics of emotions only.

Johann Gustav Droysen, to whom the voice of Prussia had become the voice of God, was less forbearing. *"Difficile est satiram non scribere,"* he exclaimed in the fall of 1866 in exasperation. "In my opinion not only fun but also common sense have ceased to exist among these stubborn Swabians, these bock beer Bavarians, these Catholicized Franconians and Alamanni. For the first time there is a new, freer organization of Germany without the command of foreign powers; for the first time there is a new, truly national organization. And meanwhile the venerated fragments of the German people surpass even the much abused dynasties in stupid resistance to the greatest step forward which we have taken in centuries, since 1517." There was at least agreement that the lower classes of Bavaria, Württemberg, and Baden remained deaf to the call of nationalism.[19]

Although particularistic loyalties were less firmly rooted in the north, they outweighed allegiance to a united fatherland. The masses, afraid that a change in the political system might threaten their way of life,

[19] Germany, *Stenographische Berichte über die Verhandlungen des durch die Allerhöchste Verordnung vom 13. April 1868 einberufenen Deutschen Zoll-Parlaments* (2 vols., Berlin, 1868) , I, 95; J. G. Droysen, *Briefwechsel*, II, 876.

remained faithful to the prince and his government. During a tour of the states of the German Confederation, Alfred von Vivenot, an officer in the Austrian army, found popular sentiment favorable to Vienna: "The observations which I have made concerning the general mood of the population in north Germany differ in many respects from those in south Germany. But also there embitterment at the arbitrariness and at the presumption and perfidy of the Prussian government is in the process of growing, even if there the mood does not make itself quite as riotously noticeable as in south Germany because of the more phlegmatic character of the northerner." Bernhardi regretfully confirmed this evaluation of the attitude toward Prussia. He discovered on a visit to Dresden that "the spirit which rules here is a thoroughly reprehensible one. Passionate particularism, whose chief element naturally is poisonous hatred of Prussia, . . . is aroused and nourished with clever calculations in all educational institutions down to the village schools." Johannes Miquel described conditions in Hanover in similar terms: "A large part of the peasantry and of the lower classes of the cities is, like the largest part of the civil servants, absolutely without national sentiment. Not Germany but Hanover is for them an end in itself." From his estate near Osnabrück Georg von Vincke wrote: "You should just once hear our handicraftsmen and peasants here inveigh against Prussia, not to mention the nobility, the military, and the bureaucracy." The Prussian agent Eduard von Ungern-Sternberg reported that in Holstein "the mass of the people still persists, to be sure, in its anti-Prussian particularistic mood." Heinrich von Treitschke, after assuming his professorship at Kiel, was shocked to learn that "the cry 'rather Danish than Prussian' is *sans phrase* the conviction of thousands." National unification was achieved not through but despite the popular will.[20]

[20] *Quellen zur deutschen Politik Österreichs*, ed. H. v. Srbik, V/ɪɪ, 787; *Aus dem Lebens Bernhardis*, vɪɪ, 362; *Zeitung für Norddeutsch-*

Yet while the lower classes favored the established system of confederal particularism, the strength of their attachment should not be exaggerated. It was a predilection rather than a persuasion. It was more apparent in the neighborhood tavern or at the village fair than at the political meeting or on the field of battle. Since the downfall of the German Confederation did not affect their basic interests, the masses could adjust to the new order as easily as they had accepted the old. At the beginning of the Seven Weeks' War the Bavarian statesman Prince Chlodwig zu Hohenlohe-Schillingsfürst noted in his diary that "the general public regards the entire crisis with a certain indifference. . . . Everyone perceives that present conditions cannot continue. Why wage war for their maintenance?" The popular attitude in the opposing camp was similar. An Austrian agent in Prussia informed Vienna that "the mood of the people is on the whole still very much against the war. . . . In the capital city itself there is not a trace of enthusiasm to be seen. On the contrary, there is unspeakable distress among families. No impartial person looks to the future with confidence in victory."

Even before hostilities came to an end the foes were becoming reconciled. Prince Friedrich Karl, commander of the Prussian First Army, wrote Bismarck that "the population in Saxony was very astonished at our advance, yet anything but hostile. It was exceedingly willing when the problem arose of billeting and of requisitions for the welfare of the troops." According to a foreign observer, "nothing can be more touching than the scenes of 'fraternization' between the Prussian invaders and the invaded Hanoverians, Saxons, and Hessians, as described in almost every letter from the seat of war." By the time of Sadowa, popular opinion in the northern states had by and large acquiesced in the

land, August 20, 1866; *Duncker: Politischer Briefwechsel*, ed. J. Schultze, p. 424; *Die auswärtige Politik Preussens*, VI, 393, n. 3; *Treitschkes Briefe*, ed. M. Cornicelius, III, 119.

destruction of the German Confederation. "So far as the North of Germany is concerned," reported the London *Times*, "it is very evident that Prussia has now gained the victory over the people's minds no less than over their armies. Even where the Prussian Government is most strongly detested, the Prussian people are the object of sympathy, and Prussian soldiers are received with open arms. In Hanover, in Hesse, in Saxony the past is blotted out as thoroughly and rapidly as it was in Tuscany, Modena, or Parma in 1860. Kings and electors are gone. . . . Many [Germans] might have preferred a Federal unity compatible with their local independence; but unity they must have—with their Princes, if practicable; if not, without them." After peace had been restored, however, Professor Julius Möller, a member of the Progressive Party, concluded that "the great mass of the people had no idea of the old confederation, and none can be conveyed to it concerning the new one which is to take its place."[21]

Here is the key to an understanding of the lower-class attitude toward unification. The masses of Central Europe were essentially neither nationalist nor particularist. Other things being equal, they would have chosen to retain the established system of state sovereignty. But their loyalty to it was not strong enough to withstand defeat. They swayed with the wind. The advocates of political consolidation deplored the lack of national consciousness among the people. The young Treitschke cried out bitterly that "the saddest thing is: only through a mass movement can a revolution succeed, but our masses think of everything except German unity." Bismarck toward the end of his life admitted: "I had believed that in the creation of the Reichstag on the basis of universal manhood suffrage I had found a corrective

[21] L. Parisius, *Hoverbeck*, II/II, 131. Cf. *Denkwürdigkeiten des Fürsten Chlodwig zu Hohenlohe-Schillingsfürst*, ed. Friedrich Curtius (2 vols., Stuttgart and Leipzig, 1907), I, 160; Eduard von Wertheimer, *Bismarck im politischen Kampf* (Berlin, 1929), pp. 219-220; *Anhang zu den Gedanken und Erinnerungen von Bismarck*, II, 399; London *Times*, June 29, July 3, 1866.

against the centrifugal force of gravitation of dynastic strivings, and thereby I had overestimated the energy of the national feeling in the mass of the voters." But the partisans of confederal decentralization could not count on steadfast popular support either. Less than two weeks after Sadowa, Max Duncker was writing that "the mood in Hesse-Kassel, except for Hanau and Fulda, is most favorable to us." In Schleswig-Holstein the population gave up the fight for autonomy even earlier. "The mass of the people," explained Ungern-Sternberg, "would without a doubt prefer the formation of the duchies into an independent state under the hereditary prince of Augustenburg over every other solution of the pending question. But we should not expect of it any sacrifices for this idea. It is tired of excitement and longs for peace at any price." The peasants and the workers, in other words, remained unmoved by either the unitarian or the pluralistic principle of national organization. As the *Gothaisches Tageblatt* pointed out, "the most significant world events, especially in the towns and villages which lie far from the cities, come to the knowledge of the inhabitants only through oral communication, and even then rather late. It is obvious, however, that under this method of transmitting information we can speak in only very rare cases about a real understanding of the state of affairs, and it is just as obvious that a livelier interest or an enthusiasm for an idea cannot even exist." Nationalism was clearly not an ideology for the lower classes.[22]

It appealed rather to men of means, most of them bourgeois, whose ideals and interests stimulated their support for political unification. They hoped to find a broader scope for individual talent in a united liberal fatherland. The form which national consolidation assumed after 1866 did not meet all their wishes, but it

[22] *Treitschkes Briefe*, ed. M. Cornicelius, II, 70; O. v. Bismarck, *Werke*, XV, 630; *Duncker: Politischer Briefwechsel*, ed. J. Schultze, p. 423; *Die auswärtige Politik Preussens*, VI, 393, n. 3; *Gothaisches Tageblatt*, January 9, 1864.

represented a compromise attractive enough to win their approval. It opened to them exciting new economic opportunities and gave them a modest measure of parliamentary authority. This was an arrangement they could profitably accept. For the masses, on the other hand, the struggle to establish a new federal union meant patriotic orations, party rallies, military parades, mobilizations, battles, and casualties. They were not consulted concerning the problems of civic reconstruction, the complexities of which they could not in any event understand. They remained mute, uncomprehending witnesses to the great achievements of the age of elite politics. Here lay the gist of the bitter attack on the new order in Central Europe which the historian Georg Gottfried Gervinus composed during the Franco-Prussian War:

> But at the founding of the sham confederation for half of Germany only the victor's command of the unapproachable Prussian government was heard. Its former small following and the former formidable opposition in the old parts of Prussia as well as the voluntary and forced servants of success in the new parts of Prussia and in the federal states simply submitted to it. That great estimable core of the whole people was neither heard nor considered in the new enterprise. Nor was it heard in the entire period since then, either in the north or in the south, either in the Reichstag or in the legislatures, in which it had only fragmentary representations. [These representations] were and are moved by one-sided party motives, which are moreover highly contradictory, and with which the simple needs of the people usually have nothing at all in common. Freedom and influence of the written word were also almost solely on the side of the dominant party, which had the hand of authority behind its voice. It was [this party] which almost alone asked all questions and answered them in the most widely circulating press. The voice of public opinion was thereby falsified, and because of this unnatural state of affairs

more than one government or political system in Europe has already perished unexpectedly in this half century.

It was a prophetic observation. In the next half century many more governments and political systems were to perish unexpectedly because of "this unnatural state of affairs."[23]

[23] G. G. Gervinus, *Hinterlassene Schriften* (Vienna, 1872), p. 16.

Alphabetical List of Cited Works

ADAM, REINHARD, "Der Liberalismus in der Provinz Preussen zur Zeit der neuen Ära und sein Anteil an der Entstehung der Deutschen Fortschrittspartei," *Altpreussische Beiträge: Festschrift zur Hauptversammlung des Gesamtvereins der deutschen Geschichts- und Altertums-Vereine zu Königsberg Pr. von 4. bis 7. September 1933* (Königsberg, 1933).

Aktenstücke zur Wirthschaftspolitik des Fürsten Bismarck, ed. Heinrich von Poschinger (2 vols., Berlin, 1890-91).

Allgemeine deutsche Arbeiter-Zeitung.

"Das allgemeine und geheime Stimmrecht vor dem Reichstage," *Die Grenzboten*, XXVI (1867), no. 1.

ANDERSON, EUGENE N., *The Social and Political Conflict in Prussia, 1858-1864* (Lincoln, 1954).

"Aphorismen zur Arbeiterbewegung," *Berliner Revue*, XXXVII (1864).

"Die arbeitenden Classen und die Arbeits- und Lohnverhältnisse," *Jahrbuch für die amtliche Statistik des preussischen Staats*, II (1867).

ARMSTRONG, SINCLAIR W., "The Social Democrats and the Unification of Germany, 1863-71," *Journal of Modern History*, XII (1940).

ARND, KARL, *Gedanken über die Fortbildung des deutschen Bundes* (Frankfurt am Main, 1860).

ARNIM, HANS VON, "Friedrich Julius Stahl," in *Deutscher Aufstieg: Bilder aus der Vergangenheit und Gegenwart der rechtsstehenden Parteien*, ed. Hans v. Arnim and George v. Below (Berlin, 1925).

"Aus dem kommerziellen Leben des Jahres 1866," *Vierteljahrschrift für Volkswirthschaft und Kulturgeschichte*, IV (1866), no. 4.

"Aus Ostpreussen," *Preussische Jahrbücher*, XXI (1868).

Die auswärtige Politik Preussens, 1858-1871 (10 vols., Oldenburg and Berlin, 1932-45).

BAMBERGER, LUDWIG, *Gesammelte Schriften* (5 vols., Berlin, 1913).

BANDMANN, OTTO, *Die deutsche Presse und die Entwicklung der deutschen Frage, 1864-66* (Leipzig, 1910).

BAUMGARTEN, H., "Der deutsche Liberalismus: Eine Selbstkritik," *Preussische Jahrbücher*, XVIII (1866).

BEBEL, AUGUST, *Aus meinem Leben* (3 vols., Stuttgart, 1910-14).

BECHSTEIN, KONRAD, "Die öffentliche Meinung in Thüringen und die deutsche Frage, 1864-66," *Zeitschrift des Vereins für thüringische Geschichte und Altertumkunde,* XXXIII (1922-24) and XXXIV (1926).

BECHTEL, HEINRICH, *Wirtschaftsgeschichte Deutschlands* (3 vols., Munich, 1951-56).

BECKER, BERNHARD, *Geschichte der Arbeiter-Agitation Ferdinand Lassalle's* (Brunswick, 1875).

BECKER, OTTO, *Bismarcks Ringen um Deutschlands Gestaltung* (Heidelberg, 1958).

"Die Bedürfnisse und Bedingungen der deutschen Handelspolitik," *Wochenschrift des Nationalvereins*, May 8, 1860.

"Beiträge zur Statistik des Deutschen Reiches," *Zeitschrift des königlich preussischen Statistischen Bureaus*, XVII (1877).

BENAERTS, PIERRE, *Les origines de la grande industrie allemande* (Paris, 1933).

"Aus den Briefen Rudolf v. Bennigsens," ed. Hermann Oncken, *Deutsche Revue*, XXX (1905), no. 3.

Der Beobachter.

BERGENGRÜN, ALEXANDER, *David Hansemann* (Berlin, 1901).

BERGENGRÜN, ALEXANDER, *Staatsminister August Freiherr von der Heydt* (Leipzig, 1908).

BERGER, L., *Der alte Harkort: Ein westfälisches Lebens- und Zeitbild*, 4th edn. (Leipzig, 1902).

[BERGHAUS, HEINRICH], *Statistik des preussischen Staats: Versuch einer Darstellung seiner Grundmacht und Kultur, seiner Verfassung, Regierung und Verwaltung im Lichte der Gegenwart* (Berlin, 1845).

402

Berlin und seine Entwickelung: Städtisches Jahrbuch für Volkswirthschaft und Statistik.

Berliner Revue.

Aus dem Leben Theodor von Bernhardis (9 vols., Leipzig, 1898-1906).

BERNSTEIN, EDUARD, *Die Geschichte der Berliner Arbeiter-Bewegung: Ein Kapitel zur Geschichte der deutschen Sozialdemokratie* (3 vols., Berlin, 1907-10).

BEUSHAUSEN, GERTRUD, *Zur Strukturanalyse parlamentarischer Repräsentation in Deutschland vor der Gründung des Norddeutschen Bundes* (Doctoral Thesis, University of Hamburg, 1926).

BIERMANN, WILHELM, *Franz Leo Benedikt Waldeck: Ein Streiter für Freiheit und Recht* (Paderborn, 1928).

Anhang zu den Gedanken und Erinnerungen von Otto Fürst von Bismarck (2 vols., Stuttgart and Berlin, 1901).

Fürst Bismarck als Volkswirth, ed. Heinrich v. Poschinger (3 vols., Berlin, 1889-91).

BISMARCK, OTTO VON, *Die gesammelten Werke* (15 vols., Berlin, 1924-35).

Blätter von der Saale.

BLUMBERG, HORST, "Die Finanzierung der Neugründungen und Erweiterungen von Industriebetrieben in Form der Aktiengesellschaften während der fünfziger Jahre des neunzehnten Jahrhunderts, am Beispiel der preussischen Verhältnisse erläutert," in Hans Mottek, Horst Blumberg, Heinz Wutzmer, and Walter Becker, *Studien zur Geschichte der industriellen Revolution in Deutschland* (Berlin, 1960).

BLUNTSCHLI, J. C., *Denkwürdiges aus meinem Leben* (3 vols., Nördlingen, 1884).

BOECKH, R., "Statistik der Urwahlen für das preussische Abgeordnetenhaus vom neunzehnten November 1861," *Zeitschrift des königlich preussischen Statistischen Bureaus,* II (1862).

BÖDIKER, T., "Die Auswanderung und die Einwanderung des preussischen Staates," *Zeitschrift des königlich preussischen Statistischen Bureaus,* XIII (1873).

BÖHME, HELMUT, *Deutschlands Weg zur Grossmacht: Studien zum Verhältnis von Wirtschaft und Staat während der Reichsgründungszeit, 1848-1881* (Cologne and Berlin, 1966).

BOEHMERT, CARL VICTOR, *Briefe zweier Handwerker: Ein Beitrag zur Lösung gewerblicher und socialer Fragen* (Dresden and Döbeln, 1854).

BÖHMERT, VICTOR, "Die Entstehung des volkswirtschaftlichen Kongresses vor 25 Jahren (Zur Erinnerung an Schulze-Delitzsch und Huber, Lette und Prince-Smith)," *Vierteljahrschrift für Volkswirtschaft, Politik und Kulturgeschichte*, XXI (1884), no. 1.

BÖHMERT, VICTOR, *Freiheit der Arbeit!: Beiträge zur Reform der Gewerbegesetze* (Bremen, 1858).

BÖHMERT, VICTOR, *Rückblicke und Ausblicke eines Siebzigers* (Dresden, 1900).

BONDI, GERHARD, *Deutschlands Aussenhandel, 1815-1870* (Berlin, 1958).

BORN, KARL ERICH, "Sozialpolitische Probleme und Bestrebungen in Deutschland von 1848 bis zur Bismarckschen Sozialgesetzgebung," *Vierteljahrschrift für Sozial- und Wirtschaftsgeschichte*, XLVI (1959).

BRANDENBURG, ERICH, *Die Reichsgründung*, 2nd edn. (2 vols., Leipzig, 1923).

BRAUN, CARL, "Staats- und Gemeinde-Steuern, im Zusammenhange mit Staats-, Heeres-, Kommunal- und Agrarverfassung," *Vierteljahrschrift für Volkswirthschaft und Kulturgeschichte*, IV (1866), no. 2.

BRAUN, CARL, "Studien über Freizügigkeit," *Vierteljahrschrift für Volkswirthschaft und Culturgeschichte*, I (1863), no. 3.

BRENTANO, LUJO, "Familienfideikommisse und ihre Wirkungen," *Volkswirtschaftliche Zeitfragen*, XXXIII (1911), no. 2.

Breslauer Zeitung.

BRUCH, ERNST, "Wohnungsnoth und Hülfe," *Berlin und seine Entwickelung: Städtisches Jahrbuch für Volkswirthschaft und Statistik*, VI (1872).

BRUCK, KARL VON, *Die Aufgaben Oesterreichs* (Leipzig, 1860).

[BULWER, EDWARD GEORGE EARLE LYTTON], *England and the English* (2 vols., New York, 1833).

BUNDESARCHIV ABTEILUNG FRANKFURT AM MAIN, *Akten der Nationalversammlung: Volksw. Ausschuss*, 21 II (Memorial of the Bremen Civic Association).

BURCKHARDT, JACOB, *Gesammelte Werke* (10 vols., Basel, 1955-59).

BUSCH, MORITZ, *Tagebuchblätter*, (3 vols., Leipzig, 1899).

CAMERON, RONDO E., "Founding the Bank of Darmstadt," *Explorations in Entrepreneurial History*, VIII (1956).

CHARMATZ, RICHARD, *Minister Freiherr von Bruck: Der Vorkämpfer Mitteleuropas* (Leipzig, 1916).

CIRIACY-WANTRUP, SIEGFRIED VON, *Agrarkrisen und Stockungsspannen: Zur Frage der langen "Welle" in der wirtschaftlichen Entwicklung* (Berlin, 1936).

CLAPHAM, J. H., *The Economic Development of France and Germany, 1815-1914*, 4th edn. (Cambridge, 1951).

CLAUSNITZER, L., *Geschichte des preussischen Unterrichtsgesetzes*, 2nd edn. (Berlin, 1891).

COLLANI, HANS-JOACHIM VON, *Die Finanzgebarung des preussischen Staates zur Zeit des Verfassungskonfliktes, 1862-1866* (Düsseldorf, 1939).

COLOGNE CHAMBER OF COMMERCE, *Jahres-Bericht für das Jahr 1849* (Cologne, 1850).

COLOGNE CHAMBER OF COMMERCE, *Jahres-Bericht für 1850* (Cologne, 1851).

Congress deutscher Volkswirthe:
Zweite Versammlung des Congresses deutscher Volkswirthe zu Frankfurt a. M. vom 12. bis 15. September 1859: Stenographischer Bericht (Frankfurt am Main, 1859).

Dritte Versammlung des Congresses deutscher Volkswirthe zu Köln vom 10. bis 14. September 1860: Stenographischer Bericht (Frankfurt am Main, 1860-61).

Die Verhandlungen des Vierten Congresses deutscher Volkswirthe zu Stuttgart am 9., 10., 11. und 12. September 1861 (Stuttgart, 1861).

405

Die Verhandlungen des Fünften Congresses deutscher Volkswirthe zu Weimar am 8., 9., 10. und 11. September 1862 (Weimar, 1862).

Bericht über die Verhandlungen des sechsten Congresses deutscher Volkswirthe zu Dresden am 14. 15. 16. 17. September 1863 (Berlin, 1863).

Bericht über die Verhandlungen des siebenten Kongresses deutscher Volkswirthe zu Hannover am 22. 23. 24. 25. August 1864 (Berlin, 1864).

Bericht über die Verhandlungen des achten Kongresses deutscher Volkswirthe zu Nürnberg am 28., 29., 30. und 31. August 1865 (Berlin, 1865).

"Bericht über die auf Veranlassung der ständigen Deputation des volkswirthschaftlichen Congresses am 4. August 1866 abgehaltene Versammlung zu Braunschweig," *Vierteljahrschrift für Volkswirthschaft und Kulturgeschichte,* IV (1866), no. 2.

CONRAD, J., "Agrarstatistische Untersuchungen: Die Latifundien im preussischen Osten," *Jahrbücher für Nationalökonomie und Statistik,* L (1888).

COUSIN, V., *De l'instruction publique dans quelques pays de l'Allemagne et particulièrement en Prusse,* 3rd edn. (2 vols., Paris, 1840).

"Die Debatte über das Wuchergesetz," *Berliner Revue,* XX (1860).

"Das definitive Resultat der Volkszählung im preussischen Staate am 3. December 1861," *Zeitschrift des königlich preussischen Statistischen Bureaus,* II (1862).

DEHIO, LUDWIG, "Die preussische Demokratie und der Krieg von 1866: Aus dem Briefwechsel von Karl Rodbertus mit Franz Ziegler," *Forschungen zur brandenburgischen und preussischen Geschichte,* XXXIX (1927).

DEHIO, LUDWIG, "Die Taktik der Opposition während des Konflikts," *Historische Zeitschrift,* CXL (1929).

DELBRÜCK, RUDOLPH VON, *Lebenserinnerungen, 1817-1867* (2 vols., Leipzig, 1905).

DEMETER, KARL, *Das deutsche Offizierkorps in Gesellschaft und Staat, 1650-1945,* 2nd edn. (Frankfurt am Main, 1962).

Denkschrift des Deutschen Handwerkerbundes betr.: den Erlass einer allgemeinen Deutschen Handwerker-Ordnung (Bückeburg, 1864).

"Deutsche Feste und Kriegsgefahr," *Die Grenzboten*, XXII (1863), no. 3.

Der Deutsche Handelstag, 1861-1911, ed. Deutscher Handelstag (2 vols., Berlin, 1911-13).

"Der deutsche Handwerkertag in Weimar vom 5. bis 8. September 1862," *Berliner Revue*, XXX (1862).

Die deutschen Parteiprogramme, ed. Felix Salomon (2 vols., Leipzig and Berlin, 1907).

Deutscher Handelstag:

Verhandlungen des Handelstages in Berlin, vom 20. Februar bis 2. März 1860 (Berlin, 1860).

Verhandlungen des ersten deutschen Handelstags zu Heidelberg, vom 13. bis 18. Mai 1861 (Berlin, 1861).

Verhandlungen des zweiten deutschen Handelstages zu München, vom 14. bis 18. October 1862 (Berlin, 1862).

Verhandlungen des Dritten Deutschen Handelstages zu Frankfurt am Main, vom 25. bis 28. September 1865 (Berlin, 1865).

Deutscher Liberalismus im Zeitalter Bismarcks: Eine politische Briefsammlung, ed. Julius Heyderhoff and Paul Wentzcke (2 vols., Bonn and Leipzig, 1925-26).

Deutsches Verkehrsbuch, ed. Hans Baumann (Berlin, 1931).

DEUTSCHES ZENTRALARCHIV ABTEILUNG MERSEBURG, *Ministerium für Handel, Gewerbe und öffentliche Arbeiten*, Rep. 120 B I 1 Nr. 62 Bd. 5, "Einladung zum Preussischen Landes-Handwerkertage in Berlin."

"Deutschland und der polnische Aufstand," *Wochenschrift des Nationalvereins*, April 10, 1863.

Deutschlands Lage und Zukunft: Ein freies Wort an Deutschlands Fürsten und Volksstämme (Oldenburg, 1860).

DIETERICI, C.F.W., *Handbuch der Statistik des preussischen Staats* (Berlin, 1861).

DROYSEN, JOHANN GUSTAV, *Briefwechsel*, ed. Rudolf Hübner (2 vols., Berlin and Leipzig, 1929).

Max Duncker: Politischer Briefwechsel aus seinem Nachlass, ed. Johannes Schultze (Stuttgart and Berlin, 1923).

[DUNCKER, MAX], "Politische Correspondenz," *Preussische Jahrbücher*, VII (1861) – IX (1862).

Durch Krieg zum Frieden (Stuttgart and Wildbad, 1859).

ENGEL, ERNST, "Die Ergebnisse der Classensteuer, der classificirten Einkommensteuer und der Mahl- und Schlachtsteuer im preussischen Staate," *Zeitschrift des königlich preussischen Statistischen Bureaus*, VIII (1868).

ENGEL, ERNST, "Die Ergebnisse der Urwahlen für das preussische Abgeordnetenhaus vom 28. April 1862 und vom 20. October 1863," *Zeitschrift des königlich preussischen Statistischen Bureaus*, V (1865).

ENGELS, FRIEDRICH, "Die deutsche Reichsverfassungs-Campagne: Für Republik zu sterben!," *Neue Rheinische Zeitung: Politische-ökonomische Revue*, I (1850), no. 3.

ENGELS, FRIEDRICH, "Gewalt und Oekomonie bei der Herstellung des neuen Deutschen Reichs," *Die Neue Zeit*, XIV (1895-96), no. 1.

ENGELS, FRIEDRICH, *Die preussische Militärfrage und die deutsche Arbeiterpartei* (Hamburg, 1865).

"Die Ergebnisse der Volkszählung und Volksbeschreibung nach den Aufnahmen vom 3. December 1861, resp. Anfang 1862," *Preussische Statistik*, V (1864).

ERNEST II, *Aus meinem Leben und aus meiner Zeit*, 4th edn. (3 vols., Berlin, 1888-89).

Die Erstrebung einer maritimen Stellung Deutschlands auf der Basis des Zoll-Vereins (Berlin, 1859).

Europäischer Geschichtskalender, ed. H. Schulthess.

EYCK, ERICH, *Der Vereinstag deutscher Arbeitervereine, 1863-1868: Ein Beitrag zur Entstehungsgeschichte der deutschen Arbeiterbewegung* (Berlin, 1904).

FISCHER, LAURENZ HANNIBAL, *Der teutsche Adel in der Vorzeit, Gegenwart und Zukunft vom Standpunkte des Bürgerthums betrachtet* (2 vols., Frankfurt am Main, 1852).

Flugblatt vom ständigen Ausschusse des Vereinstags deutscher Arbeitervereine, August 13, 1865.

"Die Fortschrittsparthei und der Socialismus," *Wochen-Blatt des National-Vereins*, April 6, 1865.

Frankfurter Reform.

FRANZ, EUGEN, *Der Entscheidungskampf um die wirtschaftspolitische Führung Deutschlands (1856-1867)* (Munich, 1933).

FRANZ, EUGEN, "Die Entstehungsgeschichte des preussisch-französischen Handelsvertrags vom 29. März 1862," *Vierteljahrschrift für Sozial- und Wirtschaftsgeschichte*, XXV (1932).

FRIEDMANN, O. BERNHARD, *Zur Einigung Oesterreichs: Eine Denkschrift* (Stuttgart, 1862).

Grossherzog Friedrich I. von Baden und die deutsche Politik von 1854-1871: Briefwechsel, Denkschriften, Tagebücher, ed. Hermann Oncken (2 vols., Berlin and Leipzig, 1927).

Kaiser Friedrich III: Tagebücher von 1848-1866, ed. Heinrich Otto Meisner (Leipzig, 1929).

FRÖBEL, JULIUS, *Ein Lebenslauf: Aufzeichnungen, Erinnerungen und Bekenntnisse* (2 vols., Stuttgart, 1890-91).

FRÖBEL, JULIUS, *Theorie der Politik, als Ergebniss einer erneuerten Prüfung demokratischer Lehrmeinungen* (2 vols., Vienna, 1861-64).

GABLENZ, ANTON VON, *Die deutsche Einheit nach des Königs Worten aufgefasst* (Breslau, 1861).

GAGEL, WALTER, *Die Wahlrechtsfrage in der Geschichte der deutschen liberalen Parteien, 1848-1918* (Düsseldorf, 1958).

GENSEL, JULIUS, *Der Deutsche Handelstag in seiner Entwickelung und Thätigkeit, 1861-1901* (Berlin, 1902).

Ernst Ludwig von Gerlach: Aufzeichnungen aus seinem Leben und Wirken, 1795-1877, ed. Jakob von Gerlach (2 vols., Schwerin, 1903).

Briefe des Generals Leopold von Gerlach an Otto von Bismarck, ed. Horst Kohl (Stuttgart and Berlin, 1912).

Denkwürdigkeiten aus dem Leben Leopold von Gerlachs, Generals der Infanterie und General-Adjutanten König Friedrich Wilhelms IV. (2 vols., Berlin, 1891-92).

409

GERMANY, *Stenographische Berichte über die Verhandlungen des Reichstages des Norddeutschen Bundes.*

GERMANY, *Stenographische Berichte über die Verhandlungen des . . . Deutschen Zoll-Parlaments.*

GERMANY, *Stenographische Berichte über die Verhandlungen des Deutschen Reichstages.*

GERSCHENKRON, ALEXANDER, *Bread and Democracy in Germany* (Berkeley and Los Angeles, 1943).

GERVINUS, G. G., *Einleitung in die Geschichte des neunzehnten Jahrhunderts* (Leipzig, 1853).

GERVINUS, G. G., *Hinterlassene Schriften* (Vienna, 1872).

Die Geschichte der Social-demokratischen Partei in Deutschland seit dem Tode Ferdinand Lassalle's (Berlin, 1865).

Die Gewerbefrage in Preussen: Zwei Petitionen an die hohen Häuser des allgemeinen Landtages (Berlin, 1861).

[GILDEMEISTER, O.], "Die Verkehrskrisis des Jahres 1857," *Preussische Jahrbücher,* I (1858).

GLASER, JOHANN CARL, "Die Arbeiterfrage und die Parteien," *Jahrbücher für Gesellschafts- und Staatswissenschaften,* V (1866).

Görlitzer Anzeiger.

GOETHE, JOHANN WOLFGANG, *Wilhelm Meisters Wanderjahre: Wilhelm Meisters theatralische Sendung* (Zurich, 1949).

GOLDSCHMIDT, "Schulpflicht und Schulbesuch in Berlin," *Zeitschrift des königlich preussischen Statistischen Bureaus,* VII (1867).

GOLDSCHMIDT, ERNST FRIEDRICH, *Die deutsche Handwerkerbewegung bis zum Sieg der Gewerbefreiheit* (Munich, 1916).

GOLLWITZER, HEINZ, *Die Standesherren: Die politische und gesellschaftliche Stellung der Mediatisierten, 1815-1918,* 2nd edn. (Göttingen, 1964).

GOLTZ, THEODOR VON DER, *Geschichte der deutschen Landwirtschaft* (2 vols., Stuttgart and Berlin, 1902-03).

GOLTZ, THEODOR VON DER, *Vorlesungen über Agrarwesen und Agrarpolitik* (Jena, 1899).

Gothaisches Tageblatt.

GRAMBOW, LUDOLF, *Die deutsche Freihandelspartei zur Zeit ihrer Blüte* (Jena, 1903).

GRUBE, WALTER, *Die Neue Ära und der Nationalverein: Ein Beitrag zur Geschichte Preussens und der Einheitsbewegung* (Marburg, 1933).

"Gutachten des Professor Dr. Goldschmidt zu Heidelberg über die Aufhebung der Wuchergesetze," *Verhandlungen des sechsten deutschen Juristentages* (3 vols., Berlin, 1865-68).

HAHN, ADALBERT, *Die Berliner Revue: Ein Beitrag zur Geschichte der konservativen Partei zwischen 1855 und 1875* (Berlin, 1934).

HAMEROW, THEODORE S., "The German Artisan Movement, 1848-49," *Journal of Central European Affairs*, XXI (1961).

HAMEROW, THEODORE S., *Restoration, Revolution, Reaction: Economics and Politics in Germany, 1815-1871* (Princeton, 1958).

Handelstag, *see* Deutscher Handelstag.

Handwerkertag:

Verhandlungen des im Jahre 1860 vom 27. bis 31. August zu Berlin abgehaltenen Preusz. Landes-Handwerkertages nebst den dabei aufgenommenen Protokollen (Berlin, 1860).

Die stenographischen Verhandlungen des deutschen Handwerkertags zu Weimar vom 5. bis 8. September 1862 (Berlin, 1862).

Der zweite deutsche Handwerkertag zu Frankfurt a. M. vom 25. bis 28. September 1863 (Frankfurt am Main, 1863).

Der dritte deutsche Handwerkertag zu Cöln vom 26. bis 28. September 1864 (Aachen, 1864).

Der dritte Norddeutsche Handwerkertag zu Hannover am 14., 15. und 16. September 1868 (Hanover, 1868).

HANSEN, JOSEPH, *Gustav von Mevissen: Ein rheinisches Lebensbild, 1815-1899* (2 vols., Berlin, 1906).

HANSEN, MARCUS L., "The Revolutions of 1848 and German Emigration," *Journal of Economic and Business History*, II (1930).

HASSELL, W. VON, *Geschichte des Königreichs Hannover* (2 vols., Bremen and Leipzig, 1898-1901).

"Die Hauptresultate der Urwahlen für das preussische Abgeordnetenhaus vom 25. September 1866," *Zeitschrift des königlich preussischen Statistischen Bureaus*, VII (1867).

"Das Haus der Abgeordneten," *Berliner Revue*, XX (1860).

Ausgewählter Briefwechsel Rudolf Hayms, ed. Hans Rosenberg (Berlin and Leipzig, 1930).

HERMES, GERTRUD, "Statistische Studien zur wirtschaftlichen und gesellschaftlichen Struktur des zollvereinten Deutschlands," *Archiv für Sozialwissenschaft und Sozialpolitik*, LXIII (1930).

HERRMANN, PAUL, *Die Entstehung des Deutschen Nationalvereins und die Gründung seiner Wochenschrift* (Leipzig, 1932).

HERSCHEL, OLGA, *Die öffentliche Meinung in Hamburg in ihrer Haltung zu Bismarck, 1864-1866* (Hamburg, 1916).

HERZFELD, HANS, *Johannes von Miquel: Sein Anteil am Ausbau des Deutschen Reiches bis zur Jahrhundertwende* (2 vols., Detmold, 1938).

HESS, ADALBERT, *Das Parlament das Bismarck widerstrebte: Zur Politik und sozialen Zusammensetzung des preussischen Abgeordnetenhauses der Konfliktszeit (1862-1866)* (Cologne and Opladen, 1964).

HOFFMANN, W. G., and J. H. MÜLLER, *Das deutsche Volkseinkommen, 1851-1957* (Tübingen, 1959).

Denkwürdigkeiten des Fürsten Chlodwig zu Hohenlohe-Schillingsfürst, ed. Friedrich Curtius (2 vols., Stuttgart and Leipzig, 1907).

HÜMMLER, HEINZ, *Opposition gegen Lassalle: Die revolutionäre proletarische Opposition im Allgemeinen Deutschen Arbeiterverein, 1862/63-1866* (Berlin, 1963).

IPSEN, GUNTHER, "Die preussische Bauernbefreiung als Landesausbau," *Zeitschrift für Agrargeschichte und Agrarsoziologie*, II (1954).

JACOBS, ALFRED, and HANS RICHTER, *Die Grosshandelspreise in Deutschland von 1792 bis 1934* (Hamburg, 1935).

JACOBY, JOHANN, *Gesammelte Schriften und Reden,* 2nd edn. (2 vols., Hamburg, 1877).

Jahrbuch für die amtliche Statistik des preussischen Staats.

Rudolf von Jhering in Briefen an seine Freunde (Leipzig, 1913).

[JÖRG, EDMUND], "Zeitläufe: Deutschland in den Spannungen des Moments," *Historisch-politische Blätter für das katholische Deutschland,* LVII (1866).

[JÖRG, EDMUND], "Zur Kritik von Lösungen der socialen Frage: Schulze-Delitzsch," *Historisch-politische Blätter für das katholische Deutschland,* LV (1865).

JORDAN, HERBERT, *Die öffentliche Meinung in Sachsen, 1864-66* (Kamenz, 1918).

K., "Correspondenz: Aus Berlin," *Deutsches Museum,* XVI (1866), no. 1.

K., H., "Der volkswirthschaftliche Congress zu Frankfurt a. M.," *Berliner Revue,* XIX (1859).

K., W., "Handelspolitische Betrachtungen aus der Gegenwart," *Deutsche Vierteljahrs-Schrift,* XXI (1858), no. 4 and XXII (1859), no. 1.

KAHN, JULIUS, *Geschichte des Zinsfusses in Deutschland seit 1815 und die Ursachen seiner Veränderung* (Stuttgart, 1884).

KAIZL, JOSEF, *Der Kampf um Gewerbereform und Gewerbefreiheit in Bayern von 1799-1868* (Leipzig, 1879).

KATZ, EUGEN, *Landarbeiter und Landwirtschaft in Oberhessen* (Stuttgart and Berlin, 1904).

KAUFFER, EDUARD, "Zur Begrüssung des Deutschen Handelstages zu Heidelberg am 13. Mai 1861," *Sächsische Industrie-Zeitung,* May 10, 1861.

KELLNER, WILHELM, *Taschenbuch der politischen Statistik Deutschlands oder Aufstellung der staatlichen Einrichtungen Gesammt-Deutschlands sowohl als der einzelnen deutschen Staaten* (Frankfurt am Main, 1864).

KERSTORF, FRIEDRICH VON, *Erfahrungen u. Beobachtungen auf handelspolitischem Gebiete, 1848 bis 1862* (Augsburg, 1862).

KEUDELL, ROBERT VON, *Fürst und Fürstin Bismarck: Erin-*

413

nerungen aus den Jahren 1846 bis 1872, 3rd edn. (Berlin and Stuttgart, 1902).

KNAPP, GEORG FRIEDRICH, *Die Bauern-Befreiung und der Ursprung der Landarbeiter in den älteren Theilen Preussens* (2 vols., Leipzig, 1887).

KNOLL, JOACHIM H., *Führungsauslese in Liberalismus und Demokratie: Zur politischen Geistesgeschichte der letzten hundert Jahre* (Stuttgart, 1957).

KÖLLMANN, WOLFGANG, *Sozialgeschichte der Stadt Barmen im 19. Jahrhundert* (Tübingen, 1960).

Königsberger Hartungsche Zeitung.

Konsequenzen des preussisch-französischen Handelsvertrages für unser inneres Staatsleben (Berlin, 1862).

"Krieg oder Friede?," *Deutsches Wochenblatt*, May 13, 1866.

KRÜGER, ALFRED, *Das Kölner Bankiergewerbe vom Ende des 18. Jahrhunderts bis 1875* (Essen, 1925).

KUCZYNSKI, JÜRGEN, *Die Bewegung der deutschen Wirtschaft von 1800 bis 1946*, 2nd edn. (Berlin and Leipzig, 1947).

KUCZYNSKI, JÜRGEN, *A Short History of Labour Conditions under Industrial Capitalism: Germany, 1800 to the Present Day* (London, 1945).

KUCZYNSKI, JÜRGEN, *Studien zur Geschichte der zyklischen Überproduktionskrisen in Deutschland, 1825 bis 1866* (Berlin, 1961).

KÜNSSBERG-MANDEL, PHILIPP VON, *Auf zur That! Ein Zuruf an meine Standesgenossen und alle loyalen Deutschen* (Dresden, 1861).

LAMBI, IVO NIKOLAI, *Free Trade and Protection in Germany, 1868-1879* (Wiesbaden, 1963).

[LAMMERS, A.], "Ein Blick auf die deutsche Genossenschaftsbewegung," *Preussische Jahrbücher*, VI (1860).

[LAMMERS, A.], "Die wirthschaftliche Reformbewegung in Deutschland," *Preussische Jahrbücher*, VI (1860).

Die landwirthschaftliche Statistik des Königreichs Sachsen, ed. K. von Langsdorff (Dresden, 1886).

LANGE, FR. A., *Die Arbeiterfrage in ihrer Bedeutung für Gegenwart und Zukunft* (Duisburg, 1865).

"Briefe Lassalles an Dr. Otto Dammer in Leipzig, Vice-

präsidenten des Allgemeinen Deutschen Arbeitervereins,"
ed. Hermann Oncken, *Archiv für die Geschichte des
Sozialismus und der Arbeiterbewegung*, II (1912).

LASSALLE, FERDINAND, *Gesammelte Reden und Schriften*, ed.
Eduard Bernstein (12 vols., Berlin, 1919-20).

LASSALLE, FERDINAND, *Nachgelassene Briefe und Schriften*,
ed. Gustav Mayer (6 vols., Stuttgart and Berlin, 1921-25).

[LAVERGNE-PEGUILHEN, MORITZ VON], "Die Doctrin und das
Gewerbe," *Berliner Revue*, I (1855).

LE MANG, RICHARD, *Der deutsche Nationalverein* (Berlin,
[1909]).

LE PLAY, F., *Les ouvriers européens* (Paris, 1855).

LETTE, W. A., *Der volkswirthschaftliche Kongress und der
Zollverein* (Berlin, 1862).

LEXIS, W., *A General View of the History and Organisation
of Public Education in the German Empire*, trans G. J.
Tamson (Berlin, 1904).

LIEBKNECHT, WILHELM, *Briefwechsel mit Karl Marx und
Friedrich Engels*, ed. Georg Eckert (The Hague, 1963).

LIEBKNECHT, W., *Zu Trutz und Schutz: Festrede gehalten
zum Stiftungsfest des Crimmitschauer Volksvereins am 22.
October 1871*, 4th edn. (Leipzig, 1874).

[LÖHER, FRANZ], *Recht und Pflicht der Bundes-Staaten zwischen Preussen und Oestreich: Zur Bundesreform auf
Grund des Bundesrechts* (Munich, 1862).

LÖWENTHAL, FRITZ, *Der preussische Verfassungsstreit, 1862-
1866* (Munich and Leipzig, 1914).

LOTZ, WALTHER, *Die Ideen der deutschen Handelspolitik
von 1860 bis 1891* (Leipzig, 1892).

LOTZ, WALTHER, *Verkehrsentwickelung in Deutschland seit
1800*, 4th edn. (Leipzig and Berlin, 1920).

LÜTGE, FRIEDRICH, *Deutsche Sozial- und Wirtschaftsgeschichte* (Berlin, Göttingen, and Heidelberg, 1952).

M., "Die nationale Partei und ihr Verhalten innerhalb der
Einzelstaaten," *Wochenschrift des Nationalvereins*, November 29 and December 6, 1861.

M., K., "Die Zukunft des Zollvereins," *Die Grenzboten*, XIX
(1860), no. 4.

Unter Friedrich Wilhelm IV: Denkwürdigkeiten des Ministerpräsidenten Otto Freiherrn v. Manteuffel, ed. Heinrich v. Poschinger (3 vols., Berlin, 1901).

MARCKS, ERICH, *Der Aufstieg des Reiches: Deutsche Geschichte von 1807-1871/78* (2 vols., Stuttgart and Berlin, 1936).

MARKOW, ALEXIS, *Das Wachstum der Bevölkerung und die Entwickelung der Aus- und Einwanderungen, Ab- und Zuzüge in Preussen und Preussens einzelnen Provinzen, Bezirken und Kreisgruppen von 1824 bis 1885* (Tübingen, 1889).

MARR, WILHELM, *Selbstständigkeit und Hoheitsrecht der freien Stadt Hamburg sind ein Anachronismus geworden* (Hamburg, 1866).

MARX, KARL, and FRIEDRICH ENGELS, *Ausgewählte Briefe* (Berlin, 1953).

MARX, KARL, and FRIEDRICH ENGELS, *Briefwechsel* (4 vols., Berlin, 1949-1950).

MASCHER, H. A., *Das deutsche Gewerbewesen von der frühesten Zeit bis auf die Gegenwart* (Potsdam, 1866).

[MATHY, KARL], "Deutsche Interessen und deutsche Politik," *Preussische Jahrbücher,* II (1858).

MAYER, GUSTAV, "Der Allgemeine Deutsche Arbeiterverein und die Krisis 1866," *Archiv für Sozialwissenschaft und Sozialpolitik,* LVII (1927).

MAYER, GUSTAV, *Bismarck und Lassalle: Ihr Briefwechsel und ihre Gespräche* (Berlin, 1928).

MAYER, GUSTAV, *Friedrich Engels: Eine Biographie* (2 vols., The Hague, 1934).

MAYER, GUSTAV, *Johann Baptist von Schweitzer und die Sozialdemokratie: Ein Beitrag zur Geschichte der deutschen Arbeiterbewegung* (Jena, 1909).

MAYER, GUSTAV, "Die Lösung der deutschen Frage im Jahre 1866 und die Arbeiterbewegung," *Festgaben für Wilhelm Lexis zur siebzigsten Wiederkehr seines Geburtstages* (Jena, 1907).

MEHRING, FRANZ, *Die deutsche Sozialdemokratie: Ihre Geschichte und ihre Lehre* (Bremen, 1877).

416

MEHRING, FRANZ, *Geschichte der deutschen Sozialdemokratie* (2 vols., Stuttgart, 1897-98).

MEISNER, HEINRICH OTTO, *Der preussische Kronprinz im Verfassungskampf 1863* (Berlin, 1931).

MEYER, GEORG, *Das parlamentarische Wahlrecht* (Berlin, 1901).

Mittheilungen des Statistischen Bureau's in Berlin.

MOHL, ROBERT VON, *Staatsrecht, Völkerrecht und Politik* (3 vols., Graz, 1962).

MOLL, BRUNO, *Die Landarbeiterfrage im Königreich Sachsen* (Leipzig, 1908).

MOLTKE, HELMUTH VON, *Briefe, 1825-1891*, ed. Eberhard Kessel (Stuttgart, 1959).

MOMBERT, PAUL, *Studien zur Bevölkerungsbewegung in Deutschland in den letzten Jahrzehnten mit besonderer Berücksichtigung der ehelichen Fruchtbarkeit* (Karlsruhe, 1907).

MOMMSEN, WILHELM, *Johannes Miquel* (Stuttgart, 1928).

MOMMSEN, WILHELM, "Zur Beurteilung der deutschen Einheitsbewegung," *Historische Zeitschrift*, CXXXVIII (1928).

MORGAN, ROGER, *The German Social Democrats and the First International, 1864-1872* (Cambridge, 1965).

MÜLLER, HUGO, *Der Preussische Volks-Verein* (Berlin, 1914).

MÜLLER, KARL ALEXANDER VON, *Bayern im Jahre 1866 und die Berufung des Fürsten Hohenlohe* (Munich and Berlin, 1909).

Nach zehn Jahren: Auch eine Rundschau (März 1848–März 1858) (Frankfurt am Main, 1858).

National-Zeitung.

Neue Frankfurter Zeitung.

Neue Preussische Zeitung.

[NEUMANN, KARL], "Politische Correspondenz," *Preussische Jahrbücher*, II (1858)–VI (1860).

Nordstern.

O'BOYLE, LENORE, "The German *Nationalverein*," *Journal of Central European Affairs*, XVI (1957).

Offener Brief an alle Innungen Deutschlands so wie zugleich

*an alle Bürger und Hausväter: Von zweiundzwanzig In-
nungen zu Leipzig* (Leipzig, 1848).

ONCKEN, HERMANN, *Lassalle* (Stuttgart, 1904).

ONCKEN, HERMANN, "Der Nationalverein und die Anfänge
der deutschen Arbeiterbewegung 1862-63," *Archiv für die
Geschichte des Sozialismus und der Arbeiterbewegung,*
II (1912).

ONCKEN, HERMANN, "Publizistische Quellen zu den Bezie-
hungen zwischen Bismarck und Lassalle," *Archiv für die
Geschichte des Sozialismus und der Arbeiterbewegung,*
IV (1914).

ONCKEN, HERMANN, *Rudolf von Bennigsen: Ein deutscher
liberaler Politiker* (2 vols., Stuttgart, 1910).

PARISIUS, LUDOLF, *Deutschlands politische Parteien und das
Ministerium Bismarck* (Berlin, 1878).

PARISIUS, LUDOLF, *Leopold Freiherr von Hoverbeck* (2 vols.,
Berlin, 1897-1900).

"Parlamentsgedanken eines Politikers a. D.," *Jahrbücher für
Gesellschafts- und Staatswissenschaften,* V (1866).

PAULSEN, FRIEDRICH, *Geschichte des gelehrten Unterrichts
auf den deutschen Schulen und Universitäten vom Ausgang des Mittelalters bis zur Gegenwart,* 3rd edn. (2 vols.,
Berlin and Leipzig, 1919-21).

PETERSDORFF, HERMANN V., *Kleist-Retzow: Ein Lebensbild*
(Stuttgart and Berlin, 1907).

PFLANZE, OTTO, *Bismarck and the Development of Germany: The Period of Unification, 1815-1871* (Princeton,
1963).

[PLANCK, GOTTLIEB], *Der Nationalverein: Seine Entstehung
und bisherige Wirksamkeit* (Coburg, 1861).

POHLE, LUDWIG, and MAX MUSS, *Das deutsche Wirtschaftsleben seit Beginn des neunzehnten Jahrhunderts,* 6th edn.
(Leipzig and Berlin 1930).

"Politische Uebersicht," *Deutsches Wochenblatt,* April 8,
1866.

POSCHINGER, H. VON, *Bankwesen und Bankpolitik in Preussen* (3 vols., Berlin, 1878-79).

418

Poschinger, Heinrich von, *Fürst Bismarck und der Bundesrat* (5 vols., Stuttgart and Leipzig, 1897-1901).

Preradovich, Nikolaus von, *Die Führungsschichten in Österreich und Preussen (1804-1918)* (Wiesbaden, 1955).

Preussens auswärtige Politik, 1850 bis 1858: Unveröffentlichte Dokumente aus dem Nachlasse des Ministerpräsidenten Otto Frhrn. v. Manteuffel, ed. Heinrich v. Poschinger (3 vols., Berlin, 1902).

Preussisches Handelsarchiv.

Prince-Smith, John, "Die sogenannte Arbeiterfrage," *Vierteljahrschrift für Volkswirthschaft und Kulturgeschichte,* II (1864), no. 4.

Prussia, *Gesetz-Sammlung für die königlichen preussischen Staaten.*

Prussia, *Sammlung sämmtlicher Drucksachen des Hauses der Abgeordenten.*

Prussia, *Stenographische Berichte über die Verhandlungen der . . . beiden Häuser des Landtages.*

Prussia, *Verhandlungen des zum 2. April 1848 zusammenberufenen Vereinigten Landtages,* ed. E. Bleich (Berlin, 1848).

Quellen zur deutschen Politik Österreichs, 1859-1866, ed. Heinrich von Srbik (5 vols., Oldenburg and Berlin, 1934-38).

Ranke, Leopold von, *Neue Briefe,* ed. Bernhard Hoeft and Hans Herzfeld (Hamburg, 1949).

Rapp, Adolf, *Die Württemberger und die nationale Frage, 1863-1871* (Stuttgart, 1910).

Redlich, Fritz, "The Leaders of the German Steam-Engine Industry during the First Hundred Years," *Journal of Economic History,* IV (1944).

Reichensperger, August and Peter, *Deutschlands nächste Aufgaben* (Paderborn, 1860).

Die Reichstags-Wahlen von 1867 bis 1883: Statistik der Wahlen zum konstituierenden und norddeutschen Reichstage, zum Zollparlament, sowie zu den fünf ersten Legislatur-Perioden des deutschen Reichstages, ed., A. Phillips (Berlin, 1883).

Die Reichstags-Wahlen von 1867 bis 1903: Eine Statistik der Reichstagswahlen nebst den Programmen der Parteien und einem Verzeichnisse der gewählten Abgeordneten, ed. Fritz Specht and Paul Schwabe, 2nd edn. (Berlin, 1904).

REIN, GUSTAV ADOLF, *Die Revolution in der Politik Bismarcks* (Göttingen, 1957).

"Religionsbekenntniss und Schulbildung der Bevölkerung des preussischen Staats," *Zeitschrift des königlich preussischen Statistischen Bureaus,* XIV (1874).

RICHTER, ADOLF, *Bismarck und die Arbeiterfrage im preussischen Verfassungskonflikt* (Stuttgart, 1935).

RIEHL, W. H., *Die bürgerliche Gesellschaft,* 2nd edn. (Stuttgart and Tübingen, 1854).

RITTER, GERHARD, *Die preussischen Konservativen und Bismarcks deutsche Politik, 1858-1871* (Heidelberg, 1913).

ROBOLSKY, H., *Der deutsche Zollverein: Seine Entstehung, Entwicklung und Zukunft* (Berlin, 1862).

[ROCHAU, AUGUST LUDWIG VON], *Grundsätze der Realpolitik, angewendet auf die staatlichen Zustände Deutschlands,* 2nd edn. (2 vols., Stuttgart and Heidelberg, 1859-69).

RODBERTUS-JAGETZOW, JOHANN KARL, *Briefe und socialpolitische Aufsätze,* ed. Rudolph Meyer (2 vols., Berlin, 1882).

Denkwürdigkeiten aus dem Leben des Generalfeldmarschalls Kriegsministers Grafen von Roon, 5th edn. (3 vols., Berlin, 1905).

ROSENBERG, HANS, *Die nationalpolitische Publizistik Deutschlands: Vom Eintritt der neuen Ära in Preussen bis zum Ausbruch des deutschen Krieges* (2 vols., Munich and Berlin, 1935).

ROSENBERG, HANS, *Die Weltwirtschaftskrisis von 1857-1859* (Stuttgart and Berlin, 1934).

Arnold Ruges Briefwechsel und Tagebuchblätter aus den Jahren 1825-80, ed. Paul Nerrlich (2 vols., Berlin, 1886).

RUIDER, HANS, *Bismarck und die öffentliche Meinung in Bayern, 1862-1866* (Munich, 1924).

SAILE, WOLFGANG, *Hermann Wagener und sein Verhältnis*

zu Bismarck: Ein Beitrag zur Geschichte des konservativen Sozialismus (Tübingen, 1858).

SARTORIUS VON WALTERSHAUSEN, A., *Deutsche Wirtschaftsgeschichte, 1815-1914*, 2nd edn. (Jena, 1923).

SCH., "Unsere materiellen Interessen," *Wochenschrift des Nationalvereins*, May 31, 1861.

SCHÄFFLE, ALBERT EBERHARD FRIEDRICH, *Aus meinem Leben* (2 vols., Berlin, 1905).

[SCHÄFFLE, A.E.F.], "Die Bundesreform und die grossdeutsche Versammlung in Frankfurt," *Deutsche Vierteljahrs-Schrift*, XXVI (1863), no. 1.

[SCHÄFFLE, A.E.F.], "Die Handelskrisis, mit besonderer Rücksicht auf das Bankwesen," *Deutsche Vierteljahrs-Schrift*, XXI (1858), no. 1.

[SCHÄFFLE, A.E.F.], "Realpolitische Gedanken aus der deutschen Gegenwart," *Deutsche Vierteljahrs-Schrift*, XXII (1859), no. 3.

SCHÄFFLE, A.E.F., "Vorschläge zu einer gemeinsamen Ordnung der Gewerbebefugnisse und Heimathrechtsverhältnisse in Deutschland nach den Grundsätzen der Gewerbefreiheit und der Freizügigkeit," *Deutsche Vierteljahrs-Schrift*, XXII (1859), no. 1.

SCHILFERT, GERHARD, *Sieg und Niederlage des demokratischen Wahlrechts in der deutschen Revolution 1848-49* (Berlin, 1952).

SCHLÖZER, KURD VON, *Petersburger Briefe, 1857-1862*, ed. Leopold von Schlözer (Stuttgart, Berlin, and Leipzig, 1923).

SCHMOLLER, GUSTAV, "Die Arbeiterfrage," *Preussische Jahrbücher*, XIV (1864).

SCHMOLLER, GUSTAV, *Zur Geschichte der deutschen Kleingewerbe im 19. Jahrhundert* (Halle, 1870).

SCHNABEL, FRANZ, *Deutsche Geschichte im neunzehnten Jahrhundert* (4 vols., Freiburg im Breisgau, 1929-37).

SCHOEPS, HANS-JOACHIM, "Hermann Wagener: Ein konservativer Sozialist," *Zeitschrift für Religions- und Geistesgeschichte*, VIII (1956).

SCHRAMM, PERCY ERNST, *Hamburg, Deutschland und die*

Welt: Leistung und Grenzen hanseatischen Bürgertums in der Zeit zwischen Napoleon I. und Bismarck (Munich, 1943).

SCHULZE-DELITZSCH, HERMANN, *Schriften und Reden*, ed. F. Thorwart (5 vols., Berlin, 1909-13).

SCHUPP, FR., and K. A. WETTSTEIN, *Die Entstehungsgeschichte des ersten Allgemeinen Deutschen Handelstages 1861: Zum 50jährigen Jubiläum des Handelstages* (Karlsruhe, 1911).

SCHWAB, RUDOLF, *Der deutsche Nationalverein: Seine Entstehung und sein Wirken* (Frauenfeld, 1902).

Briefwechsel des Botschafters General v. Schweinitz (Berlin, 1928).

Denkwürdigkeiten des Botschafters General v. Schweinitz (2 vols., Berlin, 1927).

SCHWEITZER, J. B. VON, *Politische Aufsätze und Reden*, ed. Fr. Mehring (Berlin, 1912).

SERING, MAX, *Deutsche Agrarpolitik auf geschichtlicher und landeskundlicher Grundlage* (Leipzig, 1934).

Social-Demokrat.

SOMBART, WERNER, *Die deutsche Volkswirtschaft im neunzehnten Jahrhundert und im Anfang des 20. Jahrhunderts*, 5th edn. (Berlin, 1921).

SOMBART, WERNER, *Der moderne Kapitalismus: Historisch-systematische Darstellung des gesamteuropäischen Wirtschaftslebens von seinen Anfängen bis zur Gegenwart*, 6th edn. (3 vols., Munich and Leipzig, 1924-28).

SPRINGER, ANTON, *Friedrich Christoph Dahlmann* (2 vols., Leipzig, 1870-72).

SRBIK, HEINRICH VON, *Deutsche Einheit: Idee und Wirklichkeit vom Heiligen Reich bis Königgrätz* (4 vols., Munich, 1935-42).

STADELMANN, RUDOLF, *Das Jahr 1865 und das Problem von Bismarcks deutscher Politik* (Munich and Berlin, 1933).

STAHL, FRIEDRICH JULIUS, *Die gegenwärtigen Parteien in Staat und Kirche* (Berlin, 1863).

Statistisches Handbuch für den preussischen Staat.

Statistisches Jahrbuch für das Deutsche Reich.

STEGLICH, WALTER, "Eine Streiktabelle für Deutschland, 1864 bis 1880," *Jahrbuch für Wirtschaftsgeschichte* (1960), no. 2.

"Die Stellung der Industrie im heutigen Wirthschaftsleben," *Deutsche Vierteljahrs-Schrift*, XXV (1862), no. 2.

STOLPER, GUSTAV, *German Economy, 1870-1940* (New York, 1940).

STRUVE, GUSTAV, *Diesseits und jenseits des Oceans* (4 vols., Coburg, 1863-64).

SYBEL, HEINRICH VON, *Die Begründung des Deutschen Reiches durch Wilhelm I.* (7 vols., Munich and Leipzig, 1890-94).

Tabellen und amtliche Nachrichten über den preussischen Staat für das Jahr 1855 (Berlin, 1858).

Tabellen und amtliche Nachrichten über den preussischen Staat für das Jahr 1858 (Berlin, 1860).

TEUTEBERG, HANS JÜRGEN, *Geschichte der industriellen Mitbestimmung in Deutschland* (Tübingen, 1961).

TEWS, J., *Ein Jahrhundert preussischer Schulgeschichte: Volksschule und Volksschullehrerstand in Preussen im 19. und 20. Jahrhundert* (Leipzig, 1914).

THUN, ALPHONS, "Beiträge zur Geschichte der Gesetzgebung und Verwaltung zu Gunsten der Fabrikarbeiter," *Zeitschrift des königlich preussischen Statistischen Bureaus*, XVII (1877).

THUN, ALPHONS, *Die Industrie am Niederrhein und ihre Arbeiter* (2 vols., Leipzig, 1879).

TILLY, RICHARD, *Financial Institutions and Industrialization in the Rhineland, 1815-1870* (Madison, Milwaukee, and London, 1966).

London *Times*.

TODT, ELISABETH, *Die gewerkschaftliche Betätigung in Deutschland von 1850 bis 1859* (Berlin, 1950).

TÖNNIES, FERDINAND, "Deutscher Adel im neunzehnten Jahrhundert," *Neue Rundschau*, XXIII (1912).

Heinrich von Treitschkes Briefe, ed. Max Cornicelius, 2nd edn. (3 vols., Leipzig, 1913-20).

TREITSCHKE, HEINRICH VON, "Das Zweikammersystem und das Herrenhaus," *Preussische Jahrbücher*, XXXI (1873).

"Ueber die Verschlechterung der physischen Beschaffenheit der Berliner Bevölkerung in neuerer Zeit," *Mittheilungen des Statistischen Bureau's in Berlin*, XIII (1860).

"Unsere Aufgabe," *Berliner Revue*, XVI (1859).

Das Unterrichtswesen im Deutschen Reich, ed. W. Lexis (4 vols., Berlin, 1904).

VAHLTEICH, JULIUS, "Das Leipziger Zentralkomitee und Ferdinand Lassalle," *Die Gründung der deutschen Sozialdemokratie: Eine Festschrift der Leipziger Arbeiter zum 23. Mai 1903* (Leipzig, 1903).

VALENTIN, VEIT, *Geschichte der deutschen Revolution von 1848-49* (2 vols., Berlin, 1930-31).

[VEIT, MORITZ], "Die Legislaturperiode des Hauses der Abgeordneten 1859-1861: Ein Rechenschaftsbericht," *Preussische Jahrbücher*, VIII (1861).

Vereinstag deutscher Arbeitervereine:

Bericht über die Verhandlungen des ersten Vereinstages der deutschen Arbeitervereine abgehalten zu Frankfurt a. M. am 7. und 8. Juni 1863 (Frankfurt am Main, 1863).

Bericht über die Verhandlungen des zweiten Vereinstags deutscher Arbeitervereine. Abgehalten zu Leipzig am 23. und 24. Oktober 1864 (Frankfurt am Main, 1864).

Jahresbericht über die Thätigkeit des ständigen Ausschusses für den dritten Vereinstag der deutschen Arbeitervereine (Frankfurt am Main, 1865).

Verhandlungen des Congresses deutscher Abgeordneter in Weimar am 28. und 29. September 1862 (Weimar, 1862).

Verhandlungen der deutschen verfassunggebenden Reichs-Versammlung zu Frankfurt am Main, ed. K. D. Hassler (6 vols., Frankfurt am Main, 1848-49).

Verhandlungen der Mitglieder deutscher Landesvertretungen in Frankfurt a. M., Sonntag den 1. October 1865 (Frankfurt am Main, 1865).

VIEBAHN, GEORG VON, *Statistik des zollvereinten und nördlichen Deutschlands* (3 vols., Berlin, 1858-68).

Volksblatt für Stadt und Land.

Das Volksschulwesen im preussischen Staate, ed. K. Schneider and E. von Bremen (3 vols., Berlin, 1886-87).

Der Volksstaat.

Volks-Zeitung.

"Ein Vortrag des Justizraths Wagener," *Berliner Revue*, XXIX (1862).

WAENTIG, HEINRICH, "Die gewerbepolitischen Anschauungen in Wissenschaft und Gesetzgebung des 19. Jahrhunderts," *Die Entwicklung der deutschen Volkswirtschaftslehre im neunzehnten Jahrhundert: Gustav Schmoller zur siebenzigsten Wiederkehr seines Geburtstages* (2 vols., Leipzig, 1908).

WAGENER, HERMANN, *Erlebtes: Meine Memoiren aus der Zeit von 1848 bis 1866 und von 1873 bis jetzt*, 2nd edn. (2 vols., Berlin, 1884).

WAGENER, HERMANN, *Die kleine aber mächtige Partei* (Berlin, 1885).

"Was kann Preussen thun?," *Hermann: Deutsches Wochenblatt aus London*, June 11, 1859.

WEBER, ROLF, *Kleinbürgerliche Demokraten in der deutschen Einheitsbewegung, 1863-1866* (Berlin, 1962).

[WEHRENPFENNIG, WILHELM], "Politische Correspondenz," *Preussische Jahrbücher*, X (1862) –XII (1863).

WEISS, SIEGFRIED, *An die deutsche Nation: Oesterreich, Deutschland und das Einheitsproject* (Berlin, 1860).

WERTHEIMER, EDUARD VON, *Bismarck im politischen Kampf* (Berlin, 1929).

WESTPHAL, OTTO, *Welt- und Staatsauffassung des deutschen Liberalismus: Eine Untersuchung über die Preussischen Jahrbücher und den konstitutionellen Liberalismus in Deutschland von 1858 bis 1863* (Munich and Berlin, 1919).

WIENSTEIN, FRIEDR., *Die preussische Volksschule in ihrer geschichtlichen Entwicklung* (Paderborn, 1915).

"Wir nehmen die Verantwortlichkeit, gebt uns die Freiheit!," *Berliner Revue*, XXXIII (1863).

WIRMINGHAUS, ALEXANDER, *Die Industrie- und Handelskam-*

mer zu Köln: Ihre Geschichte und ihre Wirksamkeit (1797-1914/33) (Manuscript, Rheinisch-Westfälisches Wirtschaftsarchiv, Cologne).

WIRTH, MAX, *Die deutsche Nationaleinheit in ihrer volkswirthschaftlichen, geistigen und politischen Entwickelung an der Hand der Geschichte beleuchtet* (Frankfurt am Main, 1859).

WIRTH, MAX, *Geschichte der Handelskrisen* (Frankfurt am Main, 1858).

Wochenschrift des Nationalvereins.

X., V., "Preussische Briefe: Neue Folge," *Berliner Revue,* XXI (1860).

ZECHLIN, EGMONT, *Bismarck und die Grundlegung der deutschen Grossmacht,* 2nd edn. (Stuttgart, 1960).

Zeitschrift des königlich preussischen Statistischen Bureaus.

Zeitung für Norddeutschland.

ZIMMERMANN, ERICH, *Der Deutsche Reformverein,* (Pforzheim, 1929).

ZUCHARDT, KARL, *Die Finanzpolitik Bismarcks und der Parteien im Norddeutschen Bunde* (Leipzig, 1910).

ZUNKEL, FRIEDRICH, *Der rheinisch-westfälische Unternehmer, 1834-1879: Ein Beitrag zur Geschichte des deutschen Bürgertums im 19. Jahrhundert* (Cologne and Opladen, 1962).

"Zur Arbeiterfrage," *Berliner Revue,* XXXII and XXXIII (1863).

"Der zweite deutsche Handwerkertag zu Frankfurt a. M.," *Berliner Revue,* XXXV (1863).

[ZWICKER, R.], "Die Elbzölle," *Preussische Jahrbücher,* III (1859).

Index

agriculture, modernization, 36-37; concentration, 37-38; form of ownership, 38, 59; yield, 38-39; prosperity, 39-40; part-time laborers, 41-42; and conservatism, 205-207
Alban, Ernst, 67
aristocracy, landownership, 59; army and bureaucracy, 60; social position, 181-82; indifference to politics, 270; and nationalism, 388-92
Arnd, Karl, 109
Arndt, Ernst Moritz, 340
Arnoldi, Ernst Wilhelm, 67
artisan class, decline, 77-78, 80-83; size, 78-80; structure, 79-80; living conditions, 88; aspirations, 117-19; opposition to industrial freedom, 121-23; organizations, 123-32; and conservatism, 209-10, 215-17; political allegiance, 368-71
Assembly of German Workingmen's Societies, 173-75, 226, 255, 257-59
Association of German Jurists, 355

Bachem, Joseph, 335
Bachmann, 326
Bamberger, Ludwig, 384
banking, 28-32; concentration, 34-35
Barth, Marquard, 137, 313, 342
Baumgarten, Hermann, 136, 272, 291, 362
Bebel, August, 151, 255-57, 261, 263
Becker, Bernhard, 226
Beckerath, Hermann von, 67, 352
Behrend, Heinrich, 352
Below-Hohendorf, Alexander von, 94, 183, 311
Bennigsen, Rudolf von, 159, 320, 342

Bernhardi, Theodor von, 113, 135, 146, 273-74, 285, 294-95, 300-301, 330, 372-73, 376, 394
Bernstorff, Albrecht von, 333
Beseler, Georg, 294
Bethusy-Huc, Eduard von, 183
Beust, Friedrich von, 337, 389
Biedermann, Karl, 289, 343
Bismarck, Otto von, 14, 56, 94, 135, 137, 139, 198, 212, 218, 227, 236, 240, 244-48, 250-53, 257, 262, 271, 285, 317, 353, 362, 364, 373-74, 376-77, 379, 389, 395-96
Blanckenburg, Moritz von, 14, 183, 219, 299, 311, 315, 326, 329, 372
Bleichröder, Gerson, 31
Blind, Karl, 166
Bluntschli, Johann Caspar, 339, 355
Bockum-Dolffs, Florens Heinrich von, 313
Böhlen, H., 82
Böhmert, Victor, 95, 121, 137, 141, 143, 157, 159, 171, 340, 342, 344, 348, 352
Borsig, August, 22
Brandstrup, F.M.C., 128
Brater, Karl, 137, 313, 342, 347
Braun, Karl, 156, 158, 161, 342-43, 352
Bruck, Karl von, 111, 154, 162, 382
Büttner, Hermann, 137
Bulwer-Lytton, E.G.E.L., 279
Burckhardt, Jacob, 307
Busch, Moritz, 271, 291, 314, 356, 385

Camphausen, Ludolf, 67
Cassel, Jacob, 31
Chambers of Commerce, 4, 11, 13, 72-74, 81, 84, 86, 97-98, 101-104, 130, 354

Christian Conservative Election Society, 358
Classen-Kappelmann, Johann, 352
Congress of German Economists, 358; formation, 340-41; membership, 341-43; program, 343-46; activities, 346-48
conservatism, social basis, 182-83; international relations, 183-86; and Italian unification, 186-88; and German unification, 188-90; and nationalism, 191-92; and liberalism, 192-95; and the middle class, 195-97; and royal authority, 197-98; program, 198-200; and economic reform, 200-202, 220-21; and industrial freedom, 202-203; and freedom of movement, 203-204; and usury laws, 204-205; and agriculture, 205-207; and form of society, 207-209; and the peasantry, 208-209, 214-15; and the artisan class, 209-10, 215-17; and the lower classes, 210-11; and the suffrage question, 211-13; and the industrial working class, 218-20
cooperative movement, 176-79
Cousin, Victor, 276
Cramer-Klett, Theodor von, 173

Dahlmann, Friedrich Christoph, 164
Dammer, Otto, 228
demographic change, population growth, 44-47; death rate, 48; birth rate, 48; infant mortality, 49; internal migration, 50, 54-55; immigration, 50; emigration, 50-53; urbanization, 54-57
Diest, Gustav von, 212
Dietzsch, Karl, 300
Dönniges, Helene von, 238
Dörnberg, Ernst von, 188
Dohna, Friedrich zu, 311
Droysen, Johann Gustav, 146, 164, 284, 291-92, 393

Duckwitz, Arnold, 67
Duncker, Franz, 137
Duncker, Max, 135, 147, 285, 324, 397

economic depressions, 3; 1857, 6-9; financial crisis of the 1860's, 10
economic growth, mining and metallurgy, 12-13, 19-21; capital goods, 13, 18; railroads, 14, 24-27; textiles, 16; metals, 17-19; machine construction, 22-23; imports and exports, 27-28, 85; banking, 28-32, 34-35; mechanization, 33; concentration of production, 33-34; joint-stock financing, 35; agriculture, 37-40; production, 85
economic reform, aristocratic, 94, 200-202, 220-21; middle class, 95-102, 162-63
education, expenditures, 276-78; elementary, 278-80
Eisenstuck, Bernhard, 352
elections, influences on the electorate, 298-301; participation, 301-306; results, 374-79
Emminghaus, Arwed, 137, 343
Engels, Friedrich, 7, 56, 224-27, 257, 260-61, 329, 381
Erbach-Fürstenau, Alfred, 187
Ernest II, 357

Faucher, Julius, 137, 169, 342, 352
Fein, Georg, 321
Feuerbach, Ludwig, 343
Feustel, 122
Fischer, Laurenz Hannibal, 365
Forckenbeck, Max von, 137, 281, 310, 342, 356
Francis Joseph, 189
Francke, Karl Philipp, 348
Frederick, 145, 284
Frederick William IV, 149, 191, 198, 317

freedom of movement, 98; and
  liberalism, 159-61; and
  conservatism, 203-204
Frenzel, Karl, 274
Frey, Theodor, 349
Freytag, Gustav, 140, 291, 343,
  357
Friedenthal, Karl Rudolf, 275
Friedmann, O. Bernhard, 106
Friedrich, Karl, 395
Fries, Hugo, 323, 342
Fröbel, Julius, 136, 165, 332,
  336, 338

Gablenz, Anton von, 108
Gagern, Heinrich von, 336
General Civic Society of Barmen,
  75
General German Workingmen's
  Society, 227, 229, 238, 242, 245,
  250-55, 259-60, 262-63
Gerlach, Ernst Ludwig von, 183,
  186, 190-91, 197, 203, 206, 214,
  219-20, 293, 315, 326, 391
Gerlach, Leopold von, 183-85,
  191, 198, 203, 207, 210, 212, 220,
  391
German Association of
  Handicraftsmen, 126-30, 215
German Commercial Association,
  358; background, 348-50;
  formation, 350-51;
  membership, 351-52; program,
  352-53; activities, 353-54
German Society of Gymnasts,
  356
German Society of
  Sharpshooters, 356-57
Gerson, Hermann, 42
Gervinus, Georg Gottfried, 140,
  398
Glaser, Johann Carl, 183, 193,
  218
Gneist, Rudolf, 295
Godeffroy, Johann Cesar, 66
Goertz, Karl, 187
Goethe, Johann Wolfgang von, 22
Grabow, Wilhelm, 363
Günther, 390
Guttentag, Immanuel, 137

Hammacher, Friedrich, 26, 352
Hänle, Leo, 352
Handel, Maximilian von, 210
Hanekamp, J., 128
Hansemann, David, 5, 67, 349,
  352
Harkort, Friedrich, 169
Hartmann, Richard, 22
Hatzfeldt, Sophie von, 228, 239,
  246, 249
Häusser, Ludwig, 291
Haym, Rudolf, 270, 300
Heckscher, Johann Gustav, 67
Henckel, Hermann, 215
Henneberg, Friedrich, 321
Henschel, Carl Anton, 22
Heydt, August von der, 25-26,
  119, 125, 219
Hohenlohe-Ingelfingen, Adolf
  von, 183
Hohenlohe-Schillingsfürst,
  Chlodwig zu, 395
Hoverbeck, Leopold von, 138,
  149, 167, 273, 284, 310, 356

indifference to politics, and the
  lower classes, 269-70, 273-76,
  304-306, 379-80; and the
  aristocracy, 270, 302; and the
  middle class, 270-72, 302-304;
  and the peasantry, 112-14,
  275-76
industrial freedom, 96-97, 117-23;
  and liberalism, 158-59; and
  conservatism, 202-203
industrial working class,
  development, 68-69; factory
  labor, 70-72; living conditions,
  73; wages, 74; strikes, 75-76;
  child labor, 76-77; political
  attitudes, 114-17; and
  conservatism, 218-20
International Workingmen's
  Association, 257, 259, 261
Itzenplitz, Heinrich von, 26

Jacoby, Johann, 137, 148, 167
Jhering, Rudolf, 274
Jörg, Edmund, 273

Kaffka, 330

Kamptz, Karl Albert von, 390
Kant, Immanuel, 378
Karl Anton of Hohenzollern, 285, 374
Keil, Ernst, 291
Keipp, Hermann, 200
Kerstorf, Friedrich von, 111
Kessler, Emil, 67
Ketteler, Wilhelm Emmanuel von, 127
Keudell, Robert von, 15, 248
Kiesselbach, Wilhelm, 109
Kinkel, Gottfried, 105
Kleist-Retzow, Hans Hugo von, 183, 214, 326
Klett, Johann Friedrich, 67
Krupp, Alfred, 17, 67
Künssberg-Mandel, Philipp von, 56

Lammers, August, 137, 177, 342
Lange, Friedrich Albert, 171
Langerhans, Paul, 137
Lassalle, Ferdinand, 86, 115, 170, 211; background, 227-28; founding of the General German Workingmen's Society, 228-29; attack on capitalism, 229-30; and the cooperative movement, 230-31; and producer associations, 231-34; and the state, 235-36, 241-42; and the suffrage question, 236-37; and liberalism, 239-41; and conservatism, 242-44; and Bismarck, 244-49; and death, 249-50
Lavergne-Peguilhen, Moritz von, 203
Le Play, Frédéric, 78
Leo, Heinrich, 183, 331, 369-70
Lerchenfeld, Gustav von, 335-36, 338
Lette, Wilhelm Adolf, 160, 341, 343, 345-46
Lewy, Gustav, 228
liberalism, social basis, 135-39; international relations, 140-41; problem of nationalities, 142-43; German unification,
144-45; and a parliamentary system, 145-46; right wing, 146-47; left wing, 148-49; radicals of the secondary states, 150-52; politics and economics, 152-54; and the middle class, 154-56; and free enterprise, 156-57; and industrial freedom, 158-59; and freedom of movement, 159-61; and usury laws, 161-62; and middle-class economic reform, 162-63; and the lower classes, 163-64; and the suffrage question, 165-67; and wages, 167-69; and the labor movement, 169-70; and improvement of the lower classes, 171-73
Liebknecht, Wilhelm, 226, 237-38, 255-57, 260-61, 263-64
List, Friedrich, 47
literacy, 280-83
Löher, Franz, 160
Löwe-Calbe, Wilhelm, 164

Maffei, Josef Anton, 22
Manteuffel, Edwin von, 183-84
Manteuffel, Otto von, 66, 195, 206, 320
Marcard, Heinrich Eugen, 293
Marr Wilhelm, 388
Marx, Karl, 7-8, 56, 69, 145, 224-27, 234, 237, 249, 255, 257, 261
Mathy, Karl, 104, 144
Meier, Hermann Heinrich, 66, 352
Metz, August, 363
Mevissen, Gustav, 31, 35, 67, 146, 153
Meyer, Rudolph, 218-19
Michaelis, Otto, 137, 342, 347, 352
middle class, 64-68; and economic reform, 95-102, 162-63; and liberalism, 154-56; and conservatism, 195-97; indifference to politics, 270-72, 302-304; and nationalism, 380-88

Miquel, Johannes, 145, 165, 387, 394
Mittermaier, Karl, 341
Möller, Julius, 396
Mohl, Robert von, 168
Mohrenheim, Arthur, 357
Moll, Eduard, 352
Moltke, Adolph von, 211
Moltke, Helmuth von, 211
Mommsen, Theodor, 137, 291, 300, 310
Mullensiefen, Theodor, 321

Nathusius, Philipp von, 190
nationalism, and the lower classes, 381, 392-97; and the middle class, 380-88, 397-99; and the aristocracy, 388-92
Nationalverein, 107, 142, 153, 157, 159, 171, 173, 240, 247, 272, 314, 330, 337-38, 342, 347, 356, 358, 363; program, 315-17; tactics, 317-18; and politics, 318-19; economic views, 319-20; and the lower classes, 320-22; membership, 323-25
Neuhaus, 330
newspapers and periodicals, circulation, 284-86, 290-91; government influence, 285-86; price, 291-92

occupational pattern, 57-58
Oppenheim, Abraham, 31

Panse, 330, 369-70
Parisius, Ludolf, 342
parties, beginnings, 308-309, 313-14; Progressive Party, 309-11; Conservative Party, 311-13; social composition, 314-15
Patriotic Alliance, 358
peasantry, 61-63; indifference to politics, 112-14, 275-76; and conservatism, 208-209, 214-15; political allegiance, 372-73
Perthes, Clemens Theodor, 195
Pesche, C., 81, 128, 370
Piest, 127, 370

Pilsach, Adolf Senfft von, 211, 326
Planck, Gottlieb, 272, 325, 342
political reform, middle-class, 103-104; *kleindeutsch*, 105-108; *grossdeutsch*, 108-12; and the peasantry, 112-14; and the industrial working class, 114-17; class basis, 269-70, 306-307, 357-58
Prince-Smith, John, 137, 153, 156, 168-69, 171, 342, 344
Prussia, state finances, 14-15
Prussian Commercial Association, background, 349
Prussian People's Association, 186, 198-99, 204-205, 216, 243, 287, 358, 362, 368-69; formation, 325-37; activities, 327-29; membership, 329-30; leadership, 330-32
Prussian State Convention of Handicraftsmen, 123-27, 130
public opinion, nature of, 360-61; mass meetings, 361-63; petitions, 363-64; participation in elections, 364-65; and liberalism, 365-68; and conservatism, 366-68; and the artisans, 368-71; and the peasantry, 372-73

quasi-political organization, 339-40. *See also* Congress of German Economists; German Commercial Association; Association of German Jurists; German Society of Sharpshooters; German Society of Gymnasts

railroads, 5, 11, 15, 24, 26, 34
Rakowitza, Janko von, 249
Ranke, Leopold, 190-91
Rechberg, Johann Bernhard von, 332
Reformverein, 358; background, 332-34; formation, 334-36; internal divisions, 336-37; membership, 337-38

Reichenheim, Leonor, 155, 169, 342
Reichensperger, August, 108, 335
Reichensperger, Peter, 108
Rewitzer, 80
Rickert, Heinrich, 138
Riehl, Wilhelm Heinrich, 40, 183, 208
Robolsky, Hermann, 107
Rochau, August Ludwig von, 154, 159, 269, 293, 321
Rodbertus-Jagetzow, Johann Karl, 116
Roesler, Hermann, 218
Roggenbach, Franz von, 295
Roon, Albrecht von, 14, 113, 270, 373
Ross, Edgar Daniel, 352
Rümelin, Gustav, 383
Rüstow, Wilhelm, 115
Ruge, Arnold, 150

Sänger, Karl von, 295
Saucken-Tarputschen, Kurt von, 298, 311, 372
Savigny, Karl Friedrich von, 14, 338
Sayn-Wittgenstein, Emil, 187
Schäffle, A.E.F., 6, 110, 160, 163, 336-37, 342, 352
Schloenbach, Arnold, 142, 169
Schmerling, Anton von, 332, 355
Schmettau, Captain von, 221
Schmoller, Gustav, 42, 47, 72, 81, 172, 179
Schulze-Delitzsch, Hermann, 137, 141, 149, 155-56, 164, 167, 169, 175-79, 203, 211, 230, 239, 255, 310, 319, 322, 341-42, 347-48, 356
Schweedt, C.P.C., 126
Schweinitz, Hans Lothar von, 186, 384
Schweitzer, Johann Baptist von, 252-55
Siemens, Werner, 137
Sieveking, Karl, 67
Smidt, Johann, 67
Smith, Adam, 378
Social Democratic Workingmen's Party, background, 255-58;

program, 258-59; size, 259-60, 263-64; and the Franco-Prussian War, 260-63
socialism, size of Lassallean movement, 115-17, 254-56, 263-64; and proletarian class consciousness, 222-24; General German Workingmen's Society, 250-55; Social Democratic Workingmen's Party, 255-60, 263-64; and the Franco-Prussian War, 260-63
Soetbeer, Adolf, 352
Sonnemann, Leopold, 170, 289, 342
Stahl, Friedrich Julius, 183, 193, 207-208, 366-67
standard of living, living conditions, 73, 87-88; rise in imports, 85; rise in production, 85; per capita income, 85-86; improvement of, 89-90; earnings, 91-93
Stolberg-Wernigerode, Eberhard, 187, 215, 311, 326
Streckfuss, Adolph, 170
Streit, Fedor, 322, 342, 356
Strousberg, Bethel Henry, 27
Struve, Gustav von, 50, 151, 159, 172
suffrage question, franchise restrictions, 292-96; and liberalism, 165-67; and conservatism, 211-13; and Lassalle, 236-37
Sybel, Heinrich von, 145, 147, 165-66, 278, 291, 359, 362

Testa, Heinrich von, 7
Thadden-Trieglaff, Adolf von, 211
Thüngen, Wolfgang von, 392
Todt, 119
Treitschke, Eduard von, 191
Treitschke, Heinrich von, 181, 271, 291, 385, 394, 396
Twesten, Karl, 137, 147, 310

Ungern-Sternberg, Eduard von, 394, 397

Unruh, Hans Viktor von, 137, 271, 310
urbanization, 54-57
Usedom, Guido von, 285
usury laws, 99-101; and liberalism, 161-62; and conservatism, 204-205

Vahlteich, Julius, 116, 223, 238
Vecchioni, August, 137, 342
Viebahn, Georg von, 72
Vincke, Georg von, 394
Vincke-Olbendorf, Karl von, 274
Virchow, Rudolf, 137, 310
Vivenot, Alfred von, 394
Völk, Joseph, 137, 313
voting laws, 296-98

Wagener, Hermann, 183, 189, 191-92, 195, 198, 208-209, 213, 217-18, 221, 227, 243-44, 250, 270, 287, 291, 293, 311, 315, 326, 329-31, 369-70, 391
Wagner, F., 129
Waldeck, Benedikt, 137, 167, 329
Weiss, Siegfried, 105, 153
Welcker, Karl Theodor, 341
Werner, Josef von, 337
Westphalen, Ferdinand von, 374
William I, 55, 60, 126, 186, 236, 298, 301, 340, 353
Windischgrätz, Alfred, 187
Wirth, Max, 4, 86, 137, 173, 322, 341, 343, 352
Wohlgemuth, 330
working class, *see* industrial working class
Wydenbrugk, Oskar von, 336

Ziegler, Franz, 43, 167, 170, 228, 293